Waynesburg College Library
Waynesburg, Pa. 15370

D1525524

332.15		P448f
Perkins, Edwin F.		
AUTHOR		
Financing Anglò-American Trade.		
TITLE		
109999		
DATE DUE	BORROWER'S NAME	

332.15   P448f
Perkins, Edwin J.
Financing Anglo-American Trade.
109999

Harvard Studies in Business History
XXVIII
Edited by Alfred D. Chandler, Jr.
Isidor Straus Professor of Business History
Graduate School of Business Administration
George F. Baker Foundation
Harvard University

FINANCING
ANGLO-AMERICAN TRADE
The House of Brown,
1800-1880

EDWIN J. PERKINS

Harvard University Press
Cambridge, Massachusetts
and London, England
1975

Copyright © 1975 by the President and Fellows of Harvard College
All rights reserved

Library of Congress Catalog Card Number 74-34543
IBSN 0-674-30145-5
Printed in the United States of America

For JULIA AND BRAXTON

109999

Editor's Introduction

This study is traditional business history presented in an untraditional way. It is traditional in that it is the history of a single enterprise and so is a study of entrepreneurship and management. It is untraditional in that the story is presented in a functional rather than a chronological manner. After providing a brief overview of the firm's changing strategies and internal organization, it concentrates on describing and analyzing the ways in which the firm carried out for an eighty year period its three financial functions — the handling of foreign bills of exchange, the making of advances, and the issuing of letters of credit. Such a focus permits Mr. Perkins to pinpoint and analyze more effectively the institutional changes in the financing of international trade than if he had concentrated on the more conventional chronological story of short-term entrepreneurial responses to day-to-day operating problems and situations.

The chronological overview, by being brief, helps emphasize the fact that the Browns' business success resulted from their ability to adjust their strategies, policies, and procedures to long-term shifts in trade resulting from the coming of new technology and a changing demand. The firm began operations at the moment when cotton was becoming the nation's primary export and textiles its major import. Its business expanded as the Atlantic trade grew in volume and as grain and foodstuffs came to supplement cotton as exports and metal goods, machinery and other industrial products to supplement textiles as imports. The Browns' greatest challenge and most effective response was to the new technology in transportation and communication — the railroad and steamship, the telegraph and the cable — which permitted an unprecedented speed and regularity in the movements of goods.

The Browns were the first international bankers to capture economies permitted by increased volume of trade and improved communication. They did so by transforming their interlocking partnership into a network of branch offices. Where the Barings and other competitors continued to rely on other merchants to act as their agents in different commerical centers, the Browns began to place full-time salaried employees in charge of offices in Boston, New Orleanes, Mobile, and other ports. This basic organizational innovation permitted them to modify existing business procedures in ways that made their firm predominant in the financing of Anglo-American trade by the 1860s.

In analyzing the ways in which the firm carried out its basic activities, Mr. Perkins indicates the impact of this fundamental organizational innovation on the evolution of its financial functions. The combination of branch offices and the telegraph gave the Browns an immediate dominance of the foreign exchange business in the United States since instantaneous communications quickly lowered the cost and risk of such transactions. The administrative network permitted the senior executives of the firm to expand the volume and reduce the costs of international finance through the adoption of increasingly sophisticated methods of issuing letters of credit. Their success in the exchange business and letter of credit field encouraged the firm to phase out its more risky business of financing trade through advances.

By focusing in this way on long-term functions, Mr. Perkins has been able to tell more than the story of a single enterprise. He has illuminated the institutional development of a major sector of the international Atlantic economy. By recording the history of America's foremost international banking enterprise in the nineteenth century, he has described and analyzed the changing institutional arrangements and instruments that financed international trade during the critical years of the growth of the American economy.

Alfred D. Chandler, Jr.

Acknowledgments

This study is more than the history of a single business firm. It is the most complete account to date of the financing of nineteenth-century American foreign trade. Because the Brown banking house was the leader in several Anglo-American financial markets, a review of its operations reveals much about the broad development of the mechanisms of international finance and about the various institutions which provided financial services to American importers and exporters. The subject is approached in the context of a dual organizational structure: part one is a chronological overview of the firm's growth, stressing its competitive strategies and its internal administration; part two is a more detailed discussion of the main economic functions performed by the partnership, and it is tailored more to the demands of specialists in financial history.

Most authors incur debts to librarians, colleagues, and friends in the process of writing a book, and I am no exception. First, I would like to thank Irene Neu and Tom Cochran for initially suggesting this research topic. On separate visits to Johns Hopkins, where I was then a graduate student, they told me that the business records of the Brown firms were an untapped source of information on the nineteenth-century economy and that someone with my previous experience in banking and my interest in financial subjects might find a study of the enterprise rewarding. Their wise and timely counsel permitted me to avoid the long delays so frequently associated with the selection of a worthwhile research project.

I am indebted even more to Alfred D. Chandler, Jr., for his guidance and encouragement. The decision to organize the study around the firm's main functional activities was inspired by him—both in his role as a teacher and more indirectly through the example of his own scholarly achievements. Others who read early drafts of certain chapters were Louis Galambos, Morton Rothstein, and Herman Krooss, and I have profited from their comments and criticisms. Paul Uselding suggested the inclusion of estimates of the firm's market shares, although he is not responsible for the actual calculations.

For granting me permission to consult the firm's historical files, I am grateful to the partners of Brown Brothers Harriman & Co. This year, incidently, marks the 175th anniversary of the founding of the enterprise and the 150th anniversary of the opening of the New York branch. My relationship with the firm was ideal, since the partners did nothing to disturb the atmosphere of historical objectivity. They permitted me to examine the historical files without restrictions, and I received neither financial assistance nor editorial advice from anyone associated with the firm. Indeed, I never met or even corresponded with any of the firm's executives other than its librarians Nancy O'Connell and Mary Beth Byrne, both of whom deserve a special note of thanks for their expeditious handling of my research requests. As only he can appreciate, I am particularly indebted to John Kouwenhoven, an earlier historian of the firm who gathered and organized the collection of source materials in the historical files. His systematic cataloguing of the various records saved me months, if not years, of valuable research time. In the course of my research, I also learned that a belated note of thanks is due Bennett Wall, who over twenty years ago persuaded the Baltimore branch of the Brown family to donate its massive holdings of nineteenth-century letterbooks and related documents to the Library of Congress.

Most of the final manuscript was expertly typed by Sandy Wasserman, who came into the project late, after others had lagged behind. A generous Woodrow Wilson fellowship financed the early stages of the study. I also thank the editors of *Business History* and *Explorations in Economic History* for permission to draw on material previously published.

Lastly, I would like to express my gratitude to my wife Caroline, who made her own contributions to this study from its beginning until its completion.

Contents

Financing Anglo-American Trade

Introduction

This book is a study of the business activities of an Anglo-American, merchant-banking partnership, the House of Brown, during the period from its founding, in 1800, until 1880, when the firm was at the height of its prestige in the international financial community. Over the first half of the nineteenth century, this family enterprise established a chain of subsidiary branches and associated agents reaching from the principal eastern and southern ports of the United States to Liverpool, one of the world's most active shipping centers. Concurrently, the firm followed a trend, characteristic of other urban merchants, toward increased specialization. The Browns' main commercial activities progressively concentrated on the extension of financial services to the foreign trade sector of the American economy. The firm provides a prime example of the movement from general merchandising to commission merchant and, finally, to the more specialized field of banking. By the 1840s, the Browns, with their network of representatives, had emerged as the single most important international banking house serving the trade sector of the American economy, and it remained so until very near the end of the nineteenth century.[1]

My intention is to describe the broad strategies and the operating procedures which the Browns employed in the performance of their primary economic functions. The three functions receiving individual consideration are the extension of advances to exporters on consignments, the issuance of letters of credit to importers, and the purchase and sale of foreign bills of exchange. The emphasis here is on the evolution of the firm's rules for conducting its business affairs and on the factors the partners normally considered both in formulating long-range policies and in routine decision making.[2]

The firm's changing administrative structure is examined as well. Although the House of Brown retained its fundamental character — that of a family enterprise — its wide geographical dispersion and an increasing volume of business dictated the acceptance of new men within the organization. In the most important of the subsidiary branches, some of these "outsiders" were officially admitted into the partnership.[3] The criterion for admittance, and thereby a share in future profits, was not the contribution of additional capital, a resource with which the family was amply supplied, but administrative skill. Even the sons and relatives of the founders had to demonstrate a superior aptitude in the counting house before they received invitations to join the firm as full partners. Indeed, a few members of the Brown family remained little more than salaried employees throughout their entire association with the house. Until late in the nineteenth century, little dead wood accumulated within the organization.

Because the firm had branch offices of critical importance in the United States and in England, it had no single headquarters where policy could be easily developed and quickly implemented. Instead, the partners formulated comprehensive strategies through transatlantic correspondence, a formidable task. After 1840, moreover, the English operations were predominantly in the hands of nonfamily partners who had a viewpoint on organizational matters which frequently differed from their American counterparts. Despite such apparent handicaps, the firm successfully managed its affairs through a variety of economic and political crises and through several periods of internal stress.

The achievement of managing a multibranch system is especially notable when one recalls that few early models existed for administering enterprises of even moderate scope. The main profit the partners gained from comparisons with competitive organizations was to note their mistakes and inadequacies. The Browns' internal structure, based as it was on a transatlantic ownership pattern and a chain of outlets made up in part by wholly owned subsidiaries, was original and not successfully duplicated by any other Anglo-American banking house. In fact, except for the two banks chartered by the Congress early in the nation's history, it was one of the very few nineteenth century banking organizations to develop a broadly dispersed system of branches across the borders of the respective states.

The managerial process developed to administer and coordinate the activities of the firm's branch managers and its agent representatives is also investigated. Other international banking houses created loose chains of agents that competed with the Browns in the major American ports, but there was little effort to coordinate the activities of the various outlets. Each agency was a distinct mercantile firm, normally concerned only with business affairs in its home port; moreover, such firms might themselves have a series of agency agreements with other merchants in distant cities. As a consequence, none of the competitive houses seriously attempted to prescribe a uniform system of operation for these agencies, and indeed, without a method of enforcement, it would have been impossible to establish a high degree of uniformity. An independent merchant cooperated with an associated firm according to his own proclivities, and only when it appeared to be in his interest to do so. As a rule, there was a large turnover in agency accounts. Even Baring Brothers & Co., the Browns' chief competitor for much of the century and one of the more stable banking organizations, was not immune to numerous agency shifts as well as variations in the range of services.[4] Only in Boston did the Barings emulate the Browns and employ full-time subordinates who could be counted upon to follow the instructions of superiors. The Browns, on the other hand, maintained a relatively continuous level of service in their localities, and, for the most part, through the same representatives.

In order to create greater uniformity in the operating procedures of their various branches, the Browns instituted a system of internal control. The partners' instructions to branch managers reflected their determination to adopt policies considered vital for the long-run health of the organization as a whole. The Browns' personnel frequently transferred from one location to another. The partners established an informal, but highly effective training program for the junior men in the organization. They often sent a prospective partner to one of the southern branches for an initial management trial. If he followed the instructions of the main office diligently and performed his duties competently, the younger employee could generally look forward to promotion within the organization.

Like the Second Bank of the United States under the administration of Nicholas Biddle, the House of Brown developed an informal administrative structure which may be viewed as a transitional form between the prevalent family enterprise and the more professional management systems created by the railroads and later adopted by large industrial firms.

I

The Role of the International Banker

Although the Browns' internal organization differed significantly from the normal pattern within the field, the partnership performed financial functions similar to those carried out by competitive enterprises. In the nineteenth century merchant-banking houses provided a vital financial link between the United States and the commercial centers of the outside world. Through these foreign banking houses and their agents, payments flowed back and forth across the oceans. American shippers received payments primarily for the export of raw materials and foodstuffs. In the antebellum economy, cotton was by far the most important export. By the 1870s, however, the overseas shipment of American grain and processed foodstuffs was equally important. The imports Americans bought were more varied. Dry goods and manufactured products arrived from the more industrialized countries of Europe while sugar, coffee, tea, and silk were among the raw materials and exotic foodstuffs imported from South America and the Far East. The international banker, in addition to financing trade, also facilitated the capital flows which contributed so much to the rapid development of the American economy during the last century.[1]

An international system for smoothly and efficiently handling the financial transactions required by an expanding world trade was only beginning to develop in the early nineteenth century. During the eighteenth century the increasingly widespread use of bills of exchange, drawn in sterling on English merchants and bankers, as a prime means of payment within the commercial world created the conditions for the gradual emergence of a more monetized international economy.[2] An early response to the proliferation of sterling drafts and bills was the gradual formation of markets for foreign exchange in those port cities outside the English monetary system. Usually a few firms or banks became foreign exchange dealers — buying and selling sterling bills for the local currency.

Prior to the emergence of sterling bills as the prime medium of international exchange, debts between distant merchants were settled by barter or specie or, quite frequently, a combination of the two.[3] Although barter was the prevalent form of international exchange, it was by no means as crude a mechanism as often depicted. Distant merchants shipped to one another on open account. On a single round trip voyage, merchants tried to exchange merchandise of approximately the same monetary value. Any residual balance between merchants which failed to disappear over a long period could be then settled through the shipment of gold or silver.

There were, of course, several drawbacks to this pattern of trade. First, the transfer of goods was fairly well restricted to a bilateral or, at most, a triangular pattern. Moreover, a close relationship between the bulk or physical volume of the goods traded and their monetary value was necessary if shipping capacity was to be fully employed. For example, in the normal pattern of trade between the United States and Brazil, the value of a full cargo of flour, the main export, was only about one fourth of the value of a return cargo of coffee. A shipper either returned with a ship having excess capacity or he carried specie with him to buy additional cargo. In some trade patterns, notably with China, there was little basis for exchange other than specie. Except for furs, ginseng, and sandalwood, there was little Chinese demand for foreign goods.[4] Even where there was a fundamental balance of trade between nations, merchants who sold on open account were restrained in their activities because of the difficulty in locating correspondents that could be trusted. As a result, much early trade went on between relatives located in various port cities.[5]

The chief characteristic of the bill of exchange was that it permitted sellers of merchandise to convert the amounts owed to them on open account into monetary instruments which could be immediately sold to third parties in their home ports. The bill of exchange expedited transactions between nations where there was already a basis for barter, and it was capable of overcoming the problem of a fundamental or seasonal disequilibrium in the balance of trade, without resort to specie shipments. In the United States, it meant that exporters were able to draw bills against shipments of cotton to Liverpool and to sell the bills to American importers who were international debtors.[6] The standard method of settling foreign debts eventually became the remittance to England of a sterling bill of exchange.[7]

The foreign bill of exchange also gained more esteem in England with the maturation of the London money market.[8] Most bills were time drafts; that is, they were drawn to become payable in cash at

Waynesburg College Library
Waynesburg, Pa. 15370

some future date. A few of the bills were actually assigned a specific maturity date at the time they were drawn. But the vast majority of the foreign bills were sight drafts, and there was an indefiniteness about their ultimate maturity dates. A familiar item in the nineteenth century was the 60 day sight bill, often abbreviated as 60 d/s. Sixty days sight was a shorthand for saying that a sterling bill had to be physically presented to the English firm on which it was drawn before an actual maturity date could be set; upon presentation, or sight, the drawee was obliged to establish a final payment date 60 days in the future. A bill drawn in South America at 60 d/s, for example, might not become payable for 90 to 120 days, depending on the length of time that elapsed before the bill reached its English destination.

If a bill was drawn under a letter of credit agreement, which guaranteed its ultimate payment, the drawee was responsible for formally accepting a bill at the time of initial presentation as well. In accepting a bill, merchant bankers legally acknowledged their responsibility to pay the bill at the assigned maturity date. The word accepted was actually written across the face of the bill of exchange before it was returned to the parties presenting it. Thereafter, the item was known in financial circles as an acceptance rather than a bill of exchange or a sterling draft. When the maturity date arrived, it was the responsibility of the holder to submit the acceptance to the banking house for final cash payment.

During the interim, the holder had the option, however, of selling, or more precisely discounting, his acceptance in the very active short term money market. In nineteenth century England, this market was commonly known as the discount market.[9] The growing demand for foreign acceptances as short term investments for deposit banks and private houses such as Overend Gurney & Co., who specialized in these money market instruments, enhanced the negotiability of the bill of exchange throughout the world.

In the United States, the British pound was so critical to the foreign trade sector that the term foreign exchange became almost a synonym for money obligations payable in sterling. American importers settled virtually all their international debts in sterling bills. Although exporters drew the vast majority of their bills in sterling, they also drew bills in French francs and Dutch guilders against shipments of tobacco and grain to the European continent. Because the institutional structure was such that English merchants could insist on transacting all business in sterling or other strong European currencies, there was no dollar market in England corresponding to the sterling markets in the United States. References in the early nineteenth century to such a market are actually references to specie markets; the dollar transactions were entirely in gold and silver coins. A dollar bill of exchange was a rarity.[10]

The creation of active American markets for foreign exchange was a prerequisite for the continued development of related international financial services. The authorization of advances to exporters on goods consigned to European markets for sale and the issuance of letters of credit to importers were among the most important of these complementary services. These two primary functions were carried out, for the most part, in separate and distinct geographical regions. Advances to the exporters of cotton and tobacco were an integral part of the system of marketing southern crops, while northern merchants used letters of credit to facilitate the importation of foreign goods. Seasonal variations in demand and supply complicated the situation even further. The main purchasing season for exchange dealers was winter, while the chief selling season was late summer and fall. Because the supply of bills and the demand for them were separated so widely in time and place, the early exchange markets did not function smoothly; exchange rates, meaning prices, were subject to sharp ups and downs rather than gradual movements.

Several factors were decisive in developing a more national market for foreign exchange.[11] First, there was the entry into the field of a few organizations with large capital resources and a broad system of branch offices and agents. The most important of these were the Second Bank of the United States and the House of Brown. Nicholas Biddle, during his tenure as president of the Second Bank, viewed the greater coordination of the southern and northern markets as one of his primary public responsibilities.[12] The Browns, on the other hand, conducted business in a manner that tended to achieve precisely the same result — namely, the elimination of dramatic fluctuations in the movements of exchange rates. The invention of the telegraph was the second meaningful factor; it provided the communications technology which made feasible the realization of a national market.[13] The Browns quickly recognized the potential of an improved communications system. During the 1850s the partners began the regular practice of maintaining uniform rates for foreign exchange in all their various branches.

The increasing efficiency of the foreign exchange markets encouraged an expansion of the system of advancing on produce consigned to distant ports for sale. In the main southern ports, the agents and representatives of British firms authorized a large volume of advances against cotton shipments to Liverpool. The advance was usually an inducement to gain consignments. It permitted the American shipper to draw a sterling bill of exchange for a certain percentage, often 75 to 90 percent, of the probable market value of the cotton in England. Because these bills were sight drafts on England, their actual payment date was several months away. If all went well, the British consignee would be able to sell the cotton upon arrival and use the proceeds to meet the sterling bill drawn in the United States. Had the American shipper, in practice, been forced to wait that long before converting his advance into cash, the authorization to draw would have been of little value.

What actually made the advance so valuable was the possibility of transferring the bill of exchange drawn by the consignor to a third party. In other words, the bill could be sold outright for cash. Early in the nineteenth century, exporters had difficulty finding local buyers for their bills, and many bills were sent north for sale through exchange brokers. The brokers, in turn, often had difficulty locating a buyer who required a bill drawn in the amount of the southern exporter's advance. The emergence of a more national market for foreign exchange, however, soon mitigated these difficulties. The Second Bank of the United States and those private firms who regularly dealt in foreign exchange made arrangements with their southern representatives to purchase the authorized advances, in any amount, at the original source.

The chief danger in this financial activity was the risk of overadvances. An overadvance was not generally detectable until near the end of the marketing cycle—not until the consigned goods had arrived in Liverpool and the probable proceeds of the sale were then apparent. If, because of a sharp decrease in prices, the proceeds were not sufficient to pay in full the bill drawn months ago in the United States, then it became obvious in retrospect that an overadvance had indeed been made. The party on whom the bill was drawn, the consignee or his banker, at that point had two options. If the proceeds of the sale were only slightly less than the bill of exchange, 5 percent or so, the drawee might be inclined to honor the bill on its maturity date. The small difference could be settled with the American shipper at a later date, perhaps during the next shipping season. But if, on the other hand, the proceeds were substantially less than the face amount of the bill, the consignee, or his banker, frequently had no choice other than to refuse payment. Because it was impossible to alter the face amount of the bill at the last minute, a consignee might refuse payment even though he held in his possession as much as 90 percent of the funds actually required to meet the bill.

The general pattern was for a large number of overadvances to materialize all at once, predictably after a dramatic decline in the price of cotton. The stage was then set for an international monetary crisis. The reason a spate of overadvances had such a broad effect was because the ownership of the original bill had long since been transferred from the shipper to other parties. In fact, during the interim between the date on which the bill was drawn and the date on which it was ultimately assigned to become due, the bill was likely to have passed through several hands. Once the bill was dishonored (refused payment), it proceeded to trace its steps backward over the earlier ground, with each buyer demanding immediate reimbursement from the prior seller, until the bill was finally "thrown back" on the shipper himself. Many parties, therefore, who quite innocently bought a bill which happened to be generated by someone else's unfortunate overadvance soon found themselves drawn into the panic as well. This is what happened, for example, in the panic of 1837.

In the 1860s and 1870s, a series of new developments significantly changed the pattern of the American export trade. The growing shipment of breadstuffs and provisions from northern ports was one of the factors bringing greater equilibrium to foreign exchange markets in the north. Because the number of vessels headed for continental ports also increased, American shippers offered foreign exchange dealers a greater volume of bills payable in currencies other than the pound sterling. The successful completion of the transatlantic cable in 1866 sounded a death knell for the marketing system based on consignments and advances. Foreign buyers increasingly used the undersea cable to make direct purchases of American commodities. At the same time, any problems arising from overadvances on the remaining consignment business could be easily adjusted by the transfer of funds over the cable. By 1888 the Browns' Liverpool consignments, once among the port's largest, were so small that senior management closed the branch upon the death of the sole partner tending the office. The advance as a vital financial function in the international marketing of commodities had by then outlived its usefulness.

The coming of an international money economy based on the sterling bill of exchange spurred the issuance of letters of credit as well. During the first two or three decades of the nineteenth century, the letter of credit issued through an English merchant-banking house became a standard device for arranging the settlement of an American importer's debts.[14] Although the widespread use of such credits is a relatively recent development of the modern commercial world, its precursors had been facilitating long-distance transfers in one form or another from the time men began journeying to distant towns.

In its barest form the early letter served as a means of introduction and generally vouched for the financial integrity of the traveler. An established merchant or private banker typically wrote letters to his counterparts in towns where the traveler was scheduled to visit. The letters took on greater importance if the writer indicated a willingness to reimburse distant parties for funds provided to the traveler either for living expenses or to assist him in the purchase of merchandise for his business. As vague authorizations matured into firmer guarantees of a traveling merchant's debts, then the essential feature of the modern financial instrument had evolved. Even so, specific arrangements with foreign bankers for the issuance of each credit had to be made far in advance of any given trip, and the number of places where credits could be arranged was fairly limited.

The expansion of British commerce and the corresponding growth of the great English merchant-banking houses such as the House of Baring opened up new opportunities for the utilization of the letter of credit.[15] As English bankers acquired an international reputation for fiscal integrity, the drafts they authorized to be drawn on them in payment for goods and services were readily honored by foreign merchants and bankers. Most important, the drafts were honored without the necessity of lengthy prior arrangements. The credit granting procedure was thereby significantly streamlined; the English house could issue a credit immediately upon a customer's application. As a convenience to businessmen and tourists using their credits, English bankers frequently engaged a whole chain of independent merchants and bankers to act as correspondents in distant cities. The travelers received an "indication list" naming all the foreign firms which had informally agreed, without a binding commitment, to honor drafts drawn under the issuing bank's letters of credit. By the mid-nineteenth century, the issuance of a letter of credit was no longer an isolated transaction but a regular financial service of the international banker.

Moreover, the issuance of letters of credits reinforced the acceptance of the bill of exchange. When supported by a credit from a respected banking house, the bill of exchange became a much stronger financial instrument; it acquired a feature otherwise lacking—the guarantee that it would be paid punctually on the assigned maturity date. The possession of a letter of credit thus broadened the range of an importer's overseas markets. He could now make purchases even in ports where he had no relatives, no friends, or any previous connections.

American merchants holding letters of credit also exercised greater bargaining power in overseas markets, especially in the British Isles. Because the bills drawn under a letter of credit could be

discounted in the English money market after gaining formal acceptance, buyers were in a strong position to bargain for lower prices.
Some English manufacturers considered a bill drawn under a letter
of credit the equivalent of cash payment. In many cases, the discount
an American importer received from the seller was much larger than
the commission he paid a merchant banker for issuing the credit.[16]

The regular issuance of letters of credit was the one international
banking function most subject to specialization. It was performed
mainly by established firms with impeccable reputations. A credit
was not useful to an American importer unless a foreign merchant
immediately recognized, and completely trusted, the issuing house.
Only a few of the large Anglo-American firms had sufficient prestige
that their guarantee of a customer's financial obligations was especially valued by foreign merchants. It was the performance of this
banking service which, more than any other, qualified a firm for the
informal designation as a merchant-banking house and distinguished
it from firms which performed other international financial services
such as investment banking but did not issue letters of credit.[17] Under the most favorable circumstances, it usually took several years for
a potential competitor to cultivate a reputation for financial integrity
that was sufficiently strong to permit a limited entry into the letter of
credit market. Meanwhile, business contractions and financial crises
frequently eliminated weaker firms from the field. As a consequence,
the market structure was decidedly oligopolistic; a few houses, like
the Browns, the Barings, and George Peabody & Co. (plus successor
firms), dominated the Anglo-American letter of credit market over a
significant part of the nineteenth century.

By mid-century, a fairly stable system, based solidly on well-estab-
lished precedents, had evolved for handling a wide spectrum of international financial functions. This system was centered in Great Britain. The English had initially created a sophisticated financial structure for the purpose of expediting their own trade, but English merchants later found it profitable to extend these same services to other
nationals throughout the world. Because of a common language,
close family ties, and a colonial heritage, American merchants were
in an advantageous position to benefit from the development of the
British financial system.

Whereas domestic banking in the United States was in the hands of
widely scattered commercial banks, those firms which performed financial services for the foreign trade sector concentrated in the port
cities. Acting as representatives of the great Anglo-American banking houses, these local firms were essentially offshoots of the British
banking system. The majority of the representatives were independ-

ent firms which served as the appointed agents of English bankers. In a few cities, notably Charleston and New Orleans, state chartered commercial banks also served as agents. Occasionally an agent and the parent organization did business on a joint account basis, sharing profits and risks according to a predetermined formula. Some arrangements called for the parties to handle each others' business on a commission basis. There also were agreements under which an agent received a salary for handling a minimum volume of business and, thereafter, shared in the commissions or profits on any additional business. In fact, the terms on which these cooperative ventures were undertaken were so diverse that it is difficult to make a general statement about them.

It can be said, however, that many agents did not offer the whole spectrum of financial services in their respective ports. A given firm might perform only one of the main international banking functions. Not all agents were designated as bankers in their home ports. Oelrichs & Lurman, the Barings' agents in Baltimore for many years, were usually listed in city directories as commission merchants and often failed to appear in lists of local bankers.[18] During certain periods, often after an economic disturbance, an agency might go through years of relative inactivity. In one case, the Browns spent almost thirty years complaining about the lack of aggressiveness on the part of their appointed agent in Savannah, yet the partners were reluctant to shift to another firm because the representative was considered safe, meaning business was conducted only when risks were minimal, and he could be thoroughly trusted.

On occasion, the English bankers themselves preferred to restrict the range of services in the American market. For example, the Rathbones, who managed a medium-sized merchant-banking house based in Liverpool, did not actively solicit foreign exchange accounts in the United States, yet they authorized advances on consignments and accepted bills drawn by American importers under their letters of credit.[19] On the other hand, George Peabody & Co. sharply reduced the issuance of letters of credit in the Baltimore market after 1857 although a local agent remained very active in the foreign exchange market. Some of the smaller English houses concentrated their financial activities on trade confined to a limited number of commodities or on shipments between the United States and one other continent.[20] For instance, a number of these small merchant-banking houses offered letters of credit to U.S. importers engaged in the South American coffee trade at reduced commission rates.

In the breadth of their range of services and the permanency of their broad organization, however, no other competitive organization could match the House of Brown. After the demise of the Second Bank of the United States, it was the only firm to maintain a continuous market for foreign exchange throughout the whole period under review; and it could make a similar claim for the issuance of letters of credit. In the period from 1820 to 1840 the Browns' Liverpool house was among the leading recipients of cotton consignments from the South, and the firm's southern representatives authorized a proportionate volume of advances.[21] In addition, the Liverpool office made advances against consignments of dry goods to the Browns' American branches.

In the forties and fifties, however, the Browns' consignment business declined. Correspondingly, the volume of authorized advances—the financial function so closely associated with this merchandising activity—diminished. During this period, American shippers generally pressed consignees for higher advances against the probable proceeds of cotton sales in Liverpool and demanded greater return commissions or rebates. Some of the partners became quite concerned about the danger of making overadvances, and they decided to hold the advances of the firm's southern representatives to a very conservative percentage of probable market values. The net result was that as cotton prices rose significantly in the 1850s, the Browns lost most of their former customers to the competition.

The Browns' organization was distinctive in many ways. It was one of the few Anglo-American houses tracing its beginnings to the United States. Although George Peabody, like Alexander Brown, began his career in Baltimore, he had become a permanent resident of London at the height of his firm's international fame. Indeed, the few Americans who became full partners in other prominent Anglo-American houses were generally expatriates. As the Browns began to specialize more and more in the performance of international financial functions, the Liverpool partners likewise gained a greater role in the decision-making processes of the enterprise. The English branch was in the most favorable position to keep well informed about current international developments, and the policy recommendations of the partners stationed there naturally had much influence. Still the English branch never rose to a position of superiority vis-à-vis the American branches because the men who represented the firm in New York, and at times in other ports, were themselves full partners and not mere agents. Indeed the firm, in a significant departure from the norm, had more partners in the United States than in England. In that sense, it was the only merchant-banking house which justifiably merited the identification Anglo-American.

Another organizational characteristic distinguishing the Browns from their major competitors seems so self-evident that its significance can be easily overlooked: in each port city served, the firm usually maintained only one representative. The partners employed a marketing technique that was a precursor of the exclusive territory. Although outside offers of cooperation were plentiful, the Browns rejected most of them. Other international banking houses, who worked solely through a chain of independent firms, felt no compunction about aligning themselves with several agents in the same port if it appeared to be in their interest to do so. In the New York market, for instance, the Barings often had agency agreements with several firms, although some of them concentrated primarily on the performance of only one or two financial or merchandising functions. In the early fifties, George Peabody made a grand tour of the port cities on the eastern seaboard lining up agency agreements with almost every respectable house that would sign on. In Baltimore Peabody recruited two firms, McKim & Co. and Robert Garrett & Sons, and they actually competed with one another on foreign exchange transactions.[22] McKim also issued letters of credit on George Peabody & Co., while the Garretts were closer to the investment banking end of Peabody's business.[23]

Until 1863 the Browns had no London office. It was the only major Anglo-American banking house to rely for so long on a single provincial office in Liverpool. Because most sterling bills were traditionally drawn on London, the firm paid substantial commissions to a correspondent for handling their account in the English capital.[24] Partly because of their remote location from London and partly because of the financial prejudices of a few of the partners, the firm never became deeply involved in investment banking activities. After 1840 the Browns' principal competitors participated to a much greater extent in the flotation of American securities in European markets. Their competitors' periodic preoccupation with investment banking functions contributed to the Browns' rise to preeminence in the trade sector during the last two antebellum decades.

The Liverpool location was a factor in the partners' decision to invest heavily in a line of steamers, organized principally by E. H. Collins in the late 1840s.[25] The promoters were successful in obtaining a mail subsidy from the American Congress which was expected to permit it to compete with the Cunard steamers on the choice North Atlantic run between New York and Liverpool.[26] The Cunards had received a similar subsidy from Parliament. The Browns' Liverpool branch served as the shipping agent for the so-called Collins Line at its eastern terminus and therefore received a fair volume of commissions for forwarding goods to the United States.

Although the firm had previous experience managing the affairs of its own fleet of sailing vessels and in the 1820s became a silent partner in the Cope Line of packets between Liverpool and Philadelphia, the association with the Collins Line was a most unfortunate one. Despite the subsidy, the steamers were unprofitable; there were charges of corruption, and the Browns were called upon to advance considerable sums to the line to keep it in operation. When the line ceased its runs in 1859 the Browns were left holding mortgages on the steamers far in excess of their market value. Eventually, it seems, the house recouped its investment by transferring the steamers to the Pacific Mail Steamship Co. although the evidence is far from complete.[27] Aside from the financial outcome, the most important result of the association with the Collins line was the disharmony and ill feeling it generated within the partnership for the better part of ten years. Yet, the partners did not allow disagreements about the scope of outside activities to interfere with their main task of serving the financial needs of American foreign trade sector.

In the course of the firm's rise to a position of leadership in the international banking field, the partners developed a series of business strategies and general operating policies which differed significantly from those of their competitors. However, in offering such services as the making of advances against goods consigned to overseas markets, the issuance of letters of credit to American importers, and the buying and selling of foreign bills of exchange, the partnership performed those functions closely associated with the role of the international banker in the nineteenth century Anglo-American economy.

Part One

The Historical Narrative

Because of the topical organization of later chapters, an overview of the firm's development should be helpful in providing a clearer perspective for subsequent discussions of how the Browns performed their principal economic functions. In the course of describing significant turning points in the firm's history, the narrative seeks to analyze the broad business strategies and the organizational structure which contributed so much to the Browns' success during the first eight decades of the nineteenth century. Although the partners were, for the most part, committed to a concentration on the foreign trade sector of the American economy, there were occasional disputes about the proper scope of the firm's business activities. In these controversies, a fundamental issue was the allocation of capital resources, and the partners' viewpoints on this subject are thoroughly explored.

Since nomenclature is a potential source of confusion, it may be appropriate to define terms at the outset. The business entity known widely as the House of Brown was composed of several branches which were called by different names in different ports. In the 1820s, for example, the firm was styled Alexander Brown & Sons in Baltimore, Brown Brothers & Co. in New York, and William & James Brown & Co. in Liverpool; and over the years there were even more variations in the names of these and other offices. In this study the terms branch, office, and house are used interchangeably in referring to wholly owned outposts in the Brown organization.

The partnership also did business through independent businessmen who represented the firm as agents. These businessmen were usually local merchants with commercial interests beyond the field of international banking. The agency form of association was prevalent in Charleston and Savannah, and it emerged at times in Baltimore, New Orleans, and Mobile. In the latter three cities, however, and in

Boston and Philadelphia, the firm's representatives were more frequently general partners or full-time employees, none of whom was permitted any other outside business interests.

Unfortunately, the Browns did not seek fine distinctions in their own correspondence, and the senior partners indiscriminately referred to all their distant representatives as agents. The concept of retaining permanent subordinates in remote locations was apparently so recent that no identifying term had, as yet, been coined for such representatives. In this book, however, the partners and subordinates who manned the firm's subsidiary branches are referred to as branch managers, not as agents. By way of comparison, other Anglo-American banking houses were almost universally represented by independent merchants acting solely as agents. For optimum clarity, the various outlets of these international banking houses, including those of the House of Brown, are generally identified by the port in which they were located rather than by name.

II

Growth and Expansion

The founder of this family enterprise, Alexander Brown, was already a successful linen merchant in Ballymena, Ireland, before he emigrated to Baltimore in the late 1790s.[1] That he was reasonably prosperous can be adduced from the fact that this Irish businessman sent four sons to a boarding school in England. On the voyage to America, only his wife and eldest son William accompanied him; the three other boys were left behind to continue their education. Alexander Brown probably emigrated to Baltimore because several relatives who had preceded him to the port during the prior decade gave favorable reports.[2] Not long after his arrival, Alexander Brown announced, in an advertisement of December 20, 1800, that he was the port's newest linen merchant.[3]

The business was a profitable one. By 1810 the firm's capital had increased to $121,000. In 1821 the figure topped the million dollar mark; and it stood at $3,230,000 at the end of 1830.[4] By the latter date, the Browns' total capital had actually surpassed that of their most important rival in the American trade, Baring Brothers & Co. On June 30, 1830, the capital resources of all the Baring partners was only £492,000 — or slightly less than $2,500,000.[5] Following the pattern of other successful merchants in the colonial and early national periods, Alexander Brown extended the scope of his business over a wide range of activities and products. Like other "all-purpose" merchants, he performed a variety of economic functions — buying and selling goods on his own account, selling for others on commission, managing a fleet of sailing vessels, and sometimes performing the credit functions of a banker.[6]

During the firm's first quarter century, all four of Alexander's sons became partners in the family enterprise, and without exception, they proved to be men of remarkable business acumen. Each son eventually established a branch of the organization in a separate port.[7] William, the eldest and considered by his brothers the most like his father in business matters, had tried without success to open a permanent office in Philadelphia in 1808. The failure resulted more from bad timing than poor management, for Jefferson's embargo made any new mercantile adventure in that year especially difficult. In 1810 William left for Liverpool where he had better luck. The third son, John A. Brown, managed to succeed where his brother had earlier failed, when he reopened the Philadelphia branch in 1818.[8] James, the youngest son, began his career by temporarily joining his brother in Liverpool.[9] Their house, known as William and James Brown & Co., soon became one of the two or three largest acceptors of cotton consignments in England. In 1825 James established a new branch in what was rapidly becoming the nation's busiest port city, New York.[10] There he adopted the style, Brown Brothers & Co., the name by which the partnership was destined to become best known in the United States. The second son, George, remained at home where his father groomed him to assume the leadership of the Baltimore house, Alexander Brown & Sons.[11]

Although Alexander Brown's participation in a wide range of economic activities was representative of other early nineteenth century merchants, there were, nonetheless, indications from the very start of his career that this enterprising businessman's interests were broader than those of his contemporaries. By 1803 Alexander Brown had moved beyond the linen trade and was purchasing cotton through a Savannah agent for shipment to England. At the same time, he had gained some experience in handling foreign exchange transactions. Alexander Brown began buying the sterling bills drawn by a tobacco exporter in Petersburg, Virginia, and selling them to Baltimore importers. In April 1803 he told a Petersburg correspondent that locally there were only five or six Baltimore drawers whose bills he felt absolutely safe in purchasing for resale and that: "Respecting the purchase of Bills with you & selling here, I am still of the opinion its a business that ought to be proceeded in with great caution."[12]

After the Liverpool house was established in 1810, the volume of Anglo-American financial transactions increased markedly. Indeed, the creation of a transatlantic branch was clearly one of the key factors in the firm's rapid rise to prominence in the field of international finance. In the winter of 1811 the Baltimore partners made arrangements with William to coordinate their joint dollar-sterling exchange account.[13] Since the American branch was now in a position to create its own supply of sterling bills by drawing on the Liverpool branch, it was no longer confined to the brokerage function it had previously performed. The firm graduated to the rank of exchange dealer. In Baltimore, Alexander Brown and his three remaining sons soon found to their delight that bills drawn on Liverpool in amounts "to suit the purchaser will frequently sell higher."[14]

The establishment of a Liverpool office also stimulated the solicitation of consignments. Early in 1811 the Baltimore office informed exporters that it was prepared to negotiate reasonable advances against tobacco and cotton shipments consigned to the Liverpool house for sale.[15] Two stipulations were that the bill of lading, which conveyed ownership of the produce, accompany the request for an advance and that an insurance policy on the cargo be ordered through the Baltimore office. Since underwriting marine risks was another of the Browns' complementary services, the house sometimes issued its own insurance policies.[16] In its ability to so easily "negotiate" an advance, the firm had a distinct competitive advantage. It meant that the house was in a position not only to authorize an exporter to draw a bill of exchange on the Liverpool branch but, in addition, the Baltimore office was prepared to purchase at once a bill so drawn. In short, the Browns could perform two, otherwise independent, financial functions— the authorization of an advance and the purchase of a sterling bill of exchange—all in one simultaneous transaction.

In the meantime, the Browns had become shipowners as well. A 413 ton vessel, the *Armata,* was built in New York during the winter of 1810-11. The ship had no sooner completed its maiden voyage, however, than the long-running naval dispute between the United States and England began to heat up once again. Congress finally declared war in the summer of 1812, and because of the British blockade, American foreign trade fell off sharply during the following two years. The Browns were not adversely affected by the conflict, however. Through the Liverpool outlet, they procured a British license which allowed the *Armata* to carry provisions such as flour and wheat from Norfolk, Virginia, to the English troops fighting the French armies in Spain. In December 1812 Alexander Brown was optimistic about the probable outcome of their mercantile adventures: "If the Armata gets safe to Lisbon and home again, not being insured, we cannot make less than 60 or 70 Thousand Dollars by this year's trade."[17]

By the end of 1814 the Browns had increased their American capital to $263,117. Over a three year period, it had risen just over 60 percent. In a letter to William, who had returned to Liverpool in January 1814 after visiting Baltimore, Alexander Brown outlined some of his general thoughts on the future course of the enterprise: "We once thought . . . of going largely into the Dry Goods business, this idea we have abandoned as it might get us too extensively into a business with which we are not acquainted; . . . in case of peace we think your prospects of commission business is very great and you ought to confine yourself . . . to it."[18]

The strategy proved a resounding success. In 1815 alone, the partners' earnings were sufficient to increase the capital another 50 percent. With the addition of William's capital to the amount accumulated in the United States, the Browns' overall resources passed the one-half million dollar mark. The bulk of the earnings during the war years resulted from their "shipping interests." In later years the partners constructed additional ships, and they normally maintained a fleet of four or five vessels over the next three decades.

In the postwar period the firm continued to emphasize the solicitation of consignments for the Liverpool branch. Otherwise, the Baltimore branch described its own activities in the local market as largely confined to "Irish linens and the buying & selling of foreign exchange."[19] In other markets, however, the branch arranged for the export of some cotton on its own account. On cargoes consigned to the Liverpool branch by trustworthy southern merchants who had no inclination for speculation, the Browns were frequently willing to do business on a joint account basis. On these transactions, the firm preferred to limit its risk to no more than one third of the overall cost. Except for joint account interests, the Browns did not ship cotton on their own account unless a purchase was required to give one of their own ships a full freight. The Baltimore branch explained the firm's policy to an inquiring customer in a letter dated August 1818 and then added a slight qualification: "It is only when our regular trade is interrupted by Wars or restrictions that we ever deviate."[20]

In surveying the progress of their house over the first twenty years of its existence, Alexander Brown and his sons could cite with pride the many achievements of the enterprise. The senior Brown usually attributed the family's success to the resolute devotion to prudent conservative management and to those characteristics generally associated with the attitude Max Weber identified as the Protestant work ethic. He supplemented the moralistic fare, however, with an attachment for the virtues of specialization and for the confinement of business activity to a level not in excess of one's capital resources. That this philosophy was a cardinal tenet of the Browns' business strategy is revealed most clearly in the advice the Baltimore management gave William, in 1819, concerning a proposed investment in an English cotton mill:

> However profitable the business may be now, we know of none subject to more reverse than the Cotton Spinning trade . . . and when once it's known or even suspected that you are in any way interested in such an establishment . . . shippers of Cotton might conceive there was a risk if sent to you of it being sold to your own establishment lower than it ought . . . In the management of one's business it is not only necessary to be correct, but not to be suspected of incorrectness.

The Baltimore managers also suggested that William look around Liverpool and "see those Merchants who have so many concerns that they cannot superintend themselves; how, sooner or later, it does them injury if it does not ruin them altogether." In Baltimore, they testified, "those persons who have kept steadily to one pursuit are far the richest men." On the basis of this observation, they assured William that "one business properly conducted is the surest and safest way to make money."[21]

A year later Alexander Brown summarized what he believed was the key reason for the firm's success:

> We have always held it as essential to our comfort, and we may add in the long run to our prosperity, to let our business be within our means and seldom or never have occasion to try the extent of our credit; this we believe has raised our credit as high and probably higher than any house in the United States of the same length of time in Business.[22]

Throughout the 1820s the Browns continued to place increased emphasis on the financial phase of the business and the solicitation of consignments. Even so, the Baltimore branch admitted as late as 1822 that according to its calculations the operation of the sailing fleet was the most profitable line of endeavor.

In 1821 Alexander Brown was instrumental in vetoing William's proposal that the house expand significantly its volume of insurance risks. He cited several reasons for his opposition but the crucial objection centered on the possible effects of such a move on the firm's consignment business. Because the Liverpool house would be acting in the role of both insurance underwriter and the designated agent for the insured, there was a great danger of suspicion arising in the settlement of claims. Therefore it was doubtful, Alexander Brown felt, that shippers would be reconciled to such an inherent conflict of interest.[23] Since the house had become the second largest recipient of cotton consignments in Liverpool by 1820, the firm's leading position there was clearly worth protecting.

One of the firm's greatest assets in the cotton trade was its reputation for the avoidance of speculation. The prevalent form of speculation in Liverpool was the withholding of cotton from the market in anticipation of higher prices. In 1825, for example, the excitement in the market led to a host of rumors about speculation on the part of the principal Liverpool consignees, including the Browns. The Baltimore branch vehemently denied all the accusations, but many people remained skeptical. The rumors apparently reinforced the Baltimore partners' commitment to their fundamental strategy: "These circumstances show . . . that the true policy for a Commission house is to go on selling regularly their consignments let the market rule as it may & to have nothing to do with speculation either directly or indirectly."[24]

One problem which plagued the organization for years was the recruitment of competent southern representatives, for these agents were critically important to the success of the consignment business. "We don't think its possible to get an agent in Orleans to do business satisfactorily," Alexander Brown lamented in the summer of 1818.[25] Finally, the senior Brown decided to send John to New Orleans for several winter seasons to handle the business and seek out a more reliable permanent representative. In a personnel transfer so typical of this organization, James returned from his Liverpool post to substitute for John in Philadelphia during his absences. John, as a result of his New Orleans experience, became the American partner most responsible for the firm's cotton activities. By 1823 he had found a man who met the partners' demanding requirements for a satisfactory agent. Benjamin Story soon became the Browns' chief New Orleans representative, and John Brown reassumed the permanent management of his Philadelphia house.

The opening of a New York branch in 1825 signaled a number of alterations in the scope of the business and in the firm's internal structure. At least three developments ensued with long-range significance: the family accepted, for the first time, outsiders into the firm as junior partners; the issuance of letters of credit to American importers became a regular part of the Browns' financial services; and finally the Liverpool office began sending a much larger volume of English goods to the American branches on consignment.[26] All three developments were closely interrelated.

Several factors had discouraged the partners from expanding American consignments. First, there was the depression from 1819 to 1823 that put the house on the "defensive."[27] The real blows, however, were the inability of the Baltimore trade to revive after the depression and the failure of the Philadelphia office to live up to expectations. Too many out-of-town buyers passed up these trade centers for the New York market. Thus, the burgeoning growth of the Hudson River port offered an excellent opportunity for a revival of the firm's American consignment activities.[28] To manage the merchandising phase of the New York business, James Brown invited Samuel Nicholson, an experienced merchant, to join the house.

In a circular dated January 1826 the Browns outlined the terms under which consignments would be received and at the same time advised potential shippers that the house maintained branches in Baltimore, Philadelphia, and New York. The circular contained other important announcements as well. To assist William Brown in the management of Liverpool affairs, Joseph Shipley had joined the office. Shipley, a Quaker native of Wilmington, had been employed for six years as the Liverpool agent of a Philadelphia merchant. As to the future course of business operations, the Browns stated their position forthrightly, "We have felt ourselves pledged since the American War to confine ourselves to a commission business."[29]

The Browns also distributed a second circular which invited American importers to make greater use of the firm's letters of credit. Prior to 1826 the house had been extremely cautious in managing this sphere of its business. Although it is difficult to establish exactly when the Browns issued their first credits, it may have been soon after the Liverpool office opened. In a letter to a prospective customer in January 1826 James Brown explained that "no credits are issued by the Liverpool house unless opened through partners on this side which for 16 years has proven necessary to our safety."[30] Assuming James' memory was accurate, an 1810 starting date would appear correct.

The first reference to the issuance of a letter of credit in the extant letterbooks is found in March 1820.[31] The correspondence concerned a £1,500 credit for the Baltimore firm of Peabody & Riggs; rather ironically, one of the partners in that firm, George Peabody, in time became one of the Browns' principal competitors in the credit field. Early credits were, however, isolated transactions, in small or moderate amounts, for the convenience of wealthy merchants. The strongest advocate of an expansion of the firm's volume of credits seems to have been William Brown. But late in 1821 Alexander Brown could find little in the way of encouragement after reviewing the Baltimore situation, "This is a small market compared with New York or Philadelphia & the number of Importers here whom we would guarantee are very few."[32]

The distribution of the 1825 circular was then the starting date for the Browns' serious entry into the letter of credit market. At first, the credits were mainly used by importers who purchased dry goods and hardware in England, where the Browns' name was best known. In the spring of 1826 James Brown heard reports that the firm's acceptances were passing "in Manchester as *Cash* with as much freedom as . . . any other banker in the place which cannot be said of any other Liverpool house."[33] Importers who used the Browns' credits often made their purchases at anywhere from "5 to 10% cheaper" which was more than sufficient to cover the 2.5 percent commission for the financial service.[34] By the late 1820s the Browns were thoroughly involved in the extension of financial services to both the export and import sector of the American commercial community.

Meanwhile, the Browns' foreign exchange business in the United States had grown steadily. But the Browns were not as yet full-fledged exchange dealers in the narrowest sense of the term, since they did not maintain a permanent and continuous market for bills of exchange. In the 1820s the partners were not willing to buy or to sell sterling at all times. Rather they reserved the right to decline service to customers and the general public. As their business increased, however, the Browns realized that an increasing number of merchants were becoming dependent on them and they did not wholeheartedly welcome the responsibility. The Baltimore house explained the dilemma in April 1819: "Once you consent to do a business of this kind . . . you cannot at pleasure, on any change of circumstances, break off and refuse without hurting the feelings of your friends & being thought illiberal."[35]

Once the firm became generally known in the exchange markets, the partners discovered that a very passive sales strategy usually resulted in higher profit margins on their bill transactions. A flood of bill purchases in the south, however, could result in the temporary abandonment of their normal policy. In the spring of 1820, for example, the receipt of a large volume of orders for cotton purchases from customers of the Liverpool branch threatened to force the American branches into more aggressive sales tactics. The Baltimore branch estimated that, within a short period of time, the firm would be obliged to negotiate advances on approximately 16,000 bales of cotton. The house was somewhat dismayed by the likely consequences of the heavy southern purchases: "Having so much to negotiate we shall be forced into the market on a footing with others; hitherto by keeping off until asked for Bills we generally get 1% above the current rate which we cannot expect on so large a scale."[36] Their profit margin on foreign exchange transactions normally ranged from 1 to 1.5 percent during the early twenties.[37] There are no indications that the Browns deferred to any other firm in pricing their bills, at least until the Second Bank of the United States became more active in foreign exchange markets later in the decade.

A particularly clear view of the Browns' foreign exchange activities is found in a letter of March 1821 from the Baltimore branch to the Liverpool office. The correspondence is especially significant because it touches on several important topics related to the functioning of early exchange markets. Since the currently high sterling rate offered an opportunity for substantial profits on bill sales, the Baltimore partners warned the Liverpool branch to prepare for a large volume of incoming drafts during the next few months. "If . . . there appears to be any danger of you being scarce of money," they wrote, "we will send over stock to make a temporary loan on." They did not expect the situation to last very long, however; "We think it impossible heavy importations will continue . . . in face of such a rate of Exchange."

The Baltimore partners also reported that sterling rates in New York had been higher than in Philadelphia and Baltimore in recent months: "It's the greatest market and always rises or falls there first." Therefore, they had contemplated the possibility of selling their bills in New York through an independent broker for a commission of 0.25 percent. In previous years, such an arrangement was considered unnecessary, the Baltimore partners explained, "When Exchange is stationary we have generally found Phila. and this place full as good as New York." Meanwhile, they planned to push bill sales in the last few days before the packet ship sailed for England because they feared that foreign exchange might suddenly take a turn downward. "We should feel mortified at not having realized," the Baltimore partners added, "particularly as our purchases are predicated on a high Exchange."[38]

As the correspondence indicates, the Browns managed their foreign exchange account with great care, and this involved the coordination of the activities of their various branches and representatives. In doing so, the partners transferred capital resources from branch to branch and country to country. For the most part, idle cash was held in the United States for investment because yields were higher, but the firm did not hesitate to shift assets to England if there appeared to be any danger that the Liverpool office might be subject to undue pressure in the money market. The stock proposed for transfer here was that of the Second Bank of the United States.[39]

Although the Browns and the Second Bank eventually became competitors in many financial markets, the partners continued to hold a substantial amount of Second Bank stock.

It is also clear that the Browns did not always balance their current bill sales with current bill purchases. When exchange rates were abnormally high, they were tempted to sell heavily in the north, with the expectation that later in the year their account could be balanced, or covered, at lower prices. Their profit margin might thereby be increased several percentage points. The Browns also found it profitable to engage in transatlantic specie shipments whenever exchange prices were extremely high or low, and their calculations, designed to determine the exact point at which such operations should commence, were exceedingly precise.[40]

The Browns, in short, were already "playing the foreign exchange market," and they were doing so in a highly sophisticated manner. Like a short seller in the modern stock market, the Browns often sold a bill without making an offsetting purchase for several months. This behavior is especially notable, since in other fields of economic endeavor including their own advancing and letter of credit activities, the Browns expressed the greatest abhorrence for speculation and the perpetrators of speculation. Cautious in the performance of other functions, the Browns continued to play a bold and dangerous game in the foreign exchange markets. In terms of the risks involved, the partners were, of course, aware of the many parallels between foreign exchange operations and other forms of economic activity, but for the most part, they chose to ignore them. One can only surmise, and their record bears it out, that the Browns achieved so much expertise in this field over the years and became so confident of their own ability to maintain control over operations that they did not view this phase of their business activities as inherently speculative.

Third, the correspondence clearly designates New York as the primary market for foreign exchange along the Atlantic coast. In addition the partners noted the close relationship between packet sailings in the port cities and fluctuations in exchange rates. Evidence from the mid-thirties indicates that the pattern of rate setting was essentially the same as described in 1821. "At times in a rising market we are below New York quotations & in a falling market above—the rate by one packet governs us for the next," the Baltimore partners stated in 1835.[41]

But overshadowing all else in importance is the Browns' statement that exchange rates in the three key ports, Baltimore, Philadelphia, and New York, were normally about the same. If this remark can be accepted at its face value, and there is nothing in the records to suggest otherwise, then the general impression that exchange markets in these major cities prior to Biddle's ascendancy to the presidency of the Second Bank were disorganized and uncoordinated would appear to require serious qualification. Indeed, the Browns' correspondence, taken in its entirety, demonstrates clearly that a regional market for sterling exchange was rapidly emerging in the Atlantic ports in the period from 1815 to 1825. Biddle's role in the creation of a more stable, national market may well have been over-rated.[42] The Browns were already making progress in that direction until the Second Bank decisively preempted market leadership after 1825. It is also evident that improvements in transportation and communication, which scholars have often cited as the prime explanation for the exchange market's ability to maintain stability after the closing of the Second Bank, were having an effect in an earlier period as well.[43]

The rise of the Second Bank of the United States, under the administration of Nicholas Biddle, to a paramount position in the foreign exchange market after 1825 does not appear to have been detrimental to the interests of the House of Brown. In association with the House of Baring, Biddle used the Second Bank's broad branch system and the tremendous capital resources at his command to influence prices in the exchange markets over the shortrun. Overall, the Second Bank's domineering role in the market seems to have aided the Browns in planning their exchange operations. Since the Second Bank maintained a continuous market for sterling bills, it relieved the partners of a responsibility to their own customers on that account, and it gave the firm greater flexibility in the management of its sterling account.

The Browns gained flexibility in two respects. In periods when it was difficult to purchase quality sterling bills in sufficient amounts and exchange rates were not high enough to justify specie shipments abroad, the Browns had the alternative of buying bills directly from the Second Bank. Biddle's presence in the market reduced significantly the risk of unforeseen difficulties in the execution of the Brown's seasonal operations. The partners could sell heavily during the summer and early fall with less anxiety; in the event their bill purchasing later proceeded slowly in the south, their account could always be covered quickly, with more certainty if less profit. The Baltimore house explained the situation to the Liverpool branch in August 1836: "We will try to remit promptly as we can on all fall purchases although we may be obliged to buy bills from Bk. U.S. at 8% if better cannot be done."[44]

The Second Bank's overriding presence in the market permitted the Browns to regulate with great precision the volume of their exchange sales. The controlling device here was the pricing system. Since the sterling bills of the Second Bank were the most highly valued in the economy and in the greatest demand, they correspondingly sold at the highest rates. As one of the two or three houses who represented something of a second tier of bill sellers between the Second Bank and ordinary endorsers, the Browns faced a highly elastic demand. By adjusting their own rates slightly up or down relative to the Second Bank's, the Browns could readily control the volume of their sterling sales. "We could sell largely by taking 1/4 percent less, but shall probably sell as much as we wish at their price," the Baltimore house remarked in 1828.[45] In November 1831 the same branch assessed the situation in this manner:

> We have now got to that standing that we get the same price for Exch. as the Bank U. States . . . We believe we are the only private bill drawers that are able to obtain Bank U.S. price, this arises partly from our being always ready to draw & never offering a bill for sale until asked for, even Girards & numerous bills with state Bank endorsements have recently been sold at 9 & 3/4ths whilst we are getting 10%.[46]

Even so, their sterling did not always command the very best rate as another remark made soon thereafter shows: "As we are not anxious to sell, we hold at the same rate as U.S. Bank."[47] One more sign of the Browns' increasing emergence as dealers in their own right was their growing independence from middlemen. "The credit of our Southern friends stands so high & our houses here, in Philadelphia, or New York are getting the top price for sterling without employing a broker," the Baltimore partners wrote in August 1831.[48]

Aside from their financial services to the foreign trade sector, the Second Bank of the United States and the House of Brown performed other broad functions for the general economy. Economic historians have long debated to what extent the Second Bank under Nicholas Biddle acted as a central bank for the commercial banking system. By virtue of his efforts to facilitate commerce generally and to regulate the money and credit markets, Biddle was unquestionably behaving as a central banker, but his failure to serve as a lender of last resort for other banks in times of crisis has tended to disqualify the Second Bank, in the minds of many, as a genuine precursor of the modern central bank.[49] The last function seems to have been largely relegated to the private banking houses.

The Browns, for example, frequently came to the aid of

commercial banks in desperate need of temporary reserves, and especially those banks having a Brown partner on their boards of directors. The firm's capital was, of course, inadequate to perform such tasks on a national scale, but the partners did rescue a few individual banks threatened with disastrous runs by increasingly suspicious depositors. As a rule, these banks were placed in jeopardy because of large defalcations, general mismanagement of the loan portfolio, or merely rumors of the like.

On one, well-publicized occasion Alexander Brown stood steadfastly beside a group of local banks in an effort to head off a localized monetary panic. In the spring of 1834 he publicly announced, in the wake of an anticipated run on the Baltimore banks, that his own firm's capital was committed and no fundamentally solvent firm would be allowed to fail.[50] The leadership Alexander Brown exhibited on this occasion was apparently effective because a panic was averted. In an interesting sequel, the Browns attempted to assist the Union Bank of Maryland in its search for a $600,000 loan to bolster its reserves. The Baltimore branch asked the Liverpool office, at one point, to seek out the Rothschilds and their friends as a potential source of funds.[51] When the Browns and other merchant bankers required a lender of last resort, they invariably sought the aid of the Bank of England; it was the central bank for the international houses operating in the Anglo-American economy.

At the outset of their fourth decade of operations, the Browns were very concerned about the investment of surplus capital and about the competition the Liverpool office faced in securing consignments of finished goods for the American branches. On the matter of surplus capital, the American partners strongly opposed William Brown's proposal that the firm's excess funds be invested in the English market. Speaking for the American partners, the Baltimore office told William that, despite the difficulty in locating investments which paid a "regular and well-secured interest," it felt this goal could be achieved in the United States "to better advantage and safer" than in Great Britain.

In the past the Browns had invested substantial sums in the stock of the Second Bank of the United States, but in April 1831 the Baltimore management believed the situation warranted a more cautious attitude: "The uncertainty of the charter . . . being renewed makes it a hazardous investment; if the charter should not be renewed the stock would not be worth par." The stocks of the state-chartered banks appeared to be an equally "precarious investment." Indeed, the American partners were disturbed because none of the American stocks they considered safe paid over 4 percent in dividends. Nonetheless, they felt that "Money may get scarce by & by . . . in the meantime . . . we can use considerable funds by discounting good long paper a little below the Bank U.S. rate, probably . . . from 5 to 5½%."[52] Although the wishes of the American partners prevailed on this occasion, the debate over whether to invest excess capital in England or in the United States recurred in the ensuing decades.

Meanwhile, a reduction in the commission rates of Liverpool forwarding agents in the summer of 1831 threatened the recently expanded business of securing consignments of English finished goods for the firm's branches in the northern port cities. The Browns faced the prospect of matching the lower rates or losing a large share of their current volume. Quite characteristically, they were reluctant to reduce their fees for fear of the precedent it might set, and that solution was ruled out. They finally approved an alternate plan; the Browns hired William Bowen as the firm's Manchester representative, with the explicit duty of soliciting consignments of manufactured goods for the American branches. Bowen, like Joseph Shipley, was a Quaker who had previously been employed by the Philadelphia merchant, John Welsh.

William Brown opposed the appointment of an "inland" agent, but again his brothers' wishes on the matter prevailed. The consignment business in Philadelphia and especially New York had been a source of "handsome profits," they argued in August 1831, and without these revenues Liverpool commissions and foreign exchange earnings would have to bear the whole cost of maintaining the American branch system.[53] Moreover, "without some exertion to keep up the commission business the Junior partners could not make a support . . . and would have to retire," the American partners added. At the same time, they rejected the alternative of importing merchandise on their own account as too risky; one good season like the last often led to "overtrading the next."

The inland agent discussion in 1831 illustrates the extent of the American branches' involvement in the commission phase of mercantile activities. During the last half of the 1820s, the merchandising volume had increased substantially over the low point reached in the early part of the decade. The generally depressed state of business after 1819 and the decline of Baltimore as a regional center for the import trade were, of course, causes of the earlier decrease, and the partners' desire to rejuvenate this sphere of the business motivated, in part, their decision to locate branches in the two ports farther north.

The partners' concern over the possibility that the revenues recorded in the ledgers of an individual branch might not be sufficient to cover its own operating expenses was also significant. The potential inability of an office seemingly "to pay its own way" was a disturbing factor. And it remained so despite the partners' realization that many of the commissions recorded in the Liverpool books were attributable to the efforts of their other outlets and that these same outlets also played a role in generating the exchange profits calculated once a year for the American branch system as a whole. This difficulty in measuring the contribution of a single branch to the overall profits of the partnership plagued the firm for many years. Although some progress toward a satisfactory solution to the problem of internal accounting occurred during the course of the century, the partners never developed a completely satisfactory system.

At one point there were indications that the Browns might choose to make their name in the investment banking field as well. Alexander Brown was among the more ardent promoters of the Baltimore and Ohio Railroad, and his son George actually served as the road's treasurer for several years after the first tracks were laid in 1828.[54] The family's interest in the B & O Railroad was more a matter of civic duty and community pride, however, than an all-out effort to gain a foothold in a new line of business. The firm's investment banking activities did not expand significantly again until the postbellum era. But on the strength of their association with the nation's earliest railroad and all the publicity surrounding that historic event, the Browns' role in the investment banking field during the nineteenth century has, at times, been overestimated.

As their temporary performance of investment banking functions demonstrates, the Browns were involved in a wide variety of business activities. In this respect, the firm's pattern of operation—though on a grander scale—was not strategically different from the business operations of more traditional merchants. By limiting the purchase of goods on their own account in the United States and becoming thereby largely commission merchants, the Browns followed a trend characteristic of other business enterprises. At the same time, the Browns were expanding their operations into new markets over the first three decades of the century. Coinciding with the opening of a New York branch in the mid-twenties, the firm increased the issuance of letters of credit and solicited more consignments of finished goods for the American branches. At this point in the firm's history, there were few signs that the adoption of a strategy stressing greater specialization on the performance of purely financial functions lay ahead.

III

New Strategies

In the mid-thirties the partners formulated new strategies which affected permanently the character of the enterprise. The death of Alexander Brown in 1834 precipitated a comprehensive reassessment of the partnership's business operations. Overall profits were at an all-time high. The founder's passing in his seventieth year was the catalyst for a thorough review of the firm's progress, and more important, it led to serious discussions of the future of the enterprise, the partner's individual goals, and the policies requiring implementation to achieve those goals. By the end of the decade, the partners had adopted a management philosophy and an organizational alignment which served the firm for the remainder of the century.

During the American boom of the early thirties, the Browns' letter of credit business mushroomed. In view of this growing demand for their credit services, some partners began contemplating the possibility of discontinuing mercantile activities in the northern ports and concentrating exclusively on the extension of financial facilities to other importers. Simultaneously, the difficulties encountered by the Second Bank of the United States in respect to the recharter issue enhanced the status of the Browns' sterling bills. Furthermore, the Browns believed that in the event of the Second Bank's ultimate demise, which by 1834 — given Jackson's veto of the bank bill and the President's reelection largely on the bank issue — seemed probable, they would become the logical heirs to the leadership position in the foreign exchange market.[1] Although these impersonal economic forces had been pointing the way for some time, the American partners' articulation of their intention to specialize in the performance of financial functions was clearly hastened by the death of the senior Brown.

In conjunction with a gathering of the family for the funeral in

April 1834, the American partners decided that the time had arrived to restrict, for the most part, the operations of their three northern branches to a "monied business." James, who remained in Baltimore with George for several weeks after the funeral, revealed in correspondence with William the family's thoughts on limiting partnership activities: "As to future business we all agree here we had better curtail than extend operations . . . we shall confine ourselves chiefly to our Exchange & comm^n business keeping that as moderate as we can, employment of capital being more an object now than acquisition of further wealth."[2] This rentier attitude can be associated mainly with George and John, although James agreed that the overall situation did call for extensive reflection. He also told William that the Liverpool branch, in the meantime, would not be asked to narrow the scope of its merchandising activities; William was to continue handling cotton consignments in cooperation with the southern outlets and soliciting other business that could be transacted locally on a commission basis.

Several months later a broad analysis of the relative profitability of their various activities and investments was in full swing. The fleet of sailing vessels that had yielded handsome returns in the early twenties came under review; "We believe ships are not likely to be what they have been . . . two of them lose money now but bring business to the Lvpool. house," George concluded in one letter to William.[3] In July George told the same correspondent that he had resigned the presidency of the Merchants Bank and given up his duties as treasurer of the B & O Railroad in order to devote more time to the affairs of the firm. Turning to the subject of U.S. consignments, he stated: "It would be my wish to confine ourselves more to a Banking business & have less to do with goods as I am convinced until the B.U.S. question is settled the commission on sales . . . will not pay the bad debts."[4] The foreign exchange business was safer, George argued, because sterling bills usually matured within three months while goods purchasers usually took up to eight months to pay. The New York house was already experiencing difficulties in the collection of debts arising from earlier sales of hardware in particular, and the partners generally agreed that too much capital had become tied up in this phase of business.[5]

George feared that many of these debts might turn into lockups. Lockup was a broad term that encompassed overdue accounts, tied-up assets, securities not worth either par or cost, and any other item which could not be included in a firm's normal working capital. It was a malleable term that could be easily molded to suit the purposes of the user; George and John often thought they saw lockups where James and William believed none existed. In order to prevent them entirely and, at the same time, to release more capital for exchange operations, George suggested the following course of action, "It is my decided opinion, the less goods New York and Phila. have for sale for 2 years the better."[6] Apparently the others agreed. Indeed, the mercantile sphere of the New York business was soon sold outright to a local dry goods merchant.[7]

George's point about the favorable opportunities in the exchange end of their business was well taken. In late September he urged William to keep all the firm's "spare cash" in the foreign exchange business "in which we are doing more than formerly." In addition, George offered an overall assessment of the firm's current position: "We are quite aware that taking all our business together there is no house probably in this country doing so well."[8]

The year end accounting for profit seemed to bear out his conclusion. Gross earnings on the American side in 1834 were $435,155. Because of the continued consolidation of American branch accounts in Baltimore, George wrote the covering letter that accompanied the financial statements to Liverpool: "The last year has been one of great prosperity . . . arising in part out of Jackson's hostilities against the Bank U.S. The gross earnings are much more than we could have anticipated as no part of the amount was made by speculation."[9] He also noted that during the year the house had "made loans to several Banks and to some individuals to sustain them." The insurance end of the business was gradually being phased-out, he reported, although the remaining accounts were "paying well."[10] With the addition of Liverpool profits and deductions for the partners' living expenses and $150,000 for their mother's legacy, the capital account of the four brothers stood at $4,610,321.[11] The breakdown was as follows:

William Brown	$1,678,352
George Brown	1,079,946
John A. Brown	913,006
James Brown	939,017
	$4,610,321

The absence of speculation, commented upon by George, was especially prevalent in the firm's cotton operations. In the early stages of the 1833-34 season, the Browns cautioned their southern agents about the danger of overadvances on consignments to the Liverpool house. The continued excitement in the cotton market caused George to become extremely apprehensive about this phase of their business. In August 1834 he made a statement which may be cited as an early expression of the attitude that was to prevail in the partnership some years later: "The Cotton trade is no doubt a pleasant one but the competition for it being so great, people are willing to go to any length to get consignments . . . we understand many houses will advance the whole cost."[12] In addition to the imposition of strict limits on advances, the house also refused all proposals to ship on joint account. George told Benjamin Story, the New Orleans agent, that "should the rate keep up to last year's prices . . . we would not wish to be interested in a pound of Cotton."[13] Cotton prices, of course, continued to climb and the Browns remained largely out of the market throughout the speculative mania.[14]

George Brown assumed not only his father's place as the head of the Baltimore branch, but in addition he attempted to maintain the tradition of controlling and coordinating the firm's American affairs from its unofficial Maryland headquarters. The southern agencies kept their accounts with the Baltimore branch and received most of their instructions from there. The old administrative arrangement had one serious flaw, however. By the mid-thirties, James's New York house produced by far the largest volume of business, and its location in the leading commercial and financial center made it a more natural headquarters for operations in the United States.

An organizational realignment soon followed. When the partnership became engulfed in the general economic crisis of 1837, the experience unnerved George and John; shortly thereafter both men decided to retire from the general partnership.[15] New York then replaced Baltimore as the firm's American headquarters. Despite the retirement of the two brothers, the offices in Baltimore and Philadelphia remained integral parts of the surviving organization.

The newly adopted strategy of the firm—to concentrate on the performance of financial services for the foreign trade sector—was not significantly altered by the economic crisis; indeed, the wisdom of that strategy was powerfully affirmed. In the year before the panic the firm enjoyed the most profitable period in its history. Net additions to capital in 1836 were just short of one million dollars, bringing the total capital account of the four brothers to $5,912,000. Near the end of 1836, however, after the Bank of England began discriminating against British houses involved in the American trade, the Browns began to feel some pressure in the money market. In England, William became quite concerned about the general state of partnership affairs.

Any anxiety in Liverpool was usually multiplied severalfold in Baltimore. In correspondence with William in November 1836, George expressed hope that the worst of the crisis had passed. The recent turn in events had proven, he felt, the prudence of not issuing letters of credit in the reckless manner of other houses; he mentioned Wildes, Pickersgill, Wiggen, and Morrison Cryder. The same could be said for the avoidance of speculative security transactions. "We view the regular & legitimate business as much more desirable to cultivate than the stock operations, when money becomes plenty the latter will cease but the other will be permanent," he argued.[16] In conclusion he stated, "It has been a good year for making money but I would rather make less than have the excitement we have had for the last two years."

At the end of 1836 when the annual financial statements went out to Liverpool, George was more positive in his general outlook. "The past year has been one of great prosperity on this side although at times we of course had our anxieties from the great derangement of the currency; yet this very derangement," George noted ironically, "was in our favor." From the magnitude of their present capital, he felt the firm would be able to sustain any losses that might occur in 1837. Meanwhile, George was convinced that the increased emphasis on financial activities was sound policy: "I think our abandoning the dry goods business and doing a monied business makes us more independent & less likely to make bad debts."[17]

George's optimism was short-lived. The rapid decline in the price of cotton during the winter and spring of 1837 and the subsequent return of dishonored bills of exchange to the United States as a result of the overadvances of Liverpool consignees created a panic atmosphere in the American port cities by April. George lamented these developments in correspondence with the firm's trusted New Orleans agent, Benjamin Story: "There is no knowing where these failures will end." In Baltimore, the situation appeared to be less critical than elsewhere, he reported, since "the same wild speculations have not been entered into by merchants in this city." Meanwhile, George advised Story to avoid the purchase of bills of exchange drawn on the leading merchant bankers in London. "Unless the Bank of England acts liberally toward them," he added, "it will be impossible to foresee the consequences."[18]

By the end of July, however, his reports to Story were more encouraging. "You knew Wm. & Jas. Brown & Co.'s engagements were so great they were alarmed at their situation," George wrote, "but you will have since learned that the Bank of England came forward in a spirited manner & sustain them by paying all their engagements to the end of the year." As security for the loans made by the Bank of

England, the Browns had offered "real estate, stocks, and other securities as collateral."[19]

Although the firm was saved from bankruptcy, George was severely shaken by the trying experience. In a letter to William in November 1837 he intimated that he might join his brother John in retiring from the general partnership: "If you will refer to my letters of the past few years, you will find I was always afraid we were doing too much business involving risk & a great deal of anxiety." By withdrawing and doing a more limited business, he felt his anxiety would be greatly lessened. As soon as accounts were settled in Philadelphia, John was determined to leave. The possible closing of the Philadelphia branch disturbed George, however, because he believed "it would break up a very important link in the chain as it is desirable to be apprised of the movements of the Bank of the U.S. in regard to our exchange operations." Inasmuch as the business in Baltimore had ceased its growth, George felt his retirement would also provide an opportune time to make the New York office the American headquarters: "New York being the principal place for negotiating bills . . . it has been found most advisable to have the southern accounts transferred there."[20]

John retired the next year, but George remained in the partnership until 1839. The transfer of the southern accounts to the New York house occurred in 1838, and this date marks the beginning of a new administrative era, with New York controlling and coordinating the activities of the American outlets. Nonetheless, until his actual retirement, George Brown was still involved in the decisions that shaped the firm in the aftermath of the panic.

At the end of 1837 George made the annual review of the operations of the American branches for the last time. First, he expressed gratification over the news that the loan from the Bank of England was being repaid at a faster pace than anyone had originally anticipated. George then turned to the firm's foreign exchange business: "We have no difficulty in selling our bills anywhere *notwithstanding Ward the Agent of Barings* rejects Brown Brothers & Co.'s bills with contempt as I have understood, this arises from the mortification that Barings are not to have all in their own hands as they at one time expected."[21] In Baltimore "there are no regular bill sellers except ourselves," he reported; the firm's credit standing was as high as ever.[22] In the upcoming months he anticipated the coverage of earlier bill sales at profit margins of 10 to 15 percent, an astronomical amount compared to the usual 0.5 to 1 percent margins. George felt exchange profits during the 1837-38 season would probably offset the losses sustained during the panic. He estimated those losses would not exceed $300,000 or about 5 percent of total capital. George claimed he had lost only a minimal amount on his own Baltimore accounts. His desire to avoid sharing in any future losses sustained by the other branch offices was an important factor in his decision to retire from the general partnership.

George also mentioned that in the course of the year he had declined deposits from many merchants wishing to place money with the house. Although it is difficult to determine when the rejection of strictly domestic accounts became a general policy of the Brown organization, the policy was later an important feature of the firm's overall business strategy. Since there is no evidence that the house ever had a large number of domestic accounts, there may have been a general understanding from the firm's inception that only the accounts of those merchants involved in foreign trade were welcome, and in later years the understanding became a set rule. At any rate, the policy was a hallmark of the Browns, and the partners justified it on the grounds that the acceptance of such deposits left an international house too vulnerable to domestic monetary disturbances. One qualification should be noted, however. During economic crises later in the century, when all commercial banks were under suspicion, the Browns accepted substantial deposits from various privileged clients on a temporary, principally safekeeping basis. Nevertheless, the validity of the generalization—that the Browns did not maintain interest bearing accounts for domestic depositers—still holds. The partners were known as foreign bankers exclusively.

One change following the 1837 panic was a new name for the Liverpool branch. It was largely due to the boldness of Joseph Shipley, who had served the house since 1826, that the Bank of England agreed to lend the firm sufficient funds to carry it through the crisis.[23] As a reward for arranging the two million pound loan, then an unprecedented sum for a private firm, William and James Brown & Co. became Brown, Shipley & Co., a style which has been retained by the English firm up to the present. The partners thereafter entrusted Shipley with the primary responsibility for managing the Liverpool office; William Brown became more of a senior adviser and less an active participant in the branch's administration. In time, the senior Brown was elected to Parliament and political affairs impinged on his business activities. Since none of his progeny survived him, men who were not members of the Brown family generally managed the English division of the organization for the remainder of the century.

Before making the final arrangements for his retirement from the partnership, George Brown assisted his brothers James and William in planning a number of administrative changes in Mobile, New Orleans, and Philadelphia.[24] In the two southern ports, they decided to establish permanent branches of the parent organization, thus ending the firm's reliance on independent parties acting as agents. This move was logical from two standpoints. The Browns' exchange operations were already extensive, and the prospects for continued growth, now that the Second Bank had closed, were highly favorable. Since New Orleans and Mobile were large markets for the purchase of sterling bills, the firm especially needed competent and responsive representatives in those locations. Branch offices in the two most important cotton ports became a reality, however, because the firm had the personnel available to manage them.

When the northern branches gave up their mercantile functions, two junior partners whose duties had been associated primarily with the American consignment trade were left with reduced responsibilities. In New York, Samuel Nicholson had handled most of the branch's dry goods transactions. In England, William Bowen had concentrated on the solicitation of consignments for the American market. Both men were in need of new assignments and increased responsibilities. The partners' solution was to transfer their skills to foreign exchange operations and the solicitation of cotton consignments for the Liverpool branch.

George initially favored opening a branch office only in New Orleans. In reviewing the prospects in several cities during the spring of 1838, he was especially enthusiastic about the Louisiana port: "New Orleans . . . is a place to get some good business but it requires a man of experience and judgement." In the past Benjamin Story had been "a most excellent, safe, and prudent correspondent," George acknowledged, but because he kept no clerks on the payroll, Story's accounts were frequently late. "If we could make an arrangement with Story to give him half of all commissions earned, with Nicholson or Bowen remaining there 8 months each year," George suggested, "it would be a most advantageous arrangement as his advice and information would be worth a great deal to an active partner."[25] The partners finally decided to send Nicholson to New Orleans and Bowen to Mobile. The exact arrangements Nicholson made with Story after his arrival are unknown, but the association continued for several years thereafter.

The dispatch of William Bowen to Mobile occurred at a time when the partners were also seriously considering his transfer to Philadelphia as a replacement for John A. Brown. Although John was not a member of the general partnership after 1837, it was not known publicly, and he continued to manage the affairs of his office on what might be loosely called a trustee basis, waiting until his brothers had made a firm decision on the fate of the branch. Bowen was a natural choice for the post because he was a native of the Quaker City and thus had roots in the community. The season he spent alone in Mobile the senior men looked upon as good experience for the junior partner, and his record there no doubt had a bearing on their deliberations over the Philadelphia office. In later years it became standard procedure to send younger men with management potential to the outlying branches for on-the-job training.

At first, George Brown questioned the plans for the assignment of a full partner to the Philadelphia office. He feared an expansion in the membership of the partnership might be necessary to achieve that goal. But after satisfactory arrangements were made with William Bowen, George supported plans for the maintenance of a strong Philadelphia outlet. It would prevent "a great deal of business . . . from going into other hands," he observed at one point.[26] John Brown, in the meantime, agreed to act as an informal adviser to the new branch manager. On the whole, George was favorably impressed with Bowen, "whose habits and integrity are tried." He also admitted that "an agent cannot get along as well as a partner and . . . is not looked up to in the same way."

When the partners offered Bowen the Philadelphia job, he balked somewhat, however, because the family did not propose, at the same time, a liberal increase in his share allotment. At the very minimum, he had expected to receive the same claim on profits accorded the other junior partners in the firm. George and William rejected Bowen's pleas for an increased share in partnership earnings partly on the basis of his relatively short association with the firm: "You cannot expect to be put on the same footing as those who have been in the concern 15 to 18 years." Moreover, from their view of the volume of business to be handled in Philadelphia, the senior partners could not "justify a large participation of interest to a resident there who brings no Capital into the house." George and William dismissed Bowen's efforts to equate his position with that of their brother John as well: "It was very different with our Brother John, he had a large Capital and he was our Brother if he had none."[27] However, in a gesture of appreciation for his agreeing to accept the management post in Philadelphia, the senior partners agreed to change the name of the local office to Browns & Bowen. The branch was known under that style until William Bowen's retirement in 1859, when it adopted the name used in New York — Brown Brothers & Co.

With the situation in Philadelphia progressing toward a satisfactory solution, George felt less reluctance about discussing plans for his retirement. He negotiated the terms of his departure in April 1840. In a letter to William, James explained the reasons for this change in the firm's structure: "George's uneasiness arising from the business . . . being done, or so large a portion of it being done from under his eye & control, he could not divest himself of anxiety." George expected to conduct limited operations solely on his own account under the same style — Alex. Browns & Sons, which as James pointed out, was "so well known over the world it seems certainly desirable to preserve it." In the future, the Baltimore house would serve as an agent for the main organization, dividing commissions and running the proportionate share of risks. "In this way," James remarked, "the Baltimore business would just go on as usual having George's care & superintendence & he would know the precise extent of his responsibilities." James felt the arrangement was satisfactory because "the interest & union of the family can be kept up so far as Balto., NY & Lvpool. are concerned."[28]

Finally, James summed up George's goal as the employment of his capital, then estimated at approximately $1,500,000, in a "moderate, safe business under his own control." The whole family had voiced essentially this same objective six years earlier upon the death of Alexander Brown; and it is clear in retrospect that only John and George had taken those words literally. Nonetheless, the outlets in Philadelphia and Baltimore were preserved and remained integral parts of the overall Brown organization.

By 1840 the basic features of the Browns' comprehensive business strategies and their administrative structure had evolved. The process of functional specialization and geographic expansion had gone on, with only occasional interruptions, over the first forty years of the life of the enterprise. The growth of the Anglo-American economy and the changing patterns of foreign trade were, of course, underlying forces shaping the firm's development; but the events of the thirties — the death of Alexander Brown, the closing of the Second Bank of the United States, and the crisis of 1837 and its aftermath — had hastened the emergence of an international banking organization that was, as George Brown characterized it, "second to no house" in the United States.

The firm was committed to the extension of a broad range of financial services to the foreign trade sector of the American economy. The authorization of advances against consignments of cotton to the Liverpool branch were at their height during the closing years of the 1830s, while the volume of letters of credit and foreign exchange transactions grew steadily. With the retirement of George Brown from the general partnership, the New York office assumed responsibility for coordinating the activities of the American branches and agents. Hereafter, the partners in the New York office, a branch almost completely controlled by members of the Brown family, and those in the Liverpool office, which increasingly came under the domination of administrations who had been recruited from beyond the extended family, made in concert the major policy decisions. By the forties, the partners were acknowledged specialists in the field of financing international trade.

IV

Specializing in Finance

During the 1840s and 1850s, the Browns consolidated their position as the foremost international banking house serving the Anglo-American foreign trade sector. A chain of events — the demise of the Second Bank of the United States; the similar fate of Biddle's successor bank; and the inability of some merchant bankers, along with the reluctance of others, including the Barings, to reenter the American market in strength after the panic of 1837 — left the Browns in an enviable competitive situation. The depressed state of the American economy from 1839 to 1843 further discouraged potential competitors. The massive repudiation of state debts was one more development causing a general feeling of uneasiness among businessmen about American economic prospects. While others were hesitant, or in retreat, the Browns patiently built up and improved their organization. In 1844 the partners opened a Boston branch to complement the branches in New York, Liverpool, Philadelphia, Mobile, and New Orleans, and the agencies in Baltimore, Savannah, and Charleston.

With their network of representatives, the Browns were in a unique position to make profitable use of the new communications technology that burst upon the scene in the mid-forties in the form of the telegraph. In the United States, the partners employed the telegraph to coordinate the activities of the offices in the banking chain and, most important, to communicate adjustments in foreign exchange rates. At first the Browns usually changed rates every two or three days. Hourly adjustments were, of course, a possibility as well, but except in emergencies such frequent price changes did not occur regularly until later in the century. The entire banking chain quickly adopted the rates established in the New York market. The continuous maintenance of uniform rates for foreign exchange in distant cities was an innovative strategy that only an organization which was national in scope could have initiated. Competitors who lacked such an organization were unable to make full use of the new technology. With the implementation of the new pricing policy, the Brown partnership soon became the one firm other dealers looked to for leadership in setting rates for sterling bills of exchange.

Improved transatlantic transportation, in the form of faster and more regular steamship service, also affected international banking operations. Transaction costs fell almost immediately. The Cunard Line began regular Atlantic crossings in 1844, and the Collins Line followed in 1850. Because of the shorter travel time, bill prices rose somewhat. On the average, British payees accepted sterling bills sooner, and there were smaller interest adjustments built into bill prices than formerly. William Bowen, in Philadelphia, noticed the effect late in 1845: "Now the steamers go so quick there is very little gain in interest," he wrote Joseph Shipley.[1]

Although the foreign exchange and letter of credit business continued to prosper, the Browns became increasingly disillusioned with their consignment trade in cotton during the forties and fifties. Competitors persisted in their authorizations of high advances against the probable proceeds of cotton sales in Liverpool. William Bowen described the situation aptly: "It seems as if the Cotton trade was never to be governed by the same commonsense rules that prevail in other commercial transactions, there seems to be a charm in the great southern staple that leads people out of their sober senses."[2] The demand of shippers for rebates, in the form of "return commissions," disturbed the Brown management as well. In the spring of 1856 the New York office told Thomas Curtis, the Boston branch manager, that the Liverpool office would continue to charge a sales commission of 3 1/4 percent, since the partners were "not so anxious for consignments as to make a return by way of inducement."[3] The New York branch wrote the same correspondent in 1858 that the senior partners had resolved many years ago to avoid involvement in the cotton trade whenever the price rose above 12¢ per pound.[4] But little evidence has survived that would throw light on the exact circumstances of the firm's withdrawal from this previously lucrative market.

The Liverpool partners compiled an interesting financial statement in 1845 which indicates that the curtailment of cotton operations had not, as yet, occurred. The statement compared the firm's revenues from the issuance of letters of credit with those from the consignment trade over the last four years, and the figures (in sterling) do not reveal a downward trend in consignment earnings during the first half of the decade. The statement also demonstrates how much American importers restricted their use of the Browns' letters of credit during the business contraction that ended in 1843. When the economy improved in 1844, credit commissions rebounded, and they rose steadily thereafter. By 1859 the revenues from letter of credit commissions were £74,631 compared to only £3,469 from consignments.[5]

	1841	1842	1843	1844	1845
Letter of credit commissions	15,241	12,051	9,177	18,344	19,719
Consignment commissions	8,410	13,451	14,604	11,255	11,023

The economic dislocations which upset the international trading community in the late 1840s affected the Browns' operations only slightly. The crisis reached a climax in England in 1847, but the reverberations in the United States were not severe.[6] The Browns, with business almost exclusively in the American trade, were not seriously threatened. In fact, the partners came to the aid of other British houses feeling pressure in the money market. It was a complete reversal of their position ten years earlier. At one point, the Browns made a $500,000 loan to Overend, Gurney & Co., one of London's largest dealers in acceptances.[7]

When Joseph Shipley wrote a long letter to New York early in 1848 reviewing the management of the house over the past several years, however, he was not that satisfied with the firm's reaction to recent events.[8] Although the partnership had suffered relatively little from the disturbances, he was, nevertheless, inclined to attribute the result more to fortuitous circumstances than to efficient administration. In retrospect, Shipley concluded that, by expanding the volume of business so much, the house had put itself in almost as much danger in 1847 as in 1837. Yet none of the partners, excepting himself, had been fully cognizant of the seriousness of the situation until the crisis had passed. Shipley had cautioned his associates about the ominous trends he saw in the Anglo-American economy late in 1846, and he had recommended a reduction in the volume of business transactions. But the New York partners had dismissed his warnings as overly pessimistic.

One of the firm's problems, Shipley believed, stemmed from the conviction that it was necessary to do "a large business to make the gains of the Juniors satisfactory to them." He readily conceded that there might be "more profit in the end from an enormous business," but argued, nonetheless, that recent experience indicated the house had been "incurring fearful dangers" along the way. In regard to the alleged difficulties in contracting the volume of outstanding credits, Shipley remained unconvinced: "It may be difficult to curtail as you say 'because so much is expected of us' but I maintain on the other hand that much is also expected from us by the *conservative* part of the commercial community who desire always to see a timely check to overtrading." Additionally, he found it surprising that American importers had not voluntarily reduced their volume of business after short-term interest rates climbed to 12 to 15 percent. The tendency of importers to assume that any disruption in trade would be temporary was unsettling, Shipley stated; it reminded him too much of developments in 1836.

Finally, Shipley recommended improvements in the firm's system of internal control. Much better planning would be required to handle future crises, he warned, and the partners could begin at once the formulation of new policies that would expose them to less risk. With that goal in mind, Shipley suggested the implementation of strict limits on the aggregate amount of sterling the firm would purchase against individual English payees during any given 60 day period. Such limits would ensure a diversity of names in the sterling portfolio at all times. In addition, he hoped restrictions on purchases would serve as a partial check on a payee's overexpansion. The other partners approved Shipley's plan, and the Liverpool branch assumed responsibility for establishing limits on individual English firms while the New York office took on the task of controlling and coordinating bill purchases in the United States.[9]

During the fifties two of the partners' central concerns were the allocation of capital resources and the refinement of internal administration. In one sense, the two matters were closely related. Improvements in the management of the firm's cash account reduced the amount of working capital required in the normal functioning of the enterprise and left several million dollars available for outside investment. There were several drawn-out debates over the choice of investment alternatives. One group based in Liverpool held out for an essentially defensive position; that is, the purchase of low risk securities with appropriately low yields which would serve as a secondary reserve in emergencies. They also feared that too close an association with the stock market tended to draw the firm into investment banking activities that were contrary to the established policies of the firm. James Brown led a second faction in New York which included most of his heirs in the enterprise. James favored a more aggressive investment policy emphasizing "sound" situations that offered the potential of higher returns. The New York contingent favored such investment channels as railroad securities, real estate, an iron works, and the Collins steamship line.[10]

William Brown was the key man in these internal controversies, since he and James together held approximately 90 percent of the firm's total capital.[11] Sharing his brother's desire for greater employment of their resources, William was initially inclined to line up behind James on the issue of investment strategy. But the Liverpool group had the advantage of frequent personal access to their senior adviser and he, in turn, had much confidence in their judgment. Some of James's more ambitious schemes were tempered in England, especially after a series of bad choices in the selection of railroad securities. The financial difficulties of the Collins line further discredited the American investment strategy. The firm's real estate holdings, on the other hand, were more productive and seem on the whole to have appreciated enough to offset losses in other outside ventures.

The main protagonists on the English side were Francis Hamilton and Mark Collet, two men of extraordinary administrative ability. They were the leading spokesmen for systematizing the firm's general operating procedures. Moreover, Hamilton and Collet strongly endorsed the movement toward greater uniformity in the management of the firm's branches and agencies. Customers should receive identical service from every outlet in the chain, they maintained. The Liverpool partners were the first management group to appreciate fully the uniqueness and value of the firm's organizational structure; they saw it as a source of strength in its own right.

Alexander Brown and his four sons were, of course, the original architects of the organizational framework, but it took this second generation of nonfamily administrators to recognize the full potential of such a broad organization. The founders had been far ahead of competitors during the period when the branch system was patiently put together, but Hamilton and Collet could not refrain from efforts to perfect the functioning of the organization. To achieve their goals, they expounded the benefits of a carefully planned program of administration: great care should be exercised in the selection and training of new personnel; the activities of the various branches should be closely supervised and coordinated; subordinates should be given clear and specific instructions and the performance of their duties closely monitored; and every phase of the business should be periodically reviewed and analyzed.

The Liverpool partners were so successful in their efforts to convert the operations of the enterprise to a regular routine that James Brown found enough free time to dabble in a wide variety of outside interests. This, of course, had not been one of their goals. The more effective Collet and Hamilton were in improving the business procedures of the firm, the more daring James became in diverting capital into outside investments. In England these investments were called lockups and diversions from the firm's legitimate activities. James's consistently poor record in choosing among investment alternatives led the Liverpool partners to argue even more vigorously against the expansion of outside business interests. James liked the Erie and the Illinois Central Railroads as vehicles for investment as well as several other equally weak securities. [12]

Who were these men of such organizational genius? Francis Hamilton began his association with the house early in the 1830s as an indentured apprentice. Joseph Shipley was impressed with young Hamilton's talents, and at the end of his indenture contract the partners offered him a position in the organization. In 1839 they sent Hamilton to Savannah as the firm's accredited representative. There Hamilton performed his duties so competently that he was reassigned to Liverpool in 1845 and simultaneously became a partner. He became an expert on all facets of the cotton trade including the purchase and collection of sterling bills drawn in the south.

When Joseph Shipley retired in 1850 because of ill health, the partners brought in Mark Collet to share the administrative duties with Hamilton. Collet was already a rising young man in the commercial world when he accepted a partnership in 1851. His career began in 1832 at a branch of Thomas Wilson & Co., one of the infamous houses that failed in the 1837 panic. For a time thereafter, Collet served as a submanager of the Bank of Liverpool. He was subsequently associated with several merchants in the American trade. Collet was unquestionably the intellectual of the Brown organization, speaking several foreign languages. Later in his illustrious career, he was appointed governor of the Bank of England. In the Liverpool office, Collet usually concentrated on letters of credit and other financial activities. [13]

As Collet and Hamilton assumed greater responsibilities, they began to press their case for a larger participation in partnership earnings. On an issue of such importance, they usually brought up the matter with William Brown, who spent much of his time in London on Parliamentary affairs. In April 1853 they protested with vigor James's contention that the New York partners were entitled to the most shares because of the "wear & tear of mind & responsibility and the extra expense of living in New York."

In the course of their rebuttal, Collet and Hamilton provided a concise description of the main activities of the Liverpool office.

After conceding that the New York branch bore greater responsibility for letter of credit operations, they argued that Liverpool played the more crucial role in the foreign exchange field. They maintained credit files on approximately 2,000 payees of sterling bills in England, Ireland, and Scotland: "a work the most onerous, requiring the greatest care." Since so many of the British firms participating in the American trade were speculative and therefore easily "tempted into transactions quite foreign to their legitimate business," they required "constant watching." The list of names had become so long in recent years, Collet and Hamilton boasted, that Overend Gurney & Co., one of England's leading banking establishments, had observed that "it was like asking a report on the whole commercial world."

The Liverpool managers also noted that whereas New York operations in the 1850s were almost exclusively in the banking field, their own office had, in addition to its financial functions, "mercantile transactions as large as any house in England." These too demanded judicious handling, "the class of Clerks & men being such that it requires constant superintendence." Moreover, the branch served as British agent for the Collins Steamship Line — a task which caused "more trouble & anxiety than falls to the lot of many Houses in a large way." In sum, Hamilton and Collet contended that if the work was not in truth equally divided, then, of the two, "the Liverpool House bears the larger portion of the labour & responsibility."

In regard to the cost of living, they questioned the existence of any substantial differences between New York and Liverpool. Although they admittedly did not spend much money entertaining customers, Collet and Hamilton nonetheless claimed a burden of heavy expenses because of their association with the firm. "There is scarcely a thing going on in the Town political, Religious or in any way beneficial, that we are not called on to aid — & that liberally," they explained, "as we are from our position looked on as fair play & bound to contribute." Finally, the Liverpool managers told William that James's view of their responsibilities was predicated "on a wrong impression." Consequently, there was no basis for any discrimination against the Liverpool branch in the division of partnership profits. William apparently sustained their position because James soon countered with a new proposal which called for a 20 percent increase in the shares allotted to all the junior men in the organization, including Collet and Hamilton.[14]

The Liverpool managers were similarly outspoken in correspondence with William about the firm's overall investment policy. In June of 1852 they responded forthrightly to suggestions that the partnership invest more of its capital in American securities. Both men felt the partners could employ capital to better advantage in their regular business than in stocks and bonds. In view of increasing Anglo-American trade, they thought any additional capital could be safely used in an expansion of the outstanding volume of letters of credit. Such an expansion would be in accord with the principles guiding firms in the insurance business: "The more extended & divided the accounts, using due discretion in the selection, the greater the prospect of success combined with greater security."[15]

Collet and Hamilton subsequently warned William Brown that any diversion of funds into permanent investments might impair future operations. "The House cannot extend its business unless it can fall back on these investments in case of emergency," they advised; and "from the number of lockups we estimate, the actual available Capital of the House is not more than it was four years ago & maybe less."[16] As a consequence of the strain of illiquid assets and frozen investments, the Liverpool managers became worried about the prudence of American investments generally. "We look upon the advancement of the United States as certain," they wrote, "but the Americans are an extravagant & wasteful people & inclined to forestall all legitimate advance."[17]

When it was learned in Liverpool that William Brown had consented to become a trustee for a bond issue of the Illinois Central Railroad, Hamilton and Collet were especially concerned. But not wishing to offend the senior Brown, who was known to favor limited involvement in investment banking functions, they initially voiced no objection to the plan. "As far as we can learn this appears to be a good concern," they wrote to William in London. The prospect of earning commissions on such transactions appeared very desirable if they could be "earned without undue risk, or without drawing the public into ruinous schemes." However, there were "so many schemes afloat that it will require a good deal of precaution to keep clear of the worthless," they added.[18]

On one occasion, William Brown suddenly became quite irritated by the torrent of criticism and suggested that the two men make arrangements with the New York office to protect their partnership accounts from the risk of outside investments. Hamilton and Collet would have none of it, however. It was not their wish to have separate interests, they explained: "We think the great strength & security of the House rests mainly on an identity of interest in all transactions." Therefore, they wanted "in *every instance* to be part & parcel of *all* business undertaken by the House."[19]

Their primary concern, the Liverpool managers continued, was with the fundamental business principle at issue. From the beginning they had felt that the recent transactions with the Erie Railroad bonds were likely to turn out well: "but . . . we all know that the greatest losses usually arise from operations entered into on the spur of the moment & which promise often the most favorably at the first." After all, Collet and Hamilton complained, when stock prices had been considerably lower, the New York partners had clearly stated that they did not have the time to devote to such transactions and strongly believed that there was a great risk in dealing in them. Everyone had then agreed that the house should "adhere firmly to our legitimate business." Given this basic position, "it certainly does appear that if the doctrine was good at low prices, it behooves us to be more cautious in going into large Stock operations when prices have advanced," the two men observed.

While conceding that the latest discoveries of gold in California would do much to increase business prospects in the United States, the Liverpool managers feared that the probable benefits had already been overestimated. The sanguine temperament of the American people seemed to be leading them into schemes that would require more gold than they were likely to receive, and "taking the value of money even now existing in the United States, the price of all Stocks is fully higher than circumstances justify."

In closing, Collet and Hamilton assured William Brown that their confidence in their American partners had not been impaired by the dispute over outside investments. Indeed, they heretofore had never expressed a word of disappointment at any of the losses on American securities in their correspondence with the New York office. Their reason for raising the issue now, they told William, "arose from our thinking you felt even more strongly than we did the necessity of adhering rigidly to the rules laid down by our New York House as well as by ourselves."[20]

But as Collet and Hamilton feared, the New York partners' investment activities eventually led to the firm's involvement in the management of some of the concerns faced with unexpected difficulties. The involvement with the Canandaigua & Niagara Falls Railroad, a line of less than 100 miles constructed in the mid-fifties, was perhaps the deepest. In May 1856 Collet told Hamilton of his reservations about the prospect of the firm joining in the "purchase and working" of the railroad; he pointed to the likely effect on the standing of the house in the commercial world.[21] He hoped every influence would be exerted by the more cautious partners "to prevent our being drawn into this project." Collet could not "call to mind a single large House in England or New York that had departed from its legitimate business to enter into large lockups and has not thereby been ruined sooner or later." He "trembled" at the "easy confidence with which we seem to be following the same dangerous course."

In the long-run the success of the firm rested on its credit, Collet believed; "and what is that credit but the confidence of the public in large means and judicious management." If the firm's large loans to the Collins Line, its £80,000 investment in one insolvent American railroad, and—should it take place—its further involvement in financing and operating the similarly insolvent Canandaigua & Niagara Falls Railroad were to become a matter of public knowledge, Collet feared "it would give our credit a rude shock." He also suspected that worry over these matters had brought on Hamilton's recent headaches and was partly responsible for his own ill health. The whole situation was especially frustrating, Collet concluded, because William Brown, their former ally, was "so impatient of any representation of this kind from his juniors."[22]

The Liverpool managers also argued that excessive involvement in the internal affairs of American railroads was thwarting the firm's efforts to achieve parity with the House of Baring. With so many resources tied up in Erie and Illinois Central Railroad bonds, the Liverpool office was forced to continue borrowing in the English discount market in order to finance the firm's exchange and letter of credit activities. One of the Barings' unique characteristics, and one of the key reasons for their unchallenged position in British financial circles, was their high degree of liquidity, and this factor was reflected in their ability to function without even temporary reliance on short term money markets. In February 1855 Mark Collet reminded the New York partners about how much their gratuitous loans to American railroads were undermining the realization of what, the Liverpool managers at least believed, was one of the primary goals of the enterprise: "We aim, with perfect right—at a rank & position equal to the Barings, but it is impossible that we can maintain it, if we are to be in the discount market week by week . . . whereas they never discount & are known to have always large sums lying at call."[23]

In New York a greater interest in profit maximization mitigated the partners' concern about matters of prestige. While admitting that an extraordinarily liquid position was one of the hallmarks of a great banking enterprise, many of the American partners did not feel it was an absolute prerequisite for distinguished status. James Brown, for one, did not feel that the ethereal benefits of such austerity were worth the sacrifice of the financial leverage which borrowing in the discount market added to the firm's capital structure. Appearances were, of course, important but so was the retention of a capital structure with a high profit potential. In formulating many of their operating policies, the Browns had not emulated the Barings, and from their vantage point in New York, the partners viewed their chief competitor's attitude toward discounts as an overly expensive luxury that was not justified on the basis of even the most conservative banking principles.

In this debate which raged for almost an entire decade, the New York position progressively weakened as its investments failed to yield the anticipated returns. While it is patently true that the Liverpool partners were by nature extremely status conscious, the absence of any real successes in financial fields outside the firm's niche of expertise encouraged Collet and Hamilton to marshall and to exploit to the fullest every conceivable argument in favor of reducing the volume of outside investments.

Collet and Hamilton waged a long campaign against the inappropriateness of forays into new ventures beyond the scope of the firm's normal activities. Yet it was not until the 1860s that the validity of their point of view was, in a sense, formally recognized. Stewart Brown, a cousin of the four original brothers and a partner in New York, stated as much in correspondence with James Brown in October 1864. Stewart attributed most of the credit to the English partners for the firm's "splendid position . . . *having free all our capital.*"[24] "There was a time you know," he told James "when we were locked up with the *Steamers* . . . Erie Bonds Collateral & other things." It was only after Collet and Hamilton had become active managers, he reminded James, that Liverpool began "giving us statements . . . of the active capital in the business showing how small a part of our means were free and urging us not to put out any more in unavailable things however good." At the time, William Brown had taken "very unkindly" to some of their objections but they had "proved to be right." Moreover, Stewart admitted that they had been right about the handling of the exchange account and most other things as well, although he himself had been among those who were originally "impatient at their suggestions." Their experience in the fifties had demonstrated, Stewart was convinced, the "absolute necessity of allowing the fullest liberty of discussion" and the "full expression of opinion" within the partnership.

The Browns' exemplary performance during the panic of 1857 elevated the house to a position of unquestioned preeminence among financiers of the international trade of the United States. Internal disagreement over investment policies had not distracted the partners from their main task—the refinement of procedures for handling foreign exchange and letter of credit transactions. In this phase of their operations, controversy was absent. Despite the continuance of their traditionally large volume of business, the Browns came through the most serious economic crisis since the thirties with only minimal losses.[25] During this period, the partners' policy of placing great emphasis on the minimization of risk in the issuance of letters of credit was put to the test and proved enormously successful. While other credit issuers suffered and retrenched, the Browns escaped the panic with relatively few bad debts.[26] Their achievement was the result not only of the safeguards in the terms of issuance but also of the overall effectiveness of their comprehensive organization.

George Peabody & Co., whose organization consisting of a loose chain of independent agents emerged in the fifties as the Browns' strongest competitor in the issuance of credits, did not fare as well during the crisis. At the height of the turmoil Duncan, Sherman & Co., Peabody's New York agent, actually repudiated its guarantees of its customers' outstanding credits. George Peabody himself was compelled to seek the aid of the Bank of England in order to maintain solvency. Later after international financial services were largely restored in the early months of 1858, Duncan, Sherman & Co. discreetly informed the Browns that, for the present, it was prepared to defer to its competitor in the setting of terms, conditions, and commissions in the letter of credit business. The Liverpool partners received the news calmly; indeed, they were glad to hear that Duncan, Sherman & Co. was beginning operations again: "For as we cannot do the whole business, it is better that we should have competitors who have learnt from bitter experience to be more cautious, than that we should have in the field new Houses who have their experience still to learn."[27] As this remark so clearly indicates, the Browns were never interested in absolutely monopolizing any single market. The preferred arrangement was for several responsible and reputable firms to exert a fair degree of control over a given market, whether local or international in scope.

New firms were unwelcome because they were likely to disturb too many of the precedents established by the leading houses over the previous decades. In addition, newcomers were likely to increase the pressure on larger firms to lower the general level of commission rates. Even so, there were always marginal firms who regularly competed with the established firms on the basis of price. These firms were tolerated so long as they confined themselves to normal operations and did not attempt to enter new markets outside their accustomed pattern of business. Regularity and predictability were two virtues the Browns invariably respected in competitors. The Browns' organization was so formidable in the foreign exchange and letter of credit fields, however, that there were few genuine threats to the status quo until the last decade of the century.

The rapid rise of the house to preeminence in the financing of Anglo-American trade was a source of great satisfaction to the Brown family. The men associated with the enterprise took great pride in the firm's accomplishments and its growing international renown. Already well endowed with material wealth, the Brown family especially cherished the leadership recognition it received from its peers in the commercial world. The partners were justifiably proud of the firm's general reputation, and most decisions were made with the aim of preserving and strengthening the overall organization. This sense of permanency was unique in an environment where the usual pattern was the frequent formation and dissolution of partnerships, even among close relatives. In fact, the Brown partners exhibited almost a "corporate mentality" in their approach to formulating long range strategies; the fundamental assumption was that the business entity would be perpetuated for future descendents.

The nonfamily partners shared the family's attachment to the house. Their association with the enterprise not only gave them an opportunity to amass substantial wealth, it also vaulted them to a high position within the commercial community. Their status in the informal hierarchy of the business world was enviable. New partners, both from within and outside the family, generally identified with the traits that were the hallmarks of the House of Brown. An enumeration of all these assumed qualities would be lengthy, but character, prudence, discretion, and integrity were certainly high on the list.[28] Virtually every full partner was ostensibly a model of business and social propriety; civic and religious duties played an important role in the lives of many of the partners. In the firm's financial activities, a high devotion to business principle, which almost amounted to commercial snobbery, was a vital asset. When it was matched with a great knack for organization and administration, the result was an enterprise competitors found difficult to emulate in the Anglo-American economy.

In many ways the managers of the Liverpool house, Collet and Hamilton, were more staunch in their defense of the firm's reputation than the family itself. For, while the aspirants for great renown in the United States were few in number, in England, with its larger and more established commercial community, the candidates for lofty stature were plentiful. In fact, it was characteristic of the Liverpool partners to serve as the most ardent spokesmen for the preservation of a policy that traditionally restricted the firm's operations to the more judicious business transactions.[29] As guardians of the faith, Collet and Hamilton kept their colleague's attention focused on the safety factor in every proposal. The slightest deviations from sound business principles were, at times, almost equated with moral transgressions. Even their close associates departed from the normal patterns of business behavior at the risk of a stinging rebuke. Neither Collet nor Hamilton was prone to mince words in discussions of even minor matters if a question of principle was somehow involved.

Their saving grace, despite their criticisms of associates and employees, was that both Collet and Hamilton invariably augmented their censures with specific instructions on better ways to handle similar transactions in the future. They generally moved from an elucidation of the broad principles involved in a given situation to a more detailed description of the proper operating procedures. It was, in short, constructive criticism. The Liverpool partners firmly believed that a system for handling business transactions could be devised which, if faithfully followed, would alleviate most of the dangers arising from the exercise of authority by distant employees and accredited agents. Collet and Hamilton felt the creation of an efficient system of internal management should be one of the firm's primary goals and that much progress was genuinely possible in this field of endeavor.

Meanwhile, the question of the firm's overall investment strategy was largely settled in favor of the general position long advocated by the Liverpool partners. James Brown journeyed to England in the fall of 1860 to renegotiate terms in the formal articles of partnership. The new articles provided for the establishment of a permanent Reserve Fund; its purpose, James stated in a note to his home office, was to "enable the house to pass through any commercial crises such as have occurred with unimpaired credit."[30] The fund consisted at the outset of £180,000 invested in British consols and similar amount, about $800,000, in U.S. Government bonds or other absolutely safe securities.

The allocation of a certain portion of the firm's capital to the maintenance of a permanent reserve position was one of the major goals of Hamilton and Collet. This provision in the articles of partnership did much to alleviate tensions between the New York and Liverpool branches. Thereafter, Collet and Hamilton were far less concerned about the investment of the remaining surplus capital.

James Brown continued his interest in steamship lines, and his investments in the Pacific Mail Steamship Co. were generally profitable. But the close association with bankrupt railroads ceased, partly because of a more intelligent selection of securities. During the last quarter of the century, the partners occasionally accepted invitations from J. P. Morgan to join underwriting syndicates bidding for U.S. Government and prime railroad securities.[31] Otherwise, the Brown firm performed only limited investment banking functions until the merger with the Harriman family firm in the twentieth century.[32]

V

The Mature Firm

The 1860s were years of turmoil for the partnership. First, there were the disruptions associated with the coming of the Civil War. The effects on an organization that was national and in fact international in scope were especially great. The main supply of sterling bills for the firm's foreign exchange operations was cut off abruptly. The southern branches were quickly closed, and personnel were transferred elsewhere. Meanwhile, there was much uncertainty about the risks involved in the issuance of letters of credit to northern importers. Thus many of the operating policies developed over the last 60 years had to be reformulated to meet the new political realities.

The war caused internal problems as well. The New York partners were for the most part staunch Unionists, but the Liverpool management assumed a far more impartial stance. Francis Hamilton had spent over five years representing the Browns in Savannah in the early 1840s, and during the conflict he was a strong southern sympathizer.[1] At the very minimum, Collet and Hamilton felt the partnership should adopt a fundamentally neutralist position. In New York there was much confusion and uncertainty about a partner's obligation to support his country while continuing to conduct an international business which was theoretically divorced from political considerations. The firm played such a crucial role in the Anglo-American economy, however, that whatever policy the partners pursued was likely to have political implications. Moreover, in a partnership the division between an individual's personal interests and his business activities is never clear. In a test of will, the Liverpool managers finally convinced James Brown and the other New York partners to give the joint interests of the firm the highest priority, and a disputed investment in U.S. Government bonds was liquidated because it seemed to identify the firm too closely with the Lincoln administration.[2]

Since a complete narrative of the firm's activities during the Civil War years would be extremely complex, the focus here is mainly on those developments which had a permanent effect on the partnership's functions or on its internal organization. Despite numerous temporary adjustments in the handling of letter of credit operations, this function was performed fundamentally in the same manner after the war as in the 1850s. Foreign exchange operations, on the other hand, were managed quite differently after wartime inflation drove the currency off the gold standard, but an explanation of how the partners made the readjustment is fairly technical and must be delayed. In this chapter, three topics are discussed in some detail: the basic policies adopted at the beginning of the conflict; the establishment of a London branch; and the partners' deliberations on the issue of managerial control and succession. The latter two were matters with origins in the previous decade but they became issues of greater significance during the 1860s.

In the first half of 1861 the Browns were preoccupied with the closing of their southern outlets and the general suspension of their letter of credit activities. By late summer the partners were reconciled to the possibility of a lengthy war, and a serious discussion of wartime business tactics began in earnest. Beyond the disagreement over the investment in U.S. bonds, there was a general consensus on the proper course to be followed in managing the firm's regular financial services.

The American partners agreed that the firm should not become involved in financing any business transactions which violated the terms of the British declaration of neutrality. They decided to issue letters of credit only to first-class merchants until the situation became more settled. The range of products eligible for financing was restricted to "necessaries" such as coffee, sugar, dry goods, and the like. The Browns also discouraged applications for long credits, especially those in the China and Far Eastern trade. Because of the increased risks, some partners recommended the establishment of higher commissions and fees. On European accounts, other partners suggested that a clause be added to the credit agreement stipulating that the financed goods had to be ordered through the firm's Liverpool office; in this way, the partnership could secure a buying commission beyond the normal banking commission.

In fact, the Liverpool partners favored an increase in the volume of mercantile transactions generally. "The obtaining of consignments of Grain and other produce under safe advances," they proposed as a business activity the partnership might want to consider "whilst our ordinary business is suspended."[3] Meanwhile, the New York branch reduced sharply its volume of outstanding letters of credit; by May 1863 James Brown reported that its primary business was the "buying & selling" of foreign exchange.[4]

In addition to reviewing their operating procedures and policies, the Browns also reexamined their system of branch offices. The partners closed the offices in New Orleans and Mobile and terminated the agency agreements with indigenous merchants in Charleston and Savannah. For some time, the prospects for continued shipping in the port of Baltimore appeared so poor that the Browns considered ceasing operations there as well. Indeed, in the course of the partners' deliberations, various options were freely bantered about. New branches were proposed in one or more of the following cities — San Francisco, Chicago, St. Louis, Cincinnati, Paris, London, and Havana.[5] In the last, the partners established an office early in 1862, but it failed to survive the year.

Although the Liverpool managers were not adamantly opposed to the opening of new branch offices, they were not enthusiastic. Despite their suspicion that the war would drag on, they nevertheless were thinking ahead to the reestablishment of the branch system, regardless of the outcome. Any expansion into new American cities would absorb the manpower that would be needed again at a later date in the south. "Experience shows it is not easy to get the proper people for such important positions," the Liverpool partners reminded New York in August 1861.[6] Hamilton and Collet also opposed the opening of a new office merely "as an experiment for the sake of finding occupation for a partner." On the whole, they were not satisfied with the personnel in some of the northern branches, and they hoped to transfer a few of the more competent southern employees to Boston, Philadelphia, and Baltimore. These suggestions were consistent with their general management philosophy: "Our idea is that concentration and a perfect system of management of our business are the objects to be aimed at rather than extension, for even with the Branches we have it appears almost impossible to get the business conducted as it should be." They exaggerated, of course, and later admitted that most of the branches had been manned by employees of considerable ability. Still some doubt lingered about the managers in Philadelphia and Boston: "They are not equal to difficult times," was the Liverpool assessment.[7]

Although Collet and Hamilton were hypercritical of the performance of subordinates, they were fair minded men, in the sense that they judged all according to the same standards, and most important, they were optimistic about the possibility of continued improvement. The perfection of the administrative system was to them a goal worth striving for in the organization. The original founders of the house had always demanded expertness from each other and their representatives, but until the fifties and sixties none of the partners thought of the matter in terms of a continual process or a uniform system of management. In short, except for the larger railroads, which were also geographically dispersed, few managers of business enterprises considered their affairs in the same administrative framework as the House of Brown.

While it would be an overstatement to attribute the opening of the firm's London branch in 1863 entirely to Civil War dislocations, they did release sufficient manpower to permit implementation of the expansion plan. A London office had actually been under consideration for many years. Almost every other important merchant-banking house in England had its main office in the capital. When the partners discussed the matter at length in 1855 no one questioned the premise that a branch there one day was a certainty.[8] The Liverpool managers demurred in the mid-fifties, however, for two principal reasons. A London branch would require the admission of new partners to administer the additional business. If the extra revenues did not cover the increased expenses, the earnings of the current partners would be diluted. Hamilton and Collet also used the London proposal as a vehicle for piquing James Brown and his New York allies about the firm's illiquid capital position. A London house would be expected to occupy a more independent position, they argued, and that was impossible so long as a large portion of the firm's capital was locked up in inconvertible assets.

The Liverpool managers had other reasons for opposing the transfer to London, but they only hinted at them rather than stating them outright. The English capital was the center of investment banking activities, and Collet and Hamilton feared the house would be tempted into an even further involvement with securities. William Brown's residence in London during Parliamentary sessions and his close contacts with the city's financiers had already contributed to the firm's unfortunate investments in a series of weak railroad issues. In addition, neither Collet or Hamilton relished the thought of living in a city where prominent businessmen were expected to carry on a more active social life. Unlike their counterparts in many competitive houses, the two administrators did not go out of their way to entertain visiting Americans. In Liverpool less was expected on that account, but in London they feared the social pressures might be irresistible.

Just three years later, in 1858, the London proposal was considered again. On this occasion, the proposition received a more sympathetic hearing. Collet, who was in New York for one of the firm's periodic policy reviews, cited three advantages: the access to superior credit information, the opportunity of working their cash balance more closely, and the savings on fees to London bankers for paying their acceptances.[9] On the other hand, the drawbacks still seemed formidable. Hamilton again mentioned the additional overhead costs and the necessity of admitting at least two new partners. He did not think the house could attract many consignments in the London market that would not be taken at the expense of the Liverpool branch. For the present, the firm's business seemed to be holding up well despite its provincial headquarters. Judging from the latest advices from the American branches, Hamilton concluded that the firm was likely to have its "full share of the business." Moreover, after considering the effects of the 1857 crisis on competitive houses, he asked his fellow partners bluntly, "Is not our business already as large as likely to be, or as large as we desire it to be?"

By 1863, however, the arguments in favor of the London move were more persuasive. In this instance a threat from a potentially powerful new competitor in the foreign exchange field revived the issue. A firm to be known as the British & American Exchange Banking Corporation, Ltd., had been formed in England with the expressed purpose of operating in the New York market, which was described in the prospectus as highly profitable.[10] The new venture was an unabashed effort on the part of an incorporated bank to divest a portion of the foreign exchange business from the private houses, which had considered such operations their exclusive territory. There were rumors that a second bank might be formed for the same purpose. By opening an office in London, the Browns felt they would be demonstrating to the public that they intended to protect their position in the American trade. Several months after making a decision to move to the capital, however, it became quite clear that their initial fears had not been justified. The British & American Exchange Banking Corporation, Ltd., quickly fell into the hands of a "stockjobbing clique" and collapsed before the enterprise could be got underway.

The name — Brown, Shipley & Co. — was so well known in international financial circles that the firm decided to retain it for the London office. Hamilton and Collet were to manage the new office with the assistance of Herman Hoskier, a young Englishman who had been stationed in New Orleans at the outbreak of the Civil War. During the transition period, Hamilton was to remain in Liverpool and assist Stewart H. Brown, a member of the firm's middle management who had been designated to take over the old office. There were suggestions that Hamilton, who was more familiar with the branch's mercantile activities, remain in Liverpool permanently. Hoskier pinpointed the reason all such overtures had been rejected; if the London branch proved a success, then the Liverpool operations were likely to be curtailed, he observed, and Hamilton could not "in justice to himself consent to sink into the management of a mere agency."[11] Collet and Hamilton also foresaw the likely consequences of maintaining two English outlets: "In the main, the Credit business, the Exchange business, and Deposits together with any other Commission business which the London House may attract to itself, will gradually center there." In the long run, the old office would be left with "its present Produce & forwarding business" and with that part of the foreign exchange business which required the handling of bills of lading on shipments to Liverpool.[12]

Once in London, Collet and Hamilton hoped for the duration of the war to augment their reduced American business with expanded activities inside the British Empire. Yet, they were not overly sanguine about the prospects. "The trade with most parts of the world, and in particular with India & China, to be successfully carried on, involves the necessity of taking interests in the operations," they explained, "there being little *clean* commission business to be had." Nonetheless, they believed there were some areas of British overseas trade "which an intelligent & prudent house can *conduct* on its own account as to yield steady profits with as little . . . risk [as] attends the Commission business."[13] As predicted, the firm's business never extended far beyond the American trade, although the London office did make arrangements with Olyphant & Co., an important firm in the China trade, to import a few cargoes of tea on a joint account basis.

Deliberations over the eventual managerial control of the enterprise began in the late 1850s during the lifetime of the two senior partners. It was the controversy over management succession more than disagreements about the firm's response to political developments in the United States that almost led to a dissolution of the partnership. The struggle for control was, rather predictably, between the members of the Brown family in New York and the non-family partners in England, headed by Francis Hamilton and Mark Collet. The main participants in the transatlantic discussion recognized that the central issue was not a question of personalities but the fundamental nature of the enterprise. Much effort was devoted to determining the genre of the organization—to what extent it was a family partnership as opposed to a general partnership. A clear resolution of the matter was difficult because of the firm's unusual evolution. The family, of course, held the bulk of the accumulated capital, but the nonfamily members of the partnership in England were practically irreplaceable. In addition, the house had been administered according to more or less bureaucratic principles for some time; that is, once any man joined the organization he was judged strictly on the basis of his performance on the job. For instance, several of James Brown's sons found the work too demanding or not to their taste and had retired early. The Browns' management difficulties are an early example of the problems other large family organizations faced in dealing with hired administrators later in the century.

The death of a wealthy partner and the removal of his capital from the enterprise threatened the existence of most nineteenth century business firms. Because William Brown's sons failed to survive him and none of his heirs appeared interested in a commercial career, the firm began paying out some of his capital in installments beginning in the early 1860s. He was then in his seventies and in failing health; James, just seven years younger, was still extremely active in the firm's management. By adjusting the capital structure in anticipation of William's death, the remaining partners would be able to state at the time of his passing that the operations of the firm were not seriously affected. Thus, his death in 1864 was calmly accepted in the business community. The wisdom of such long-range planning was clearly demonstrated, and James Brown spent much of the next fifteen years planning his affairs so his own death would be received with similar calm. His position was less critical, however, because several of his heirs, in particular his son John Crosby Brown and his son-in-law Howard Potter, were expected to replace him as the heads of the New York house, and perhaps the entire organization.

The latter possibility disturbed the English partners. Fundamentally, Collet and Hamilton wanted to preserve, and if possible to expand, their role in the decision-making processes of the house, and they became increasingly apprehensive about where the internal power would lie when the younger men in New York, who in the sixties ranked below them in the informal organizational hierarchy, finally inherited James Brown's immense capital. Therefore, much energy was expended in drafting new partnership agreements that would preserve the independence of the English sphere of the business but leave the family in control of an important part of its heritage, the firm that bore the Brown name.

Serious discussions on the status of the British partners in the enterprise began in the spring of 1858 when preliminary arrangements were made to reduce William Brown's capital in the house. Mark Collet came to New York to confer with the American management and to draw up a new partnership agreement. Francis Hamilton directed his private letters to Collet but, as was the usual practice in the firm, he gave permission to his close associate to share the correspondence with the other partners. In May, Hamilton made an overall assessment of the firm's present form of leadership: "So long as Wm Brown & James Brown live they are perfectly right in reserving to themselves the power of apportioning shares; omitting or dismissing partners, for with so large an interest in the concern, it would be contrary to prudence to forego these powers."[14] However, he then qualified the statement somewhat; a few men should not completely dominate a firm because it prevented "free discussion and unreserved expression of opinion on the part of Juniors on the course of business which is desirable." Since every partner had a stake in the firm, he should have a "fair influence." Furthermore, Hamilton added, "My own view is that such distinctions are prejudicial to the good management of a concern," although he admitted there were exceptions, "as in our own case . . . so long as Seniors live such distinctions are inevitable."

But Hamilton worried more about what would happen when there were no longer Senior partners on each side of the Atlantic to balance one another. James, he assumed, would live longer, and unless James stated a willingness to share his powers in the firm, Hamilton felt there would be no alternative but to resign. "If things are not arranged properly I might be forced to remove my capital from the firm," he threatened — and then added, "but I of course have confidence in J.B." The issues he raised were not resolved at the time, however, and they arose again in 1864 after William Brown died.

Hamilton and Collet believed the partnership agreement of 1858 had given them what they had demanded — an equal voice in the management of the firm vis-à-vis New York. But by the summer of 1864, they began to suspect that the New York office was withholding important information having a bearing on the conduct of the business. In October they claimed that the lack of information had become "so irksome & wearing" that it seemed impossible for the firm to be "carried on."[15] And as if to demonstrate that their threatened withdrawal was no bluff, the London managers asked the New York partners to consult their lawyers about the possible terms of dissolution.

James Brown waited several months before replying to the charges of his English associates. After opening with a perfunctory paragraph citing the lawyers' preliminary report, he adopted a very conciliatory

tone.[16] First, he denied that the New York administrators had failed
to answer any of the London partners' questions squarely or neglect-
ed to pass on any information that was pertinent to the affairs of the
firm. He also reminded them that some of their past actions and
statements had "annoyed us exceedingly," because they indicated a
"want of confidence." Their accusations of bad faith were completely
unfounded, James assured them. In conclusion, he offered to submit
the entire dispute to Joseph Shipley, who was living in retirement in
Delaware, for arbitration. "There is no man more capable of indicating the duties each partner owes to the other," James stated; and he
pledged to accept Shipley's judgment in the event their former associate determined that the New York office had been negligent or eva-
sive about sharing control of the organization with the London
branch.

The dispute was ironed out temporarily, but the price of constant
internal stress began to tell on the organization. Herman Hoskier,
the young aspirant whose training tour in New Orleans had been so
rudely interrupted by the war, found the pressures almost unbearable.
When James sent his son John Crosby to England to soothe the London
management in the summer of 1865, he conferred with Hoskier on a
number of occasions and reported the conversations to his father.
John Crosby was favorably impressed with Hoskier's abilities and
supported a plan to admit him to the partnership forthwith. Hoskier,
for his part, intended to press for a higher allotment of shares than
was usually accorded a new member of the firm. John Crosby
sympathized with Hoskier. He told James in mid-July that the
prospective partner had been thinking very seriously "of leaving us
entirely, to be clear of a concern which is continually in hot water
within itself."[17] Hoskier's idea of a partnership corresponded more
with their own, he wrote: "For a partnership to be successful &
pleasant, the men composing it must have mutual respect & confidence & be a kind of family together, which H & C never will be with
anybody because it is not in their nature."

Respecting Hoskier's request for a substantial allotment of partnership shares, John Crosby responded positively: "There is no doubt
about it he must have some extra compensation for having to work by
the side of those gentlemen." Overall, John Crosby felt Hoskier was
invaluable and worth the extra compensation. Although the London
managers had proven to be masters at directing the activities of employees in distant ports, in their own office Collet and Hamilton
could not hold good men. Hoskier, it was hoped, would be an exception.

When negotiations over another partnership agreement began in

1868, the London partners were still on the offensive. Hamilton and Collet now believed the business could not be properly administered so long as the American partners held a disproportionate amount of the firm's capital. By the end of 1867, capital stood at $10,525,000 Cy. (see Table 1).[18] James Brown alone held 65 percent of the capital, while the combined holdings of the four partners residing in England accounted for only 16 percent of the firm's resources.[19] In a bold move, Collet and Hamilton indirectly proposed James Brown's retirement from the firm, or alternatively, a transfer in his status to that of a special partner, with no claim on earnings beyond the minimal 5 or 6 percent interest paid yearly on the capital acounts of retired partners.

Since the largest proportion of the senior Brown's estate was to pass to other members of the firm upon his death in any event, it was never clear to the New Yorkers why their London counterparts were apparently so intent on maneuvering James Brown into a position where the only practical solution would be his retirement. Undaunted, Collet and Hamilton also suggested that limitations be placed on the right of certain partners (in effect John Crosby Brown and Howard Potter) to accumulate future earnings until the relative capital deficiencies on the English side were corrected. On the face of it, their proposals were unrealistic. In the partnership form of organization an individual's personal and business assets were legally inseparable. So long as James Brown or his heirs remained in the organization, any arbitrary division of their wealth into various segments would have been meaningless from a legal standpoint.

If the New York partners themselves found the proposals irresponsible, their incredulousness did not prevent them from responding in a serious and logical manner. The family began with an examination of the likely consequences of James Brown's withdrawal from the firm. Howard Potter stated that the result "would be fatal to the credit of the house"; the firm might continue "but it would not be Brown Brothers & Co. the first House in the United States, any longer."[20] James Brown subsequently wrote a long letter to the London partners reviewing his lifelong association with the enterprise. At the outset, he indicated his own preference for retirement. But after discussing the matter with others, he had become worried "that the prestige of the house in point of credit would be seriously effected by my withdrawing; my death would not so effect it as it would soon be known that three-fifths of my property would remain in the house."[21] James then reminded Collet and Hamilton that since William's death his own wealth had been the backbone of the organization. "I suppose it is mainly due to my supposed means, which are usually

Table 1. A comparison of share allotments and capital, in currency and in gold, owned by the respective partners of the firm as of December 31, 1867

Country	Shares [b]	Capital (in thousands) [a]	
		Currency [b]	Gold [b]
United States			
James Brown	100,000	$4,879	$ 931
Stewart Brown	80,000	245	568
James M. Brown	52,902	112	219
Charles D. Dickey	39,296	210	138
Howart Potter	36,000	175	79
John Crosby Brown	22,500	210	74
Clarence S. Brown	10,000	80	45
Subtotal	340,000	$5,911	$2,054
England			
F. A. Hamilton	60,959	82	458
Mark Collet	58,179	142	431
Stewart H. Brown	35,000	-	136
Herman Hoskier	20,000	10	50
Subtotal	174,138	$ 234	$1,075
Total	517,336	$6,145	$3,129

Sources: Historical Files, Brown Brothers Harriman & Co., New York, and Wesley C. Mitchell, *Gold, Prices and Wages under the Greenback Standard* (Berkeley, 1908).

[a] *Total Capital in Greenback Currency*

$ 3,129 Gold dollars X 140 percent premium =	$	4,380
Greenback capital (from above)		6,145
Total	$	10,525

[b] Column one under "Shares" represents a partner's claim on future earnings. Columns two and three measure a partner's accumulated capital from prior years in greenback and gold dollars.

overestimated, that the house enjoys their present standing," he concluded. James estimated his total net worth at five and a half million dollars in greenback currency, not counting those amounts he had previously given his children.

Two months later John Crosby Brown wrote a letter to his brother-in-law Howard Potter, in London, that turned the tide in the family's relationship with the English partners. It was now time, he felt, to discard any pretense that the partners with the largest capital would do anything less than exert an overriding influence in the firm. The "theory of the partnership" had always been that the partners with the largest capital investment would control the organization. Moreover, it was clear that all the American members of the firm regarded "father's private fortune as well as his active capital essential to the continuance of the concern on its present footing."[22] If the theory that the firm was fundamentally a family enterprise was abandoned, then "our interest and pride in the house as a family institution ceases and our connection with it . . . becomes . . . simply a question of dollars and cents. It becomes a matter of calculation . . . whether it will not pay us better to withdraw . . . and go at something else." Given the present situation, John Crosby believed some arrangement for sharing power should be formulated that would remain in force until the nonfamily members retired. Thereafter the family would be assured of regaining full control.

In a review of alternative solutions, John Crosby touched on some of the likely consequences of a dissolution of the firm as presently organized. If a breakup occurred, James and his heirs would probably be affected the least, he reasoned, since they had "not only a fortune but also a position as high as any in the land quite independent of their connection with the house." The remaining partners, in contrast, would probably suffer financially and even socially. Many of them depended on the firm not only for their means of support but also "to some considerable extent for the position they hold in the community." It was true, John Crosby conceded in an uncharacteristically philosophical statement, that capital needed to combine with labor for their mutual benefit. Yet if one partner removed his labor, the firm could suvive without being seriously damaged; while if the capital was removed, the firm's position would immediately decline. Thus, as a rule, capital generally had the upper hand over labor. However, in this instance where the family looked "to the perpetuation of the house at all hazards," it seemed that labor was in a unique position to exercise much greater leverage.

John Crosby also recommended that the English partners consider some of the consequences of his father's withdrawal from the house.

In the past the firm had used James's private holdings as security for loans during critical times. Moreover, when unusually large losses had occurred, the senior men had magnanimously assumed the bulk of the reverses.[23] Given these circumstances, he felt the others should be proposing terms to induce them (meaning James, Potter, and himself) to remain in the partnership rather than the other way around. "I want everyone connected with us to get rich as fast as possible," he remarked, "but there was no justification for restricting the right of the wealthier partners to accumulate capital in the firm as opposed to the right of those who have been admitted to do the work." It should be stated forthrightly, he told Potter, that certain partners were in a superior position, and this fact should be clearly established in any new partnership agreement. A new agreement should cover a ten-year period, he added, so that the issue would be unlikely to arise again during his father's lifetime. "I think my views are reasonable and would stand before any impartial tribunal," John Crosby concluded.

In May, Howard Potter reported that the negotiations for new articles of partnership were being carried on "with a view to the consolidation & perpetuation of the House."[24] The articles were to be firmly based on the theory "that they form a contract between Mr. James Brown, as surviving owner of that concern, & certain other persons who are his employees for carrying it on." Nonetheless, the London partners were to retain full responsibility for managing the affairs of the English branches during their lifetime. Potter found the whole experience trying; "I feel in fact as if I was handling a business ready to drop to pieces in all directions," he told John Crosby in July.[25] Hamilton, he stated, had taken the recent death of his two sons remorsefully — none of his family would now be coming along to join the firm at some future date. As for Collet, if the firm was wound up, he would take the whole thing philosophically. Collet's position was already "made": "His Directorships in the Bank of England & the Insurance Company, blue & red ribbons of the City, would give him, if he went out of business, honours & occupation enough & he would be sought as paid Director in as many companies as he chose to serve in." Herman Hoskier believed he was entitled to a larger share allotment, and he too was "disposed to stand for what he considered his rights & to go it he does not get them."

It took great patience and considerable skill to mollify the London residents, but Howard Potter finally succeeded in drafting an agreement that was satisfactory to all parties. Despite the controversy, little change took place in the day-to-day operations of the firm; but the partnership had come through a crisis during which management passed to a new generation. The basic character of the enterprise was now established in favor of the heirs of James Brown. The point was thereafter understood by all and accepted by all. If the attitudes and initiatives of Francis Hamilton and Mark Collet had set the tone of the business over the previous 15 years, then that distinction now belonged, for the most part, to John Crosby Brown and Howard Potter who were equally able administrators and, moreover, men of broader vision. The maturity they exhibited in handling the firm's internal problems earned them the respect of the London partners.

For the future the Brown family was established as the supreme arbitrator. Yet so few disagreements arose over the firm's policies during the next 20 years that, in practice, the main branches on each side of the Atlantic managed their affairs almost independently, with little interference. A consensus on business matters and the absence of political controversy resulted in a lessening of the tensions related to the determination of status within the firm. The correspondence during the 1868 crisis differed from that in the past because, for the first time, the family defended its prerogatives openly and indicated firmly that it had no intention of relinquishing them. The plain talk cleared the air and led to better understanding.

The causes of the long series of partnership disagreements, which culminated in the late 1860s, were always perplexing to the New York partners. Communication with the London residents was at times frustrating because the motives behind the complaints of Hamilton and Collet were never adequately perceived. Some of their goals even appeared to be contradictory. No one in New York could understand how the withdrawal of James Brown would do anything but work to the detriment of all parties concerned, including the partners who managed the London office. Their proposals were paradoxical because for years Hamilton and Collet had chided the American management about the firm's inadequate working capital and the absence of a secondary reserve position.

The net effect of their recommendations, if followed faithfully over the years, would have been a lessening in the family's identification with the house and the creation of a more general partnership. In a more general firm, their own status in London's financial circles would have been enhanced, since they would have appeared more independent — and less like the employees of the American Browns. A change in the name of the house would not have been out of the range of possibilities. For Hamilton and Collet, it became a question of self-respect; commercial justice demanded that partners performing tasks of equal importance in a business enterprise should enjoy equal standing, with no exceptions. In essence, they had carried the emerging bureaucratic standards the organization had tacitly accepted in its system of administration to their logical conclusion — if not beyond.

Despite all their achievements, Collet and Hamilton retained an inferiority complex vis-à-vis their wealthier associates. The closer they came to attaining equality in the decision-making processes of the firm, the more the one remaining characteristic distinguishing them from their American counterparts, a substantial fortune invested in the house, gnawed at them.[26] This form of resentment was never really comprehended in New York because it seemed to be such a fundamental fact of life; it was a reality that could not be negotiated away. In the end the London residents apparently became reconciled to their inferior status. Meanwhile their pride and obstinacy almost caused the dissolution of the House of Brown at a point when the firm was reaching the pinnacle of its influence in the Anglo-American trade.

The 1870s and Beyond

By comparison, the 1870s were years of internal calm and steady, uneventful progress. The Browns successfully adjusted their foreign exchange operations to meet the complications resulting from the inconvertibility of the greenbacks into gold at the prewar rate. The southern connections were reestablished soon after the close of the Civil War. The men who had previously manned the branches in New Orleans and Mobile were by 1865 set in other posts, however, so the firm no longer used its own employees in those locations. Instead, independent agents represented the firm in those Gulf port cities, and in Galveston as well. The partners also revived the agency arrangement in Baltimore, after the founder's grandson, George Stewart Brown, brought new life to the original house, Alexander Brown & Sons. Only the Boston and Philadelphia offices remained under the direct administrative control of the New York office.

Both external and internal factors were responsible for the reduction in the firm's administrative control over the branch system. One exogenous force was the increase in the exports of northern ports. The shipment of large quantities of breadstuffs and other provisions to Europe did much to offset the high level of northern imports. The net result was a greater equilibrium in the foreign exchange markets of the north. The Browns were, therefore, less dependent on southern sources for their supply of sterling bills. Thus the possession of southern branches was no longer a matter of such critical importance.

From an internal standpoint, the time and energy previously devoted to managing the activities of the individual branches from New York had been considerable. The tremendously increased volume of business in New York during the postwar period strained the capacity of the main office personnel and left little time for reestablishing the former pattern of supervision.

Furthermore, the firm's overall policies had been fairly well established by the late sixties. The great degree of control over subordinates, which the partners required during the period when the various components of their business system were initially formulated, now seemed unnecessary. In fact, throughout the entire organization the main concern became the routine handling of the larger volume of transactions according to the precedents that had evolved by the 1850s. With the benefit of hindsight, it is evident that financial functions in the international trade sector had generally reached a stage of maturity in the period just prior to the war. Thereafter, it was a question of refining the techniques of management and control; the innovative era, what some might cite as the Schumpeterian stage of entrepreneurship, had passed.

The demand for the firm's letter of credit services continued to grow in the postwar period. Commercial credits to importers were, of course, the mainstay of their operations, but the issuance of travelers letters of credit to Americans visiting other parts of the world increased at a rapid pace. In the antebellum period, travelers credits had accounted for only a small volume of the total business. A second great wave of affluent American tourists reached Europe in the 1870s and 1880s, spurred on in part perhaps by the improved financial services of the Browns and other international banking firms.[27] Over the last quarter of the nineteenth century, the name Brown Brothers & Co. was as synonomous with traveling credits in foreign countries as the name American Express has become with travelers checks in the twentieth. By the mid-seventies the Brown's list of correspondents included banks in over 250 cities throughout the world. An advertisement which appeared in the 1873 edition of the *Banker's Almanac* featured their travelers credits.

The Browns also advertised their services for consignors of cotton which shows clearly that the mercantile phase of the firm's operations in England had not, as yet, ceased. Indeed, the Browns' consignment activities experienced a brief revival in the postwar period. For instance, the Baltimore agency arranged for the consignment of numerous bales of cotton to the Liverpool office in the late sixties and early seventies. Some of the cotton came directly to Baltimore over the Baltimore and Ohio Railroad, but much of it

BROWN BROTHERS & CO.

59 WALL STREET, NEW YORK,

211 Chestnut Street, PHILADELPHIA,   66 State Street, BOSTON,

ALEXANDER BROWN & SONS,

Corner Baltimore and Calvert Streets, BALTIMORE

Issue against cash deposited, or satisfactory guarantee of repayment, CIRCULAR CREDITS FOR TRAVELERS, in *Dollars* for use in the United States and adjacent countries, and in *Pounds sterling* for use in any part of the world.

   These credits, bearing the signature of the holder, afford a ready means of identification, and the amounts for which they are issued can be availed of from time to time, and wherever he may be, in sums to meet the requirements of the traveler.

   Application for credits may be made to either of the above houses direct, or through any first class bank or banker in this country.

THEY ALSO ISSUE COMMERCIAL CREDITS.

MAKE CABLE TRANSFERS OF MONEY BETWEEN THIS COUNTRY AND ENGLAND,
**DRAW BILLS OF EXCHANGE ON GREAT BRITAIN AND IRELAND,
AND MAKE ADVANCES UPON COTTON OR OTHER APPROVED
MERCHANDISE**

To the consignment of MESSRS. BROWN, SHIPLEY & CO., *London and Liverpool.*

was exported from Norfolk, a port city that began to thrive in the second half of the century.[28] Both the Liverpool and London offices handled consignments of breadstuffs from Baltimore and the northern branches. Even so, it is doubtful that any of the Browns' mercantile activities ever accounted for more than 5 percent of their total revenues during this temporary postwar spurt.

   The completion of the transatlantic telegraph cable in 1866 heralded the coming of a new marketing system for American produce. European buyers purchased produce directly from American sellers, and many commission merchants were eliminated as middlemen.[29] By the mid-1880s, the volume of business handled by the Browns' Liverpool branch had declined significantly. Howard Potter strongly advocated closing the office. However, Francis Hamilton and a few others felt the office might prove marginally useful for a time.

   During a visit to his old home port in 1885, Hamilton was greatly concerned about the general state of business in Liverpool. "There is evidently growing up an entirely new system of Finance in all Produce," he reported: "Everything is changing, old modes of Business & ideas vanishing & the minutest details calling for constant supervision."[30] Hamilton's remark suggests that the breakdown in the consignment system for marketing American raw materials and breadstuffs, which has generally been attributed to the completion of the transatlantic cable in the mid-sixties, may not have accelerated rapidly until the early 1880s.[31]

Based on Hamilton's testimony, Howard Potter urged his partners to accept the inevitability of a cessation of operations in Liverpool. "It seems only necessary to recognize fully that *Brown, Shipley & Co.* is a London House now," he stated. Given the trend toward the "elimination of middlemens' services," Potter saw little hope for the future. His own analysis of Liverpool profits indicated that the branch did not "return its costs." It served instead as a drain on the profits of the London office, Potter calculated.[32]

Finally, the New York office offered an interim solution. The Liverpool branch would remain open, but its staff would be sharply trimmed. Stewart H. Brown, the only full partner assigned to the branch, could then be transferred to London leaving the existing business to someone holding only a power of attorney. Thus organized, the old office might still be useful. There was such competition in the U.S. foreign exchange market and profit margins were narrowing so much that the time could come when the New York partners might welcome the opportunity of making remittances to England in produce rather than in bills of exchange. If such a situation arose, it would be important to have a strong foothold in Liverpool.[33]

The New York proposal was accepted in principle, although Stewart H. Brown was permitted to remain at his old Liverpool post. In fact, in retrospect, it seems that Stewart's reluctance to give up his association with the office he had served for over 30 years was probably the prime reason for keeping the branch open in the mid-eighties. When he died in 1888, the Liverpool office was summarily closed. The closing of the office William Brown founded in 1810 brought to an end one era in the history of the House of Brown.

In the early seventies, the firm's foreign exchange and letter of credit business expanded enormously; indeed, the lack of capital resources placed a temporary restriction on further growth. The problem was serious by the spring of 1871. Inasmuch as Collet and Hamilton had previously recommended the withdrawal of a portion of James Brown's resources from the firm, it is ironic that they were among the first to perceive the weakness of the overall capital position. John Crosby Brown visited London in February to discuss the matter with the English partners. The overriding issue was the magnitude of the firm's outstanding acceptances. In light of the current demand for their financial services, the consensus was that further increases were likely. "We are afflicted with too much prosperity," John Crosby observed.[34]

To meet the firm's capital requirements, the partners were encouraged to convert their outside investments into cash and to deposit the funds in their respective capital accounts. Over the last three years, James Brown had not allowed his earnings to accumulate in the firm because he was satisfied that the partnership had ample resources and because he believed the gesture would help in placating the English partners. Now that circumstances had changed, John Crosby told Hamilton and Collet that his father was prepared to do his part in bolstering the firm's working capital position.

The New York partners, at the same time, investigated one possible source of new capital. They opened negotiations with Alexander Hargraves Brown, a grandson and heir of William Brown, on the terms under which he might be induced to join the firm. His net worth was approximately $1,500,000 in 1872. During the early stages the negotiations were strictly 'a family affair; none of the English partners were privy to the correspondence. There was much talk about ensuring that the enterprise would remain under the control of the Brown family. A number of the women in the family followed the activities of the firm with great interest, and several of them were anxious to see a descendant of William Brown enter the house on the British side of the business.

There was one stumbling block, however, in the way of Alexander's joining the firm. He was determined to emulate his grandfather's political career rather than his business career. By 1872 Alexander had already served three years in Parliament, and he had no burning ambitions in the commercial world. In New York the family also feared the reactions of the London managers to any proposal for admitting a new partner who had no intention of sharing fully in the administrative duties. There was no precedent for such an arrangement. From Alexander's viewpoint, on the other hand, it was mainly a matter of assessing the likely affect on his political aspirations.

After the terms for his admission had been fairly well settled within the family, the process of feeling out Hamilton and Collet on the proposal began in the spring of 1873. Much to their surprise, John Crosby and Potter met little resistance from their English colleagues on the matter. When the prospective new partner demurred at the last moment, Hamilton even helped Potter persuade Alexander to join the house. Hamilton assured the young MP of the safety of his investment in the firm by stating that "as regards the character of the business done by the House & the management of it," he knew of nothing better or safer. Moreover, Hamilton did not appear to be overly disturbed at the prospect of a reduction in his allotment of shares although he expressed hope for some relief at the office. He made it clear that he was prepared to do whatever "in the general judgment should be considered most conducive to the interests of the House." "Such an example & spirit on his part will naturally have its effect with the others," Potter observed.[35]

From several standpoints, the welcome Collet and Hamilton extended to Alexander H. Brown was not all that difficult to explain. They had long advocated greater balance in the capital accounts of the American and British partners. With the addition of their new associate's assets, the English members of the firm now accounted for approximately 25 percent of the total resources, or $1,500,000 more than previously. From the way the two senior men in London tenaciously remained at their posts over the next 30 years, it is doubtful that they really were very disturbed about the new partner's reluctance to participate actively in the day-to-day operations of the house. Despite Hamilton's disclaimer, the two administrators were probably relieved to learn no one from the family would actually be interfering greatly with their management of the branch. Since Alexander was expected to remain a novice in the commercial world for some time, they did not foresee any difficulty in influencing him to their own advantage on any important issues that might arise again between themselves and the New York partners.

A dearth of capital was something the house had not experienced since the 1820s. From 1830 to 1870, capital surpluses, beyond the firm's requirements in its normal activities had been a fundamental reason for the involvement in so many peripheral business ventures. The change from surplus to deficit was a dramatic one, and as the New York partners foresaw — a permanent one. With every available dollar tied up in the exchange and letter of credit business, there were few opportunities for disputes to arise about deviations from the main strategy of the enterprise. Increased specialization in response to rising demand pressed the capital resources and narrowed the range of alternatives.

By the 1880s the Browns had reached what was to be the zenith of their prestige and influence. In the realm of providing financial services to the international trading community and the foreign traveler, their name was the most esteemed among the great private banking houses of the era. The firm's publicly posted foreign exchange rates became virtually the unofficial American standard. Mark Collet was appointed governor of the Bank of England in 1887 and, like

William Brown before him, knighted by the Crown in 1889. The near collapse of Baring Brothers in 1890 left the Browns as one of the few remaining pillars of the nineteenth century merchant-banking tradition.

Although the absolute volume of their business continued to grow during the last quarter of the century, in terms of its relative importance the firm had entered a gradual decline. While the factors responsible for their diminishing influence are manifold and go beyond the time boundary of this study, a brief glance at some of the broader factors may aid in highlighting some of the reasons for the firm's earlier success. The Brown's specialty was providing a channel through which the American foreign trade sector could expedite its financial transactions in the nineteenth century's chief medium of international exchange, the pound sterling. As the London money market eventually began to lose its exclusiveness as the world's dominant financial center, the role of the great Anglo-American bankers correspondingly diminished. Concomitantly, other American financial institutions increased their number of foreign contacts, and some of the mystery of international transactions disappeared.

For several decades the Browns were unable to detect the signs of their own relative decline. The volume of business activity and profits continued to expand. Nevertheless, the house failed to keep pace with the phenomenal growth of the American economy and the increasing number of international transactions. Neither their personnel nor capital was enlarged to encompass all the business they might have previously claimed. In the early 1890s only nine partners administered this vast enterprise whereas 13 had felt pressed on a smaller volume of business 25 years earlier. The London office atrophied under the direction of Hamilton and Collet who were by then elderly men — and out of touch with new developments. The same personnel that had previously given the house such extraordinary organizational strength now refused to be dislodged from their posts at a time when fresh minds and new initiatives were desperately required. The longevity of the first and second generation of managers and owners, which had brought so much stability to the firm in its formative years, proved a liability as the next century approached.

The New York partners were aware of the growing seriousness of the firm's internal situation, but they could not muster the will to impose the requisite reorganization upon their London counterparts. In New York they were in a position to witness at first hand the rise of new competitive financial institutions which threatened to siphon off much of the business private bankers had traditionally reserved for themselves. In the mid-nineties John Crosby Brown cited competition from several sources, "great Life Insurance Companies with their affiliated concerns, the Trust Companies with their enormous capital & cheap money, concerns manned by active and competent men always on the lookout for business & even from second class banking houses who have twice the number of partners we have, all on the watch for good business."[36] Yet the London partners continued their preoccupation with the activities of the older and more established English bankers. Their conservatism, which had served the house so well during its rise to preeminence, restricted the firm's activities unnecessarily in the last decade of the century. John Crosby referred to the consequences of their narrowness in a letter to Howard Potter in 1897, "In our fear of dealing with so-called Trusts such as Standard Oil & Sugar, managed by able & rich men, we have in the past lost good customers & much good & safe business."[37]

In sum, the Brown organization had reached maturity by the seventies and eighties. In the next two decades the partnership saw its position as the premier Anglo-American banking house progressively weakening. Despite the continuance of substantial profits, the leadership recognition of the firm diminished. A capital and organizational structure that had been sufficient to dominate the narrower financial markets of an earlier commercial era proved inadequate for the maintenance of a similar position in the emerging industrial economy.[38]

During the early part of the twentieth century, the problems associated with the London office were alleviated somewhat after Montagu Norman, a grandson of Mark Collet, joined the firm. Norman brought new life to the English half of the enterprise, and his growing reputation as an able banker soon earned him an appointment to the board of directors of the Bank of England. Like his grandfather before him, Montagu Collet Norman was later appointed deputy governor and then served as governor of the Bank of England from 1920 to 1944. In this respect, the heritage of leadership continued.

Despite the revitalization of the London office after Norman's arrival, close ties with the New York branch were never fully restored. The strain of the First World War proved too great, and the Anglo-American partnership dissolved in 1918. The London office operated as an independent partnership until 1946 when the firm was incorporated as Brown, Shipley & Co., Limited. The firm has remained active in international finance, and as recently as 1972 it joined with the largest American brokerage house to form Merrill Lynch-Brown Shipley Bank for the purpose of engaging in short and medium-term financing in the sterling and Euro-currency markets and world wide investment banking.

Meanwhile, the American partners merged with the Harriman family's investment banking house in 1931 to form Brown Brothers Harriman & Co. The firm survives today as one of the most important financial institutions in New York. Its unique characteristics remain. Brown Brothers Harriman & Co. was, for instance, the only commercial bank in the United States permitted to retain a seat on the New York Stock Exchange after the federal law separating investment and commercial banking took effect in the 1930s. More notably, however, the firm retains the partnership form of organization and thereby upholds the agelong private banking tradition.

Part Two

The Functional Activities

In the second part of this study, the discussion shifts from an emphasis on important events and general strategies to a more detailed analysis of the firm's operating policies and business procedures. Each of the following three sections focuses on one of the partnership's main functional activities. These topics are advancing and merchandising, the issuance of letters of credit, and foreign exchange operations. Several benefits derive from examining separately the firm's participation in the three markets which were traditional strongholds of Anglo-American merchant bankers. With a narrow focal point, it is possible to analyze in much greater depth the managerial processes that were associated with each phase of the partners' business activities. At the same time, there are frequent opportunities to survey the Browns' position vis-à-vis competitive firms and to delineate the overall shape of the three markets.

Section 1

Advances and Merchandising

During the early decades of the nineteenth century, one of the Browns' primary functions was the extension of credit facilities to American producers of raw materials and English manufacturers of finished goods. It was through the advancing mechanism that merchants choosing to consign their inventories to distant markets received sufficient credit to finance operations during the long interval between production and final sale. The financing provided by the House of Brown and other merchant-banking houses was absolutely critical to the foreign trade sector and, therefore, to the economic growth and development of the Anglo-American community.[1] The Browns' close connection with the extension of credit through the advancing mechanism came about as a natural outgrowth of the firm's early participation in merchandising activities generally.

Any discussion of the firm's involvement in merchandising activities must begin by stressing the highly competitive nature of markets on both sides of the Atlantic Ocean. In contrast to their relatively secure position in the foreign exchange and letter of credit fields later in the century, the Browns were only one of many firms engaged in the bilateral Anglo-American trade in finished goods and raw materials.[2] The market structure is perhaps best revealed with reference to the English market for raw cotton. Because the size of the cotton market expanded so swiftly in the first half of the nineteenth century, the British distribution system was characterized by a significant degree of specialization. Indeed, the Browns initially earned the reputation as responsible businessmen from their association with the cotton trade.

Yet specialization in the field did not lead to a significant degree of concentration.[3] During the period from 1820 to 1840, when 80 percent of England's cotton imports entered through Liverpool, none of the port's leading firms had a market share of over 10 percent. In the three years for which precise calculations of market shares are available, the Browns stood either first or second in the rankings. In 1820 they were the second leading importer of cotton in Liverpool with 3 percent of the market; in 1830 they were second again with 5 percent of the market; and finally in 1839 the Browns headed the list with a 7.2 percent market share.[4] By comparison, data on Baring Brothers indicates a market share approaching 10 percent in the 1837 season;[5] by 1839, however, they had slipped back to a 3 percent share and a ranking of seventh on the list of cotton importers.[6]

The market for finished goods and raw materials in the United States and England were characterized not only by their competitiveness but also by the numerous variations in their patterns of distribution. Therefore, no analysis of the Browns' advancing and merchandising activities would be meaningful without a preliminary outline of the context within which this phase of their business was conducted.

American Exports-English Imports

In the first half of the nineteenth century, cotton was by far the most important commodity exported by American shippers and imported by English merchants and manufacturers. In the U.S. merchandising system, cotton factors, who advanced funds to southern planters in the major port cities, were the key businessmen throughout the period.

In England, on the other hand, different groups predominated in various stages of the market's development. In the first quarter of the century, firms acting as commission merchants handled the vast majority of the cotton imports. These commission merchants generally made advances to the American cotton factors in order to attract consignments. Under this arrangement, the risk of ownership remained with the shipper.

In the second half of the century, there was a trend toward more outright purchases of cotton by the leading merchants in the import trade. The Barings, for example, transacted the majority of their cotton business after 1840 on their own account. Concurrently, English spinners made more direct purchases in the American south, bypassing completely local commission merchants. After the completion of the Atlantic cable in 1866, direct purchases by the cotton mills soon became the normal practice.[7] Many American firms that had previously functioned as factors now acted as buying agents for English manufacturers. Cotton was increasingly purchased in the inland markets and shipped to buyers on the basis of "through bills of lading." The same system of direct purchasing via the cable predominated in the grain trade between the two nations. Exports of bread-stuffs expanded rapidly in the last quarter of the century and rivaled cotton as the most important commodity in the bilateral Anglo-American trade.

English Exports-American Imports

Finished goods of all description were the leading English exports and chief American imports. In the period from 1800 to 1815, all-purpose merchants on both sides of the Atlantic performed most of the marketing functions and bore the risks of ownership. English manufacturers sold the bulk of their goods outright to merchants in the local port cities. After filling the specific orders of their American counterparts, these English merchants often sent out surplus goods to the same correspondents on consignment.

In the period from 1815 to around 1830, however, there were numerous changes in the traditional distribution system for manufactured goods on both sides of the Atlantic. In the United States, imported goods were increasingly sold at public auction. Meanwhile in England, there was a tendency among the manufacturers of finished goods to send out more merchandise on consignment. Some manufacturers consigned goods to English merchants who were active in the export trade. Other manufacturers preferred to deal directly with American commission merchants and auctioneers. The Browns' Liverpool branch, for example, willingly advanced funds to English manufacturers in an effort to obtain consignments for the American outlets.

After 1830, however, the auction system in the United States lost some of its vitality; more goods entered the country on the account of American merchants who now specialized in importing activities. The leading Anglo-American merchant-banking houses aided the trend through the issuance of letters of credit to U.S. importers. Thereafter, representatives of American importers traveled abroad and purchased merchandise directly from English manufacturers. Both buyers and sellers were thereby able to bypass British commission merchants. As a result of this change in the distribution system, few English goods were entering the United States on consignment by the middle of the century.

VI

Anglo-American Consignments

American Imports

When Alexander Brown arrived in Baltimore at the turn of the nineteenth century, the port was experiencing the most prosperous period in its history.[1] From 1785 until the embargo of 1807, Baltimore's foreign trade boomed. Many of the successful merchants in the port were men who had emigrated from Ireland, Scotland, and Germany during the last quarter of the eighteenth century.[2] The linen goods Alexander Brown imported came mostly from his former business associates and relatives in Ballymena, a small town about 25 miles north of Belfast. His largest supplier was William Gihon, a Ballymena merchant with whom the Browns maintained a close relationship for over three decades. The tie was strengthened in 1809 when Alexander's eldest son William returned to the homeland and, a year later, married Sara Gihon. Because the firm's letterbooks covering the period from 1804 to 1810 have not survived, little is known about the details of Alexander's activities as a linen merchant. On the other hand, financial records indicate that he had increased the firm's capital to $120,000 by the end of the decade.

The existing evidence indicates that Alexander Brown tended to deemphasize American imports during the years following the end of the war of 1812. In January 1814 he told his son William that after considering for some time the possibility of "going largely into the Dry Goods business," he had finally decided that the firm could use its resources most effectively by concentrating on a commission business in Liverpool.[3] Writing to a correspondent in New Orleans in October 1818, Alexander described his merchandising activities in Baltimore as confined almost exclusively to Irish linens.[4] His decision to forego any expansion in the volume of imports was almost certainly influenced by the general decline of Baltimore as a trading center relative to New York and the increasing resort to the public auction as a means of disposing of imported goods in the port cities along the northern coast.

The severe downturn in Baltimore's foreign commerce, which coincided with the general economic contraction from 1819 to 1821, underlined the soundness of Alexander Brown's judgment.[5] In March 1819 the times were so bad, he reported, that even wealthy houses discouraged consignments from England by denying all requests for advances.[6] Two years later the Baltimore office learned that the Liverpool branch had begun the solicitation of consignments from English manufacturers. Since most of the sales were at auction, the Baltimore partners reasoned that they could "manage the business as well as anyone."[7] Moreover, they thought "manufacturers would be pleased to have a safe house to send" goods to in Baltimore. A greater incentive, however, was the willingness of the Liverpool office to make advances against the merchandise consigned to the firm's branches in Baltimore and, after 1818, in Philadelphia.

Despite the advantages associated with the maintenance of a branch office in Liverpool, Alexander Brown was nevertheless discouraged about long-run prospects in the import sector. Late in 1821 he was concerned about the probable increase in the tariff on linen goods. "This will have the effect of lessening the consumption," he warned. "Domestic cottons which are now made in this country good & cheap in great quantities are already substituting & will be more so."[8] Brown's review of the Baltimore branch's business in 1822 had a similar theme: "We think the Linen business is declining so much that it will continue to fall off, indeed the general Business of this place is falling off greatly."[9] Meanwhile, the situation in Philadelphia showed little improvement. In the winter of 1822 the Baltimore partners learned that auctions were becoming a regular way of doing business in Philadelphia.[10]

The establishment of a branch office in New York signaled the firm's renewed interest in handling American imports on a consignment basis. Within a year of the 1825 opening, James Brown made an agreement with Samuel Nicholson, which called for Nicholson to join the office as a junior partner and manage the branch's mercantile affairs. In circulars announcing the new arrangements, the New York branch stated that it would be "happy to receive & attend to Consignments . . . of any English, Irish or Scotch Goods" which were shipped to the American market through the firm's Liverpool branch. The charges for these services, in the circular dated January 1, 1826, were listed as follows:

> Our Charges will be for Sale & Guarantee Six per Cent, for Storage, Postage & Advertising one half per Cent, and one eighth

per Cent for Insurance against Fire. — In cases where we deem it the Interest of the owners to sell at Auction, our charge will be only 2 1/2 per Cent. Should our friends wish the remittances guaranteed, we will do so for 1 per Cent.[11]

The circular then cited some of the benefits a consignor would derive from allowing his merchandise to be handled by the partnership: "Messrs. Jn. A. Brown & Co. of Philadelphia & A. Brown & Sons Baltimore receive consignments on the same terms, & as we keep each other advised of our respective Markets, consignments to either of our establishments can have the advantage of all should the owner so direct."

In addition, the Browns promised liberal advances to owners on all goods consigned to them for sale. The circular explained that if the English shipper wished the net proceeds from the sale of finished goods remitted to him in cotton or any other produce, the New York office would attend to the purchase either in the local market or in the south "as will be most advantageous." Otherwise, the partners announced that they intended to limit their activities "solely to the sale of British goods," and not to engage in the purchase of American produce for overseas buyers. The implication being, of course, that those buyers who wanted to purchase cotton could do so at the firm's convenient outlet in Liverpool.

In a subsequent circular issued in the summer of 1826, the Browns raised their commission fee on auction sales from 2 1/2 to 3 percent. In the late twenties almost one half of the goods imported by New York merchants were sold on the auction block. In a letter to an Irish consignor in October 1826, James Brown explained that the house could often obtain as high a price at auction as by private sales.[12] His associate, Mr. Nicholson, always attended the auctions, James assured his correspondent, and bid up the price if it seemed likely that the goods would not bring a fair return. Whenever merchandise would not move in the private market, it was best to sell at auction and save the interest costs on carrying inventory, James reasoned in closing.

The success of the "dry goods department" in New York under the management of Samuel Nicholson led the firm to cancel exclusive agreements with two linen suppliers in Ballymena. For years the partnership had received most of its linen goods from William Gihon and John Patrick, the father-in-laws of the Brown partners in Liverpool and Philadelphia respectively. In a letter to John Patrick, James explained that the policy of welcoming consignments from other suppliers would actually benefit all sellers: "We are confident the greater variety of goods we have, the better it is for our correspondents as it draws more customers."[13] In a note to a new supplier in Belfast written a few weeks later, James reiterated the point about a wide assortment of merchandise: "You should never ship the same style of goods a second time if you can avoid it, always giving a decided preference to anything that is new."[14]

In sum, the rejuvenation of the partnership's activities in the American import sector was closely related to the establishment of an outlet in New York. With the beginning of packet line service to Liverpool and the later opening of the Erie Canal, New York was already far outdistancing its Atlantic rivals in the competition for the major share of the nation's foreign commerce.[15] It became the one market large enough to sustain a steady business for the commission merchants handling British dry goods.[16]

In an effort to increase their commission business further, the partners decided in 1831 to employ a permanent representative in Manchester with instructions to obtain consignments from the region's textile manufacturers. The young man selected for the post was William Bowen, who had previously worked as an auctioneer in Philadelphia and was familiar wih the requirements of the American market. The Browns' decision to place a representative in the factory district who could authorize advances against consignments coincided with the general movement among English manufacturers to deal directly with American merchants.

Indeed, the Browns' unique organizational structure permitted them to solicit consignments through two, normally independent channels. While Bowen cultivated accounts seeking direct imports of goods for the American branches, the Liverpool office actively solicited business on the basis of its position as one of the leading commission houses in the British export trade. Although Bowen was technically an employee of the entire partnership, his role in Manchester was primarily to act as agent for the American branches. It was one of the rare instances where an interior agent and a Liverpool house did not compete in the solicitation of consignments but actually complemented one another. The same could not be said of other commission merchants in Liverpool who, with few exceptions, had no branch offices in the United States and were therefore increasingly bypassed in the shipment of finished goods across the Atlantic.

At the same time the American branches were expanding the volume of mercantile activities, they were also increasing the issuance of letters of credit to other importers. This revival of the traditional, but now much more specialized merchant was linked to the decline of the auction system and the rapid growth of the letter of credit mechanism. The letter of credit was gaining greater recognition overseas from merchants and manufacturers and their issuance expanded accordingly in the United States. The Browns were, of course, among the largest issuers. In fact, some of the importers the partners financed later turned up as competitors in the merchandising end of the business.

The renewed emphasis on the solicitation of finished goods consignments for the American market temporarily reversed the trend toward greater functional specialization. Indeed at no other time in its history was the firm so heavily involved in such a multiplicity of financial and merchandising activities as in the ten years from 1825 to 1835. Over this period the family's capital grew from $1,531,000 to $4,957,000, and the House of Brown became, in every sense of the word, one of the premier merchant-banking firms in the Anglo-American economy.[17]

The firm had no sooner reached this exalted status than the partners decided to phase out mercantile activities in the American market. This decision emerged from a thorough reassessment of the partnership's goals and strategies after Alexander Brown's death in 1834. The main objection to consignments for the American branches was that they tied up too much of the firm's funds in illiquid accounts receivable. It often took as long as eight months to collect debts generated by the sale of imported merchandise. Meanwhile, the advances to English manufacturers remained outstanding. In the summer of 1834 James Brown estimated the total of past due accounts in New York alone at over $500,000.[18] Hardware sales were responsible for most of the slow debts. In Baltimore, George Brown became quite apprehensive about what appeared to be an ominous trend. "From the way this business has been pressed," it would, if continued, "get all our means locked up," George warned.[19]

But the most persuasive argument against the continued handling of American consignments was that the funds released by a cessation of this activity could be used more advantageously in the performance of the firm's other financial functions. More resources were needed to finance the partnership's letter of credit activities, its foreign exchange operations, and finally its advances in the South against cotton consignments for the Liverpool branch. At this point, the partners did not consider any plan to contract similarly the mercantile activities of the Liverpool office.

American Exports

During the first decade of business operations in Baltimore, Alexander Brown periodically purchased cargoes of tobacco, grain, and cotton for export to friends and relatives in England.[20] As early as January 1803, he wrote a correspondent in Savannah to arrange a modest purchase of cotton.[21] At the same time, he kept in close contact with a number of tobacco merchants in Petersburg, Virginia. Thus almost from the founding of the enterprise, he and his sons exhibited a keen interest in transacting business beyond the confines of the port of Baltimore. Yet the establishment of the Liverpool branch in 1810 was the cardinal event which hailed the beginning of the firm's rise as a leader in financing and marketing American exports to Great Britain. By 1820 William & James Brown & Co. was the second largest recipient of cotton consignments in Liverpool. In that year, the branch handled 12,696 bales of cotton—or 3 percent of the total bales imported.[22] Of almost equal importance, however, were the firm's activities in the flour and tobacco markets.

Among the thirty Liverpool firms identified as the port's leading cotton importers in 1820, the Browns received the largest volume of flour shipments—20,560 barrels. The 475 hogsheads of tobacco were the second highest recorded by commission merchants within the same category of importers. How the Browns' totals compared with the figures for other commission merchants who were also involved in the flour and tobacco trades cannot be determined. On the other hand, since there is little evidence of specialization on the part of Liverpool merchants at the time, it seems likely that the port's chief cotton importers were fairly representative of the leading commission merchants generally. Indeed, it is entirely possible that the Browns' branch conducted the largest overall commission business in Liverpool around 1820 and for many years thereafter.[23]

In the following discussion, however, our attention will be focused primarily on the Browns' association with the cotton market. In terms of its long-run significance to the Anglo-American economy and to the firm itself, the cotton trade overshadowed all others in importance during the antebellum decades.[24] The firm functioned through its own "cotton triangle"—its southern representatives, the northern headquarters in Baltimore and later New York, and the Liverpool office, with each outlet having a series of distinct responsibilities.

One of the earliest business letters between Alexander Brown and his eldest son William described the arrangements which had been made in May 1811 for a shipment of cotton from New Orleans to Liverpool. The cotton was ordered by a Baltimore shipper who agreed to consign the cargo to William in return for an advance on the anticipated sales proceeds. Alexander Brown told William that once he was "in possession of the Bills of Lading & order for Insurance," he would endorse a draft drawn "for a reasonable amount on property shipped to you."[25]

In this context it should be emphasized that Alexander Brown did not agree to purchase the draft drawn on William Brown & Co., but merely to endorse it. The endorsement was valuable nonetheless because it appreciably enhanced the standing of the bill of exchange and thus made it far easier for the shipper to sell the bill to an importer with overseas debts. By endorsing a bill for the agreed advance, Alexander Brown in effect certified—for the benefit of all potential buyers of the bill of exchange—the genuine authenticity of the transaction. At the same time, he joined the drawer (the shipper) in becoming legally responsible for restitution in the event the drawee ultimately refused payment.

Alexander Brown's offer merely to endorse a bill of exchange points up a crucial distinction between "authorizing" an advance and "negotiating" an advance. The authorization of an advance was the first step in the financial process. Generally speaking, it was the English consignee who set the terms under which he would be willing to accept bills drawn against merchandise sent to him for sale. The English commission merchants usually appointed representatives in the United States who were delegated the authority to endorse, in an agency capacity, the aforementioned bills.

To negotiate an advance, on the other hand, meant going one step further. The American representative now indicated his willingness to purchase outright for cash the authorized bills. This latter service required a substantial amount of capital, or access to supplemental funds through letters of credit and the like. In negotiating advances, the representatives of English consignees performed some of the functions of a foreign exchange dealer. The distinction between authorizing and negotiating advances must be clearly drawn because too often in the past the two functions have been joined together under the broad terminology of "making" advances. The vagueness of this latter term, as used in the description of activities in the foreign trade sector, has contributed to our failure to achieve a thorough understanding of these financial processes. In short, there was more than one way, in the informal jargon, to make an advance; and a delineation of the various stages is crucial to an appreciation of the Browns' changing role in this market over the years.

The advancing mechanism was further complicated by the existence of a middle ground between the extremes of a simple endorsement or an outright purchase. After complying with the endorsement procedure, the American representative might agree to aid the
shipper in seeking an outside buyer for the bill of exchange. In this
role the representative served as an exchange broker rather than a
full-fledged dealer. Depending on the competitive situation in a
given market, he might or might not charge the shipper a commission for the ancillary service. As a rule, there was little hesitancy
about participating in this business activity, since the agent or representative was not forced to commit any of his own funds to the
transaction. In a letter to a Savannah correspondent in 1819 Alexander Brown & Sons stated that they would not "take it upon ourselves to sell sterling bills for anyone unless predicated on property
actually shipped to William & James Brown & Co."[26] For those who
did ship cotton or other produce to the Liverpool house, on the other
hand, the branch was glad to oblige. If sufficient funds were available, the Baltimore branch generally negotiated the advance; otherwise, it only endorsed the bill and sought an alternative purchaser.

This system of marketing cotton through a chain of consignees,
who by one means or another granted advances, was fundamentally
a carryover from the institutional arrangements in the colonial
tobacco trade.[27] Because tobacco plantations were typically located
on navigable rivers, there had been no middlemen between the
growers and English commission merchants. Cotton, in contrast, was
grown farther inland, and most planters shipped their produce to an
intermediary commission merchant in a nearby port city, who was
commonly referred to as a cotton factor. Although the Browns occasionally accepted consignments directly from planters, their business, for the most part, was confined to transactions with cotton factors in the major ports.[28]

During the formative years of their organization, the Browns conducted their southern business through a network of agents. These
agents were factors who shipped cotton almost exclusively to William
& James Brown & Co. Concomitantly, they were expected to solicit
consignments for the Liverpool branch from other cotton factors in
their respective ports under the terms set forth by the Brown partners. A key question was always how large an advance might be allowed on a given cargo. Although the authorized percentage varied
from season to season, the advance generally ranged from two thirds
to three fourths of the cost of cotton in the local market. Higher percentages were sometimes allowed to special correspondents when
prices were not unusually high and to cotton factors generally when

prices were abnormally low. The Browns' goal was to preserve at all times a sufficient margin between the bills of exchange negotiated under their advances and the ultimate sale proceeds of the cotton in Liverpool. In other words, they hoped to avoid the risk of a possible overadvance and a subsequent "reclamation" on the shipper, who retained ownership.

During the first quarter of the century South Carolina and Georgia were the leading states in cotton production, and the Browns' strongest ties were with the agents in Charleston and Savannah.[29] Adger & Black represented the firm in Charleston, while Campbell & Cumming performed similar duties in Savannah. As the center of cotton production moved rapidly westward, New Orleans began demonstrating its potential as a great cotton port. The Browns were anxious to establish a solid position in this growing market, but for several years they had difficulty locating a reliable representative. Consequently, John Brown, Alexander's third son, who had opened the Philadelphia branch in 1818, was sent to New Orleans for three marketing seasons, beginning with the fall of 1820. His assignment was to promote the firm's business among the local cotton factors and to lay the groundwork for a more permanent arrangement with a resident merchant.

When John Brown left for New Orleans, he carried along a letter of credit that had been arranged through the Baltimore branch of the Second Bank of the United States. Alexander Brown was a director of the local branch, and the relationship between the Bank and the firm was then quite friendly. The letter of credit was obtained primarily as a precautionary measure; it was to be used only in a period of unusual need. Public knowledge of its existence was expected to enhance the Browns' standing in the commercial community, however. In March 1821 the Baltimore branch noted that John was doing well in New Orleans, "since he is known to have unlimited means."[30]

In Benjamin Story, the Browns found the representative they had been seeking. Based on John's initial impressions, the Baltimore branch described him for the Liverpool office in a favorable manner: "Story we understand is a peculiar and very particular man; he won't buy a bale of Cotton unless with funds in hand."[31] The Browns interpreted his disdain for transactions based on credit rather than hard cash as a sure sign of his nonspeculative character.

When John Brown left the south in 1823 and returned to his permanent post in Philadelphia, Benjamin Story became the firm's chief representative in New Orleans. The Browns maintained agency agreements with two other factors in New Orleans—Joseph Fowler,

CIRCULAR.

October, 1825.

FOR some time past we have had it in contemplation to establish a house in New-York, with the view of promoting the interest of Messrs. WILLIAM & JAMES BROWN & Co., *of Liverpool,* and of affording greater facility, and the choice of markets, to our southern friends, who are disposed to give them or us their business; for that purpose, our JAMES BROWN has established himself, at *New-York,* to conduct a Commission Business, under the firm of BROWN, BROTHERS, & Co.

The partners in that house, are the same as those composing our respective firms.

ALEXANDER BROWN & SONS, *Baltimore.*

JOHN A. BROWN & Co., *Philadelphia.*

New-York, 31st October, 1825.

IN announcing our establishment, allow us to offer you our services. Should you send us Cotton or other produce, we will either dispose of it in this market, or re-ship it to our Liverpool house, Messrs. WILLIAM & JAMES BROWN & Co., as you may direct.

If a sale is made here, we charge a Commission of 2½ per cent.; and if we guarantee, the customary charge will be made. Should the property be re-shipped to our friends, Messrs. WM. & JAMES BROWN & Co., no charge will be made for our agency.

We are willing, at all times, to make reasonable advances, on property consigned to us, or our Liverpool house, on receiving Invoice, Bills of Lading, and orders to have Insurance effected, either here or at Liverpool; and to reimburse ourselves for any advances we make, and expenses incurred on shipments to Messrs. WILLIAM & JAMES BROWN & Co., we will draw on them, for which we charge a Commission of 1 per cent., but make no charge for effecting Insurance on property consigned to any of our establishments.

Your obedient servants,

Brown Brothers & Co

REFERENCES.

BENJAMIN STORY, Esq.
JOSEPH FOWLER, JUN., Esq. } *New-Orleans.*
MESSRS. JOHN HAGAN, & CO.
MESSRS. MC LOSKEY & HAGAN, *Mobile.*
MESSRS. ADGER & BLACK, *Charleston.*
MESSRS. JOHN CUMMING & SON, *Savannah.*
MESSRS. F. T. MASTIN. & CO., *Huntsville, Alabama.*
(*Brown Brothers Harriman & Co. Historical File*)

Jr., and John Hagan & Co., but Story was the only agent who could commit them to a participation in a cotton shipment on a joint account basis. On any cargoes Story deemed safe, he was authorized to commit the Liverpool branch to a one third share of the risk and profit. Otherwise, the Browns promised to allow their agents a flat 1 percent fee for procuring consignments to the Liverpool office.[32] This allowance was a rebate of the 1 percent commission that the Browns charged customers for negotiating an advance. In Liverpool they normally charged customers an additional 3.25 percent for selling the cotton and guaranteeing the credit of the English buyer.

During the same period New Orleans was emerging as the leading port in the southern states, New York was also becoming increasingly involved in the cotton trade.[33] The cotton moved via coastal shipping to New York, where it was either sold immediately or placed on board ocean transport for consignment to the Liverpool market. According to the circular the Browns issued in October 1825, expanded services for cotton trades had been the main consideration in opening a New York branch.

The establishment of the New York outlet coincided with the outbreak of a speculative mania in the cotton market. The average price of a pound of cotton in New York rose from 11.4¢ in 1823 to a high of 18.6¢ in 1825, before plunging back to 12.2¢ in 1826.[34] In Liverpool the drop in prices was even more dramatic — just over 40 percent. Based on the calculations in Appendix C, shippers of cotton from New Orleans and New York to Liverpool lost an average of 15 percent and 13 percent respectively in 1826. The Browns had anticipated the likely consequences of the sudden spurt in prices in 1825, and they were not at all surprised by the outcome. In June 1825 the Baltimore partners told the Liverpool office that they could see "no good cause for the prices rising to the height they have done with you or here . . . , except the madness of speculators."[35] In another note written a few days later, they urged the Liverpool branch to press sales, since "the small accumulation you have cannot affect the market that much — it would be different with large holders whose stocks would excite alarm if thrown on the market."[36]

In July the Baltimore branch informed all its regular customers in southern ports that the firm wanted no more joint interests in cotton shipments during the coming season. Despite their efforts to avoid the accumulation of a large inventory in Liverpool, rumors persisted in the business community that the Browns were also holding cotton off the market in a bid to obtain higher prices for their stocks. The Baltimore and New York branches categorically denied the accusations and denounced the spread of the misleading reports. James Brown told an important New Orleans factor — Reynolds, Byrne & Co. — that "W. & J. Brown & Co. never did, and never will, speculate in an article so long as they continue to do a commission business."[37] The rumors to the contrary did the house a "great injustice," he argued, and especially among potential customers who were not well informed about the firm's actual operating policies. James told another customer one year later that the Liverpool office had been free sellers throughout the entire 1826 season. "We believe it is the best course 9 times out of 10," he added.[38]

By foregoing the risk of ownership during what was an otherwise disastrous season for shippers, the Brown family earned profits of $196,974 in 1826; at year end the family's capital account stood at $1,788,702.[39] Beyond the short-run financial gains, the Browns hoped the cautious attitude they had displayed throughout the speculative boom would enhance their reputation and stand them in good stead during the years ahead. James Brown had predicted such an outcome in correspondence with Benjamin Story in November 1825: "Such a year as this will no doubt cause some to change their correspondents and we shall no doubt get our share."[40]

The Browns followed the same cautious tactics in the period from 1834 to 1836. In December 1833 the Baltimore branch told John Cumming & Son, the firm's Savannah agent, that cotton prices were already too high and that it would be unsafe to advance over 9 to 10¢ per pound.[41] The suggested allowance was about 60 percent of the average price of cotton in the New Orleans market that December. The Browns were, of course, aware that a conservative policy on advances might restrict the volume of consignments, but that result seemed preferable to becoming caught up in a surge of speculative activity. "Others who have little to lose may be willing to promise imprudent advances for the sake of business as they did in 1825," the Baltimore partners told the Savannah agent; "if so we must let them go . . . if the shipper will risk shipping to such people we cannot help it."[42] At the beginning of the 1834-35 season, they explained to Benjamin Story that the firm would not "wish to be interested in a pound of Cotton" on joint account shipments if prices remained as high as in the previous year.[43] And as events unfolded, cotton prices not only remained high but moved up to an even more elevated level in the next two seasons.

The Browns ceased virtually all purchasing on their own account in the months leading up to the panic of 1837. In January 1836 they informed Benjamin Story of their plans in unequivocal terms: "As regards Cotton we have made up our minds to do nothing in it this season except to put a few hundred Bales in our ships to give them a start in freight."[44] The letters sent to other cotton factors about the regular consignment trade were similarly cautious. "At the present high price of Cotton in Orleans it would be the height of folly for Planters to ship to Liverpool," the Baltimore partners told a correspondent in Huntsville, Alabama. "We would not be willing to advance over 3/4 or 4/5 of the present value as all accounts agree that the crop will be about 1350 [000] Bales which will be more than sufficient for the consumption."[45] To another factor in New Orleans the message was much the same: "We think the article far above its value & heavy losses must be the result of shipments at such high rates."[46]

The rival Barings, interestingly, had just opened a branch in Liverpool when this latest upsurge in cotton prices got under way. During the first year of operations, the Baring partners were extremely disappointed in the small volume of consignments their new branch office had been able to attract from the United States. But after agreeing to handle shipments on joint account and changing several other policies for the 1834-35 season, the Barings' business showed a dramatic increase. By August 1835 their Liverpool branch had received 30,000 bales of cotton with 6,000 more on the way, and it was reported that only the Browns had received a larger volume of consignments during the first six months of the year.

One of the Barings' goals in establishing a Liverpool outlet was to become more competitive with the Browns and other merchant-banking firms in the Anglo-American cotton trade. Yet despite their successes during the 1834-35 season, the Barings worried about the persistence of rising prices for raw cotton. The partners thought they saw ominous signs that a major crisis might be approaching. Thus, they had no sooner developed an effective system for handling cotton consignments than they began to have misgivings about the market outlook for the upcoming seasons. Consequently, the Barings virtually suspended the promotion of cotton consignments in the 1835-36 and 1836-37 marketing periods.[47] In sum, both the Barings and Browns pursued conservative merchandising policies in the months leading up to the panic which finally materialized in the spring of 1837.[48]

After cotton prices had fallen substantially, the Browns slowly re-entered the market. In April 1837 the Baltimore branch told the New Orleans agent, Benjamin Story, to use the firm's funds "in making advances on consignments to W & J Brown & Co. . . . the advances to be kept low & to good houses."[49] A few days later, Story received new instructions giving him greater latitude. In view of the depressed market, the Baltimore management suggested that it might be advantageous to forego consignments and to concentrate instead on making outright purchases of cotton for overseas shipment. But the final decision was left entirely to Story, who was on the spot and therefore in the best position to judge the situation. Meanwhile, the Browns instructed Story to avoid the purchase of sterling bills drawn on other English merchant-bankers: "It is impossible to say what bill may be paid and the only safe way . . . of getting our funds remitted is by purchasing or advancing on Cotton, now that it has got so low and . . . must be at safe prices."[50]

During the remainder of the year, the Browns delegated to Benjamin Story a great degree of discretionary power over several million dollars of their funds. In October the Baltimore branch expressed the partners' appreciation for his "services on our behalf." As proof, they invited Story to debit the firm for any losses he might have sustained "due to interest . . . we know you will do what is right."[51] In contrast to their normal pattern of operation, the Browns decided to stockpile the year's cotton purchases and wait for a rise in Liverpool prices. "We hope the cotton bought for us the past season will make near a par remittance altho we have not received sales of any of the shipments," the Baltimore office told Story in December 1837.[52] The next month, however, the Liverpool branch reported that cotton prices were advancing and Story's purchases were proving profitable.

The Browns entered the 1838 season aggressively seeking consignments. Because so many competitive houses had suffered financially during the previous year's panic, the firm obtained as much business as the partners could handle by offering advances of only two thirds or three fourths of cost. In March 1838 the Baltimore branch told James Adger, the Charleston agent, that the Liverpool office would have "more cotton than ever," based on the preliminary estimates of probable receipts.[53] How many bales they actually received in 1838 is unknown, but the following year the Liverpool branch imported 73,876 bales and topped the list of importers with a 7.2 percent share of the market.[54]

Yet for reasons that are not wholly understood, the Browns drastically curtailed their cotton operations in the late 1840s and subsequently dropped almost completely out of the market in the closing years of the antebellum period. In 1845 the Liverpool branch's commission revenues on consignments were $53,000; but by 1852 the revenues had fallen to approximately $5,000—a drop of 90 percent.[55] Unfortunately, the general absence of source material on the firm's business activities in the forties makes it difficult to determine the exact reasons for this important shift in the partners' strategy.

Nonetheless, there were several concurrent developments, both internal and external to the firm, which undoubtedly had some influence on the actual timing of the partnership's withdrawal from this market. In the late 1840s the firm became heavily involved in the promotion of America's first transatlantic steamship line, popularly known as the Collins Line. E. K. Collins, one of the nations' earliest and boldest shipping entrepreneurs, managed the line while the

Browns, along with some of their mercantile friends, financed its operations. When the steamers commenced runs in the spring of 1850, the Browns' Liverpool branch assumed the duties of British agent for the line. The private notes of the Liverpool partners, which are extant after 1851, indicate that these agency responsibilities consumed an enormous amount of time and energy.

Thus, administrative constraints may, in part, have forced the Liverpool partners to choose between a continued presence in the cotton market and their new role as overseers of the operations of the Collins Line in Britain. In a suggestive letter written two years before the steamers left port, George Alexander Brown, who held a middle management post in the Liverpool office, told his brother Stewart in New York that all signs indicated the steamers would be a success and might become a better business than "cotton consignments."[56] That the Liverpool partners, who never numbered above four during the first three quarters of the century, would have given up the performance of one of their major functions to concentrate on other duties at this juncture in the firm's history seems entirely plausible, since the partnership was simultaneously involved in the largest foreign exchange and letter of credit operations in the Anglo-American economy.

An exogenous factor of some importance was the trend among other merchant-banking houses to handle a greater share of their cotton business on their own account. The Barings supplanted the Browns as the leading recipients of cotton during the 1840s, and over one half of their total imports represented direct purchases for the firm's own account. From 1842 to 1848, the Barings tried to maintain an even balance between purchases and consignments, although the ratio varied with the condition of the market. In the fifties, Ralph Hidy relates, "The policy of emphasizing purchases of cotton instead of advances on consignments was continued."[57] If consignors were demanding advances almost equal to the full cost of cotton in the American market, the Barings and others may have reasoned that the risk of actual ownership could not be that much greater. Moreover, the profit potential associated with ownership was far higher than a commission of 2.5 to 4 percent for handling all the details of a sale for a third party. Since the Browns considered themselves to be primarily commisssion merchants, they apparently decided to forego the risks and profits altogether.

Furthermore, the Browns had long-standing complaints about competitors who allowed advances that the partners considered too liberal (often the full cost of the cotton) and those who permitted customers "return commissions," or rebates, on even a moderate volume of business.[58] The rising price of cotton after the mid-forties also inhibited the partners' operations. At one point in the late 1850s, the New York office revealed that the firm had long ago decided to have little to do with the staple whenever it sold at over 6 pence per pound in the Liverpool market.[59] The maintenance of prices above that level the partners presumably interpreted as a sure sign of speculative activity; under those circumstances, the prudent merchant would be wise in curtailing operations until the commodity had fallen back to its more "legitimate," or at least traditional, value. In this case implementation of the 6 pence price limit would have automatically eliminated the firm from the cotton market in the years from 1855 to 1859 when prices were high.

Perhaps no single explanation for this change in the firm's broad strategy is satisfactory. A combination of new administrative responsibilities, the allegedly irresponsible tactics of competitors, a concern about the absolute level of cotton prices, and the trend toward a greater emphasis on transatlantic purchases may, together, have accounted for the partners' decision. But whatever the reasons for the curtailment of their cotton operations, the Browns left a market which was extremely competitive and, after 1850, concentrated on other fields in which the market structure was closer to oligopoly.[60]

VII

Managing Cotton Operations

In the management of their cotton operations, the Browns took full advantage of their unique organizational structure. The branch in Liverpool was the cornerstone of their involvement in the Anglo-American cotton trade, but the role of the northern branches in coordinating the activities of their southern representative was almost equally important. Since the partners' activities in the cotton market were the most extensive from 1815 to 1850, the discussion here focuses on the partners' management techniques during those years.[1]

In the performance of their duties as the English consignee of American cotton, the primary responsibility of the Liverpool partners was, oddly, to the one party with whom they generally had the least personal contact: the southern planter, who was the original consignor and the actual starting point in the merchandising chain. No matter what route the cotton followed in reaching Liverpool, or how many hands it passed through in the process, the planter retained ownership over the entire marketing cycle; and it was he who was most concerned about the ultimate cash proceeds of his shipment.

Thus the strategies and tactics which various Liverpool commission merchants employed in marketing consignments were important factors effecting directly the southern planters who decided to ship their cotton to overseas markets. Some English consignees tried to maximize the sales proceeds by holding cotton in local warehouses and waiting for prices to reach what they hoped would be a seasonal peak. If a consignee was skillful in selling his customers' holdings at the most advantageous prices for several seasons, then he could generally look forward to an enhanced reputation and an increased volume of new business. On the other hand, the consignee who held cotton off the market ran the risk of falling, instead of rising, prices; and the market might never recover sufficiently to make up for lost ground. The Browns considered the voluntary withholding of cotton from the market an inherently speculative activity, and, as a rule, they avoided such dangerous tactics. Their policy was basically to sell a customer's cotton soon after it arrived in Liverpool, irrespective of market conditions.

The partners' commitment to this conservative marketing strategy was strong, and it is illustrated in their correspondence with customers over the years. Writing to one customer in Huntsville, Alabama, in 1827 the Baltimore office explained the principle concisely: "The safest plan is to meet the market in the regular way, as soon after it arrives as a fair demand will justify without forcing; any other course adds certain losses, Interest on money, storage & loss of weight, which is seldom compensated by holding."[2] Sometimes, however, it was the American exporter who set a price limit below which the Liverpool consignee could not legitimately negotiate sales. The Browns discouraged customers from establishing limits or placing any conditions whatsoever on the Liverpool partners which might unduly restrain their flexibility during a period of market uncertainty. In a note to the New York office in August 1844, the Liverpool managers expressed surprise at the lengths to which some American shippers would go in their efforts to obtain even slightly higher prices for cargoes; "It is strange how cotton operators on your side seem to fancy that they may with safety hold cotton here," they wrote.[3] Those shippers who were unwilling to accept small losses occasionally, they observed, often ended up with even greater losses in the long run.

To obtain consignments for the Liverpool branch, the Brown firm relied on its network of representatives in the major southern ports. In the correspondence with agents and cotton factors, two topics were perennially important: the terms under which the Browns would be willing to handle consignments during the current season and the manner in which the southern representatives would receive compensation for their services. In determining the exact terms under which cotton operations would be conducted in a given year, the partners considered a wide range of information on the probable supply of raw cotton in the market. The starting point in the analysis was the number of bales held over in Liverpool from the previous season. To that figure, they added estimates of the probable production in the southern states and in other parts of the world where cotton was under cultivation. As new information became available, the partners updated their estimates of the likely supply. During the summer months, they closely monitored weather conditions. Later, the number of bales arriving in southern ports at

Waynesburg College Library
Waynesburg, Pa. 15370

the very beginning of the fall shipping season was another good indicator of the volume of activity the partners could expect in the coming months.

Despite a fair degree of accuracy in estimating the sizes of cotton crops, predicting the probable course of prices proved a more difficult, if not impossible, task. The difficulty was that there were no reliable techniques for assessing the aggregate worldwide demand for cotton goods, or what was commonly called the consumption.[4] With only a limited number of forecasting tools and little else to base decisions upon beyond the estimates of crop sizes, the Browns and other businessmen focused most of their attention on the supply side of the market equation. The rule of thumb was that short crops meant high prices while a bountiful harvest signaled the coming of a weakened market.

But because of the volatility of demand, there were many years when the anticipated correlation between output and price failed to materialize. For instance, small crops during the early 1840s did not stimulate prices significantly; instead they coincided with a series of new lows for cotton prices in 1843 and 1845. In assessing the overall situation at the beginning of the 1843 season, William Bowen, the managing partner of the Philadelphia branch, commented on the likelihood of low production, but he then hastened to qualify the implications of such a forecast: "Experience has taught us a lesson not soon to be forgotten, that short crops do not always make long prices."[5]

Since production levels were unreliable indicators of seasonal price behavior, the Browns were forced to adopt alternative techniques for judging market trends. The one method on which the partners placed the greatest reliance was, from a conceptual standpoint, a very simple tool. The partners simply compared the absolute level of prices with what they considered to be the normal, or intrinsic value of raw cotton in the Liverpool market. Such a technique did not require detailed calculations; rather it relied on the partners' intuition that prices had moved beyond the bounds of their traditional pattern of fluctuation. The underlying assumption was that the market went through a series of ups and downs and that sooner or later prices would return to their "legitimate" level.

The Browns' assessment of the prevailing prices relative to the supposed norm was the basis for important decisions concerning the percentage of the total cost or market value that the partners would advance against consignments in a given year. Whenever the market was in a reasonably stable state, the Browns were generally willing to authorize advances of from 75 to 80 percent of the cost of the cotton in the immediate locale. In a period of rapidly rising prices, however, the partners frequently reduced their advance to two thirds of the local cost. As a rule, the Browns did not advance the full cost of a shipment unless the market had apparently bottomed out after a long decline or a substantial margin existed between prices in the United States and the latest quotes from the Liverpool market. At the same time, there were a few southern agents who regularly advanced the full cost of the cotton on consignments to the Browns' Liverpool branch. Under these special arrangements, the agent assumed responsibility for any advance made beyond the firm's normal 75 to 80 percent limit. In these cases, the risk of an over-advance fell on the shoulders of the agent, not on the Browns.

The price level also influenced the Browns' attitude toward purchasing cotton on their own account. During years when prices were not abnormally high, the partners often participated in joint account shipments with other firms. Usually their participations were restricted to one quarter or one third of the total cost. The Baltimore partners described the firm's policy in a note to a Fayetteville, North Carolina, correspondent in 1824: "We seldom ship Cotton solely on our own a/c as so many of our friends . . . prefer giving us Interests in their purchases . . . we have no objections to take 1/3 Interest in any purchases you may make."[6] On other occasions, the Browns instructed their agents to purchase a little cotton if a few bales were needed to give one of the firm's own ships a full freight. When prices were abnormally high however, as in 1825 and then again in the years preceding the panic of 1837, the partners suspended all activity on their own account.

As in the other spheres of their business activities, the Browns preferred to restrict the extent of their cotton transactions to those parties in whom they had a high degree of confidence. The partners automatically labeled as speculative and unreliable those shippers who expected large advances or pressed for reduced commissions. James Brown advised the New Orleans agent, Joseph Fowler, in 1825 to make sure he obtained all sets of the bills of lading from the consignor at the time he negotiated an advance. This precaution was necessary, James explained, because fraudulent shippers often used the second and third copies of the bill of lading to negotiate more than one advance on the same cargo. "Where you have the least doubt of the integrity of the parties . . . it would be best to decline the business," he told the New Orleans agent.[7]

Possession of the bill of lading was of crucial importance to every commission merchant and factor because the cotton itself served as security for the advance. In a key legal decision, which incidently involved the Browns, the U.S. Supreme Court in 1840 confirmed the right of a consignee, under certain circumstances, to dispose of the merchandise in order to protect his position even if the transaction ran counter to the specific instructions of the consignor. Speaking for the court, Justice Joseph Story made it clear that by virtue of the advance, the consignee had acquired a vested interest in the merchandise, and his possession of the bill of lading gave him what was in essence a lien on the property.[8]

The practical effect of this ruling was to legitimize the right of a commission merchant to ignore the minimum price limit stipulated by a planter if, under the circumstances, the cotton market was already weak and seemed headed for further deterioration. In that situation, the consignee was within his rights to sell the cotton and use the proceeds to meet the bill of exchange generated by the original advance. By selling the cotton, the consignee might prevent an overadvance from materializing, or at least hold the size of the overadvance to its current level. When one customer inquired about the firm handling a few consignments without the immediate receipt of the bill of lading, the Liverpool partners rejected the proposal out-of-hand: "It would deprive us here of absolute control over the property confided to us for sale by our friends, & it is essential to the proper discharge of the duty we owe them. We would prefer to leave the cotton business otherwise."[9]

Besides the size of advances and the handling of bills of lading, another topic frequently discussed in the three-cornered correspondence among the Browns' office in Liverpool, their branches in the northern states, and their agents in the south was the procedure for moving advances beyond the authorization stage and into the negotiation stage. This transformation was a crucial step in the financial process, since it involved the conversion of a mere commitment on the part of a distant consignee to honor a bill of exchange into what was a more tangible form of investment—namely, spot cash. In this respect, the Browns' complementary role as one of the major foreign exchange dealers in the Anglo-American economy provided them with a distinct competitive advantage. The sterling bills drawn on the Liverpool branch could usually be converted into cash with ease, and transactions invariably took place at favorable exchange rates.

In practice, advances could be negotiated either by drawing a sterling bill directly on the Liverpool house or, alternatively, by drawing a domestic draft, in dollars, on one of the firm's northern branches. In the latter case, the northern branch usually offset incoming drafts from the south with sales of sterling bills for similar amounts. As a rule, the Browns preferred this method of operation because the demand for foreign exchange centered in the northern ports. By instructing their agents and customers to draw primarily domestic drafts, which could be readily discounted at any commercial bank, the northern offices were able to maintain far greater control over their sterling account with the Liverpool office. According to the Browns' reports, sterling bills per se rarely were drawn in New Orleans prior to 1820.[10] In later years the volume of foreign bills of exchange drawn in New Orleans increased markedly, partly because of the expanded purchasing activities of foreign exchange dealers like the Second Bank of the United States. The Browns, however, continued to negotiate the majority of their southern advances through the intermediate medium of domestic bills of exchange.

An issue of vital importance in the correspondence with southern representatives was the agent's compensation for the solicitation of business or influencing consignments as this service was commonly called in the nineteenth century. A variety of agreements were in force over the years, and it is difficult to characterize them in any way, other than to indicate that they were all based on some commission formula. During some periods, separate arrangements were worked out with each representative. At other times the Browns created a uniform schedule of compensation, which stipulated the terms under which the Liverpool branch would accept consignments from any reputable cotton factor in a given port. This latter method of compensation was confined largely to New Orleans, where after 1830 the number of bales shipped overseas exceeded the exports of all the other southern ports combined.[11] Regardless of the exact details spelled out in the agreements, the agent's fee for soliciting consignments came out of the gross commission the Browns charged the customer for negotiating an advance and for managing the sale.

When John A. Brown left New Orleans in 1823, after spending three shipping seasons in the port, the following agreement remained in force: the Browns passed on to the factor procuring the consignment the 1 percent fee that they charged the planter for negotiating an advance.[12] The implementation of this plan signaled the beginning of their policy of extending equal privileges to all their correspondents in New Orleans who solicited consignments for the Liverpool branch. Simultaneously, the partners gave Benjamin Story, their most reliable representative, exclusive control over the firm's purchasing activities for its own account. Story also served as an intermediary between the Browns and the other cotton factors who regularly directed business to the Liverpool branch.

During the early 1830s, the partners made several changes in the compensation schedule for cooperating factors. To all reputable New Orleans firms obtaining consignments for the Liverpool office, the Browns proposed the following arrangement: the 1 percent charge for initially negotiating an advance was to be equally divided, with the factor receiving an immediate 0.5 percent commission while the partners kept the other half to cover the loss of interest, brokerage, and incidental costs; later, after the cotton was sold, the procuring agent was to receive a 1 percent participation in the commission charges of the Liverpool branch. For their part, the Browns agreed to assume all the risks associated with insuring the cotton and guaranteeing the buyer's credit. For his overall compensation of 1.5 percent, the factor was expected to assume the risk on any funds advanced beyond the partners' stated limits, which then ranged from 65 to 80 percent of cost. [13]

In Charleston and Savannah, on the other hand, the Browns generally conducted cotton operations almost exclusively through a single, officially designated representative, who also handled foreign exchange operations and performed the other financial services normally associated with the Brown organization. The compensation these agents received for procuring consignments often varied from one transaction to the next, depending on whether or not the agent elected to share with the Browns the risk and commission for guaranteeing the credit of Liverpool buyers.

The agreement with James Adger, the Charleston agent, called for the equal division of the net commission on most transactions. The net commission was determined as follows: from the 3 percent gross commission, the partners subtracted a 0.5 percent fee for brokerage, 0.75 percent for guaranteeing the buyer's credit, and 0.25 percent for bankers' fees — leaving a net commission of 1.5 percent. Adger could increase his earnings above the normal 0.75 percent, however, if he elected to participate in the guarantee risk. The partners permitted the Charleston agent to retain whatever fee he charged the customer for negotiating an advance as well.

In addition to handling consignments for American shippers, the Browns also served English textile manufacturers and other foreign buyers who wished to purchase cotton in the United States. Purchasers usually specified the quality and quantity of the cotton required and set an upward limit on prices. Since the overall cost of acquiring cotton, including transportation, was generally lower in the United States than in Liverpool, foreign buyers hoped to realize savings through these arrangements. When William Brown initiated this service in 1820, his American partners were not completely sold on the proposal. They warned that the execution of cotton orders for English buyers might "cause some jealousy with your American consignment friends and may be the cause of losing some business, which at present has the appearance of growing into great magnitude, & which we think would be more stable than the English orders."[14] Despite these reservations, the American partners consented to give the plan a fair trial in the 1820-21 season.

The results of the first year's operations were mixed. Fortunately, American shippers expressed little resentment over the firm's handling of English orders, but some overseas buyers were not wholly satisfied with the outcome of their transactions. A few textile manufacturers complained about the purchase of cotton in the South Atlantic ports rather than in New Orleans, where lower prices had reportedly been quoted. The Baltimore partners expressed regret about any losses overseas buyers might have suffered in a note to the Liverpool office in April 1821. "The uncommonly long passages vessels had coming this way all this winter unfortunately occasion'd the . . . purchases in Charleston & Savannah," they explained. "One thing is certain," the Baltimore management added, cotton prices were nonetheless "fully within the Limits of the orders on hand at the time of execution."[15]

Over the years, the Browns improved their facilities for serving the foreign buyer. In addition to handling regular purchase orders, they also opened letters of credit for English firms through the Liverpool office; these credits were then used in the south by the manufacturers' traveling agents. For this purely financial service, the Browns charged a fee of only 1 percent compared to the standard 3 or 3.25 percent commission for handling the merchandising portion of the transaction as well. In New Orleans, the partners lodged the credits with Benjamin Story, and they authorized him either to endorse the bills of exchange drawn by the manufacturers' buying agents or to purchase the bills outright. A few of the partners' remarks suggest that they implemented this program in order to match the competitive services of the Bank of Liverpool, which reportedly began lodging letters of credit with commercial banks in New Orleans during the 1834-35 season for a 1 percent fee.[16]

One of the main reasons for the firm's success in the cotton market over the years was the quality of its southern representatives. John A. Brown's recruitment of Benjamin Story in the early twenties gave the partners a strong representative in New Orleans at a time when that port was emerging as the most important in the south. The relationship with Story was based on a mutual confidence that was often reinforced by word and deed. For their part, the Browns went out of their way to make certain that business transactions were handled fairly and honestly. Take, for example, their offer to Story in the spring of 1838, a period when the volume of purchase orders and letters of credit to English manufacturers were both increasing. Writing for the family, George Brown told Story that the partners felt he should hold some of their securities as collateral against those drafts drawn in the course of complying with their instructions. The explanation George gave for this generous, and totally unsolicited, offer reveals much about the Browns' attitude toward their business associates. "Although we do not think you would hesitate to draw on us for such amounts as are required," he wrote, "yet we know it's absolutely necessary you should feel quite easy in that respect." Moreover, "we would not like to send you orders and confirm credits if there is not the most implicit confidence on your part," the Baltimore partner added.[17]

In the Browns' scheme of management, the retention of cooperative and competent agents like Benjamin Story received the highest priority. Indeed, the Browns maintained remarkably harmonious relations with most of their agents over lengthy periods of time. Close ties with reliable southern agents were essential for the effective implementation of the firm's strategies in the various cotton markets. It was through these representatives that the partners' directives on the terms under which business would be handled reached planters and cotton factors. The reports coming in from these agents on local market conditions influenced, in turn, the partners' decisions on seasonal tactics.

The same spirit of cooperation which characterized the firm's cotton operations was also exhibited in the organization's handling of overseas consignments of other goods in the Anglo-American economy. The Browns' basic strategy was to perform the financial and merchandising functions of middlemen in the most expeditious manner. In these activities, the partners generally eschewed speculation and condemned those who withheld goods from the market in anticipation of a rise in prices. For the most part, they resisted the demands of shippers for larger advances and reduced commissions. By the standards of the day, the Browns' merchandising policies were considered unusually conservative.

Summary and Conclusion

Beginning his career in Baltimore at the turn of the century with a modest capital, Alexander Brown soon expanded the scope of his mercantile interests beyond the linen trade. After his eldest son William opened a Liverpool office in 1810, Alexander Brown began authorizing advances against consignments of American produce. Although the firm continued to handle a wide variety of foodstuffs and raw materials, in the years following the War of 1812, the partners increasingly concentrated on the cotton market. By 1820 the firm's Liverpool branch was the second leading recipient of cotton shipments in the port, and it ranked high among the leaders in the Anglo-American cotton market throughout the next two decades. After adding a New York branch in the mid-twenties, the firm enlarged the volume of finished goods consignments to the American outlets. Thus, during the late twenties and early thirties, the Browns were heavily involved in merchandising activities on both sides of the Atlantic.

After reassessing their overall business strategies in 1834, the Browns decided to phase out the handling of finished goods consignments in the U.S. market. At the same time, they strengthened their southern organization by adding subsidiary offices in Mobile and New Orleans and continued the active solicitation of cotton consignments for the Liverpool branch. However, because of increasing competition and the press of other duties, the partners reduced their participation in the Anglo-American market during the early fifties.

When their involvement was at its height, the Browns offered American shippers and English buyers comprehensive merchandising and financial services. The cash advances associated with the solicitation of consignments provided a credit base for the international exchange of goods. In the United States the firm not only endorsed the bills of exchange drawn by American shippers, but, as a result of its complementary role as a leading foreign exchange dealer, it also purchased most of the sterling generated through its merchandising activities. The experience gained in financing consignments was invaluable in later decades when the Browns became more involved in the specialized letter of credit and foreign exchange markets — where credit factors were equally important.

Section 2

Letters of Credit

Commissions from the issuance of letters of credit were a major source of revenue when the Browns emerged as the leading international bankers serving the foreign trade sector of the Anglo-American economy. The Browns' credits were welcome in commercial centers throughout the world. Because the partners performed their tasks smoothly and efficiently, U.S. importers participated more effectively in the rewards of an expanded foreign trade.

In the course of their rise to preeminence in the letter of credit market, the Browns developed a distinctive system of account management which later became the standard against which other firms were measured. The policies and procedures the partners employed in managing letter of credit operations in the 1850s, when international banking functions were already fairly well-developed, are the main focus here. The previous half century had been a period of refinement in the use of letters of credit and of innovation in business management as well.

In earlier studies of Anglo-American merchant banking, there is an absence of quantitative data on relative market shares. In fact, information has been so sparse and diffuse that estimates of the actual percentage of American imports financed by letters of credit in the nineteenth century are not available. However, the Browns' financial records in the late 1850s are exceptionally complete, and taking into account the existing evidence on competitive firms, it is now possible to make some tentative, and partly impressionistic, estimates of relative market shares.

After 1840 the Browns were recognized as the leading Anglo-American house within the select fraternity of letter of credit issuers. But the vagueness of this statement and similar ones about the leading or dominant firm in the various financial markets has disturbed many scholars. Even when such judgments have been accepted as valid, questions lingered about the actual market position of the leading firm. The term "leading" might be valid over a broad range of market shares — from 75 to perhaps only 25 percent of the aggregate volume of business.

The Browns' financial statements include a detailed report on letter of credit activities in 1859, and a comparison of the firm's figures with total U.S. imports in the same year is revealing. The Browns' credits financed $25,500,000 of the $344,586,000 of goods imported in 1859, or about 8 percent of the total amount.[1] Since most customers were required to finance up to 25 percent of the cost of a shipment from their own resources, it is likely that merchants holding the Browns' credits imported up to 10 percent of the goods passing through the U.S. customs houses. Whether 8 or 10 percent, it was a substantial volume for a single firm. Yet in terms of aggregate imports, it was a moderate figure.

One major competitor, Baring Bros. & Co., financed approximately one half of the Browns' volume in the late fifties.[2] Most of the Barings' credits were issued to China traders in the port of Boston, where the Barings and the Browns shared the letter of credit business on a fairly equal basis. Together they financed about one half of all the merchandise passing through the Boston customs house. No other American port had so high a percentage of its imports financed through the letter of credit mechanism. The Boston statistics are consistent with our expectations, since letters of credit were most prevalent in bilateral trading patterns where there was a narrow base for barter. For many years there was little Chinese demand for American exports.

The volume of credits handled by George Peabody, another important competitor, is unknown. The panic of 1857 seriously affected his operations, and his business was depressed for several years thereafter. But there is indirect evidence in the Browns' correspondence indicating that, for two or three years prior to the panic, the partners believed Peabody's volume was approaching their own.[3] No data at all is available on the aggregate financing of marginal competitors, but they probably accounted for no more than 50 percent of the Browns' volume.[4]

When the Browns' totals are combined with the other estimates, the resulting figures indicate that letters of credit financed no more than 30 percent of all U.S. imports in the mid-fifties. The Browns' market share ranged from one third to perhaps one half later in the decade. Despite the increasing use of letters of credit by American merchants, approximately 70 percent of all antebellum imports continued to enter the country under the open account system or some variation of the traditional barter mechanism. Only in the trade with China and South America can it be said that the letter of credit predominated.

VIII

The Rise to Preeminence

The firm's initial letters of credit were an internal arrangement between father and son. Not long after William's Liverpool branch opened in 1810, he began accepting the drafts of English and Irish merchants against the authorized shipments of linens to his father's house in Baltimore.[1] Alexander Brown later instructed William to extend the same service to other wealthy Baltimore merchants on a commission basis. By the 1820s, the issuance of letters of credit was an expanding phase of the Browns' overall business activities. American importers found they could obtain liberal discounts when they purchased goods in overseas ports where the Brown name was known and respected. The Browns' credits were soon carried on voyages to South America as well as to England and the continent. But until the firm began actively soliciting business in the mid-twenties, there was no established routine for handling accounts.

The fragmentary evidence on the Browns and other banking firms suggests that most of the letters of credit issued in the first quarter of the century were handled on an ad hoc basis. During the fifteen year period after the end of the War of 1812, a large portion of the goods entering the United States was sold at auction for the account of English merchants and manufacturers, which lessened the importance of the American importer and curtailed the demand for credit facilities. It is noteworthy that the expanded issuance of letters of credit in the late twenties and early thirties coincided with the decline of the auction system and the rise of the more specialized merchant who concentrated on imports. The exact extent of the causal relationship is not known, but clearly these two developments in the foreign trade sector reinforced one another, since the availability of broader credit facilities enabled American importers to purchase goods in a wider range of markets and on more favorable terms. By selling goods directly to American buyers, English manufacturers could avoid the auction process.

The Barings were apparently the first large scale issuers of letters of credit in the American market. Both Thomas Ward in Boston and the Second Bank of the United States from its headquarters in Philadelphia had authority to grant credits on the Barings' London office.[2] Many credits were issued to merchants trading in China, where the sterling bill of exchange began to replace silver as the primary means of payment in the late twenties. By 1834, however, the Baring partners had lost confidence in the ability of the American economy to sustain a high level of prosperity, and they instructed their representatives to reduce sharply the opening of new credits.

During the next two years of the inflationary boom, half a dozen aspiring houses supplanted the Barings in the American market, and they issued a tremendous volume of credits on exceedingly liberal terms. Among the challengers for a healthy share of the business were the Browns. Although equally guilty of overexpansion, the firm did not match its competitors in their almost total disregard for safety in the terms of issuance.

The audacity of issuers climaxed during the summer of 1836. In early August George Brown cited the aggressiveness of competitors in Baltimore. He singled out a representative of George Wildes & Co. as an agent offering liberal credits to importers "for whom under no circumstances would we do anything without sufficient collateral."[3] By November, there were signs that a crisis might be imminent. George believed the firm had been prudent in not extending credits in the same manner as houses like Wildes & Co., Wiggen & Co., and Morrison, Cryder & Co. At the same time, he felt the firm had followed the proper course in emphasizing the letter of credit phase of the business — and especially as an alternative to seemingly more lucrative opportunities for profit in security speculation. "We view the regular & legitimate business as much more desirable to cultivate than the stock operations," George remarked in November 1836, "when money becomes plenty the latter will cease but the other will be permanent."[4]

When the panic came in 1837, primarily because of the restrictive discount policy of the Bank of England and the fall in cotton prices, the major letter of credit issuers found themselves in serious difficulties. Many of their American customers were unable to sell inventories at prices high enough to cover all the drafts previously drawn in purchasing merchandise overseas. Sterling remittances from importers to English bankers dwindled rapidly. After one or two months, the strain of living up to their guarantees of their customers' debts became critical. As a consequence, many bankers exhausted their capital attempting to meet their financial obligations. Yet, like an unabated run on a community's commercial banks, the process could only go on so long without relief.

In the end only a few of the leading Anglo-American merchant-banking houses were able to avoid the wholesale dishonor of outstanding acceptances and the repudiation thereby of their guarantees of customers' debts. Even those firms managing to survive the crisis found their financial resources severely depleted. The Browns, almost miraculously, were rescued from a similar fate by timely aid from the Bank of England.[5] Buttressed by the bank's support, the firm faithfully liquidated its outstanding acceptances. The year's losses were finally put at $300,000, or less than 5 percent of capital.

With the panic and its aftermath behind them, the Browns found themselves in an enviable position in the letter of credit market. Many competitors were eliminated in the crisis, while the depressed state of the American economy in the early forties discouraged others. The Barings, meanwhile, did not attempt to recapture the lion's share of the market which they had claimed prior to 1834. Instead, the Barings became increasingly involved in the flotation of American securities and other investment banking transactions. Thus, the Browns were confronted with slight competition in every American port except Boston, where the Barings remained active. There Thomas Ward and his son Samuel, who also served as resident managers of all the Barings' various American business operations, continued to hold a fair share of the prime accounts for the parent organization.

In the management of letter of credit accounts, the Browns and Barings employed somewhat different strategies. The Barings uncompromisingly demanded all the credit business of a given importer, never allowing him to maintain an ancillary account with any other merchant banker. The partners adopted a policy against "double accounts" so that they could stay informed, at all times, about the overall extent of a customer's overseas committments. In addition, the Barings granted credits almost exclusively to established, wealthy merchants with whom they felt safe in conducting business on a completely unsecured basis.

The Browns, on the other hand, believed the danger of loss was lessened by spreading the risk over a wide range of accounts. At the same time, the partners generally insisted on some form of collateral as partial security for every credit granted. George Brown described their policy succinctly in 1837: "We do not care how many credits a firm has with other houses so long as we have proper security for our own."[6] If one customer failed, the Browns were doubly protected; in the first instance they generally held sufficient collateral to offset part of the debt, and beyond that they usually shared any uncovered losses with other creditors. The partners felt their policy of spreading risks gave them a definite competitive advantage. "One reason why we need not fear Barings as competitors is that they require to have the whole of a house's account," the New York partners explained in February 1858.[7]

Since they conducted business on a secured basis, the Browns were more inclined to grant credits to less experienced importers who initially had only a moderate capital. By welcoming instead of shunning the small account, the Browns eventually built up a large clientele of appreciative customers. On this issue the Barings were fully cognizant of the potential long-run weakness of their more restrictive policies. Just one year after the opening of the Browns' Boston branch in 1844, a worried Thomas Ward addressed the problem straightforwardly in correspondence with his superiors in England: "If we deal only with persons of wealth, and some one else takes all the rising generation, where shall we be 10 years hence when Browns have got all the now small but then great merchants?"[8] A satisfactory answer was not forthcoming.

The Browns' performance in Boston ran true to Thomas Ward's prediction. Thomas Curtis, the Browns' branch manager, revealed as much in an 1852 review of business operations during his first eight years in the port. When he arrived in Boston, Curtis stated, the Barings had all the substantial importers as customers. But he had been willing to open small credits for men of "ability and integrity," and most of his business was now with younger merchants who had risen in the last fifteen years.[9]

The contrasting strategies the Browns and Barings employed in letter of credit operations were not the result of contrasting attitudes toward risk taking, since both firms were equally conservative; rather they were the result of differing organizational structures and varying degrees of specialization. The partners in Baring Brothers were involved in so many financial, and even political, activities that few of them were prepared to expend the time and energy required to administer a business encompassing a large volume of credits to customers whose standing demanded constant scrutiny. Nor did the Barings have representatives in the major American ports who could be relied upon to make thorough investigations of marginal accounts. The Barings did not adjust their administrative structure to meet the challenge of the Browns. They continued to function through the traditional agent system rather than through the more responsive subordinates the Browns employed in their branch offices.

Only the Browns had the manpower to handle a large number of accounts efficiently. Moreover, the Barings valued the services of the Ward family so highly that they retained Boston as their American headquarters, whereas the Browns had recognized the necessity of transferring their headquarters from Baltimore to New York in the 1830s. And finally, despite the occasional heat of the internal controversy between the New York and Liverpool partners over the proper scope of operations, no other large merchant-banking house in the Anglo-American economy specialized so narrowly on the foreign trade sector as the House of Brown.

George Peabody, by comparison, conducted his letter of credit business in a totally different manner. Entering the credit field in the early 1850s, Peabody's business increased rapidly, and by the middle of the decade his firm had replaced the Barings as the Browns' principal rival. In regard to policy formulation and systemization, his stance was passive. His agreements with independent agents in various port cities left the management of credit operations largely in the hands of his American associates.[10] They were, therefore, at liberty to alter the terms of issuance in order to make their credits competitive in local markets. Peabody's duties were restricted almost entirely to accepting and paying the bills of exchange customers of his authorized representatives drew on his London office. For the use of his name and the provision of accounting services, Peabody charged his agents a flat commission on every transaction. Meanwhile, he could not be bothered with how each American correspondent chose to manage its credit business.

Peabody's lack of control over his chain of representatives dismayed the Browns and the Barings because it meant that collusive agreements were more difficult to enforce. Neither of them believed much was gained from price competition among the larger issuers. However, Peabody and some of his American associates thought differently. William Brown discussed the matter with Peabody late in 1852, but with little result. Peabody explained that his only interest was in the fee he received from his American agents; the fee they, in turn, decided to charge their own customers was not his concern. Nor was he very concerned about the precautions his agents took in issuing letters of credit on his firm.[11]

A few years later, in the 1857 financial crisis, George Peabody was faced with some of the serious consequences of his cavalier attitude toward the activities of his American agents. On that occasion, only firm support from the Bank of England saved him from bankruptcy. Yet given the lack of any organizational structure through which he could have enforced his will, it is not surprising that Peabody chose to interfere so little in the affairs of the independent firms in his banking chain.

To appreciate the advances the Browns had made in organizational and administrative techniques, it is only necessary to examine momentarily the management structure of George Peabody & Co. and its chain of allied firms. Compared to the Browns', Peabody's organization was merely a shell. Beginning around 1850 it mushroomed dramatically, but the organization cracked under the strain of the first serious economic downturn it faced. The Peabody chain functioned with nothing even approaching a uniform system of operation, and its central administration was, for all practical purposes, nonexistent.

During the 1830s the Browns began developing in earnest what became a distinctive set of rules for handling letter of credit operations. The stimulus was, not surprisingly, the panic of 1837. That experience demonstrated the need for policies and procedures which might significantly reduce the risk of losses on future business. Equally important, the Browns resolved to maintain the established rules without variation throughout the ups and downs of subsequent trade cycles. The partners advocated greater uniformity in the range and quality of services available to importers at their various branch offices. The firm's basic rules were not to be waived for any customer, regardless of his credit standing. Preferential treatment on minor matters was recognized as unavoidable in their relationship with important customers, but the goal was to eliminate as much as possible all such distinctions.

In view of the Browns' generally restrictive policy on the holding of collateral, it is rather remarkable that the firm captured such a large share of the market so rapidly in the 1840s. In the letter of credit phase of the business, the partners were far more concerned about conducting a safe business than an expansive one. Indeed the firm's rise to preeminence in this field of economic endeavor hardly fits the model of the daring entrepreneur. The Browns' great strength was the stability of their organization; customers came to depend on them for financial services and counted on them to provide those services year-in and year-out. In the meantime, adherence to their restrictive policy not only protected them from losses but, in the long run, aided in the expansion of their volume and the retention of old accounts.

Foreign sellers highly valued the reliability of the Browns' guarantees. The New York partners cited with pride numerous reports that foreign merchants welcomed their credits despite the considerable red tape associated with their use; "We believe our bills and credits under them have a preference because it is known we guard them with security." they told the Boston branch manager.[12] It was not unusual for "commission houses on the other side to object to our restrictive credits," the New York house confided to the Baltimore branch. "Every few years we hear the same objections. Nevertheless we get a very good share of the business and are not willing to deviate from our regular rule without security placed in our hand."[13] In short, the safety of their letters of credit more than offset the occasional inconveniences associated with their use.

The firm's rise to a position of preeminence in the letter of credit market occurred in the last twenty years of the antebellum era. After establishing a branch office in Boston in 1844 and soliciting the accounts of the younger merchants, the Browns, within a decade, had achieved parity with Baring Bros. & Co., in the former market leaders' primary stronghold. In the fifties, George Peabody and his American allies temporarily supplanted the Barings as the Browns' most active competitors. But the Peabody chain suffered from serious organizational deficiencies, which became embarrassingly apparent during the panic of 1857. The collapse of the Peabody chain and the disinclination of the Barings to commit themselves too heavily to the American trade sector left the House of Brown as the undisputed leader in the letter of credit field on the eve of the Civil War.

IX

Managing Credit Operations

A superior organizational structure provided the framework for efficiently managing letter of credit operations. Among the select number of firms composing the Anglo-American merchant-banking fraternity, the Brown organization was the only one in which the issuing parties in the United States and those responsible for guaranteeing final payments in England were all partners in the same business entity. The Browns' transatlantic pattern of ownership made any distinction between the British wholesaler of credits and the American retailer totally meaningless. Furthermore, the existence of a system of subsidiary branches in those port cities where the demand for letters of credit was strongest permitted the senior partners to implement policies quickly and uniformly. This overall unity of purpose was especially important during the period from 1835 to 1850, when the partners formulated many of their innovative strategies.

An uneasiness about the possible consequences of another major economic crisis tempered somewhat the partners' elation over controlling so much of the letter of credit business after 1840. The fear of a reenactment of the 1837 disaster haunted the more cautious members of this conservative firm for many decades thereafter. While the firm had significantly altered its procedures in the meantime, still in earning the largest share of the commissions, the Browns were likewise assuming the preponderance of the potential risks. Until the firm had actually passed through another financial panic, no one could be sure that the new protective measures would prove effective. Thus, despite their inclination to finance all sound proposals, there were times when the partners felt economic conditions dictated a curtailment in outstanding credits.

The routine accumulation of information on the character and extent of the firm's financial obligations aided the partners in their deliberations over expanding or contracting their volume of credits. Over the years the partners introduced a series of internal reports to guide them in the management of credit operations. The regular exchange of detailed information did not begin in earnest until the mid-thirties. Joseph Shipley confirmed that date in correspondence with the New York partners in the late 1840s. From 1826, when he joined the firm, until 1835, the Liverpool branch had not bothered to report regularly on conditions in the English money market. "We never gave the state of our finances a moment's concern," Shipley confessed.[1] The business expansion after 1834 and the subsequent panic had changed that policy, however.

An early effort to accelerate the flow of information within the firm was the implementation in 1836 of a plan to render the bookkeeper's statements of customer accounts more frequently than once a year. Since the accounts of U.S. importers were maintained on the books of the Liverpool office, the American branches found it difficult to keep up to date on the status of all their customers' accounts. George Brown enthusiastically supported the proposal to render statements semiannually; he felt the new procedure would bring importers "more under our immediate notice" and would enable the American partners "to see at once who are backward in remitting."[2]

The difficulties in keeping tabs on importers' accounts continued to plague the firm even after the record keeping system had been greatly improved. By the 1850s, the branches maintained tickler files on the monetary transfers made for each customer to the Liverpool office. The Browns expected importers to arrange all remittances through the American branches—but the rule was impossible to enforce. In 1857 the New York partners cited the problem of "keeping up to date . . . when parties remit to Brown, Shipley & Co. direct instead of through one of our offices."[3] Accounts believed to be deficient often proved current after it was learned that customers had disregarded the normal channel for making remittances.

The partners introduced new reporting procedures following the 1857 financial crisis as well. Although the Browns weathered the panic with relative ease, some partners believed there was still room for further improvement in the techniques of managerial control. In the summer of 1858 the branches in Philadelphia, Boston, and Baltimore received instructions to begin the preparation of monthly summaries of their outstanding credits. The New York partners told Thomas Curtis, the Boston manager, to compile a complete list of all the letters of credit he had issued over the last three or four years so they could "tell at a glance the comparative amt. of various credits issued."⁴ Most of the 1857 losses had occurred on Boston accounts associated with the East India trade. In order to compete with the Barings, the firm had relaxed its policies against issuing unsecured credits. The New York partners blamed their poor record in the New England port mainly on lack of experience: "The East Indian credit business was new to us & we suffered there, but we attribute to the influence of 1837 our comparative exemption from loss in the bill business & English credits."⁵

During periodic assessments of the extent of their overall commitments, the partners considered external information on general economic conditions as well. While the state of the Anglo-American economy was the main concern, political or economic disruptions in any part of the world where American merchants regularly traded were also considered. Because of its pivotal position near London, the Liverpool branch assumed most of the responsibility for keeping the American partners informed about important international developments. The Liverpool managers closely watched changes in the Bank of England's prime discount rate because of the effect on their borrowing costs and because sharp increases in the Bank Rate frequently signaled the emergence of a period of financial stringency. The Bank Rate influenced the rate of interest the Browns assessed American importers on debt balances in Liverpool and the prices at which the firm sold sterling bills of exchange in the United States.

The Browns also accumulated published statistics on the American balance of trade. They followed with great interest reports of specie flows among nations and especially news of gold movements involving the Bank of England or the Bank of France. Because of the firm's position as the leading foreign exchange dealer in the U.S. market, the Browns generally had a good "feel" for any sudden shift in the Anglo-American balance of payments. For instance, the partners often discussed the likely affect of large international capital movements on sterling rates. They viewed depressed sterling rates as a probable stimulus to overseas purchasing on the part of U.S. importers and, therefore, the prelude to an increased demand for the firm's letters of credit.

The problem with such indicators, however, was that they were often contradictory. In July 1859, for example, the Liverpool management suggested that the New York partners take note of the views of one Englishman whose analysis of current developments led to a prediction that "the balance of trade against the U.S. will become so large as to bring about a convulsion more serious than in 1857."⁶ Yet only two weeks later, Collet and Hamilton emphasized information in a fresh report which indicated a general stagnation of business lay ahead. The predicted stagnation was attributed to the overall "absence of speculation" in the Anglo-American trade. This second report was apparently more reassuring to the Liverpool partners. So far as Collet and Hamilton were concerned "the Trade of the Country is healthiest & most prosperous when there is 'stagnation' in this sense."[7]

Despite the difficulty of distinguishing fact from rumor, the Liverpool partners were in the most favorable location to advise their colleagues on the appropriate volume of outstanding letters of credit relative to general economic conditions. The business originating in the various American branches eventually converged on the Liverpool office, giving the partners there the best picture of the firm's overall activities. In addition, only the Liverpool partners had current information about the firm's position in the English short-term money market. Their warnings about overexpansion, therefore, were not taken lightly in New York even though Collet and Hamilton had earned a well-deserved reputation for being overly cautious.

The fall of 1851 was one period in which the Liverpool partners became concerned about the large volume of acceptances then being generated through letter of credit operations. A general review of the firm's recent progress revealed that outstanding credits in September had more than doubled over the corresponding month in 1848, rising from £679,000 to £1,500,000. "We fear credit is too easy & before long there will be trouble," the Liverpool partners warned.[8] Similar alerts of possible economic dislocations streamed forth from Liverpool following the spread of rumors about wars involving any of Europe's great powers. Important financial developments on the continent were reported as well; in 1855 the partners labeled the organization of the Crédit Mobilier in France a "most dangerous experiment" that was "likely to encourage undue speculation."[9]

Perhaps of greater importance than the actual contents of the firm's internal reports was the broad commitment to cooperate fully in the exchange of information and opinion. The partners placed a high premium on forthrightness in intrafirm communications. Subordinates who failed to keep the senior partners well informed about developments affecting the financial standing of customers were open to sharp criticism for their inadequacies. As a rule, the partners exhibited fairly thick skins in the give-and-take of delicate decision making, yet the slightest implication of negligence or worse the willful concealment of pertinent information invariably caused great offense and often led to bitterness and retribution. That an implied "lack of trust" or "want of confidence" was considered such a serious violation of the spirit of the firm indicates how devoted the partners were to the practice of keeping their associates well informed on routine matters as well as on more vital administrative affairs.

Some partners felt strongly that, by virtue of its prominent position in the letter of credit field, the firm had a responsibility to the American commercial community to discourage excessive purchasing abroad. Joseph Shipley, for one, believed the leading houses were obligated to set an example for others to follow. In an earlier period the Second Bank of the United States under the administration of Nicholas Biddle had tried to play the role of guardian over the U.S. economy, and after the Second Bank's closing the Browns occasionally wondered whether they had, at least in part, inherited those duties. Such discussions were based on the assumption that the firm's behavior might have a significant influence on the economy and were, therefore, as much ego enhancing as altruistic. Nonetheless, there was genuine dismay over the general structure of the American financial system in comparison with its British counterpart. James Brown expressed those sentiments during the 1857 crisis: "What a comfort to business to have such a regulator as the Bank of England and managed with such judgment, what a contrast to our Bank managers here. The power for mischief is too tremendous to be placed in such incompetent hands."[10]

Regardless of their good intentions, there is no evidence that any of the Browns' decisions ever exerted the slightest countercyclical effect on American trade cycles. And despite all their efforts at controlling the aggregate of outstanding credits, there was, in the short run, very little that could be done to halt their customers' purchasing activities. The plain truth was, as Collet and Hamilton readily admitted, that "with the credit business past experience has shown . . . it takes nearly twelve months to contract it materially."[11] Once a credit had been granted in the United States, it usually did not expire for six to eight months. The drafts drawn under the credit did not, in turn, come due for another three to four months.

In order to bring about a significant change in its overall position, an international banking house had to anticipate an economic downturn far in advance of its actual occurrence, since last minute measures invariably came too late to have any appreciable effect. By the time of Overend, Gurney & Co.'s failure in 1866, the Liverpool partners were reconciled to the situation: "Experience has shewn that it is hopeless to attempt to limit our own engagements under Credits within any period in which the reduction would be of service."[12] About all the firm could realistically do in a period of apparent overtrading, Hamilton and Collet finally concluded, was to advise the American branch managers "to implant caution in the minds of their customers."[13] One proposal to set an absolute limit on the aggregate credits outstanding at any given time had been rejected twenty years earlier, because as Joseph Shipley put it, "The amount ought & must greatly vary with times & circumstances."[14]

For the Browns the surest protection was in the character rather than in the extent of their outstanding credits. With sufficient safeguards in the credit granting process, the partners believed the firm would have a fair chance of maintaining its strength notwithstanding the variations in the business cycle. The events of 1857, when their system of managing letter of credit operations was severely tested, demonstrated that their faith had not been misplaced. The firm's ability to meet every financial commitment from its own capital resources and to come through the crisis with relatively few losses were together an overwhelming victory for those partners who had painstakingly formulated the terms of issuance and carefully nurtured the branch organization handling the business on a day-to-day basis.

"It is surprising how well our customers are able to pay us," the New York partners remarked in October 1857.[15] "At no time did the house stand higher than at present," was Hamilton's overall assessment of the situation.[16] He mentioned the suspension of the Bank of England's charter, the failure of Dennistouns, and the embarrassment of Peabody as examples of the adversities of others. Except for losses in the East Indian trade, the Browns' setbacks had been minimal. By 1863, in fact, collections on past due accounts had reduced the 1857 losses to $169,000.[17]

What the Browns proved in 1857 was the following: with vigorous administration, fairly strict adherence to predetermined rules, and careful management, an international banking house could continue to grant a large volume of credits year-in and year-out without fearing the consequences of fluctuations in business activity. Success, therefore, did not necessarily rest solely on a firm's ability to read with great accuracy the signs of an imminent contraction. The Browns demonstrated that an international banking house was not completely at the mercy of the whims of the trade cycle. On the contrary, even a firm with widely dispersed branches could do much to determine its fate after adopting a rational, well-conceived internal structure. The seemingly uncontrollable outside forces which played such a key role in the life of the old-line merchant banker, commonly designated as "luck," were no longer such an unpredictable foe. The era when enterprises associated with the commercial world were totally dependent on "fresh news" as the chief ingredient for long-run health was brought nearer to its end as the new techniques of administration eventually spread from the Browns to other financial and mercantile organizations.[18] In later years, other organizations, in various fields of economic endeavor, would similarly reap the benefits accruing from the adoption of more sophisticated managerial techniques. In the financial world much of the pioneering was done by the House of Brown.

The Details of Administration

One of the first requirements for success in the letter of credit market was the establishment of an effective system for collecting and appraising credit information about current and potential customers. The reliability of a customer was as important a safeguard in this business as the precautions in the terms of the letter of credit agreements themselves. Even on small accounts, the Browns normally restricted their credits to merchants who were men of integrity. The hint of a speculative bent in a potential customer was a signal for exercising great caution. A merchant could earn no higher compliment than to be deemed "safe" or "out of the power of chance" by the Browns; it was comparable to a triple A bond rating in the twentieth century.[19]

Since letters of credit were issued primarily in the four northern cities, the branches in Baltimore, Philadelphia, Boston, and New York gathered most of the credit information on American importers. An application for a letter of credit from a new customer at one of the three subsidiary offices was invariably forwarded to the New York partners for final approval. To aid his superiors in the assessment procedure, the branch manager had instructions to provide the New York office with all pertinent information on the new applicant. Unusual requests from regular customers were handled in the same manner.

In compiling semiannual summaries on the standing of local customers, the partnership employed a rating system that ranked firms on the basis of a numerical scale ranging from one to four, with an "A #1" position reserved for prime accounts. For further clarification, a short, marginal note appeared beside most of the names. The Browns were already using such a format in the 1820s; the earliest surviving list is dated May 1821.[20] Later reports included lengthier remarks on the rated firms. The additional information was primarily for the benefit of the Liverpool branch, since it was occasionally called upon to extend financing to an American importer beyond the period normally allowed for reimbursement.

George Brown drew up a semiannual summary in 1837 that was extremely thorough. The report listed sixty-one Baltimore merchants.[21] William Wilson & Sons, a good customer for over twenty years, George singled out as the only firm receiving unsecured letters of credit, and it headed the list of importers. Besides William Wilson & Sons, five other houses received an "A#1" rating, among them Peabody, Riggs & Co. George told the Liverpool office that it might safely accept drafts against any of the favored six even in the absence of a regular letter of credit authorization. Fourteen firms received a flat 1 rating, and George indicated that he had not required them to submit collateral in advance "when the sum was not larger than we thought them entitled to." Firms assigned a 2 rating numbered thirty-four. On these accounts, he expected a collateral deposit at the time the credit was opened. Five houses with a 3 rating he judged as "good for shipping charges," meaning freights, but little else. George gave two former customers a 4 rating; "It would be well to have nothing to do with them," he commented. In summary he stated: "We do not expect any of the foregoing houses will expect you to accept for them without a confirmed credit from us [prior arrangements] unless it should arise from some unexpected circumstances & we give you this scale that you may know how to act in case it should occur."[22]

Over twenty years later, the Baltimore branch still used the same numerical scale, but it was tied more closely to specific dollar amounts. William Graham, the branch manager, cited his cutoff points in correspondence with the Philadelphia office during the spring of 1859:

We class A 1 here at	any amount
1 here at	$20,000-40,000
2 here at	5,000-10,000
3 here at	1,000-2,000

For intermediate amounts, the Browns used fractions. A firm rated 1 1/2 would presumably be good for around $15,000, 2 1/2 for $3,500, and so on.[23]

The Browns took advantage of their association with various commercial banks to obtain information on importers. The partners were on the boards of directors of many banks. Branch managers were usually considered men of standing in the local community, and they too served on the boards of financial institutions. However, the Browns rarely used the services of mercantile agencies in the accumulation of credit information. "We give little information and take less," the New York partners stated in 1858. They understood a "good standing" could be bought, since mercantile agencies pursued the business for profit and were not always careful about their sources. "We prefer opinions of merchants who deal with the classes we want to know about," the New York partners explained.[24]

The range of goods imported under the Browns' credits was broad. The partners could usually arrange terms for the importation of any item that a merchant expressed an interest in purchasing. Even perishable items such as Mediterranean fruits were sometimes financed. However, the partners did discriminate against certain classes of dry goods merchants. "As a rule, carpet men who sell in the city are safe, but dry goods jobbers whose customers are in the country we avoid," the New York partners remarked in 1858.[25] "Importing goods for cash or nearly so & selling on time always appeared to us incompatible."[26] Hardware dealers, on the other hand, the partners felt were safer: "Their goods are more stable & they sell on shorter terms."[27]

The pattern of trade in a port determined the character of credits a given branch issued. Boston was best known for is association with the China trade. Philadelphia and Baltimore had close ties with South American sugar and coffee merchants. New York, of course, attracted the largest and most varied trade, but importers especially concentrated on British and European dry goods.

During the first six decades of business operations, virtually all the firm's letters of credit were sterling obligations payable in England. Credits issued in other currencies were rare. However, a few antebellum importers of Cuban sugar found dollar credits on the firm's New York or Baltimore branches almost as negotiable as sterling credits. The partners first issued credits payable in French francs in 1879, with their use restricted to the Caribbean islands, Guadeloupe and Martinique. Authorization for their issuance came soon after the partners made arrangements with a Paris firm, Comptoir d'Escompte, to begin full scale foreign exchange operations in francs. Following the pattern of evolution in sterling, the regular issuance of letters of credit in French francs followed the emergence of a wider market for bills of exchange payable in francs and drawn on Paris.[28]

Because of the Browns' many outlets, local importers were not restricted to shipments bound only for the home port. A Philadelphia merchant, for example, might obtain a credit to finance a cargo from Rio de Janeiro to New York or to any one of the other port cities where the Browns retained representatives. Northern coffee merchants often shipped produce to New Orleans under the Browns' letters of credit. Shipments to California, on the other hand, were not encouraged. When one of the firm's Baltimore customers wanted to send coffee to the West Coast in 1855, the New York partners rejected his application on the grounds that the house had no agent in San Francisco.[29] Six months later, however, another customer offered the firm solid collateral for a credit to finance a shipment of sugar from the Philippines to San Francisco. "We do not fancy it much," the New York house remarked, "but with undoubted security we suppose we should give it."[30]

The volume of credits issued in *England* to *British* importers of cotton and grain for use in the United States was relatively small. The Liverpool partners and the firm's London banker, J. P. Kennard, discussed the possibility of expanding such credits in 1851. "Your suggestion as to granting Letters of Credit on the United States is not new to us," Mark Collet wrote Kennard, "we have recently had it under consideration."[31] The firm had already issued a few credits to British importers, he continued, and it appeared as if the business was "capable of considerable extension." But there was one major stumbling block: most English bankers paid their customers interest on the funds left as an initial deposit. Several bankers allowed 2 percent on funds deposited against credits, and it seemed to Collet that the practice would "take away any profit." In order to compete, he realized the firm would "have to meet the terms of others," and those terms were not very inviting.[32]

The fees the Browns charged for the issuance of letters of credit (and for their other financial services) were generally higher than, or at least equal to, those of other houses. Because they were known as a "first-class" house, the partners invariably felt entitled to the best rates. Although there was no precise method for determining the "standing" of any given firm in the Anglo-American economy, two prerequisites for a superior rating were a long tradition of responsibility meeting one's obligations and a large "means," or amount of capital. The Browns, of course, rated high on both accounts.

Equally important was the Browns' reputation for abstaining from speculation. The firm's standing was further reinforced when the house stood up through a series of economic crises. In an era when financial panics were commonplace and merchants realized that every few years another was likely to wrack the economy again, many importers thought it a wise investment to pay a little extra to deal with a solid, experienced house. Moreover, many firms felt they gained stature in the international business world because their financing was arranged through the House of Brown.

The Browns were well aware of the influence their name carried in the commercial world. In 1866 they discussed at length whether or not to reopen letters of credit for a former customer "whose failure was so little credible" during the war.[33] The London partners were hesitant because they feared the move might be misinterpreted in the commercial community as implicitly condoning the importer's disreputable behavior. The resumption of their association with the party, so soon after the bankruptcy, would undoubtedly give him "an advantage of character implied by our moral support," the English partners stated, "and thereby lessen the fear of consequences from such conduct on the part of others." Despite their reservations the New York partners finally opened a new credit, but only after an outside guarantor of the importer's debts had been obtained.

Over the century the trend was toward lower fees, but the movement was not linear. Rates were frequently raised to their former level during a period of economic uncertainty, and they generally remained high until an improved commercial climate led to a new round of price competition. During the period reviewed here, the Browns and other issuers employed three distinct rate structures.

In the 1820s the fee structure was relatively simple. For accepting and paying bills drawn under their letters of credit, the Browns' commission was 1 percent of the amount drawn, provided a customer made arrangements to reimburse the Liverpool branch prior to his bills' final due dates. If the customer made a late remittance, on the other hand, the fee was 2 1/2 percent plus interest.[34]

In the 1840s commission rates varied according to the geographical location of distant ports; each port had a "customary" rate. By this date, the Browns based their commissions on the expectation of prompt customer reimbursement, since they no longer tolerated late remittances. Under the schedule in force at the mid-century, China and East Indian credits earned commissions of 2 to 2 1/2 percent, South American credits earned 1 to 2 percent, and European and English credits carried fees of 1 to 1 1/2 percent.[35] The more remote areas carried the highest rates because the letters of credit and the bills drawn under them were usually outstanding longer than those credits negotiable in ports closer to the east coast of the United States and the British Isles. The longer a credit was outstanding, the greater the risk normally associated with it.

The following table summarizes the fee schedules on the most important trade routes. By 1880 the rate schedule had shifted from geographical to time determinants. The new system was more flexible because it allowed importers trading in distant ports to save on commissions. By agreeing to settle debts with great dispatch, a customer could move into the brackets where lower fees prevailed. The change, however, was not a significant one. The new time op-

Table 2. Commission rates on letters of credit (in percent)[a]

Year	European and English	Caribbean and E. Coast of S.A.	West Coast of South America	China and East India
1840	1–1.5	1–1.5	—	2.5
1850	1–1.5	1–1.5	1.5–2	2–2.5
1860	1	1	1–1.5	1.5–2.5
1870	1	1	1	1.5–2
	60 days sight	90 days sight or 3 months date	4 months	6 months
1880	0.5	0.75	1	1.5

[a]Fees charged by Browns & other prime issuers. Other prime issuers would at various times include Baring Brothers & Co., George Peabody & Co., Dennistoun & Co., J. S. Morgan & Co., N. M. Rothschild & Sons, Morrison, Cryder & Co., and a few of the larger commercial banks in London and Liverpool.

tions corresponded closely with the standard number of months that were normally required to complete transactions in each quarter of the globe.

The initiative for the last across-the-board reduction in rates came in the spring of 1879 from Drexel, Morgan & Co., a major competitor in the postwar period. When George Peabody retired from active business in 1863 the Morgan-Drexel alliance assumed many of his former accounts, and they can be considered as, more or less, the successor organization.[36] Yet, for several years immediately after the Civil War, there was ill will between the two families who had been closely allied with Peabody's firm. The Drexels actually transferred their London account from the Morgans to the Browns from 1865 to 1868. The senior Morgan apparently made what the Browns considered some highly slanderous accusations upon learning of the Drexels' defection to the competition in 1865, intimating that the Browns had stooped so low as to *solicit* the account.[37] Among international bankers in the nineteenth century, such statements were serious affronts and not dismissed lightly or soon forgotten.[38] The Browns, of course, denied the charge and expressed resentment at being so blatantly maligned. Aside from its humor, the episode is important because it demonstrates the extent of the Morgan family's involvement in the American trade sector. J. P. Morgan, like George Peabody, eventually became best known for his investment banking activities, but both men received much of their early training and experience in the more mundane world of commerce.

There were always a few firms in the field issuing letters of credit at lower rates. Houses of moderate capital — such as Rathbone Bros. & Co.; Pickersgill & Co.; Fletcher, Alexander & Co.; Huth & Co.; McCalmont & Co.; Fruhling & Goschen; Stuart & Co.; and Drake, Kleinwort & Cohen — frequently set their fee schedules at one half a percent below the corresponding rates of the prime issuers. Marginal competitors were generally more amenable to customer proposals for rebates and other discounts. The Browns suspected that many of their customers who returned from long voyages with unused credits on Brown, Shipley & Co., had actually negotiated bills of exchange under letters of credit granted by competitors charging lower commissions.

If an importer did not make use of the opportunity to draw bills of exchange under his credit, the Browns assessed no charges against his account. Customers, in other words, only paid for what they used regardless of the amount authorized on the face of their credit. This leniency made it advantageous for an importer to take out a credit for a greater amount than his probable requirements and, in addition, to take out a duplicate credit with another house, especially if the other credit could be negotiated at lower fees. Some merchants carried along a credit on Brown, Shipley & Co. to use only in the event the foreign seller refused, or was unable, to draw under the cheaper credit. At other times an importer did not arrange a credit on a less expensive English house until he had finally reached his foreign destination.[39] Bankers elsewhere apparently felt safe in assuming that any firm holding a letter of credit from the Browns was likely to be a good risk.

During the antebellum era, the Browns firmly resisted the demands of their largest and strongest customers for preferential rates or secretive rebates. To a remarkable extent, the Browns pursued the goal of extending equal treatment to all importers, and there were few deviations from the standard schedule of commissions.[40] They opposed subterfuge not so much on principle as on the quite legitimate ground that such secrets were extremely difficult to keep in the commerical community. As it was, the Browns' branch managers were often called upon to deny charges that importers in another port were receiving some form of preferential treatment from one of their counterparts. Rumors of rate allowances, however, were quite rate; importers apparently realized that discussions of rebates were taboo when transacting business with the House of Brown.

After the Civil War, the partners reassessed their policy. The pressure to grant some customers special consideration grew and finally reached the breaking point. First, the Barings lowered their standard rates for a privileged class of customers. In correspondence with the New York branch in 1866, the London partners outlined their reasons for favoring a new policy similar to the Barings':

> With reference to the general question of adopting a discriminating charge of commission for the same class of credits, we entirely concur with you in the expediency & propriety of such a discrimination, making it apply according to the means & standing of our several clients and the length of time they have been upon our Books. We see no injustice in drawing such distinctions, and quite concur with you also in the advantage it will give you in being better able to regulate accounts as well as the aggregates of the business; it must rest with you to decide to whom you will make the concessions . . . but looking at the magnitude of our credits at the moment, we should suppose you would not require to make the concession very extensively; nevertheless we should prefer to risk the loss of an account which you do not class among the best & safest . . . You may be able to win back . . . some . . . that have previously left us by intimating your readiness to place them, ex-

ceptionally, on as good terms as they can obtain from any other House of equal standing with our own — or in other words from Messrs. Barings, who are the only competitors likely to draw such accounts from us.

The time may come when we shall have to revert to the scale of Commissions they [Barings] charge uniformly as we did before the troubled times; but so long as our obligations under credits continue so large as they are now, there would seem to be no necessity for any *general* reduction . . . this system appears to have worked well in Philadelphia & we hope you will find it equally convenient & practical in New York.[41]

The Browns' ability to sustain a higher rate schedule than the Barings for several years after the war further emphasizes the extent to which the firm had become the premier banker in the American trade sector.

Competitive behavior in the letter of credit field was characteristic of that in oligopolistic markets dominated by one or two acknowledged price leaders.[42] Collusion between the Barings and the Browns, and at times other firms, was "imperfect" in the sense that it was the result of tacit agreements rather than formal arrangements. Whenever the Browns discussed a proposed change in their rate schedule, the likely response of competitors was thoroughly analyzed. The leading firms generally confined their competitive activities to differentiations in the terms of their credits and in the quality and range of service. In the absence of any evidence to the contrary, it appears that the demand curve for the industry was relatively inelastic. Since each of the prime issuers was prepared in the long run, to match any general reduction in rates initiated by its peers, the major houses soon realized that little was to be gained from vigorous price competition.

In selective markets, however, price competition among the leading international banking houses did occur. In the early fifties, various firms acting as agents for George Peabody & Co. began issuing credits to coffee importers in the Rio trade at 0.5 percent below the Browns' regular 1.5 percent rate. The partners spent over a year assessing the effect of Peabody's initiative.[43] While the Browns procrastinated, Peabody's agents busily garnered a substantial share of the South American market. Finally, the Browns assented to the inevitable and lowered their own rate to 1 percent.[44] In this case, the delayed reaction was due in part to some indecision about whether Peabody's entry into the market was a serious threat to the firm's position.[45] Later in the 1850s, the Barings offered lower rates to a few of the Browns' customers on credits negotiable along the western coast of South America. On this occasion the partners did not hesitate in matching the Barings' reduced commissions. By acting promptly the Browns retained the accounts of two large copper refiners in Baltimore who purchased the bulk of their ore in Chilean ports.

The Browns were more apt to introduce the rate increases which often emerged during periods of economic uncertainty. In November 1861, for example, the partners decided to resume the issuance of credits in the Far Eastern trade, which had been suspended after the outbreak of the Civil War, and they used the occasion to boost commissions from 2 to 2.5 percent.[46] They felt the increase was justified because of the wartime situation. In an effort to prepare the way for the change, the firm gave advance notice of their intentions to Dennistoun & Co. and to the most important of Peabody's American agents, Duncan, Sherman & Co. The Liverpool managers called it an experiment because of their apprehensiveness about how the Baring and Peabody firms would react to their trial balloon. If their main competitors refused to follow suit, the partners doubted their ability to sustain the higher rate. In short, their behavior was quite typical of a dominant firm in an oligopolistic market which is never certain of its latitude in exercising price leadership.

The firm's market power was demonstrated forcefully, however, in the late sixties when the firm was the last merchant-banking house to retreat from the higher rates which had been imposed during the war.[47] During this period their volume of business grew so rapidly that the Browns began to worry about a shortage of capital resources. The maintenance of a high rate schedule, which allowed some leeway for discrimination, permitted the house to maximize revenues without taking on a larger volume of business than was prudent for the existing capital structure. After Alexander H. Brown subsequently returned a portion of the senior William Brown's fortune to the house, the partners were less reticent about increasing the magnitude of acceptances generated through letter of credit operations.

Until the pricing system was significantly altered in the 1870s, geography was the main factor in determining the number of months a credit would remain outstanding, or be "open," and the length of time bills drawn under the credit would run before their maturity dates. As transportation and communication improved, the length of time customarily permitted to complete transactions in distant ports correspondingly declined. At the mid-century, for example, credits issued to China traders usually remained open anywhere from six to twelve months, and issuers allowed foreign merchants to draw drafts at four to six months. Importers shipping from South America were given three of four months to make purchases, and bills could be drawn at either 60 or 90 days. European dry goods credits usually expired at the end of the calendar year regardless of the opening date. Bills drawn on the continent were generally payable 90 days after the *date* on which a transaction occurred rather than after sight. Final payment on goods purchased in England was usually due in three months plus 10 days, with some merchandise calling for more rapid settlement.

The Browns discouraged customers who requested authorization to draw bills of exchange with extended maturities. In 1826 James Brown told one customer he had no intention of authorizing bills of exchange at eight months, regardless of the extra commission offered for the privilege of a lengthened maturity.[48] The same negative attitude was evident in the mid-thirties when a Baltimore auctioneer asked for a three year credit. A credit open that long, George Brown explained, was something he "would not grant to any house."[49] The customer left in a huff, but George Brown was not perturbed; their "paltry commissions" were not worth retaining, he assured the Liverpool branch. Several years later, George Brown strongly recommended that the English partners reject all bills drawn under the expired credits of his Baltimore customers. Too often, he stated, the goods reached a "late market."[50] The Browns also disapproved of the practice of postdating drafts beyond the actual sales date. A foreign merchant sometimes postdated the bills of exchange in order to accommodate customers and to increase thereby his volume of sales. The net effect of this action was to lengthen the importer's credit period. During the 1860s the Browns finally inserted a provision in their credits that eliminated the postdating loophole.[51]

The financial standing of the applicant and the degree of risk associated with the merchandise to be financed also influenced the terms of issuance. A prerequisite for opening any letter of credit was that there be no doubt about the honesty of the applicant. The Browns, throughout the century, preferred to confine their guarantees to those importers about whom there were no reservations from an ethical standpoint. The moral risks were left to others, and according to their testimony, some competitors were far less fastidious.[52] At the same time, the Browns were willing to assist a new firm of untested business ability or limited capital. But their initial credits were generally for small to moderate amounts, and the partners expected applicants to offer a reputable endorser or strong collateral.

In fact, it was unusual for the firm to extend financing to any customer without taking some form of security for at least a part of the total obligation. A comparison with the Barings' policy during the antebellum era is informative: the Barings regularly issued credits that were totally unsecured. To reduce their risks, the Barings relied completely upon their selectiveness in choosing responsible customers. The Browns simply went them one better; they too screened their customers for reliability, but then secured themselves as well in order to reduce further the risk of loss in their credit operations. In the postwar period, the Barings and other bankers adopted many of the precautions which had proven so effective for the Browns, including a greater reliance on the receipt of bills of lading and other forms of security.

Most of the customers applying to the firm for credits had dealt with the house for a number of years, and the partners handled their requests in a routine manner. The Browns generally expected an importer to open a separate credit for each individual voyage. In addition to such information as expiration dates and face amounts, the American branches' letters to Liverpool designated the vessel by which the shipment would be made, the foreign ports where the credit might be used, and the names of the foreign merchants, if specified, who were authorized to draw bills of exchange under it.[53] Each credit received an official number, and all the details were forwarded to Liverpool by steamer. The successful laying of transoceanic telegraph cables and the worldwide spread of overland wires made possible the almost instantaneous opening of credits in the 1870s. In 1878, for example, the Baltimore agency expedited two overseas transactions for important customers on the same day: first, it advised the London branch of the openings; then it assisted its customers in cabling authorizations to draw to merchants in Brazil and Japan, respectively. Cable advices were expensive, however, and the vast majority of credits continued to be handled through the mails. The international telegraphic network gave importers and bankers a new option for use in emergencies, but it did not fundamentally alter the normal letter of credit routine.

Prior to 1840 many of the Browns' customers held running credits. Financial arrangements of this sort are usually referred to as revolving credits today. A running credit was generally in force for an entire calendar year, and it could be used to finance a whole series of transactions. By the fifties, these arrangements had fallen into disfavor. "We open very few running [credits], confining ourselves as much as possible to the specific foreign credits," the New York branch explained in 1855.[54]

The partners objected to running credits for several reasons. During a period of business uncertainty, there was no effective way of curtailing the activities of importers holding running credits so long as the customer remained within the maximum amount originally authorized. But of equal importance was the firm's inability to keep track of the various transactions involving the holders of such credits; the very nature of the relationship minimized the frequency of personal contact. Thus, the uncertainty associated with running credits led the house to discourage their issuance.

The successful management of letter of credit operations was essentially a task of planning strategies with a view to their intermediate and long-run effects. Once a credit was actually issued, it was likely to take six months or more until a customer finally settled all his debts with the Liverpool branch. During the interim between issuance and final settlement, the economy was susceptible to indeterminate variation. When a downturn did occur, it was invariably too late for the Browns to take any action that would have any more than a marginal influence on the scope of the credit business. The cure, in this situation, had to be preventive in character if it was to have any effect.

As a result, the Browns concentrated on the formulation of sound terms of issuance, in particular the stipulation of fully secured transactions with adequate margins. Beyond their conservative rules, they maintained credit files that were current and thorough. An integrated branch system and a stable administrative structure created an environment in which thoughtful long range planning was genuinely possible. Other, loosely formed banking chains which might have benefited from a similar degree of forward planning lacked the coherence to sustain a comprehensive program. With the possible exception of the Baring partnership, no other firm in the field could compare with the House of Brown in terms of the permanence of the managerial staff and the ability of the partners to administer letter of credit operations.

Summary and Conclusion

Alexander Brown began opening letters of credit for his own account and those of a few favored merchants soon after his son William established a Liverpool branch in 1810. The gradually increasing volume of credits was part of an overall trend toward a much greater emphasis on the performance of financial services for the American foreign trade sector. The active solicitation of new accounts coincided with the opening of a New York branch in 1825. When the founder died in 1834, the letter of credit business had grown to such an extent that his four surviving sons decided to eliminate their merchandising activities in the United States and to concentrate instead on financing the overseas purchases of other American importers. In the aftermath of the panic of 1837 the Browns introduced several new rules to govern the handling of credit operations. With the exception of the China trade, the firm conducted business exclusively on a secured basis. The Browns also shortened the period of debt settlement; the Liverpool branch expected to have a remitted bill of exchange in its possession before final payment was made on a customer's acceptance. The privilege of a cash advance largely ceased, and the operations became a strictly commission business.

During the 1840s and 1850s, the Browns made considerable inroads on the market share of their leading competitor, the House of Baring; they opened a Boston office in 1844 and within ten years the firm had achieved parity with the Barings in their primary stronghold. George Peabody mounted a challenge to the two leading houses during the early fifties, but the panic of 1857 seriously damaged his position. The Browns suffered few losses, on the other hand, and their preeminence in the field was firmly established.

By the mid-century, the basic operating procedures in the letter of credit field were well developed, but the Browns continued to devote much effort to improvement and sophistication. The partners worked assiduously at maintaining uniform rules in all their branch offices, and by keeping in constant communication, they were largely successful. Importers who dealt with the Browns received credits that were welcomed by foreign merchants throughout the world. Despite the firm's high fee schedule, many importers, nevertheless, arranged their financing through the Browns because of the unparalleled service which was available to them after they had become regular customers. In addition, an importer gained access to credit information that was as current and accurate as any in the Anglo-American economy. Moreover, merchants liked to maintain an association with an international banking house which was blessed with ample capital and proven intelligence. Based on their performance in 1857 importers believed the Browns would be able to withstand future financial crises.

The Browns' network of offices could efficiently coordinate trading activity involving numerous port cities. A merchant could open a credit in Philadelphia, purchase merchandise almost anywhere in the world, send his cargo to any major American port (except San Francisco), settle his account with any office that was convenient, and finally have his bills accepted and paid in England. In the United States no other banking house could provide such broad and comprehensive service to the international trader.

In retrospect, it is surprising how rapidly financial services developed to meet the demands of American importers. The shift in the marketing system during the early thirties from auctions to the direct importation of foreign goods by resident merchants coincided closely with a broad expansion of letter of credit facilities in the United States. In the three or four years prior to the panic of 1837, many importers gained access to credits which a host of merchant-banking firms issued on exceedingly liberal terms. The Browns believed the response of competitors had been too accommodating, if not outright overgenerous.

Within the letter of credit field, there seems to have been little institutional lag in the response of international bankers to the new opportunities for service and profit. Unlike their more regulated counterparts in the domestic economy, these unincorporated firms were completely free to tailor their financial services to the demands of the marketplace, and the history of the Brown firm suggests that innovation in the foreign trade sector was stimulated quickly. Moreover, the letter of credit facilities the Browns and other bankers extended to small and medium-sized importers on a secured basis almost certainly contributed to the general expansion of American foreign trade during the last two thirds of the nineteenth century.

The growth of the import sector, in turn, had an effect on the Browns' overall strategies. The threefold increase in the value of imports between 1845 and 1859, from $115 million to $345 million, paved the way for increased specialization. This growth in the size of the market presented the Browns with an incentive to emphasize more strongly their strictly financial services. During the corresponding period, the partners increased their revenues from the issuance of letters of credit by 350 percent—from $95,000 in 1845 to $346,000 in 1859. Commissions on consignments of cotton and other produce, in the meantime, fell by two thirds to less than $20,000. Through an evolutionary process, the firm had risen from its humble beginning in the linen trade to a position of leadership in the specialized field of international banking.

Competition among the major firms in the letter of credit market focused mainly on the eligibility of customers for financing and the terms of issuance. The Barings maintained, by far, the narrowest standards for customer eligibility. Since they solicited only the accounts of wealthiest merchants, their share of the total market was, by design, fairly limited. The Browns, on the other hand, maintained the strictest terms of issuance, and competitors found them especially vulnerable in this area. In Boston, the Barings' offer of unsecured credits to the Browns' prime accounts eventually forced the Browns to surrender to customer demands for similar consideration. The Barings made formidable challenges in other ports too, but with less success.[55]

After the outbreak of the Civil War, however, there was less differentiation in the credit terms of the main issuers. When the Barings resumed the issuance of credits in November 1861, after a temporary suspension, the Browns' Liverpool house reported that their competitors had decided to insist on the privilege of bills of lading in all future transactions and that the "Barings had now adopted this condition as a uniform system."[56] Thus ended what had been a long standing tradition of conducting business almost solely on an unsecured basis. Yet it took an extraordinary political crisis to convince the Baring partners that there was merit in the Browns' standard procedures for handling credit activities.

Some of the changes brought about by wartime exigencies proved lasting. When business conditions returned to normal, the Barings did not revert to their antebellum strategies but adopted instead policies which were far more flexible. Daniel Curtis, who had replaced his father Thomas as the Browns' Boston branch manager, described these policies in August 1867. The Barings no longer restricted themselves to the issuance of clean credits to the best houses, he reported, but "now compete with us by offering [secured] credits to firms of every scale." Since the Browns' rate structure was one half a percent higher than the competition, Curtis had difficulty holding many of his old customers. "In other cities your policies are more successful since the offices do not meet head on the Barings who are so well established in Boston & now offer better terms."[57] Curtis also cited the increasing competition of the local firm—Kidder, Peabody & Co. (no relation to George Peabody) who issued credits on the London banking house of McCalmont & Co. Four years later Curtis complained that Kidder, Peabody & Co. was constantly "drumming our customers" and was "ingenious in invention of small inducements to such of our Credit and Exchange customers as are open to them."[58]

The Barings' lower rates in the immediate postwar years and their greater willingness to accommodate younger merchants eventually gave them the competitive edge in the Boston market. Upon hearing of the loss of another customer to the Barings in November 1868, the London partners expressed a desire to become more competitive in the terms of issuance: "It has struck us before that there is a want of flexibility in applying general rules to particular cases there which must militate against the retention and certainly against the extension of business."[59] Without recommending a general relaxation in rules on security, the London partners nonetheless observed that in

Boston the same rules "appear to bear a more stringent & inflexible application." Whatever the cause, the firm was losing out in the Boston market. Finally, as they had been forced to capitulate in the antebellum era as well, the Browns relaxed the terms of isssuance in the competitive Boston market.

However, the partners failed to mention similar difficulties in either Baltimore, Philadelphia, or New York; the inference being that in the latter cities the Browns had things just about their own way.[60] The main emphasis was on diversification in their accounts. The London partners stressed that any extension of the credit business should be in the form of "*new* safe accounts, rather than in the enlargement of the lines of our existing constituency, so as to preserve the principle of an insurance system — *many moderate* safe lines rather than *fewer large* ones."[61]

Despite their differences, the international bankers participating in the Anglo-American trade were in fundamental agreement on the basic principles and terms under which business was transacted in the letter of credit field. The operations of the Barings and the Browns, for the most part, set the standard against which the policies and procedures of other houses were judged. When the two firms agreed on the appropriateness of a new rule or procedure, it was usually not long before the change was adopted as the customary practice. After the panic of 1857, for instance, there was much talk in London about reducing the normal maturity date for bills drawn in the Eastern trade from six to four months, and the matter remained up in the air for several months. Meanwhile, the New York partners reassured the Boston manager that the question would be settled soon. "Whatever we & the Barings think proper for the American trade," they stated emphatically, "we can force the thing."[62]

Section 3

Foreign Exchange

In performing their function as foreign exchange dealers, the Browns and other international banking houses provided a specialized service that was vital to American participation in an expanding world economy. The spectrum of customers requiring adequate facilities for the international transfer of monetary assets was broad and varied. In the foreign trade sector, the nation's importers and exporters were regular buyers and sellers of bills of exchange drawn in foreign currencies. But periodically, foreign exchange dealers handled a diversity of other transactions as well. The range of monetary transfers extended from large international capital movements to the merest remittances of recent immigrants to their overseas relatives.[1]

When the antebellum foreign exchange mechanism was at the height of maturity in the 1850s, the Browns' operations were very seasonal. The effective performance of this business function relied heavily on interbranch cooperation. From approximately May to November, the firm's northern offices were predominantly sellers of foreign exchange to those merchants who imported finished goods. The Browns temporarily invested the cash these sales generated in short term commercial paper. In the late fall, when the cotton crop began to move to market, the partners systematically liquidated their short term investments and put the funds at the disposal of the southern branches. The southern branch managers purchased bills of exchange over the winter at seasonally low prices and remitted them to the Liverpool office. The Liverpool partners, in turn, used the remittances to cover the previously overdrawn sterling accounts of the northern branches. The seasonal cycle was then complete. For the firm as a whole, profits were maximized: the Browns sold a disproportionate volume of exchange when rates were high; they covered many of those sales later in the year when rates were low; and during the interim the partners invested the accumulated cash in the U.S. money market where interest rates were normally higher than in England.

Although outside sources generally confirm the Browns' assertions of their commanding position in the field around the mid-century, even rough estimates of the probable market shares of the major foreign exchange dealers do not exist. The actual extent of the firm's leadership or dominance has thus remained obscure. Fortunately, some extremely useful data on the aggregate of the Browns' volume of activity in the 1850s survives. Included in the partnership records are precise statements of the foreign exchange sales in the five years from 1851 through 1855 along with informal references in the correspondence to the approximate volume of transactions in 1859 and 1860. Sales to importers were of course only one half of the exchange equation; in order to balance its account, the firm offset its sales with an equivalent volume of foreign exchange purchases, supplemented occasionally with specie shipments. The following table indicates the absolute *minimum* of the Browns' market share in the years for which information is available.

Inadequate data seriously handicaps the overall analysis, however. The actual volume of bills drawn in the United States was certainly less than the potential flow of foreign exchange because some international accounts were not settled through monetary payments. Yet there are no statistics available on the extent to which international debts were cleared by offsetting shipments of merchandise rather than through the transoceanic transfer of bills of exchange. In short, the size of the foreign exchange market itself cannot be accurately determined. Only the Browns' minimum share of 12 to 15 percent can be estimated with any degree of certainty. Still, with these figures as a base, it is nonetheless possible to draw inferences about the probable upward limit of their market share. Even if as much as one half of all U.S. foreign trade was carried on through barter, which seems unlikely, the Browns' share of the remaining foreign exchange market would not have risen above 30 percent at any time during the 1850s. And the Brown's correspondence confirms what these figures indicate — that the structure of the foreign exchange market at the mid-century was far more competitive than the market structure for letters of credit.

Table 3. Estimate of minimum market shares

Year	Browns' volume of activity 1	Potential outflow of exchange 2	Potential inflow of exchange 3	Column 1 as a percentage of column 2 4	Column 1 as a percentage of column 3 5
1851	$28.4	$232	$232	12 %	12 %
1852	28.4	231	221	12	13
1853	35.8	290	234	12	15
1854	41.6	330	301	12.5	14
1855	38.2	290	278	13	13
1860	49.0[a]	392	401	12.5	12

Sources and notes: The data on the Browns comes from two letters—BB&C, New York to T. Curtis, Boston, January 2, 1856, *BB&CP* and BS&C, Liverpool, to BB&C, New York, February 11, 1860, HF. The figures on the potential inflow and outflow of foreign exchange were derived from various tables in the appendices of Douglass North's *The Economic Growth of the United States.* The composite figures correspond closely with the aggregate debits and credits on the American balance of payments account. Imports account for the bulk of the potential outflow and exports the inflow. Specie shipments, the overseas payment of interest and dividends, and transportation earnings also enter into the calculations. Capital movements show up as a debit in balance of payment statements, but in this chart they are lumped in with the figures for the potential inflow, since monetary assets were transferred into the United States during the period.

[a] The Browns estimated their current volume of transactions to be running at a rate of approximately £10,000,000 early in 1860.

X

The Assumption of Leadership

When Alexander Brown first opened his doors at the turn of the nineteenth century, the foreign bill of exchange was already a familiar device for the payment of international debts, but an active and continuous market for bills had only begun to develop in the major port cities. In the late eighteenth and early nineteenth centuries, the foreign exchange markets were strictly local in organization, and fluctuations in the rates were often sharp and unpredictable. Following the pattern of other contemporary merchants, Alexander Brown's entry into the field was at first limited, and the function he performed was essentially that of a broker. He bought bills of exchange from exporters in Maryland and Virginia, endorsed them, and quickly sold them to Baltimore importers. Exporters often resorted to such an intermediary when they were unable to find a buyer among their importing counterparts. As a consequence, Alexander Brown engaged in foreign exchange transactions irregularly, and the inventory of salable bills was held to a minimal figure. It was not until William Brown opened a Liverpool branch in 1810 that the firm had the facilities for creating its own supply of sterling bills.

Thereafter, the Browns progressed steadily toward the status of full-time foreign exchange dealers. The American branches increasingly forwarded their bill purchases to the Liverpool office for collection — no longer were bills merely endorsed and resold. The ability to draw its own bills of exchange promptly in response to demand was an added benefit for both the firm and its customers. Freshly drawn sterling bills on the Liverpool office could be sold in amounts individually tailored to each customer's requirements. This feature enhanced their marketability and, therefore, their price. Buyers were also prepared to pay higher rates for bills in which they had greater confidence. If an importer decided to purchase bills directly from exporters or brokers, he always had the problem of making a judicious selection from a variety of bills drawn on a diverse group of English drawees about which he probably had little current information or personal knowledge. By purchasing a bill freshly drawn on the Browns' English office, the importer could concentrate his effort on merchandising functions and shift the vast proportion of the foreign exchange risk to the dealer specialist.

The establishment of an English branch on which sterling bills could be freely drawn also gave the Browns' foreign exchange operations a new dimension of flexibility. From that date, the firm had the option of handling its account on either a "covered" or "uncovered" basis. There were fundamental differences between these two general methods of conducting a foreign exchange business, and at this point in the analysis, the distinctions must be clearly drawn. One matter of absolutely critical importance was the timing of foreign exchange sales vis-à-vis foreign exchange purchases. The Browns' interbranch account could be described as covered whenever the bill purchases of the American outlets exceeded, or were equal to, the current volume of exchange sales. In other words, aggregate sales were always adequately covered by prior bill purchases. From the standpoint of the Liverpool branch, it meant that the cash inflow generated through the collection of remitted bills was sufficient to offset the cash drain which resulted from honoring the bills the American branches routinely sold. Overall, the risks involved in operating a covered exchange account were not unusually great. It was mainly because of their relative safety, in fact, that the vast majority of the business agreements between other Anglo-American merchant bankers and their various U.S. agents were maintained on the basis of a strictly covered account.

The operation of an uncovered foreign exchange account was, on the other hand, a far more dangerous business venture. The normal order of activity was completely reversed: the dealer sold sterling bills in amounts that temporarily exceeded the volume of bill purchases and remittances. When the Browns elected to leave their account uncovered, the partners were, in effect, gambling that future purchases could be made at substantially lower prices. Their net profit margin on foreign exchange sales might be improved by several percentage points if transactions were advantageously timed. During the interval that the firm's account remained uncovered, the Liverpool partners were called upon to finance a steady stream of payments with little relief. If later remittances from the American branches came forth slowly and their collection proved difficult, the Liverpool management could suddenly find itself in a serious dilemma. It was this same fear of delayed or inadequate reimbursement that led most of the other Anglo-American banking houses to decline proposals from their U.S. agents for the maintenance of uncovered foreign exchange accounts.

One additional feature of the international exchange account mechanism should be clarified here. Although the remittance of a sterling bill was the most commonly employed method for covering an account, there were alternative means of accomplishing the same result. Coverage was sometimes achieved through specie shipments. On other occasions the partners sent a cargo of cotton or tobacco to balance a deficient account. When the Liverpool branch required reserves to bolster its position, the firm often transferred stocks and other securities across the Atlantic to serve as the collateral for a temporary loan. In fact the Browns were apt to consider a wide variety of reimbursement devices during an economic crisis or a period of high sterling rates. Indeed the methods Anglo-American bankers in general employed in covering foreign exchange sales in the U.S. market varied considerably. This diversity was most pronounced in the early decades of the nineteenth century when foreign exchange markets were still in the process of development.

Initially, the Browns were cautious about operating their foreign exchange account on an uncovered basis even for short periods of time. In the 1820s, they rarely delayed covering remittances for prior sales for more than two or three months. The tactics planned in the summer of 1824 called for, at the most, a two month lag. The Baltimore branch explained the basic plan to the Liverpool office in May: "We think Exchange will continue high . . . with this view we intend to increase the balance we owe you in *all* June, calculating on Exchange getting lower in July & August . . . at some gain."[1]

Interest rate differentials between the English and American money markets occasionally influenced the length of the delay in covering a deficient account. In the spring of 1825 the Baltimore partners felt that the current rate of interest on short term loans was sufficiently high to merit the temporary investment of excess funds in the U.S. market. At the same time, they told the Liverpool branch that the anticipated 6 percent return was "still . . . no inducement to keep you short of money." If William Brown saw any possibility of his funds running low, the Baltimore partners told him, "advise us & we will remit on the best terms we can."[2]

As a rule, the firm followed a flexible policy in the management of its exchange account. A flexible policy permitted the firm to take advantage of opportunities for profit as they arose. In the summer of 1825, for example, the American partners were undecided about whether their account should be operated on a covered or uncovered basis during the upcoming months. Consequently, they could, at the time, provide little guidance for the Liverpool branch. If sterling rates remained low, the American partners told the Liverpool office they planned to maintain a covered position. If, on the other hand, rates turned higher, they intended to sell sterling bills over and beyond their current remittances.[3]

To finance temporary deficits, the Liverpool partners often borrowed funds from their London bankers, Denison Heywood Kennard & Co. In the period from 1816 to 1836 stock of the Second Bank of the United States frequently served as collateral for these loans. Indeed, one stock certificate might finance a long chain of Anglo-American credit. In Baltimore and elsewhere, the Browns sometimes accepted the stock of the Second Bank and other reliable financial institutions as security for loans to local merchants. Occasionally, the Browns, in turn, transferred a customer's collateral to England to serve as security for their own borrowings.

The Browns contemplated such a transfer in the fall of 1825. Exchange rates were high, and the Baltimore branch planned to press bill sales. Meanwhile, a transfer of stock certificates to Liverpool was proposed. "We have plenty of stock here on which we have loaned money," the partners reported.[4] Apparently, these transoceanic shipments of stock certificates were not uncommon. At one point, the Baltimore partners warned the Liverpool office about the danger of losing certificates when they were sent "backward & forward" too often.

By the late twenties, the management of the foreign exchange account was becoming increasingly complex. In the course of decision making, the partners regularly considered a whole series of external and internal factors. For instance, the relationship between exchange operations and the firm's mercantile activities is plainly revealed in the correspondence of December 1827. Although the American branches were heavily overdrawn at the time, they nonetheless hoped to delay remittances to Liverpool for several more weeks. The Baltimore partners explained the rationale for the delay: "We . . . hope heavy shipments of specie & the probable war in Europe will bring Exchange down."[5] Then they added a qualifier. If this plan seemed likely to cause a severe cash shortage in Liverpool, the Baltimore management was prepared to abandon its delaying tactics. They feared an inadequate reserve of liquid assets might force William Brown into "premature sales" of his cotton inventories. The Baltimore partners wanted to prevent such a development at all costs; "We would remit you at a loss rather than have you too tight," they assured the Liverpool office.

Despite the Browns' increasing managerial sophistication in the field, the organization that contributed most to the maturation of the American foreign exchange market was the Second Bank of the United States under the leadership of Nicholas Biddle. Biddle did much to centralize the foreign exchange market and make it national, as opposed to local and regional, in scope.[6] In doing so, he moved to dampen the degree of seasonal fluctuation in bill prices. In the antebellum economy seasonal variations were a predictable result of the American foreign trade pattern, with the demand from importers for foreign exchange greatest during the summer and fall while the supply of bills peaked in the winter and early spring when the cotton crop moved to market. By offering large amounts of sterling for sale during the summer and buying heavily in the winter, the Second Bank acted as a stabilizing influence.

The explanation for Biddle's many accomplishments in the foreign exchange market are manifold, but a few of the major factors contributing to the Second Bank's successes can be mentioned briefly. First, the Second Bank had a branch organization that reached into every important port city. This network of branch offices supplied Biddle with the information he needed to coordinate activities in the various local and regional markets. A given branch was not asked to balance its exchange sales with an equivalent volume of bill purchases. The northern offices were free, therefore, to concentrate on sales, while the main responsibility for bill buying rested with the Second Bank's southern outlets. The geographical specialization practiced within the framework of this centrally managed, national organization made the Second Bank an important factor in the greater unification of local and regional exchange markets.

The Second Bank also possessed far greater capital resources than any of its competitors in the foreign exchange field. Moreover, it operated its account in alliance with the House of Baring. Each financial institution was, in its own right, among the most powerful in the Anglo-American economy. United in a joint business venture, they presented a formidable foe for potential rivals. Under the terms of their joint account agreement, the Barings permitted Biddle to draw against an uncovered credit line of £250,000.[7] The Second Bank's market power was so great that Biddle could exert tremendous pressure on exchange rates. The Browns, for one, used the Second Bank's prices as a touchstone in their own rate setting procedures.

Another important factor in defining the Second Bank's role was Biddle's belief that he was responsible for providing the nation with a stable foreign exchange market.[8] When he assumed the presidency in 1823, this was one of the goals he set out to accomplish. Biddle felt his interference in the market was justifiable insofar as he was protecting the domestic currency and counteracting unhealthy business disturbances. As a result, the Second Bank was an innovator when it came to buying and selling foreign exchange according to a seasonal pattern.

With the Second Bank's failure to gain a renewal of its charter in 1836, no other firm remained with sufficient capital to exercise decisive control over the foreign exchange market. The history of Biddle's successor bank is a case in point. For several years, the bank was able to exert some influence over exchange rates, but its overall position became more precarious every year. Finally the overextended bank, with Biddle in retirement, collapsed.[9] In the meantime, the other half of the once invincible alliance — the House of Baring — had lost much of its enthusiasm for transacting business in the United States. Although the Barings continued to play an important role in the foreign exchange market, they did not try to reestablish their formerly dominant position in the field.

Insofar as it affected the foreign exchange market, the end of the Second Bank of the United States was by no means a national disaster. The anticipated fragmentation did not materialize; nor did the market revert to a more disorganized condition. Indeed the quantitative evidence indicates that, on the whole, the process of maturation continued. Measured by the narrowing of price deviations from the gold par standard, the trend toward stability, which became increasingly noticeable during the 1830s, went on unabated throughout the remainder of the century — the greenback years excepted.

In the past, scholars explained this damping in the amplitude of price fluctuations primarily with reference to factors external to the American economy: the reduced costs of ocean transport; the increased speed and reliability of transportation and communications; and the development of adequate ocean insurance. While conceding that these factors were important, Lance Davis and J. R. T. Hughes more recently stressed two fundamental changes taking place within the American economy itself.[10] As the overall banking system developed greater stability, the suspension of specie payments occurred less frequently. Because suspensions effectively revoked the gold standard mechanism in the areas affected, "early financial crises produced extraordinarily wide fluctuations in the exchange rates." In addition, they argued, "As communication and transportation facilities improved, the U.S. financial market became better integrated." Variations in domestic exchange rates lessened, and foreign exchange rates in one port city were conditioned by the corresponding rates in contiguous areas. "This widening of the 'extent' of the exchange market," Davis and Hughes stated, "also tended to damp the amplitude of the fluctuations."

From an institutional standpoint, the firm most active in creating a more integrated market structure during the 1840s and 1850s was the House of Brown. During the lifetime of the Second Bank, the Browns had been Biddle's chief competitors, and there were occasions when they had sold sterling at comparable rates. From 1832 to 1836 when the Second Bank's recharter was seriously in doubt, the Browns rapidly expanded the volume of their foreign exchange transactions. The partners quickly overcame their inhibitions about participating in uncovered seasonal operations. At the beginning of the 1832 winter buying season, the American branches had overdrawn their account in Liverpool by $2,400,000; in 1836 the figure had reached approximately $5,000,000.[11] The U.S. branches derived the vast majority of their 1836 profits of $438,527 from foreign exchange operations.[12]

The House of Brown promptly moved into the leadership vacuum left by the expiring Second Bank of the United States. Thereafter the Browns used most of the managerial techniques Nicholas Biddle had formerly employed. By the end of the decade they had outlets in most of the major port cities—north and south; their capital, while not unlimited, was nonetheless substantial; and they had in England an established branch on which sterling could be sold against an open, uncovered line of credit. In his relationship with the Barings, Biddle, by timing withdrawals and deposits to the Second Bank's advantage, had often imposed on the good will of his English associates. Within the Brown organization, on the other hand, the partners had nothing to gain from such transatlantic maneuvering. Since each partner held claims on the profits of every branch office in the chain, the firm functioned with more unity of purpose than competitive organizations.

The Browns were in a favorable position to exploit a technological breakthrough in the communications field that became an important tool in the further centralization of the foreign exchange market. A telegraph line connecting Baltimore and New York was completed in 1846.[13] As the network of telegraph lines spread along the Atlantic coast and down through the southern states to Mobile and New Orleans, foreign exchange dealers were able to monitor closely the quoted rates in the major port cities.

The availability of instantaneous communications facilities brought nearer the realization of a genuinely national foreign exchange market. Theoretically, a firm's operations might have been managed from any point along the telegraph line, but as a practical matter, New York remained the hub for all the major dealers. Because the pattern of trade in New York was chronically unbalanced in favor of imports, the greatest demand for foreign exchange emanated from that port, and for most of the year, conditions there set the tone for the entire U.S. market. During the winter months, however, the supply side of the market exerted more influence on the rate structure, and the telegraph was especially useful in relaying to New York the current prices for sterling bills in New Orleans and Mobile.

The telegraphic network permitted the Browns to implement one of their most innovative strategies: the maintenance of uniform rates throughout the branch system. By the early fifties, the New York partners regularly used the telegraph to communicate adjustments in the firm's exchange rates to the branch offices and agent representatives. At first, the partners normally changed their rates no more than once every two or three days. Because these messages went out over a public wire, the Browns devised a secret code for relaying information. The code contained symbols related solely to bill prices, however, since during the early years of the network's existence, the partners rarely employed the telegraph for any administrative function other than rate setting.

As organized by the Browns, the seasonal pattern of buying and selling foreign exchange became an extremely complicated operation. An analysis of the firm's management of its cash resources reveals something of this complexity. The partners' general plan called for the northern branches to retain a substantial portion of the cash proceeds from their summer and fall sterling sales until winter, when the southern offices needed those funds to make covering purchases at generally lower rates. Of course the cash accumulated in the American branches was offset, for the enterprise as a whole, by the cash drain in Liverpool, but to the extent that the firm's working capital permitted, the partners held funds in the United States and invested them in interest bearing assets. An integral part of the Browns' foreign exchange cycle was therefore the temporary investment of the seasonal cash surplus.

Because it was necessary to liquidate the entire portfolio in order to purchase a sufficient volume of bills to cover prior sales, a primary consideration in choosing investments was the preservation of principal. Thus the partners were not interested in investment situations where there was a high degree of risk. One form of investment well suited to the Browns' internal requirements was commercial paper. In the antebellum era, the term included a broad range of negotiable instruments. Most of the paper, however, represented debts between two mercantile firms, and arose out of the normal course of trade. The terms — business paper, mercantile paper, acceptances (domestic), and commercial paper — were often used interchangeably. The Browns generally referred to this entire class of investments as bills receivable. One common characteristic of all the variants was a short maturity date, which meant that the risk of loss was slight. Most of the paper, or bills receivable, came due within 90 days, although some paper ran on for as long as six months.

The New York partners were responsible for managing the short term investments of all the northern branches. The branch managers in Baltimore, Philadelphia, and Boston transferred their excess cash to the main office. They made local investments only with the explicit approval of the New York office. There were two main reasons for marshaling the firm's cash resources in New York. The Browns wanted to minimize uncertainties about the quality of their investments and, at the same time, to maximize the control of the senior partners over this phase of their financial activities. In New York the volume of paper associated with first rate mercantile firms was usually adequate to meet the firm's investment requirements. There were frequently opportunities to invest funds in other cities at slightly higher interest rates, but the partners were extremely cautious about taking paper from any merchant who was not unquestionably a first class credit risk. Safety was a more important factor than earning power in the seasonal portfolio.

Equally important was the ability of the New York partners to plan a portfolio with properly staggered maturity dates. Funds would then become available gradually in accordance with the needs of the southern outlets. The southern representatives usually purchased sterling by drawing domestic drafts on the New York branch at sight or three days sight. If southern purchases proceeded at a faster rate than anticipated, the New York partners generally raised additional funds through increased sales of sterling bills in the northern branches. Excessive southern purchases could force the firm to reduce selling rates drastically in order to stimulate additional sales. One alternative method of raising cash on short notice which the Browns might have employed was the sale, or rediscounting, of the firm's short term investments before their final maturity dates. But the New York partners refused to resort to "discounting" because such a practice had been customarily associated with houses of lesser standing in the financial community. Without an "acceptable" means of generating a prompt cash inflow other than through exchange sales, the New York partners' timing of maturity dates in their short term investment portfolio became critically important.

One point of possible confusion should be clarified here. There was absolutely nothing in the foreign exchange mechanism that, of necessity, linked the maintenance of an uncovered account with seasonal operations. To operate under a seasonal, covered account, a dealer could always begin his participation in the market by purchasing sterling bills during the winter months and remitting them to his English correspondent for collection. The offsetting sales could then be delayed until the summer months when exchange rates generally rose 1 to 2 percent. The risk of a seasonal gain or loss was essentially the same whether a dealer maintained a covered or an uncovered account. By the same token, an uncovered account was sometimes employed to take advantage of high interest rates in the U.S. money market and not because of the seasonality of bill prices. There were also occasions when exchange rates rose so high that dealers felt little hesitancy about selling uncovered bills because they could be sure of at least a minimal profit through specie shipments.

The main deterrent to the working of uncovered accounts was that the risks involved in their maintenance were not evenly distributed between cooperating firms in England and the United States. The English participant in a cooperative effort bore the brunt of the risk because there was always the possibility that, in a crisis, he might receive only partial reimbursement, or none at all. Significantly, the Brown firm was a unique enterprise, for such risk considerations were totally irrelevant, since the partners had pro rata interests in the branch offices on both sides of the Atlantic.

For the Browns, therefore, the choice between the operation of a covered or an uncovered, seasonal account was purely a question of profit maximization in light of given interest rate differentials. Since the firm did a volume of business far in excess of its own capital resources, short term borrowing in either the U.S. or English money markets was unavoidable. Had the American branches maintained a fully covered exchange account, it would have been necessary to borrow additional funds in the United States to finance each winter's bill purchases. If, on the other hand, the American branches maintained an uncovered account, the burden of financing a temporary deficit in the summer and fall was passed on to the English partners. Because short term interest rates were, as a rule, lower in London than in the New York money market, the Browns preferred the latter alternative. The operations of an uncovered foreign exchange account was the logical choice from the Browns' standpoint because it minimized the firm's overall interest costs and, thereby, contributed to the total earnings.

One feature of a more integrated market was a narrowing of profit margins. In the early twenties, the Browns usually realized margins of 1 to 1.5 percent of foreign exchange transactions. By the forties, that figure had been reduced to approximately 0.5 percent. An analysis of operations in the spring of 1860 revealed a further shrinkage of net profit margins of a level of one quarter to one eighth of a percent. The partners became extremely concerned about the decreasing profitability of this phase of their business activities, and they launched a comprehensive review of the firm's general position in the foreign exchange market.

The trend toward smaller returns in the exchange phase of the business alarmed the Liverpool partners in particular. By comparison, they noted that commission earnings on letter of credit accounts were already approximately five times greater than the profits derived from sterling operations, and the disparity was increasing.[14]

Indeed, there was general agreement that new strategies were necessary to rejuvenate earnings in the exchange field. If the prospects for improvement seemed slight, the English partners were prepared to discuss a reduction in the volume of transactions or perhaps even a complete withdrawal from the market. Their letter to the New York branch, dated February 11, 1860, covered several policy options, but its overall tone was decidedly pessimistic:

> Even 1/4 percent does seem a very inadequate compensation for the risk, labor, & anxiety attendant upon our large turn over of 10 Millions Sterling. Only 4 Millions belong to the Credit business [settlements], which would not be in any way affected if the remaining 6 Millions — which are purely Exchange business — were entirely dropped, supposing it were thought proper to do so. And it occurs to us to be deserving of consideration & investigation whether, in the altered circumstances of the Exchange business our plan is the one now calculated to yield the best return for a given measure of labor, risk, and Capital. Whether . . . it would not pay us better, instead of being always buyers & sellers under all circumstances, to circumscribe our transactions within the limits to which they would be reduced by declining all that did not yield a stated margin (of say, for instance, 1/2 percent) and to look to draw for the bulk of our Capital in the Summer & Autumn at the high rates that then prevail, & employ it in New York at good interest in paper that would be available about the time when the decline almost invariably occurs at the height of the shipping season . . .

> We offer no opinion . . . on these points, but merely . . . suggest
> for consideration whether, as the present system does not compen-
> sate us fairly, some other plan can be devised that will pay better;
> or that, whilst yielding only the same result, will diminish the risk
> & labor.[15]

In short the Liverpool partners proposed a strategic shift to a more
exaggerated version of the seasonal pattern of buying and selling bills
of exchange.

Beyond these policy implications, the Liverpool correspondence
discloses much about the relationship between the firm's two most
important functional activities. By 1860 letter of credit customers
generated, internally, 40 percent of the firm's sterling sales. In fact,
one justification for a merchant banker's involvement in foreign
exchange operations was that such activities provided a ready source
of good remittances for importers using the banker's letters of credit.
Every credit issuer appreciated the emergence of strong exchange
dealers whose bills could be taken with impunity. This explains in
part the Browns' failure in an earlier period to express too much dis-
pleasure over the Second Bank's leading position in the foreign
exchange market. The Second Bank's sterling bills on the Barings
made excellent remittances for the Browns' credit customers. Later
the circumstances were reversed. The Barings' resident manager,
Thomas Ward, did not consider the firm's inability to establish satisfactory joint exchange accounts with independent agents in the
major ports during the 1840s a serious deficiency, since his letter of
credit customers still had the alternative of remitting good bills on
Brown, Shipley & Co.[16]

The profit figures, revealed a few weeks later in the completed
1859 income statement, underscored the need for a realignment in
the firm's overall strategies. Profits on foreign exchange operations
dropped from $194,836 in 1858 to $64,073 in 1859. The profit
margin on $44,639,198 of sterling remittances was closer to 1/8
percent than the 1/4 percent figure originally estimated by the New
York partners. Again the response of the Liverpool partners was
pointed and far reaching: "You will no doubt agree with us that this
is not in any sense an adequate . . . compensation, and that some
change is indispensible." It was easier however "to arrive at these
conclusions than to point out the remedy."

Collet and Hamilton felt that there were two fundamental problems. In the south, they argued, the firm faced "excessive competition," while in New York there were problems with the short term
management of cash balances. Their analysis of southern operations
had an unusual twist. To the degree that vigorous competition

rendered the business unprofitable, "it has occurred to us as a fair inquiry whether it is not caused perhaps as much by ourselves as by others; whether in fact our anxiety to extend the business, at even reduced margins, has not materially contributed to the high rates which have prevailed in the South." Their ideas of prudence had prevented them from taking the riskier classes of bill which could be purchased at lower prices, and as a result of the increasing demand for the better class of bills, the partners had apparently "helped to raise & maintain the rate against ourselves."

The Liverpool managers willingly accepted their share of the blame for this unfortunate outcome. They had been among those urging increased business at smaller margins in the southern markets. It was now time to admit that this tactic had failed; "We have neither beaten our Competitors out of the field, nor made a satisfactory result for ourselves." As an alternative, the Liverpool partners suggested the adoption of a system of "buying only at the South (as you do in New York on all ordinary occasions) such Bills as leave a definite margin."

Turning to the second part of their analysis, the Liverpool partners questioned "whether the mode of raising funds in New York is not a source of more serious injury to the result of the Exchange business than the Competition in the South." Traditionally the only method the New York branch had employed to raise cash for its short term requirements was the sale of sterling. Collet and Hamilton cited the absence of supplementary sources of short term funds as an inhibiting factor in the search for higher profits: "It seems hopeless to carry on a large business in Exchange profitably, if the main reliance for funds is on drawing without immediate reference to the rate, or even to the desirableness of drawing at all, as a matter of profit." In former years, when profit margins were larger, the situation had not been viewed as critical to the firm's success; but now, they argued, when margins were much narrower, the lack of additional sources of ready cash had become an acute problem.

The Liverpool partners quickly dismissed several alternatives: "We are aware of the difficulty of lending money out safely at short call in your market, of the impossibility of any arrangement to supply yourselves temporarily by short loans, and of the insuperable objection to discounting." But, they queried, why not begin dealing regularly in commercial paper, or what they referred to as bills receivable? If the plan was adopted, the New York partners would be in a position to sell short term investments whenever money was needed, "in preference to drawing sterling at a disadvantageous rate." The branch could then draw beyond its requirements when exchange rates were high and still have the funds available later to invest in sterling at lower rates. Moreover, the Liverpool partners argued, "the character of the transaction, in reselling Bills Receivable, which can only have come into your possession by *purchase* for *Cash*, is so unexceptionable in its own nature, that we are quite disposed to recommend your trying it, if no greater objection exists than the comments it might excite." The branch would be a buyer as often as a seller in this market, and it would soon be apparent that the firm's becoming a more active dealer in commercial paper was "solely a means of making interest on [cash] balances."

If this plan was impractical and the New York partners had no other means of improving their method of fund raising, the Liverpool managers felt a smaller aggregate exchange business would probably "leave a *better* result, with diminished risk." "It may also involve your yielding the present pre-eminent position you hold as regulating to a great extent the Exchange market," they added, "but we do not attach great value to *that*, if the pecuniary result attending it is so unsatisfactory."

Collet and Hamilton further suggested that an improved result might be achieved "by seeking to regulate your Exchange business according to the views you may entertain of a probable rise or fall, instead of being at full stretch throughout the season." "We are not unmindful of your oft-repeated maxim as to the impossibility of foretelling the course of Exchange," they continued, "but within certain limits it never fails that Sterling is high in Summer & Autumn, & relatively low during the shipping season, and to this extent at least the known changes might be availed of."

Before closing, the Liverpool partners turned to another matter of potentially great importance. Earlier the New York house had forwarded overseas a copy of a letter from a businessman who proposed the establishment of a Cincinnati branch under his management.[17] Collet and Hamilton wrote in response: "Mr Knight's very interesting letter . . . further suggests the enquiry whether as the simple exchange business in Sterling has become so bare, it may not be expedient to combine with it the domestic business which appears to admit of such handsome profits. If Cincinnati be really the stable, sound, & wealthy place Mr. Knight represents, it seems to offer a far better sphere than any of the Southern points; & by combining it with them might apparently be made very profitable." At this point, however, they were not prepared to make any specific recommendation on the proposal. It was, they stated, only "one element in the reconsideration of the whole Exchange business, which has been forced to our notice by the investigation of the past year's result."[18]

Because of its broad scope, Collet and Hamilton's letter ranks among the most informative in the entire Brown collection. Their remarks show clearly that the partners planned their strategies in the foreign exchange market from the vantage point of leadership. The correspondence indicates that seasonal fluctuations in bill prices were becoming far less pronounced in the late 1850s. Indeed, on the basis of the Browns' experience in 1859, it appears that little seasonality remained in the prices of first class bills.

The profit picture was bleak. In March the Liverpool partners predicted a continuation of meager earnings in the field: "It is quite clear . . . that competition is forcing down margins in a way that we fear must be regarded as permanent."[19] Despite the seriousness of their discussions, the Browns adopted no new policies in the last year before the war. They finally put aside the preliminary plans for opening a new outlet in Cincinnati, and another in Galveston. But the debate on the proper management of the firm's cash position in New York continued.

The need for alternative methods of fund raising in an emergency was shown again during the brief "political panic" that occurred in mid-November on the heels of Lincoln's victory in the presidential election. Because of the disrupted exchange market, the New York branch sold sterling at embarrassingly low rates in order to raise sufficient cash to meet the incoming drafts from the south. When the Liverpool partners received an account of these latest difficulties, it disturbed them greatly.

In December Collet and Hamilton repeated with added force some of their earlier recommendations. They suggested the negotiation of a standing agreement with a large commercial bank which would entitle the firm to borow $500,000 at any time against the security of U.S. Treasury Bonds or bills receivable. After its negotiation, Collet and Hamilton hoped their transatlantic partners would freely use the new line of credit: "You . . . should exercise your right to put in & draw against your Bills Receivable, maturing within 14 or 21 days, whenever it suits your convenience; using this power from time to time, so as not to make it a mere matter of Reserve in times of difficulty."[20] After all, they asked, "What harm is there in *discounting paper* that you have held to within a fortnight of maturity ! Why, in fact, should you not buy and sell domestic paper as much as Sterling!" Upon reflection, the traditional stigma placed on exchange dealers who occasionally discounted seemed overly restrictive and in some ways irrational. In fact, they now argued that such borrowings "on real trade paper" were a "sign of strength" and not "weakness," as previously supposed.

One of the problems the partners faced in analyzing foreign exchange operations was the absence of meaningful internal reports on the sources and timing of profits. There were no breakdowns of earnings on either a month-by-month or a branch-by-branch basis. In fact, it was only at the end of the calendar year that the partners consolidated the branch accounts in New York and determined the overall profit figure. Yet, given the seasonal nature of their operations and the absence of a balance between selling and purchasing in the individual branches, the firm's use of one consolidated account was sensible from an accounting standpoint. The more sophisticated accounting techniques which might have aided in the analysis had not as yet been developed in the banking field.

The partners fully recognized the potential value of such reports, but no one in the organization knew how to approach a financial problem so complex. Who was to say, for example, whether the purchases of the New Orleans branch in the first week of the season were meant to cover the overdrawn account of the Baltimore, Boston, Philadelphia, or New York office? One thing can be said about the partners' general approach to the problem: they realized that artificial allocations between branches were meaningless for the organization as a whole and that superficial efforts at approximating a monthly or branch profit, under circumstances where purchases did not equal sales, was as likely to be misleading as enlightening. An appreciation of the complexities, however, did not compensate for the frustrations the partners experienced in attempting to examine their exchange account in a rational manner. Without adequate financial statements to guide them, the Liverpool partners had little to rely upon in identifying the underlying reasons for the firm's poor profit performance in 1859.

The Brown firm was not the first Anglo-American banking house to decry the increasing tempo of competition in the foreign exchange field. Baring Brothers & Co. concluded in the mid-1840s that the profit potential was insufficient to justify an expanded volume of joint account business with their American agents. Nor did the situation improve noticeably over the next fifteen years. The Barings reduced their aggregate credit line for uncovered exchange accounts from £125,000 in 1845 to £40,000 in 1860.[21] By comparison, the Browns maintained an uncovered account that was at times over twenty times larger, reaching a high point of £851,000, or just over $4,000,000 in the fall of 1859.[22]

The relative position of the two leading dealers in the foreign exchange market around the mid-century was not a matter of crucial importance, however. Competition flowed from too many directions.

The Browns did not single out one or two houses or even a group of firms as the perpetrators of the so-called excessive competition. Their opposition in the field was broadly based and included brokers and commercial banks as well as a host of private merchants who combined a limited foreign exchange business with their regular merchandising activities. So long as a dealer confined his activities to transactions that were completely covered (exchange was bought before it was sold), entry into the market was relatively easy.

The Browns also felt the effects of a gradual shift in the geographical destination of cotton exports. A larger percentage of the cotton crop left for continental countries each season, and exporters drew a corresponding volume of bills in Dutch guilders and especially French francs. Of course the Browns had bought a limited volume of continental bills since 1803, but the firm's southern branches did not have the authority to make large scale purchases in any currency other than sterling. In analyzing the condition of the local market for the New York office in December 1857, the New Orleans managers described the general demand for exchange, including continental bills, as unusually heavy. The demand even extended to bills on "fourth rate spinners without reference to Bills of Lading" or any other form or security. Houses they listed as active in the purchase of both sterling and francs were Vobs Lecesue & Co., Voights & Leausemand, Charles Kock & Co., and Shroeder & Co. as well as two chartered institutions, the Canal and Louisiana Banks.[23]

An underlying cause of the increased competition was the unprecedented prosperity of the entire American cotton market in the decade before the Civil War. Although advances on consignments remained high throughout the fifties, English payees dishonored very few of the bills drawn in the south against cotton shipments. Even the panic of 1857 failed to disturb unduly the southern economy. In fact, the region's ability to pass through a general crisis with relative ease after a sustained period of well-being seems to have convinced many enterprising businessmen that the risk of nonpayment on cotton bills had been significantly lessened. The predictable results of this reassessment were an expanded volume of transactions on the part of existing dealers and the entry of new firms into the market, even in the face of reduced profit margins. The Liverpool partners were less than sanguine about these developments in the summer of 1860: "Although many have lost on Exchange business this year there appears to have been only a temporary check — the facilities for passing Exchange are as great as ever from what we hear."[24]

Perhaps the main conclusion one draws from an analysis of the partners' operations in 1860 is the following: in the years immediately preceding the Civil War, the value of the southern outlets to the Brown organization was diminishing. The firm's consignment business had almost disappeared, and the purchase of sterling bills was virtually the only activity of the southern outlets. The profits accruing from the operation of a seasonally uncovered exchange account had reached a point where they appeared insufficient to justify the enormous amount of time required to manage the activities of the southern branches. Merely keeping the offices staffed with the proper personnel had become a burdensome task. When the outbreak of hostilities cut off the supply of southern exchange, the northern offices were forced to limit bill sales to the corresponding volume of their local purchases. Ironically, the political crisis dictated the adoption of a strategy very similar to one the Liverpool partners had proposed a year earlier. As a last resort, they had recommended the handling of a smaller volume of business at improved profit margins. Whether the southern outlets would have eventually lost their crucial role in the firm's exchange cycle in the absence of the war, of course, cannot be determined. But, in Liverpool at any rate, Collet and Hamilton had already concluded that the traditional pattern of managing the firm's foreign exchange account was losing its viability and less reliance on southern purchases was a possible remedy for sagging profits in this sphere of the business.

XI

Management and Administration

One of the important differences in the administration of the firm's letter of credit business and its foreign exchange activities was the degree of managerial control. In the letter of credit field, the partners soon learned that it took from six months to a year to effect meaningful changes in the total of their outstanding obligations. Foreign exchange operations, in contrast, could be turned around within as little time as sixty days, and significant adjustments were possible on a weekly or even daily basis. With their account responsive to a considerable amount of fine tuning, the English and American partners continually discussed monthly tactics as well as broad market strategies.

Although the senior men on opposite sides of the Atlantic jointly shared some of the responsibilities for managing the firm's foreign exchange operations, each branch was also charged with a certain number of specific duties. One of the prime responsibilities of the English office was to accept upon presentation the sterling bills sold through the firm's U.S. outlets and to arrange for their later payment. Equally important, however, was the Liverpool partners' participation in the correspondingly reverse process—that is, they themselves presented for acceptance the covering bills on other payees which their American counterparts regularly remitted for collection. In the short run, the associated inflow and outflow of cash was rarely in equilibrium. As a result, the Liverpool managers were expected to regulate their position in the English money market with skill whether they faced a cash deficit or a periodic surplus.

In addition, the Liverpool partners maintained credit files on a diversity of British firms frequently named by bill drawers in the United States. Their information on the standing of these payees guided the American representatives in their daily purchasing activities. Indeed, their reports were absolutely crucial to the firm's success in the field. The quantity and quality of credit information flowing in from overseas determined in large part the degree of risk inherent in any banker's foreign exchange operations.

The New York partners, on the other hand, were generally responsible for directing and coordinating the routine buying and selling activities of the American outlets. From an operational standpoint, they established the firm's quoted selling rates and communicated all the adjustments in those rates to the various representatives. In addition, they managed the investment of cash resources which seasonally accumulated in the north and later oversaw the transfer of those funds to the southern outlets. At the same time, the New York partners usually consulted Liverpool before making a decision to cover the exchange account with specie or merchandise shipments in place of bill remittances.

The Responsibilities of the English Partners

In the process of planning the firm's market tactics, the role of the Liverpool partners was essentially an advisory one because the actual implementation of shifts in the firm's overall position could only be initiated on the American side. Meanwhile, the mix of sterling debits and credits converging on the Liverpool branch in any given week was difficult to foresee. As a consequence, Mark Collet and Francis Hamilton had the strictly operational task of managing the exchange account in light of the most recent transatlantic advices of bill sales and purchases. Thus, the major responsibility for meeting the firm's immediate financial obligations rested squarely upon the shoulders of the Liverpool partners. When the partnership's plans went awry, they were the ones who felt the pressure most intensely.

Since they were regularly burdened with the task of financing seasonal deficits, it is little wonder that Collet and Hamilton were consistent advocates of a strengthening in the firm's overall liquidity. In correspondence with the New York office in February 1852, they discussed the procedures customarily followed in raising funds to replenish a temporarily weakened cash position. Since their letter was written during the height of the southern buying season, the Liverpool managers strongly urged their New York counterparts to keep them well supplied with bill purchases over the next few months. The American branches were already slow in covering their overdrawn accounts, and the Liverpool partners were concerned about the delay. Collet and Hamilton wanted to work their way back to a position where they would not have to discount any acceptances that they had not held in reserve for at least twenty to thirty days. "All we wish to avoid is to be *obliged habitually* to convert our remittances immediately after they are accepted, as it might be construed as arising from a paucity of means, of which we would not even wish to be suspected," they explained.[1]

In a further statement on their overall management philosophy Hamilton and Collet outlined their attitude toward raising funds through borrowing against security holdings:

> With regard to *borrowing on Stock* we should be *decidedly* averse to resorting to such a course, if *we had to do it in the open market,* & nothing short of *necessity* would induce us to take a step so unusual for a House occupying the position we do; but so long as we can get any advance upon them we may want, from our *own Bankers,* who know our circumstances & position, we should simply consult our own convenience in using these securities or not; but even with our Bankers we should first exhaust our Bills — as being the usual, recognized & legitimate mode of raising money.[2]

Throughout the fifties, the Liverpool managers argued for a reallocation of capital resources away from speculative investments and into more liquid assets that would build up the firm's working capital and secondary reserves. Although the Browns did not use modern terminology, they did distinguish between capital that was "available" for use in their normal business transactions in the trade sector and that which was "locked up" in real estate, steamship lines, and questionable railroad issues. The Liverpool partners considered investment funds locked up if they could not be used as an immediate source of cash in a time of need. Collet and Hamilton thought that only those assets which might readily serve as collateral for loans from respectable English bankers actually qualified for placement on a list of the firm's so-called legitimate reserves. This question of the allocation of capital and the quality of investments remained a divisive issue within the firms for many years because some of the partners felt the maintenance of a high degree of liquidity was not critical to the firm's success.

Collet and Hamilton offered two lines of argument in support of their proposals to enlarge the working capital of the Liverpool branch. First, they contended that the firm needed to put aside additional funds in order to prepare more fully for unforeseen monetary panics and other emergencies. Beyond that, the Liverpool partners hoped the increased liquidity would enhance the firm's prestige in British financial circles.

The New York partners, in contrast, favored the allocation of only a moderate amount of the firm's capital resources to the management of foreign exchange operations. Naturally they conceded that the English branch needed sufficient funds to maintain solvency and retain at least some degree of flexibility in the handling of the firm's account. At the same time, they felt a certain amount of pressure in Liverpool could be expected periodically, and a partial reliance on borrowed funds, whether obtained from other bankers or in the open market, was appropriate. Since large deficits were only a seasonal phenomenon, the New York partners saw little reason to keep a large portfolio of cash and near-cash assets at the service of the Liverpool office on a year-round basis. The holding of large cash balances was costly in terms of the potential foregone profits from alternative investment channels. Moreover, the New York partners had much confidence in the ability of their overseas associates to manage the account proficiently without excessive reserves.

Mark Collet and Francis Hamilton, on the other hand, had a more ambitious goal: in the long run they planned to elevate the firm (and themselves) to the stature of the House of Baring in the eyes of the commercial world. By keeping sufficient funds available in cash or near-cash assets so as to eliminate entirely their reliance on the discount market, they hoped to achieve that goal. On this point, an earlier quote is worth repeating: "We aim, and with perfect right — at a rank & position equal to the Barings, but it is impossible that we can maintain it if we are to be in the discount market week by week . . . whereas they never discount & are known to have always large sums lying at call."[3]

In view of their own more extensive foreign exchange operations, however, the New York partners questioned whether the Barings' conspicuous liquidity was a valid basis for a realistic comparison. The issue was clouded because the correspondents did not discuss the needs of the Liverpool branch in terms of specific amounts. As a result, the New York partners had difficulty determining how much working capital was realistically required for normal business operations and how much had been sought for window dressing and other nonquantifiable factors relating to prestige.

Although they failed to attain their maximum goal, Collet and Hamilton finally convinced their New York associates to bolster the liquidity of the Liverpool branch. A decreased reliance on discounts for seasonal financing in the late 1850s was one sign of the improvement in their position. In the first half of the decade, the Liverpool managers often raised from £300,000 to £500,000 per month through discounts.[4] The vast majority of these loans were negotiated directly with their London bankers, Denison Heywood Kennard & Co. and successor firms. The Browns' policy was to confine most transactions to the private discount market and to avoid, thereby, borrowing in the more visible "open" market for foreign acceptances. In December 1852 the Liverpool partners reported that they rarely turned to the open market more often than twice during the year.[5]

Two financial statements from the late fifties illustrate the strengthened working capital position of the Liverpool branch. One statement shows that the Browns relied on discounted acceptances for no more than 40 percent of their financial requirements during the panic of 1857 — a period when many Anglo-American bankers, including George Peabody, were on the verge of insolvency. The Liverpool branch presented the figures for the final quarter of 1857 as follows (M = thousands):

In Oct., Nov., & Dec. our payments were	£2,235 M
Toward which discounts supplied . . .	854
Of these discounts we took from:	
Bk of England	129
Alexanders	170
Overends	37
	£ 336 M

The Liverpool partners took the remaining £518,000 in discounts from their London bankers, Heywood Kennard & Co.[6]

A second statement prepared one year later summarized the branch's experience in the money market over the last half of 1858. The summary broke down their monthly payments as follows:

July		£ 729 M
August		651
September		607
October		465
November		582
December		475
	Total	£3,509 M

These figures are especially valuable because, given a two to three month lag, this payment schedule roughly paralleled the earlier pattern of sterling sales in the United States. Another part of the statement listed the monthly discounts:

July		£ 86,030
Aug-Oct.		None
November		149,753
December		135,472
	Total	£371,263

During the last quarter of 1858, discounts had provided only 20 percent of the branch's requirement. In their analysis the Liverpool managers pointed with pride to the fact that only £40,000 of their borrowing occurred in the open market.[7] But the Liverpool partners also disclosed that at times they had borrowed funds from the Bank of Liverpool which were repayable on demand. Secured by bills receivable (or acceptances receivable), these loans carried a favorable interest rate of one half a percent below the market rate for prime acceptances.

The tone of their remarks indicates that the arrangement with the bank was a new departure from the established mode of raising funds. At the same time, the Liverpool partners revealed that they had occasionally returned the favor and loaned money to the bank on call when their cash account contained a temporary surplus. In previous years, the branch had used idle balances to pay off outstanding acceptance liabilities before the normal sixty day expiration date. By paying in advance, the Liverpool managers liquidated their liabilities at less than face value, and the cost savings were the equivalent of interest revenue. In other words, the partners occasionally entered the money market on the supply side and discounted bills on themselves for other borrowers. The informal agreement with the Bank of Liverpool, possibly the first close business relationship with a strictly commercial bank, thereafter provided an alternative channel for putting idle cash balances to work temporarily.

A close analysis of the Browns' financial statements for 1858 reveals the improved position of the Liverpool branch. First, the total borrowings of £ 371,263 over the entire last half of the year were lower than the branch often required in a single month at the beginning of the decade on approximately the same volume of transactions. The schedule of monthly discounts shows how the deficiencies in the Liverpool account began to build up during the late fall and early winter. Real relief came later in the spring when the remittances of the firm's southern branches finally began to mature. Here in 1858 complete coverage of the interbranch account had not occurred until July.

By the end of the decade, the Liverpool partners had persuaded their New York counterparts to redirect the firm's resources away from speculative investments and into assets with greater safety and more liquidity. The partnership curtailed its involvement with a diversity of outside business interests and resumed the movement toward further specialization in foreign exchange operations and other financial services for the trading sector of the American economy. In August 1858 the New York house took $500,000 of a new U.S. government issue for the recently created reserve fund.[8] The new articles of partnership drawn up in 1860 provided for the acquisition of £180,000 in British Consols for the English Reserve Fund.[9] All in all the firm assumed more of the attributes of a conservatively and prudently managed banking house. The Browns communicated their greater financial independence to the business community through a decreasing reliance on the discount market.

A second major responsibility of the Liverpool partners could be broadly described as information gathering. In this sphere, the scope of their interests was extremely varied. However, most of the information they accumulated can be classified into two main categories: that which was likely to have an effect on the economy generally or a broad group of businessmen within the economy and that which was related to the credit standing of individual firms active in the Anglo-American trade. Within the first category, the Liverpool branch communicated to New York virtually every economic and political development in Europe or the British Empire which might have an impact on business conditions or foreign exchange rates. In fact, the developments they reported on were so diverse that they defy characterization. Only a few of the more important topics can be mentioned here. They usually attributed special significance to large specie shipments, large capital movements, changes in the Bank of England's rediscount rate, the state of the cotton market, major business failures, and war rumors. At the same time, the Liverpool partners generally emphasized those developments which they expected to have a detrimental effect on international trade. On these occasions they advised caution and sometimes an actual reduction in sterling sales.

A series of letters written during the spring of 1854 after the outbreak of the Crimean War illustrate both the range of factors the Liverpool partners considered and the policy recommendations they proposed in response to emerging developments. Six of the notes recorded in the partners' "private letterbook" from March through

June 1854, which are presented below in capsule form, give some insight into the nature of their concerns:[10]

March 25, 1854 — Collet and Hamilton to BB&C, New York
The Crimean crisis only shows that the best policy is to keep large means in England & not locked up in the U.S. Two main reasons are more safety in case of stringency & greater ease in expanding the letter & exchange business.

March 27, 1854 — Collet and Hamilton to William Brown in London
We fear war and high interest rates. We have asked New York to send us many first class bills so we can stay clear of the discount market or at least not have to rely on it for upwards of £500,000 per month as now. Their sales of exchange should be appropriately limited. We hope our government will keep on friendly footing with the U.S. The government & ministers should not meddle in trade but let it take care of itself or it is sure to involve them in trouble.

March 29, 1854 — Collet and Hamilton to William Brown in London
A review of our financial condition shows £585 M— in lockups of one sort or another & only £385 M— of available capital. The London bill brokers will do nothing at under 5 1/4%. With cotton declining in price, we see a disposition of payees to refuse acceptance. We worry about the drain in gold which will no doubt be caused by a foreign war.

May 12, 1854 — Collet and Hamilton to BB&C, New York
The Bank of England raised its rate one-half a percent yesterday to 5 1/2%. We are glad to learn you are considering borrowing against some of your securities. We would concur in a loan of substance for 12 months even at an interest rate of 7%. The money could be used here as a reserve; our greatest desire is to be prepared.

May 30, 1854 — Collet and Hamilton to BB&C, New York
There are many houses here who would extend us broad facilities, but it is best to prepare for the worst. If, on the other hand, we could come through a crisis with little resort to the open market, it would be a source of much pride. We think you should avoid opening all letters of credit which have the slightest chance of becoming lockups — even with regular customers.

June 9, 1854 — Collet and Hamilton to BB&C, New York
We would not object if you temporarily increased your sales in working a profitable exchange operation so long as it was at a rate that could be covered profitably in gold if we are short of

remittances. We appear to be in good shape this month even without gold.

Despite the urgency of their dispatches, a serious financial crisis never materialized, and by midsummer it was again business as usual. One false alarm did not, however, outweigh the advantages of an almost constant monitoring of new developments in the Anglo-American economy. The value of such information to the Brown organization was incalculable; in 1857 it helped bring the partnership through a genuine panic with ease — so much so in fact that the house achieved the lofty stature Collet and Hamilton had been so actively seeking.

The most time consuming phase of information gathering was the maintenance of credit files on the host of English firms who were frequently named as payees by American bill drawers. The Browns disseminated the credit ratings based on these files throughout the banking chain, and the ratings guided the outlets in their purchasing activities. The Liverpool partners quickly communicated any significant change in the status of British payees to the various American representatives. By the early fifties, the Liverpool files included reports on approximately 2,000 names. The list of firms ranged from major competitors in the foreign exchange field to wholesalers and manufacturers who regularly purchased American raw materials and foodstuffs on their own account. Without up-to-date information, large scale foreign exchange operations were an extraordinarily risky venture because the purchase of only one or two bad bills drawn in moderate amounts could easily wipe out a whole year's profits.

In assessing a firm's credit position, there were three major considerations. The means, or wealth, of the enterprise was a factor of critical importance. During the second half of the century more firms began to employ the limited partnership form of business organization, and the Browns had to keep closer track of the exact amount of capital individuals invested in each separate enterprise. A firm's reputation for promptly and judiciously meeting its obligations was almost equally important. The third factor for consideration was a firm's volume of business relative to its estimated resources. Even large businesses with solid reputations might come under sharp scrutiny if suspected of overtrading. But the reason for most alterations in a firm's standing was a change in the partnership alignment. Shifts in a firm's membership were common in the nineteenth century commercial community, and staying apprised of the latest additions and withdrawals was a meticulous task.

The sources of the Liverpool office's credit information are not fully known. Much of it came from the investigated firms themselves;

and more came from their bankers and other creditors. Because many of the firms were located outside Liverpool, the Browns relied on correspondents in other cities to provide them with a fair amount of information. One exchange of letters in 1859 with the National Bank of Scotland in Glasgow provides a good example of the handling of credit inquiries. Brown, Shipley & Co. wrote on April 18, 1859:

> We shall feel much obliged by your particular confidential report upon the *means & present standing* of Peter Buchanan & Co. of your city . . . The immediate object of our inquiry is to arrive at some *amount* which we might safely & prudently hold of their acceptances at one time running . . . we should esteem it a favor if you could suggest a *line* which it would be prudent to keep running.[11]

The bank's answer, dated April 21, read in part:

> *PB&Co.* enjoy a good reputation *here,* we may almost say of undoubted credit. We do not know the precise capital of the Coy., but we learn, on very good authority that P.B. is worth £200,000 chiefly in the business. He is a bachelor, cautious to a degree, careful, clear headed & saving. Mr. Harris . . . has at least £80,000 in the business . . . We may mention that . . . Drafts pass through our Hands, from time to time, for acceptance on account of one of our Banking Correspondents — the *aggregate* fluctuating from £3 or £4,000 to £10,000, or thereby, current at a time.[12]

Upon receipt, the Liverpool partners made a copy of the letter and sent it to the New York office for reference. On the basis of the "strength" indicated in the report, they wrote, "You cannot go wrong with a line of £10,000 [$48,000] running."[13] The suggested limit was only 3 percent of the reported capital and appeared to be a safe figure.

The acceptance line mentioned in the correspondence was one of the Browns' key managerial tools. The partners' decision to establish revolving lines on British payees came in response to the economic disturbances of 1847. Because the U.S. economy was not seriously affected by that European recession, the Browns and other Anglo-American bankers did not suffer too many setbacks. But the experience frightened the Liverpool partners, and they began examining their overall operations with an eye to improvement. One of the proposals receiving a favorable reception was the establishment of definite limits on the amounts of bills that would be purchased in the U.S. on specific payees during any given sixty day period.[14] The Browns felt the limits would impede a payee's overexpansion; more importantly, they would guarantee a well-diversified portfolio of acceptances in Liverpool. As the adoption of this plan illustrates, the concept of spreading risks over a broad spectrum of names was common to both their letter of credit and foreign exchange operations.

The actual setting of limits, or more accurately guidelines, was a shared responsibility, but in practice the New York partners generally deferred to the judgment of the Liverpool managers. A given line might call for either clean bills or documentary bills depending on a firm's capital, the nature of its transactions, and the extent of its business activity. Some lines were a combination of the two—for example, clean bills up to £20,000 and an additional £15,000 with bills of lading attached. As the years passed, the trend among exchange buyers was to insist on the bill of lading in a higher proportion of transactions. Eventually, the stigma of inferiority that was originally associated with the documentary bill of exchange faded. In the postbellum era, dealers invariably insisted on receipt of the bill of lading when they purchased drafts drawn against the country's two most important exports—cotton and foodstuffs. The Browns were not overly rigid in the enforcement of guidelines, thus there was generally room for some leeway on individual payees.

The identity of the original drawer could also be an important factor in determining the extent of the Browns' purchases. In May 1859, for instance, the Liverpool house told the New York office that they wanted "to keep as low as possible" certain classes of bills. Among them were Harper & Co. on E. Ridings & Bros., Don Rose on Wm. Anderton, and Thos. Rogers, Jr. & Co. on John Greaves. On the last named payee, they added the following:

> We have now £40,700 running upon him & he has probably as much or more through other channels, and we do not know how much of his Cotton he holds. Still he ought to be good upon his own means, & we would not imply that you might not take some more on him with B/Ldg from *sound* drawers, but that you should keep your eye on the line.[15]

The Browns exhibited the same cautious attitude in regulating their holdings of bills on the other Anglo-American banking houses. The only exception was, of course, the Barings whose bills, in any amount, they never questioned. With George Peabody & Co., on the other hand, they were far more careful. Doubts about the eagerness with which they had taken Peabody's bills arose as early as 1852. At a dinner party William Brown gave in November 1852, Peabody told his host in confidence that his outstanding acceptances stood at approximately £1,000,000 and that earlier in the year they had been as high as £1,200,000. The Liverpool partners relayed the details of the conversation to the New York office and added a note of caution: "It is strange if his engagements are only a million that we should hold one fifth — certainly more than our share."[16]

In the late 1850s, a mild controversy arose over the handling of confidential credit information — such as that volunteered by George Peabody. At issue was the proper relationship between the Brown partners and their subordinates and agents in outlying ports.

In correspondence with the New York branch in January 1859, the Liverpool partners wrote:

> Your private letter . . . is before us, and we sincerely regret to ob-serve the difference of opinion that still obtains between us, as to the mode of dealing with information about parties communica-ted to us in confidence, which we transmit to you under the same reserve. We must suppose that it arises from the different footing & understanding upon which such confidential information is given & received on the two sides of the Atlantic, for you are clear-ly in error when you express your belief that "Banks & others com-municating to us in confidence" *facts* relating to the *means* & transactions of parties (of which we could have knowledge thro' no other channel), suppose that we shall communicate the same to all our agents throughout the U. States!

On the contrary, the Liverpool partners wrote, the supposition in England was that they would form their own estimate of the parties based on the information given in confidence and thereupon give instructions to their agents and subordinates about the handling of the bills in question. The facts per se, on the other hand, they could not "in good faith or honor give . . . a wider circulation" than among the bona fide partners of the firms. An argument advanced earlier in New York, Collet and Hamilton completely rejected:

> The line you draw . . . that all Agents you have . . . are entitled to *all* the information bearing upon the standing of drawees, that come into your possession, includes not only the Agents them-selves, but the clerks . . . [left] in charge during their absence — un-known to us sometimes even by name — as deserving of the same confidence in the use of such information, as those who are your own partners; this surely is an assumption quite beyond the fact.

Moreover, the branch managers did not need to know all the con-tents of the private correspondence, the Liverpool partners claimed, "since after all it is *you*, not they, who regulate the lines you take on these names & the conditions on which they are taken." Although they were devoted to the proposition that subordinates should possess all the facts required for the safe conduct of the business, Collet and

Hamilton believed, in this instance, that limits were necessary. If the firm failed to impose reasonable limits on the dissemination of confidential credit information, it was in danger of losing the confidence of informants.[17]

The Liverpool partners drew on the accumulated credit information in making decisions on the release of bills of lading attached to the bills of exchange remitted to them for collection. So long as the partners held the bill of lading, the Browns in effect owned the merchandise associated with any documentary bill of exchange. Upon receipt of a documentary bill, the Liverpool managers checked closely the payee's credit standing. If his rating was satisfactory, they usually released the bill of lading at the time of acceptance. Otherwise, the Liverpool partners held the bill of lading until the actual payment date.

Besides the Browns, there were others who had a direct stake in the acceptance and payment of a remitted bill of exchange. In the United States, the firm's representatives always insisted on the seller's endorsement of a bill of exchange, and on those occasions when the British payee dishonored the bill, the Browns had recourse to the seller for reimbursement. Therefore, it was as much for the protection of their American customers as for their own protection that the Liverpool partners exercised judgment on the release of bills of lading. In most cases, the U.S. bill sellers left the whole matter in the hands of the Liverpool partners, but some sellers specified the preservation of their lien until the final payment date. Although the vast majority of remitted bills were processed routinely, the risk of nonacceptance or nonpayment was always present. Regardless of the cause of an irregularity, the Browns invariably acted swiftly and expertly in seeking a solution to the problem.

The amount of time and energy expended in the collection of one dishonored bill was often sizable. Inevitably, some English importers failed in the interim between shipment and a bill's due date. In some cases, a sharp drop in the price of a commodity encouraged British payees to discover excuses for nonacceptance. The reason payees most frequently gave for nonacceptance of a bill of exchange was the receipt of a cargo of allegedly inferior grades of cotton or grain. Some situations were not resolved until the Liverpool managers could transfer the cargo and the financial obligation associated with it to an alternative importer. On other occasions, they sold the cargo outright through local brokers. In settling many of the disagreements between English buyers and American sellers, the partners sounded as much like lawyers as bankers.

Problems associated with the handling of bills of lading increased rapidly after the middle of the nineteenth century. In the postbellum

decades the volume of documentary bills on American exports mul
tiplied on both an absolute and relative basis. While the undersea
cable was useful after 1866 in resolving some of the differences between buyers and sellers, any improvement was overshadowed by the
frequency and complexity of new disputes. Indeed, the cable seemingly stimulated as many disagreements as it settled. Higher
advances and a narrowing of price differentials on the major commodities in the English and American markets, which were arbi-
traged out through cable transactions, were contributing factors to a
higher percentage of international quarrels into which foreign exchange dealers were often drawn.[18] In fact, the inability of small and
intermediate-sized dealers to cope with the demanding task of
handling documentary bills may have been one of the key reasons for
the emergence of a more oligopolistic market structure in the last
four decades of the century.

One of the most effective weapons the Browns had at their disposal
in dealing with recalcitrant drawees was the threat of a damaged
credit rating. In an aggravated situation, the Liverpool partners
could instruct their American representatives to suspend an English
buyer's acceptance line. The cessation of their purchases of bills of
exchange drawn on the designated payee would soon become a
matter of public knowledge, and there are indications in the partners'
correspondence that the Browns believed other exchange dealers
were likely to react in a similar manner.

In one notable controversy during the late 1870s, an English grain
importer — Schroder, Walsh & Co. — balked at accepting a bill presented by the Liverpool partners because of an alleged infraction of
the sales contract by a Baltimore grain dealer. As compensation,
Schroder, Walsh & Co. demanded a rebate. After exchanging
numerous letters and cables about the matter with Liverpool, the
Baltimore partners sized up the situation this way: "It looks as
though parties were endeavoring to take advantage of our position to
force an allowance of a rebate to which they are not strictly entitled."[19] The rebate figure was, as it happened, just sufficient to reduce the importer's net purchase price to the current market price in
England. The Baltimore branch did not think the similarity was
merely coincidental:

> If a respectable house, after ordering a cargo & fully accepting
> the terms by letter, can on the presentation of bills, repudiate
> the whole & claim to pay only what the market value may be, a
> new risk certainly is developed in the business. Such an attempt
> we have heard our oldest shippers say would be sufficient cause
> for expulsion from the Corn Exchange, and when known here, we

think Schroder, Walsh & Co. will find it an obstacle to further purchase, as we will consider it a grave objection to bills upon them by whoever they may be drawn.[20]

Eventually, the matter was settled satisfactorily, without injuring the payee's reputation.

However, in this case, and many like it, the Liverpool partners assumed the role of mediator between the buyer and seller of an American cargo. And as a rule, they received little direct compensation for their efforts. Although bill sellers were often lavish in their praise of the Liverpool partners' handling of seemingly hopeless entanglements, their appreciation was not always in evidence in the final financial settlements. Once the crisis had safely passed, sellers sometimes criticized the Browns for not maximizing their return, and at times the partners had difficulty obtaining reimbusement for out-of-pocket expenses. Baltimore exporters, at any rate, were often a thankless lot.

The Liverpool partners' ability to protect the value of the collateral standing behind their foreign exchange holdings was one manifestation of the skills they employed in assuming their share of the responsibilities for the firm's transatlantic account. From the management of the partnership's position in the money market to the accumulation and assessment of credit information, the Browns' English partners had few peers in the field of foreign exchange operations.

The Responsibilities of the New York Partners

After the firm's reorganization in the late 1830s, the responsibility for directing the foreign exchange activities of the American branches moved from Baltimore to the New York branch. In the following two decades the New York partners, with the aid of the telegraph, intensified their control over the operations of the subsidiary branches. A major goal of the organization was the development of a more coordinated, standardized system of management. One policy instituted to achieve this goal was the maintenance of a uniform rate structure throughout the banking chain. The partners established their selling rate in the New York market and communicated adjustments to the subsidiary branches over the telegraph. In the early fifties prices changed only once or twice a week, but by the late seventies the firm's outlets received rate adjustments as often as four or five times each day. Except in unusual circumstances, the branch managers outside New York had no control over the prices at which they offered sterling bills for sale.[21]

Broadly speaking, there were two fundamental factors influencing the Browns' pricing tactics. The partners began with an assessment of the competitive situation in the New York market. In analyzing their current rate structure, the partners generally reviewed the outside market forces which were likely to develop over the next week to ten days. A second consideration was the firm's internal priorities. Whether the partners decided to stimulate or discourage sales might depend on their overall cash position, the status of the account with the Liverpool branch, the level of interest rates on short term paper, or their intuitive feeling about the future trend of business.[22]

In truth, there is no precise way of describing how the partners settled on a specific rate. Fundamentally, a given rate was merely a reflection of the New York partners' best judgment in light of all the relevant variables. In the meantime an obvious mistake could be quickly rectified. For instance, a premature drop in rates could attract such a flood of buyers that the New York partners might be forced to send out cancellations of their previous instructions to all the branches. In short, the rate setting mechanism was sufficiently flexible that adjustments were possible on a trial and error basis.

The quotation of sterling rates is a topic that, despite its peculiarities and technicalities, must be clearly understood. The prices of sterling bills were quoted in terms of percentage deviations from an official par that by the mid-nineteenth century no longer had any real economic significance. Despite its lack of relevance, the quotation system survived because merchants had become accustomed to it over a long period of time, and they had no difficulty in extrapolating its underlying monetary importance. This official, but fictitious par, was fixed at the rate of $4.44 to the British pound. There was, however, another rate of exchange which did have real meaning. After the coinage act overvaluing gold in relation to silver passed Congress in 1834, it took exactly $4.86 in gold to coin a British sovereign. When the exchange market was in a state of equilibrium, the $4.86 rate was the actual par figure. Yet in a very confusing practice, foreign exchange dealers continued to quote the new par in terms of the old. That is, the equilibrium rate was stated as the ratio of $4.86/$4.44 or 109 1/2 percent. As a result, deviations from this par figure were quoted in terms such as 107 1/4, 108 1/2, 112, 106 3/4, and so on. In order to convert these percentage deviations into a meaningful price, the quoted rates had to be multiplied by $4.44. Under this system a sterling discount of 108 1/2, for example, was equal to $4.8174, while a premium of 112 equaled $4.9728. As the century wore on, there was greater precision in the quotations; the differentials narrowed from one half a percent to quarter percents, to eighths, and finally one sixteenths of a percent. It eventually took an act of Congress in 1873 to force merchants and exchange dealers to abandon this anachronistic quotation system. Beginning in 1874, sterling was quoted in terms of American gold dollars; thereafter typical quotations were listed as $4.8425, $4.88375, $4.87 less 1/16, and the like.

Because there were two variables incorporated in the price of every bill, dollar-sterling exchange rates were rarely equal to the theoretical equilibrium rate of $4.86 or 109 1/2. One variable was the premium or discount on British currency which reflected the fundamental balance of payments between the two countries. The other variable incorporated in the bill price was an interest component which compensated the buyer for the delay in realizing the proceeds of the bills in sterling. Regardless of the inherent discount or premium on any given bill of exchange, the interest component *always* served to *depress* somewhat its price. The built-in interest component had a similar effect on other monetary obligations not payable upon sight or demand, but at some date in the future. It was only after 1866, when funds could be cabled to England almost instantaneously, that transactions occasionally took place largely unaffected by interest rate considerations.

In the antebellum decades, the Browns quoted rates for sterling bills drawn only at 60 days sight. Although customers could also negotiate purchases of bills with other maturities, the partners generally asked very steep rates for bills drawn for periods shorter than the standard 60 days. Within this category of "short bills," the two most commonly in demand were those payable 3 days after acceptance in Liverpool and those payable immediately upon presentation. Through the practice of discriminatory pricing, the partners deliberately tried to discourage the sale of short bills and to restrict transactions to the customary sixty day sight bill.[23] This policy was adopted for the convenience of the Liverpool branch. The payment of short bills disturbed the regular pattern of business in Liverpool and consequently the customer paid an abnormally high rate in order to compensate the partners for the "costs" of portfolio adjustments.

By the late 1860s, however, the costs of portfolio adjustments had fallen to zero on three day sight bills, and the Browns regularly quoted selling rates for both 3 d/s and 60 d/s bills. In this later period customers paid no penalty when purchasing bills drawn at the shorter maturity date; the differential in the two rates was entirely a function of the interest rate component built into the lower priced sixty day bill. At the same time the Browns retained discriminatory rates for bills payable on demand and for cable transfers.[24]

Although conditions in the New York market usually had an overbearing influence on the firm's sterling rates, there were occasions when the partners explicitly took into account the situation in an outlying market. In October 1859 the New York partners told the Baltimore manager that there was a heavy demand for sterling at the current rate, and they had considered an increase, but in the end they had decided to maintain the same price for a while longer. The reason given for this decision was quite interesting: under normal circumstances, they said, rates would have been raised at once "were it not that we don't want to interfere with our purchases at the South."[25] In other words, the partners compared the probable increased revenues in the northern branches to the probable increased costs of southern purchases after the news of a boost in rates reached Mobile and New Orleans and concluded that the southern costs outweighed the northern revenues. A sudden rise was still a real possibility, they cautioned the branch manager, and he was therefore urged to "*sell as little as possible* . . . submit any offers to us." On another occasion in 1859 the New York partners postponed a planned drop in their rate because the Philadelphia branch was continuing to do a "good business" at the old rate.[26]

Occasionally, the New York partners made private sales to exchange brokers at discount prices. In their haste to raise cash in December 1859 the partners arranged a large sale of sterling with a New York broker without giving the outlying branches any forewarning. In Baltimore the ramifications of the sale were far reaching. Within a few days the branch manager, William Graham, heard reports that his chief competitor, McKim & Co., was not only selling sterling on Brown, Shipley & Co., but at rates below his own. Writing to the main office the next day, Graham protested this turn of events: "I think it would be greatly to your advantage in the long run to put your agents upon the same footing as yourselves . . . as parties will go elsewhere when they find you make discriminations."[27]

In response, the New York partners expressed much sympathy with Graham's plight in Baltimore. They then spelled out the circumstances of the private sale and went on to explain why the transaction was handled in the way it was:

> As a general thing we place our branches on the same footing in regard to sales of Exchange as ourselves . . . but there are special times when we cannot help ourselves and are obliged to take the best advantage of the market that we can . . . as it was necessary to meet heavy drafts on us, we were obliged to accept subrosa offers for large amounts under our regular rates and where we *knew* that the orders were from out of town people and might interfere with our agents, we declined them—had we put down our rate at the counter and authorized you to do the same, our ob-

ject would not have been accomplished, as others who were also anxious to sell would have given away still more and thus would have interfered with us. On a falling market when anxious to sell freely, it is difficult to regulate exactly as we would wish.[28]

Other scholars have pointed to the Browns as a price leader in the 1880s, but this passage suggests that they had already attained that position in the 1850s.[29]

These examples illustrate the Browns' market power and their ability to interfere, at least temporarily, with the normal rate adjustment mechanism which operated among the various port cities after the telegraph system was completed. Of course, the fundamental basis for their competitive advantage was a superior, more centralized information system. Nonetheless, it must be emphasized that the occasions on which it was both possible and profitable to manipulate foreign exchange rates were the exception—not the rule. Aside from the partially seasonal aspect of their operations, the Browns' main function was that of a broker, or middleman, between the current sellers and buyers of exchange. And from that standpoint, the absolute level of rates, except for exceptionally high premiums or low discounts, was not a matter of crucial importance. Their primary concern was the maintenance of a sufficient margin between any given selling rate and the price simultaneously paid for covering bills of exchange. In fact, an analogous argument explains their lack of concern over the level of the interest rate component in bill prices; so long as the same rate was built into the prices of the bills they bought as well as sold, the interest revenues and expenses offset one another. This factor is important in explaining why the competition among foreign exchange dealers drove the interest component in bills down to a figure which corresponded more closely with the generally lower short term English rates than with U.S. interest rates.

One further point related to the pricing mechanism for sterling bills during the antebellum period should be mentioned. In addition to the variations in rates for foreign exchange, there were, at times, also differing rates for domestic exchange. That is, the currency issued by the banks in one American city, or more often in the banks in one state or section of the country, was not always accepted at par—or face value—throughout the United States. There were weeks when domestic exchange on Baltimore, for example, passed at a slight premium in New York; a slight discount in Charleston; a moderate discount in Mobile; and a rather heavy discount of 1 to 1.5 percent in New Orleans. And what was true of Baltimore could also be said for every other port city where the Browns had representatives. During those periods when exchange rates on domestic bills fluctuated, the partners faced even greater difficulties in maintaining uniform prices throughout the branch system for sterling bills.

By requiring customers in outlying cities to pay for their sterling purchases in the equivalent of New York funds, the Browns solved the problem of fluctuating rates on domestic exchange. If, for example, Philadelphia funds passed at a 0.5 percent discount in New York, then Philadelphia merchants in effect paid that much above the quoted rate for sterling bills. On the other hand, when Philadelphia funds were a 0.5 percent premium, the local merchants paid that much less. In theory, the pluses and minuses might have balanced out except that the exchange of outlying areas passed at a discount in New York more often than at a premium. Thus, on this account, the Browns were invariably net gainers over the course of any given year.

Complications involving domestic exchange were the greatest during the southern buying season. The southern outlets paid for most of their foreign exchange by drawing domestic drafts on the New York office. So many other dealers followed the same procedure during the winter months that New York funds often passed at a discount in the New Orleans and Mobile markets. When this happened, the effective purchase price of sterling bills increased by an amount equal to the discount. For example, in the first week of 1860 the sterling rate in New Orleans was reportedly 107 1/8, with the discount on New York funds ranging from 3/4 to 7/8 of a percent.[30] The New York partners calculated their net cost on purchases at 108 to 108 1/8 and set their selling rate in the northern branches at 109. Whenever the discount on New York funds fell below 1 percent, the firm began contemplating specie shipments as a substitute for domestic bills. In December 1859 the New York partners told the Baltimore manager they were seriously considering such a transfer: "We shall likely have to send some gold to New Orleans . . . the sight rate there for drafts on New York having gone to 1 1/4% discount."[31]

During the height of the buying season, the New York partners sometimes had such difficulty avoiding a cash shortage that they asked the southern representatives to draw on them at from five to ten days sight. Hearing a rumor to this effect in January 1860, the Baltimore manager queried them about the practice; and the New York partners confirmed the story:

> All our Southern friends draw on us for a portion of their wants at 5 days & 10 days sight . . . they do so at our request so as not to have large amounts drawn at sight which is inconvenient when the

business is large in the South, forcing us at times to sell exchange at lower rates than we would if we were more independent. Drawing at 5 days sight gives us two steamers to provide means to pay with.[32]

It was this same problem of inadequate supplementary sources of cash that the Liverpool partners complained about at length in the previous chapter.

Administering the purchasing activities of the various branch offices was in many ways a more burdensome task for the New York partners than the formulation of sales tactics. Although the quality of bills bought and remitted to Liverpool was generally high, a subsidiary office exercised far more latitude in its purchasing activities than in its selling activities. Whereas the firm sold a homogeneous item, namely its own sterling, the partners had to reimburse their account through bill purchases in an open market where various grades of bills circulated freely. In the northern branches, the firm generally bought acceptable bills at 0.5 percent less than the current selling rate. For bills drawn on their own Brown, Shipley & Co. and sometimes those on the Barings, the American branches normally offered the holder an additional 0.25 percent.

The New York partners assumed responsibility for holding the volume of bills purchased on individual payees to the guidelines suggested by the Liverpool house. To maintain control, the main office regularly gathered information from each outlet on the character of its bill purchases. The partners listed the bill purchases in a tickler file so that they could "keep posted up on the position of every account."[33] They also noted whether bills of lading or any other documents were attached to each bill. Whenever a payee's line was temporarily full, the New York house advised all the offices in the chain to avoid the name or to take it only with bills of lading attached. If there was any urgency about closing down a payee's line, the partners sent the message out over the telegraph. Later, when a sufficient amount of the payee's bills had been paid in England, the partners reopened the line and their representatives received authorization to resume purchases.

Although restricting the volume of purchases on individual payees was a useful technique for partially reducing the risk of loss of dishonored bills, another consideration of equal importance was the reputation and financial strength of the bill seller. A trustworthy party on the American side was necessary in most transactions because in the event a bill was dishonored in England, the Browns then looked to the previous endorser, that is the seller, for reimbursement. All their bill purchases were, in a sense, conditional because the Browns always had recourse to their customers whenever a bill returned to the United States unpaid. Therefore, the partners instructed their representatives to purchase bills only from responsible parties.

Among the other factors the Browns considered in purchasing a bill of exchange were the number of days to its maturity and the city on which it was drawn. In a quite logical reversal of their posture as bill sellers, the Browns — as bill buyers — had no objections to the purchase of bills drawn at short maturity dates. Long bills, or those over sixty days, they categorically would not take unless all those associated with the transaction enjoyed exceptionally good credit. In fact, they rarely bought any long bills other than those drawn on the Barings. In neither category, however, was there any price discrimination; the relative prices paid for covering bills drawn at varying maturities were solely the function of the built-in interest component. Indeed, it is only with reference to purchasing activities that one can adduce the presence of English interest rates in American bill prices during the antebellum era.[34] Sterling bills payable outside London, on the other hand, did not receive full rates. During the late 1850s, the Browns took bills on other English cities at one quarter of a percent below the prevailing rates and Scottish bills at discounts ranging from three eighths to one half of a percent.[35]

In another significant variation from their sales procedure, the Browns occasionally purchased foreign exchange drawn in European currencies other than sterling. The three most important were Dutch guilders, French francs, and German marks. Their purchases of bills drawn in these currencies roughly corresponded with changing patterns in the export trade. When Alexander Brown first entered the foreign exchange market at the turn of the century, he was a regular buyer of Dutch guilders drawn against tobacco shipments leaving Baltimore and ports in Virginia for the continent. By the second quarter of the century, the firm also bought a few French francs and German marks associated with the tobacco trade, but in comparison with the volume of sterling purchased, the extent of their transactions in continental currencies declined. Among the factors discouraging the negotiation of continental exchange were the laws on the handling of documentary bills. For many years dealers on the continent were required to release bills of lading when a French payee accepted a bill of exchange, and without the option of maintaining control over the merchandise until the final payment, the Browns and other dealers were reluctant to handle obligations payable outside Britain.[36] In fact, many of the continental bills they bought were actually payable in London, where the objectionable laws could be circumvented.

To guide them in the management of the foreign exchange account, the New York partners compiled regular summaries of the American offices' position vis-à-vis the Liverpool branch. The main office prepared a statement of the overall "sterling balance" each week after digesting the outlying branches' reports of their recent sales and purchases of bills of exchange. The partners used the statement as a tool for decision making, and they then passed it on to the branch managers. One report taken from their letter of September 21, 1859, to the Baltimore manager showed a substantial deficit:[37]

Sterling Balance[a]

Due by BB&C (to BS&C)	£419.529	Available Rems.	£162.886
Due by B&B (Phila)	324.620	of which with B/L 10.135	
Due by Wm H. Graham (Baltimore)	61.500	on demand 22.000	
	805.649	as 3 d/s 18.000	
Increased (Over last week)	£42.484	Rems on themselves (BS&C)	£4.300
		Drawings not remitted	£49.039

[a] My additions in parenthesis

According to the statement, the accounts of the three branches in New York, Philadelphia, and Baltimore, had overdrawn their Liverpool account by approximately $3,864,000.[38] Of the available remittances, less than 10 percent had bills of lading attached; almost 25 percent were drawn at short sight; and about 2 percent were on Brown, Shipley & Co. itself. The £49,000, or approximately $235,000, listed as drawings not remitted was the amount due in Liverpool from the firm's letter of credit customers during the upcoming weeks. Weekly reports like the above were instrumental in creating a sense of involvement. Given the limited role of subordinates and agents in the decision-making process, the main office kept them surprisingly well informed about the status of the overall foreign exchange account.

Joint Responsibilities

Some managerial decisions were rarely made without extensive consultations between the New York and Liverpool branches. One important topic falling within the area of shared responsibilities was the coverage of the foreign exchange account through any form of remittance other than bills of exchange. Thus the partners on both sides of the Atlantic generally participated in the discussions which — on occasion — led to the partial coverage of the Liverpool account with the proceeds from a transatlantic transfer of securities, specie, or merchandise. Of these three alternatives to the bill of exchange, specie shipments were the most significant because of their frequency and their relationship to movements in the dollar-sterling exchange rate. Therefore, a brief review of the firm's early experience in the Anglo-American specie markets is the logical starting point for an analysis of the alternative modes of exchange account coverage.

The Brown collections provide a substantial amount of evidence on a broad subject which has long interested economic historians generally and monetary historians in particular: the sensitivity of the nineteenth century international monetary system to the so-called gold point mechanism.[39] During the antebellum era, the price of sterling normally varied in a fairly narrow interval around the British mint par, which was $4.86 or 109 1/2 after 1834. In theory, the cost of importing and exporting specie determined the amplitude of the fluctuations away from the par figure. The main costs of transfer were freight charges, insurance fees, and the loss of interest revenue while the specie was in transit. Any tendency of exchange rates to move beyond these so-called "specie points" would discourage the continuance of transactions involving bills of exchange and, alternatively, lead to the shipment of gold or before 1834 silver. However, monetary economists have noted periods in the first half of the century when the observed sterling rates fluctuated away from par by an amount greater than the estimated costs of specie shipments. These violations of the supposed limits of price variations have inevitably raised serious questions about the precise levels of the "effective" specie points and about the actual degree of responsiveness on the part of merchants and bankers to what appear, in retrospect, to have been profitable opportunities to settle financial accounts in specie rather than bills of exchange. On this issue, the Browns' records seem to have a special, and perhaps unique, relevance. They include a series of calculations of specie points and the details of various specie shipments. In addition, the partners' correspondence often reveals the rationale that lay behind the timing and extent of their transatlantic shipments.

Despite some enlightening features, the Browns' data cannot be relied upon to resolve all the points at issue in the debate over the effectiveness of the early gold point mechanism. Not all of the firm's activities, for example, can in fact be understood strictly with reference to such externalities as the general level of exchange rates and transportation costs. The partners initiated some shipments solely in response to internal pressures for liquidity, while they undertook others in partially altruistic efforts to ease the consequences of a financial panic. At times, the American partners also failed to maximize what were, according to the calculations of the Liverpool house, profitable opportunities to cover their exchange account with specie instead of bills of exchange.

The Browns' calculations of specie points date from the early 1820s. The timing of their interest in such transactions coincides, predictably, with the Bank of England's resumption of specie payments in 1821, after a long suspension due to the disruptions of the Napoleonic Wars. For the next thirteen years—until the passage of the 1834 law—exchange rate movements were such that the Browns contemplated specie imports as well as exports. Because the knowledge of specie points was only relevant during a period when the price of exchange was either unusually high or unusually low, the partners made calculations periodically on a more or less ad hoc basis.

The low sterling rates which prevailed during the first six months of 1823 stimulated the Browns to consider the possibility of specie shipments to the United States. After allowing for the loss of five months interest, the Baltimore partners estimated that the break even point on silver importations would be reached when the sterling rate had fallen to 104 1/2, a figure roughly 5 percent below par.[40] In order to allow for a reasonable margin of profit and to hedge against the risk of a later rise, however, the partners settled on a lower rate of 103 as the actual figure at which specie imports would begin. As it happened, exchange rates began rising in the second half of 1823, and the Browns undertook no specie shipments.

The firm faced a similar situation in the summer of 1830. The Baltimore partners calculated a break even rate on specie imports at 106 or 106 1/4.[41] Their analysis of a hypothetical transaction reveals the procedures foreign exchange dealers employed in estimating specie points:[42]

$21,000 weighing 18.151 oz. at 4/9 p. oz.	£ 4310.17.3
Brokerage 1/4, Freight 3/8, Ins. 5/8 (1 1/4)	53.17.8
5 months interest at 4%	72.14.8
	4437. 9. 7

at 6%	$20,905.45	
Amt. invoice	$21,000.00	
gain	94.45 [sic]	Import rate = 6 to 6 1/4%

The partners estimated the total transfer costs at approximately 3 percent of the sum involved. They expected shipping costs to account for 1.25 percent of the total, and lost interest revenues, or what economists call opportunity costs today, they put at slightly over 1.75 percent.[43]

When the new law lowering slightly the gold weight of dollars, and thereby overvaluing gold in terms of silver, went into effect in 1834, the Baltimore office promptly calculated a new break even point for gold importations.[44] At sterling rates below 105 3/8, the partners estimated that gold shipments would be profitable. Because bill prices during most of 1834 were, in fact, below that figure, gold shipments to the United States were extremely heavy. In a letter to the Liverpool house in July 1834, the Baltimore partners expressed their willingness to continue such importations as long as the "rate of bills will allow it."[45]

In contrast, the Browns' records include few calculations of break even points for the export of specie from the United States in the 1820s and early 1830s. Their relative absence lends support to the hypothesis, advanced by other scholars like Lance Davis, J. R. T. Hughes, and Peter Temin, that the sterling rate in the period from 1821 to 1834 rarely approached a figure sufficiently high to induce a flow of specie from the United States to England. In other words, there were apparently few occasions when such calculations had any practical value. However, an exception to this generalization must be made for the fall of 1831. In October the American branches reported a shipment of $700,000 in specie to the Liverpool house against a substantial volume of bill sales at a rate of 111.[46]

One month later, in November 1831, the Baltimore partners told their Charleston agent that silver dollars were still advancing on the London market and they expected further shipments until the exchange rate fell a little more. At the same time, they wrote, many people believed the Second Bank of the United States would lower its rate soon "so as to prevent dollars going."[47] Their remarks suggest that the break even point on specie exports was slightly below the prevailing rate—perhaps in the range of 110 1/2 to 110 3/4.

The exact figures are not especially important; what is significant here was the Browns' sensitivity to the opportunities for profit in specie transfers. Although the band within which exchange prices might fluctuate without stimulating shipments was fairly wide in this period, there were still definite limits to the variations; and at least one of the leading banking houses of the day calculated these limits with precision. Nonetheless, the relationship between the firm's normal foreign exchange operations and specie movements was not a particularly close one at this time. Sterling rates, as a rule, were not high enough to make coverage of the Liverpool account with specie a profitable substitute for the standard bill remittance. At the same time, those specie transactions which periodically took place during the twenties and thirties were initiated strictly with reference to price, and not to internal pressures for liquidity.

In the succeeding two decades, however, gold exports became almost a regular feature of the firm's foreign exchange cycle. The sterling premium was consistently higher during the 1840s and 1850s, and the Browns' operations were much more seasonal in character. Most shipments to the Liverpool house occurred in the six months from June to November when bill sales normally exceeded bill purchases by a wide margin. With a well-timed schedule of gold shipments, the Liverpool partners were rarely forced to rely too heavily on the discount market for financing. Institutional arrangements in the foreign exchange market were responsible, in part, for the frequency of international specie transfers in the antebellum era. Until the undersea cable became operational in 1866, communications were so poor that few bills in the United States were drawn at short maturities; the only method of achieving liquidity rapidly was through the transfer of specie. After the Civil War, in contrast, the supply of three day sight bills was abundant, and the pressure on the gold stock diminished.

A series of letters from the Liverpool partners to the New York branch in 1859 illustrate the planning of specie transactions. In correspondence dated April 29, Collet and Hamilton spoke of the need to begin the seasonal discounting of acceptances within two or three weeks.[48] For their maximum convenience in meeting commitments, they suggested a specie shipment in preference to bill remittances. The gold proceeds would be used "to supply our first heavy deficiency in June," they explained. Interestingly enough, Collet and Hamilton did not suggest a sterling rate at which such an alternative mode of coverage would be justified. In correspondence one week later, however, the Liverpool partners were more explicit about the conditions under which gold should be shipped. Specie was their first choice, "even if you have to send it without profit," but they were "not yet prepared to ask you to ship any at a loss."[49] From his vantage point in New York, James Brown attributed Collet's nervousness about the firm's position to the fact that outstanding acceptances against the house were "upwards of 3 millions [£], a larger sum than ever before." Even so, James felt "all will probably go right unless there becomes a panic in the cotton market."[50]

Later that year, the Liverpool partners indicated that there were still many situations in which relative prices might be a prime consideration in determining the coverage mix. The low costs one of the firm's major competitors had reportedly incurred on a recent series of specie transfers came up for discussion in the correspondence of July 29. The freight rate on gold bars carried by the latest steam-powered screwboats was put at only 1/8 to 3/16 of a percent. If the bars had been bought at par in the United States, Collet and Hamilton noted, the gold remittance would "stand" at under 110 in England and perhaps as little as 109 3/4, provided the specie had been immediately resold for export. Maybe, they suggested, the New York partners had been unaware of these low freight rates. Since the firm's selling rate had been recently reported at 110 1/2, the Liverpool partners argued that it "would be better to have gold than bills at 10 to 10 1/4%."[51]

In their response, the New York partners maintained that difficulties in obtaining gold in bar form had deterred them from shipping specie. And gold coin they did not like to ship "except at a profit on the worst result of it when melted and sent into the Bank [of England], which you calculate at 10 1/4%."[52] The Liverpool managers took exception to this statement. They now claimed that it was "*always* worth while to give Specie the preference over Bills when at the worst result of the coin or Bullion you can do *as well* as with Bills."[53] And based on the subsequent actions of their American counterparts, the arguments of Collet and Hamilton were apparently persuasive.

When, in the face of rising demand, the New York partners jumped their selling rate from 110 to 110 1/2 in the last days of October, they did not miss the opportunity to cover a portion of their sales with a transfer of specie. The New York office divulged the details of the transaction to the Baltimore branch manager: "We sent per *City of Washington* $300,000 gold at 1/8th a percent freight to BS&C which remits us equal to 60 d/s bills at less than 10%."[54] A gold shipment at this time of the year had not been been originally planned, the New York partners explained a few days later, but "the early cold snap of weather did not extend far enough south to effect the rate of exchange as we had anticipated, causing a temporary scarcity of bills."[55] A month later, the firm was actively purchasing sterling in the south at 108 or less, and all talk of gold remittances ceased for the next four or five months. For the year as a whole, the New York branch shipped gold valued at $2,908,992 to the Liverpool office. This sum accounted for approximately 6 percent of the firm's remittances in 1859.[56]

The Browns' experience strongly indicates that the gold adjustment mechanism functioned almost exclusively through the foreign exchange dealer. Very few of the firm's customers initiated specie transfers on their own as an alternative to the sterling bill. Although many buyers complained of steep rates and energetically sought lower prices from competitive dealers, a thorough search of the records over several decades did not reveal a single instance in which a customer threatened to ship gold rather than pay the Browns' rates. Even at prices as high as 110 1/2 to 111 1/2, sales were often brisk. In fact, it was only during a serious financial panic that the sterling premium ever climbed sufficiently high to induce the general public to attempt the settlement of international debts with specie. When this happened in 1837 and 1857, the commercial banks promptly suspended specie payments, and the price of gold floated upward along with the foreign exchange rate. Any incentive to substitute specie for bills of exchange was quickly thwarted.[57] The gold points, it seems, had no practical relevance to any group other than the larger foreign exchange dealers like the Browns and the Barings. The costs of smaller, more irregular specie shipments were such that the commercial banks had invariably suspended payment before the typical merchant found it profitable to forego bills for gold. In sum, it might be said that there were limits to the gold points themselves. A moderately high premium might stimulate a specie outflow through the exchange dealers, but an extremely high premium inevitably led to suspension and a reversion to the bill of exchange.

During periods of financial uncertainty, the Browns sometimes turned to commodities as an alternative means of covering the Liverpool account. When the 1837 crisis reached the panic stage, the Browns instructed their New Orleans agent, Benjamin Story, to use their funds in making conservative advances on consignments or in buying cotton outright. Transactions in cotton itself seemed the safest way of remitting funds, the Baltimore house wrote, since "no dependence can be placed in bills."[58]

These tactics proved successful, and the firm continued them in a modified form throughout the remainder of the year. In this operation, the New Orleans agent exercised broad discretionary powers.[59] Story could choose from among as many as four options: he could buy "unquestioned" sterling bills on other drawees; deal in domestic exchange; make prudent advances on consignments; or, if prices were considered to have fallen to bargain levels, he was authorized to purchase cotton. In December 1837 the Baltimore office told Story that the firm expected his cotton purchases during the past season would "make near a par remittance."[60] Since many of their prior bill sales had been at rates as high as five to ten percent above par, Story's cotton shipments proved to be extremely lucrative remittances — irrespective of any profits the firm may have earned on the mercantile transaction in its own right.

The Browns responded to the panic of 1857 in virtually the same manner. Early in November the Liverpool partners began suggesting alternative modes of coverage. Hypothesizing a scarcity of good bills in the south combined with low cotton prices, Collet and Hamilton told the New York partners that the purchase of up to $1,000,000 worth of cotton would be entirely justified.[61] A few weeks later, after the difficulties of many Anglo-American banking houses had become a matter of public knowledge, the Liverpool managers felt the southern branches might temporarily concentrate their purchasing activities on domestic exchange. In the meantime, the New York branch sent $50,000 of the firm's Erie Railroad bonds to England for sale. A gold shipment to bolster the liquidity of the Liverpool house went out in mid-December. On its arrival, Collet and Hamilton labeled it, "a losing remittance," but they welcomed it nonetheless because the funds reduced further their reliance on the discount market.[62]

In the management of their foreign exchange account, the Browns benefited greatly from the advantages inherent in their organizational system. The firm maintained outlets in all the major American markets, and it possessed an outpost of unparalleled importance in England itself. Of course, the organizational structure alone was not sufficient to boost the Browns to a position of leadership in the foreign exchange field. It also required personnel who were thoroughly trained; who could exercise sound judgment in difficult situations; and who were attuned to the cooperative spirit which permeated the whole organization.

In addition to their collaboration in determining market tactics, each of the two main offices performed a series of operational tasks for the other outlets in the banking chain. In Liverpool the partners were responsible for meeting the firm's financial obligations and the collection of information on both the state of the international economy and the credit standing of individual drawees. The New York partners established the firm's selling rate, supervised the seasonal investment of idle cash, transfered these funds to the south in the winter, and generally administered the buying and selling activities of the American branches. The partners in both offices joined in planning transatlantic specie shipments. All in all, there was no other field of endeavor in which the firm's ability to coordinate its activities was more prominently displayed than in the partners' careful and continuous management of foreign exchange operations.

XII

Formulating New Policies:
The Sixties and Seventies

The events leading up to and surrounding the Civil War had as profound an effect on the House of Brown as on any business enterprise in the Anglo-American economy. The Brown partnership was one of the few organizations in any field of economic endeavor in the United States which maintained an extensive chain of branch offices and representatives throughout the states along the Atlantic and Gulf seaboards. Four of the links in their banking chain were located in southern ports. When the Union forces successfully blockaded those ports and restricted the outward flow of cotton, the supply of foreign exchange dwindled accordingly.

Cut off from the major source of sterling bills, the Browns had to reformulate their elaborate seasonal strategies. Then the flight of the dollar from a fixed specie standard in 1862 completely extinguished whatever life remained in their former pattern of operations. Thereafter, exchange rates were, for all practical purposes, completely free to float as far beyond the gold point limits as monetary conditions dictated, and the maintenance of an uncovered account for a week, or even a day, became extremely hazardous. Eventually, the Browns refused to handle any transaction unless they could negotiate a sale and purchase simultaneously. Despite all the disruptions associated with war, the Browns — as in other periods of crisis — found the years from 1861 to 1865 highly profitable. Indeed the trend toward decreasing profit margins on sterling sales, which had developed during the late fifties, was completely reversed during the war, and the Browns earned higher returns throughout most of the next two decades.

The discussion here focuses on several of the more significant changes in the Browns' foreign exchange activities in the period from 1861 through 1880. The managerial tactics that were introduced in response to a depreciated currency and a floating exchange rate are an obvious choice for analysis. In the administrative category, the abrupt disbandment of the southern branch system, which had concentrated almost exclusively on the purchase of sterling bills, and the subsequent reestablishment of that network in a modified form receive close examination. The partnership's expanded volume of transactions in French francs and its first exposure to the complexities of the nascent futures market for foreign exchange are also reviewed.

Operational and Administrative Readjustments in the 1860s

The actual outbreak of hostilities occurred during a transitional period in the Browns' annual foreign exchange cycle. By April, most of the cotton crop had gone to market, and exporters had drawn bills of exchange against overseas shipments. Meanwhile, the political crises over secession had not adversely affected the Browns' operations in the southern states, although the situation, of course, had been very tense. Acting in unison, the American branches easily covered their overdrawn account in Liverpool. Thus, by late spring the foreign exchange slate was wiped clean for another year, and the partners entered the early months of the war with a substantial degree of flexibility.

After the firing on Fort Sumter, the fate of the firm's organizational structure in the south became a matter of overwhelming importance. The partnership faced a genuine dilemma. The Browns had been closely identified with both sections of the country for decades. But over the years the American partners gradually had concentrated in New York, and most southerners viewed the firm as principally a "northern house." The problem was least serious in Charleston and Savannah where independent merchants, whose families had served the Browns as agents for years, represented the firm. The Browns' association with James Adger, in Charleston, and George Cumming, in Savannah, was suspended by mutual agreement, since all agreed that a continued alliance might prove politically embarrassing.

In New Orleans and Mobile, on the other hand, the offices were styled Brown Brothers & Co., since they were wholly owned subsidiary branches of the parent organization.[1] These two Gulf port outlets handled a far larger volume of business than their counterparts along the Atlantic seaboard. Several of the firm's employees served in Mobile and New Orleans with the understanding that this training would lead to promotion to one of the main offices and perhaps admission into the partnership. Without exception, the men in managerial posts in the two branches demonstrated their primary devotion to the Brown organization rather than to the Confederacy when they left the south for new appointments elsewhere. Before their departure, however, they became involved in some controversial activities.

Within days of the firing on Fort Sumter both governments began actively soliciting subscriptions to their imminent war loans. In New York, the partners promptly pledged to take at least $2,000 of the Union issue. In the confusion over the firm's proper role in the conflict, the southern branches proved even more zealous in their devotion to the cause — and immediately subscribed $3,000 to the Confederate loan. Whether the branch managers were motivated by genuine conviction, or responded to the pressure from their business associates in the community, or acted out of fear for their own safety is not known, but some combination of all three factors seems reasonable. Although the Liverpool partners were generally sympathetic to the southern cause, they immediately recognized the folly of such a course when they heard of the events that had transpired. Thus they were glad to learn in the New York partners' letter of April 27 that instructions had gone out to close, at least temporarily, the offices in Mobile and New Orleans. "We hope our Southern Friends are safely in New York by this time," Collet and Hamilton wrote on May 10, "and thus free us from contributions to both sides."[2]

As partial compensation for the indiscretions of their subordinates, Collet and Hamilton agreed that the New York house would "have to take some of the Government securities & contribute in other ways freely." But the matter did not end there. In December 1861 the Liverpool partners expressed concern about the legal status of Charles Dickey, the former head of the Mobile branch who had transferred to England: "Mr. Dickey has been discussing . . . the position in which he may be placed now that *Subscription to the Southern Loan* is regarded as a cause for arrest & a penal offense, — by his having in April last subscribed at Mobile in behalf of the House to the Southern loan, the Certificates for which stand registered in his name."[3] Although Dickey was ultimately absolved of all wrongdoing and later became a valuable partner in the New York office, the episode — in addition to its irony — was important because it demonstrates so clearly the uniqueness of the Browns' organizational structure on the eve of the war.

While the beginning of hostilities precipitated an early abandonment of the firm's network of southern outlets, the economic consequences of the north's blockade of the cotton ports eventually would have dictated a suspension of foreign exchange activities in the south in any event. Exports of American cotton to England fell from 2,580,000 bales in 1860 to 72,000 bales in 1862.[4] For some time the partners considered utilizing their excess manpower in opening new branch offices in other cities. Among the sites mentioned were San Francisco, St. Louis, Cincinnati, Chicago, Louisville, and Paris. A London office finally became a reality in 1863; but prior to its founding, the partners opened an Havana office on an experimental basis early in 1862.

Although a Havana outlet had been under consideration for three or four months, the Browns did not act until the Trent Affair in November 1861 seriously strained diplomatic relations between the Lincoln administration and England. If war actually erupted between the northern states and Great Britain, the Liverpool partners hypothesized in December, then a Cuban branch might prove especially valuable: "Havanna may become a point of vital importance to us in resuming our Southern business, as soon as the Gulf ports are opened. If cotton could not be shipped with safety direct to Europe, no doubt it would freely go to Havanna for reshipment in neutral vessels."[5] In such an eventuality, they suggested the dispatch of Charles Dickey and Herman Hoskier, a young man who had been undergoing training in New Orleans the past two years, to Havana to manage the business.

In the end, most of the Liverpool partners' theorizing went for naught. Diplomatic relations between the Lincoln administration and England improved in the early months of 1862, and the northern blockade became increasingly effective in halting the outflow of cotton. The Havana branch, headed by Andrew Morrill, the former manager of the New Orleans branch, folded in less than a year. Except for the London house, the partners undertook no other new ventures. The partners were hesitant because they intended to reactivate the southern branch system at the end of the war, no matter what its outcome. Therefore, they did not want to risk having their foreign exchange specialists tied down in other posts. In voicing their opposition to other expansion proposals, Collet and Hamilton reminded their New York associates that the services of Charles Dickey and Herman Hoskier, particularly, would be needed "when we open in the South again." On this matter they warned, "Experience shows it is not easy to get the proper people for such important positions."[6] As a result of these and other considerations, the Browns shunted aside proposals for expansion into unfamiliar territories, leaving them free to concentrate on the problems arising from the issuance of the greenback dollar.

After dragging on for over half a year, the on-again, off-again negotiations between Secretary of the Treasury Salmon P. Chase and the New York banking community over financing the Civil War finally reached an impasse in December 1861.[7] During the last week of the month, the commercial banks in the northern states voted to suspend specie payments; and they were not resumed again for another seventeen years. A bill authorizing the issuance of an irredeemable paper currency passed the Congress in February 1862, marking the beginning of the so-called Greenback Era. The effects of these events on the foreign exchange market were extremely far reaching. The country soon adopted what was in essence a dual monetary standard — the greenback dollar and the gold dollar. Because the two kinds of money were not interchangeable at a fixed legal rate of exchange, they were able to coexist in the economy without either one driving the other out of circulation.[8]

Since England remained on the gold standard throughout the period from 1862 to 1879, gold dollars became almost the equivalent of sterling exchange, and the premium on gold in terms of greenback dollars was, for all intents and purposes, the basic dollar-sterling exchange rate.[9] In fact, the major demand for gold dollars arose from the foreign trade sector. Foreign exchange dealers, like the Browns, continued to transact all their business on a specie basis.

In Liverpool news of the suspension of specie payments and the probable passage of a bill authorizing the issuance of a fiat currency failed to upset Francis Hamilton and Mark Collet. In February they reviewed the latest developments and proposed new tactics that served the house well in future years. The reportedly wide fluctuations in exchange rates provided an opportunity to make handsome profits, they confidently predicted, because the firm would be able to exert "more control" over the supply side of the market.[10] Given such an unstable market, the Liverpool partners advised each northern branch to avoid naming a specific buying rate for a prospective customer until it had been allowed sufficient time to negotiate an offsetting scale. Otherwise, they cautioned, bills should only be purchased at very wide margins.

The fundamental strategy, then, was to maintain a very close balance between bill sales and bill purchases. The uncovered account of former years was absolutely ruled out. "Exchange is so hard to make judgments about, it will not pay to speculate," observed the Liverpool managers.[11] If speculation did occur, they recommended that the New York house work for a rise in exchange rates rather than a fall; in other words, purchases should be made in advance of sales. Indeed, they believed that, if the Lincoln administration persisted in its plan of raising money by borrowing heavily and keeping taxes low, "Exchange may go to fabulous rates before many months have passed."[12] In the short run their judgment was somewhat premature, but ultimately, of course, the prediction proved accurate. Even so, the rise in sterling rates had no detrimental effects on their own foreign exchange activities, since, by transacting all their business in gold dollars and maintaining a balanced account, the partners insulated themselves from the shifting value of a volatile greenback currency. The Browns performed primarily the functions of a broker, and the absolute level of the sterling rate, or by analogy the gold premium, was largely irrelevant to their business.[13] In short, while the rest of the economy went off specie from 1862 to 1879, the Browns and other foreign exchange dealers remained on it.

Although the character of the firm's business during the Civil War years underwent a dramatic change, the volume of foreign exchange transactions did not diminish. Despite the loss of the cotton trade and the large foreign exchange earnings that normally accompanied it, the northern states found other ways to finance a fairly high level of imports.[14] In analyzing their operations in May 1864, the Liverpool partners expressed much satisfaction with the results of the past few years. Exchange profits, which had dropped below the one hundred thousand dollar mark in 1859, reached $308,540 Cy. in 1863.[15]

The daily balancing of sterling sales and purchases eased the pressures on the Liverpool partners. Overall, Collet and Hamilton noted, "this is a much safer position especially as now we hold in hand actual cover for the whole of the balance drawn on the Exchange account which was not the case (except on rare occasions) before 1857."[16] In addition, they wholeheartedly agreed with a suggestion from the New York house that the firm might be prudent in keeping its outstanding acceptances limited to three times the partners' combined capital.[17] Although there was at the time "a wide margin before we reach anything like the proportion of three times the capital," the Liverpool partners observed, the figure would establish a sensible guideline where none had previously existed.[18]

The general success of foreign exchange operations during the war years paved the way for a permanent change in the organizational structure. The southern branches, which only a few years before had been thought indispensible, were hardly missed after the firm adjusted to new circumstances. In the meantime, the changes in for-

eign trade patterns and in financial conditions indicated that a reestablished branch system would play a less important role in the future
than in the past. The increased export of foodstuffs from northern
ports enlarged the local supplies of foreign exchange and produced a
greater balance in the regional market. Moreover, the suspension of
specie payments had eliminated, from a practical standpoint, any
possibility of reviving the firm's previous seasonal strategy. Because
of the length of the conflict and the overall magnitude of wartime
business, most of the southern employees were established in new
posts on a more or less permanent basis. One of the promising young
men in the organization, Herman Hoskier, who had been slated to
return to New Orleans, instead joined the staff of the London branch
when it opened in 1863.

As a result of these and other factors, the partners decided not to
reopen subsidiary branches in the south but to establish agency
agreements with independent houses in the ports where they previously had been represented. By the fall of 1865 the firm had agents
in Charleston, Savannah, New Orleans, and Mobile.[19] Their
arrangements with A. J. Ingersoll, the Mobile agent, for the 1866
season illustrate the character of the firm's postwar business. For
purchasing sterling exchange with bills of lading attached, the
Browns paid their agent a commission of 0.25 percent. The partners
expected Ingersoll to act exclusively for them in his regular
purchasing activities. However, they gave him permission to execute
occasional orders from other dealers for clean bills "such as he could
not under his instructions take for us." Ingersoll felt most of these
orders would come from August Belmont, the Rothschilds' American
representative. The Liverpool partners had no objections to these
transactions, since "Belmont's orders were 'chiefly' for Francs, which
we do not touch."[20]

One of the benefits the Browns derived from a greater balance
between sales and purchases was an improved system of internal
accounting. The partners could now make fairly accurate estimates
of the profits generated by each outlet in their network. The new
accounting tool was very useful in controlling the activities of the
various outlets and in generally assessing the strengths and
weaknesses of the organization. According to the analysis of
operations in 1866, the southern agencies as a group contributed
earnings of $69,690 Cy. to the firm's total exchange profits of
$388,004 Cy., or about 18 percent.[21]

By 1868 there were signs that the foreign exchange market was
becoming more competitive. In considering several possible re-

sponses, Collet and Hamilton, at one point, suggested that the southern agents might be able to improve their overall profits if they would agree to work for lower commissions. Intrigued by their recommendations, the New York office asked for a further clarification. In their next letter the London partners explained the proposal in greater detail: "As respects the compensation of the Southern Agents, we never contemplated that they should work for $1/8$ Comm^n., unless the reduction from $1/4\%$ held out a prospect of *at least* doubling the business in *safe* paper." The competition was "now so sharp" that these agents were unable to buy the best class of bills at the profit margins which had prevailed since the end of the war. "As your own Exchange profits have scarcely averaged more than $1/3\%$ for some time past, it does not seem likely that the Southern Agencies should be able to secure a margin of $5/8\%$ which they must do to give you this minimum margin & secure for themselves $1/4\%$ beyond," the London partners observed.[22]

As these remarks indicate, the New York partners maintained a profit margin of just under three eighths of a percent on foreign exchange transactions in the late 1860s. This margin compares favorably with a net return of between two eighths and one eighth of a percent which prevailed in the late 1850s. Based on the Browns' 1867 profit figure of $313,000 Cy. and an estimated profit margin of 0.35 percent, the firm's total volume of transactions were somewhere in the neighborhood of $90,000,000 Cy., or about 80 percent larger than in 1860.[23] Since the potential outflow of foreign exchange from the United States in 1867 was approximately $550,000,000 Cy., the Browns' minimum share of the market was probably very close to 16 percent of total sales.[24] This figure represents a three or four percentage point improvement over similarly derived estimates of the firm's minimal market shares in the 1850s.

The general tone of the partner's correspondence, the improved profit margins, and the larger market share all lend credence to the proposition advanced by earlier scholars of the U.S. foreign exchange market — that an irreversible trend toward greater specialization and concentration emerged in the 1860s.[25] Whereas the firm previously had been the market leader among a diverse group of exchange dealers, it now held the same position of leadership within a market that was becoming increasingly oligopolistic.

Although numerous forces were responsible for these new institutional arrangements, the Browns' records suggest that several factors were of key importance. First and most obviously, the war was a crisis of such gigantic proportions that it broke the familiar patterns of exchange activity and led many marginal firms to abandon the market. Of course, an extensive exodus of firms from the market had occurred during earlier financial and commercial crises. Yet the departures had always proved temporary; eventually economic stability and increased trade enticed many firms back into the market. In the sixties, however, the trend toward greater concentration was not reversed.

The wartime crisis differed from its predecessors because the suspension of specie payments lasted for almost two decades — not just a few months. Since sterling rates were subject to sharp fluctuations from day to day, or even from hour to hour, any dealer who wished to avoid undue risks had to maintain an extremely close balance between bill sales and purchases. To preserve this equilibrium, a large volume of transactions was necessary. Unlike the situation in the antebellum decades, a firm could not easily make a gradual entrance into the foreign exchange market of the sixties and seventies. The coming of the greenback dollar complicated the sterling mechanism, and this complexity favored the established dealers with experienced personnel and ample capital resources.

The expanded use of documentary bills of exchange reinforced the competitive advantage of the established dealers. There were additional complications associated with the collection of remittances with bills of lading attached, and the higher proportion of documentary bills drawn in the United States discouraged a broad participation in the exchange market.[26] Knowledgeable exporters who valued the comprehensive services offered by the experienced and more specialized firms discriminated against those dealers lacking a comparable degree of expertise. Because the Browns had been closely associated with mercantile functions in the past, they were especially skillful in the handling of bills of lading and other commercial documents.

Although the barriers to entering the exchange market were unusually steep in the Greenback Era, some new firms did venture into the field for the first time. One newcomer offering the Browns vigorous competition in the late 1860s was J. & W. Seligman & Co. The Seligmans were one of a number of German-Jewish families that made their mark in Anglo-American finance during the last half of the nineteenth century.[27] After opening a house in Frankfurt under the style of Seligman Brothers in 1862, the partners soon established wholly-owned branch offices in London and New York.[28] Like the Browns, the Seligmans preferred to do business through their own employees and thus avoid the use of independent agents.

Waynesburg College Library
Waynesburg, Pa. 15370

According to the correspondence of the Browns' London managers, the Seligmans' aggressive business tactics irritated many members of the English banking fraternity. In July 1868 Collet and Hamilton discussed their new competitor in some detail. One of their complaints about the house stemmed from the Seligmans' failure to discount remittances from the United States in their own name; instead they used the endorsement of an independent London correspondent whose connection with the house, Collet and Hamilton claimed, had been misrepresented:

> The same system of passing Bills without recourse on themselves . . . is continued under a false representation of the facts, & it seems evident that no reliance can be placed upon their statements, & therefore we cannot give credence to their unsupported statem^t . as to their means & mode of business.
>
> With houses who act fairly, it has never been a question with us whether it would be to our advantage or not to give them the benefit which might accrue to them in their competition with you, from the Credit they gain in consequence of your purchasing their paper; but in this case where the competition is not fairly conducted, it becomes quite a question whether . . . it is not better for you to forego any trifling profit you can make on their Bills, than to help them in this unfair competition by becoming buyers of their drafts & so helping their Credit.[29]

Then Collet and Hamilton came to what was apparently the heart of the dispute:

> They have been among your most active opponents at New Orleans, & of course can afford to work for very much smaller margins than you can (quite apart from the low-Agency [fees] they pay) because they only run a risk of ten or fifteen days, against your 75 or 80 days; and when the remittance is once discounted they can turn it over again. Their only difficulty is to pass their own paper freely in your market and this they are seeking to overcome by getting you to take it regularly & so give them currency. We have seen no business of theirs except Exchange business — & this they did their best to spoil for everybody else last season.[30]

This passage reveals much about the relationship between two important firms competing in the foreign exchange market. One firm was an established fixture in the market, its adversary — an intruder seeking a foothold in the field. In this context, the charges of "unfair competition," advanced by Collet and Hamilton, must be accepted with a grain of salt. The Seligmans' real transgression, one strongly suspects, was the introduction of a discounting policy which ran against the traditional, ingrained business procedures of the English merchant-banking elite. Moreover, such price cutters have never been popular among competitors—and especially in market structures characterized by oligopoly. At the same time, part of the London managers' animosity can be attributed to the partnership's oft revealed anti-Semitism. This attitude they shared with most of the members of the English financial community.

Despite the sour grapes, the London partners nonetheless raised a valid point about the wisdom of aiding a competitor in New York who was severely damaging their business in New Orleans. But instead of justifying their proposed retaliation in strictly economic terms, they chose to emphasize the Seligmans' supposedly unethical tactics or, what they called, "unfair competition." At the summit of high finance, there were moral sanctions against certain forms of business behavior, and banking houses violated them at the risk of their credit rating. Because of their market power, the Browns and other leading firms had the informal means of enforcing most, although not all, of their standards of conduct. Eventually, however, a few firms like Seligman Brothers successfully entered the market and then proceeded to join the "club" themselves.

It is difficult to determine exactly how many firms were arbitrarily counted as full members of that distinguished club in the late sixties, but many of them certainly could be found on a list of the major bill drawers in New York. In 1868 the list would have included the following names:[31]

Brown Brothers & Co.	on Brown, Shipley & Co., London
Dabney, Morgan & Co.	on J. S. Morgan & Co., London
Duncan, Sherman & Co.	on The Union Bank, London
Hallgarten & Co.	on The Union Bank, London
James G. King & Sons	on Baring Bros. & Co., London
John Munroe & Co.	on Munroe & Co., Paris
W. C. Pickersgill & Co.	on Fielden Bros. & Co., Liverpool
J. & W. Seligman & Co.	on Seligman Brothers, London
Philip Speyer & Co.	on Speyer Brothers, London
J. & J. Stuart & Co.	on Smith, Payne & Smith, London
Simon de Visser	on Drake, Kleinwort & Cohen, London

One name notably absent from the list was Drexel and Co. The Drexels were heavily involved in investment banking activities during the immediate postwar years and were not active participants in the foreign exchange market. It was only after the Morgan-Drexel merger in 1871 that they emerged as the Browns' most serious challenger in the field.[32]

Baltimore Operations in the Sixties and Seventies

After conducting business activities in Baltimore for fifteen years through a subsidiary of the parent organization, the Browns reverted to the agency form of representation in 1867. At one point during the early months of the Civil War, the foreign trade of the Maryland port deteriorated to such an extent that the partners talked about closing the office. But after adjusting to wartime conditions, Baltimore's trade rebounded sharply and the branch did a larger volume of business than the partners had anticipated. It was therefore in an atmosphere of improved expectations that the original family firm of Alexander Brown & Sons reassumed the agency duties it had relinquished back in 1852. The Baltimore firm was now headed by the founders' grandson George Stewart Brown, who had inherited the reins of leadership after his father's death in 1859. On the day the changeover was made the branch manager, William Graham, left the employ of the parent organization and joined his brother-in-law's rejuvenated house as a senior partner.

The new agency arrangement worked out very satisfactorily. The basic agreement called for the two firms to share equally in the profits and risks of all the business originating in Baltimore, including foreign exchange operations. As an independent agent, the local office exercised far more managerial autonomy, and the frequency of consultations with the New York office about administrative matters declined. Ironically, however, the foreign exchange market had developed in such a manner that the Baltimore office was more dependent that ever on the price guidelines of the New York house.

The pricing strategy was the same one that had been in force for over a quarter of a century: namely that the local office would match its sterling sales with bill purchases at a margin of 0.5 percent. But there was one important new stipulation. If the agency was unable to achieve a daily balance in its buying and selling activities, the New York partners were obligated to cover its position in either direction at a guaranteed minimum margin of 0.25 percent.[33]

Because of the fluctuating price of gold dollars, the Browns' quoted rates did not reflect the full price of sterling in terms of greenback currency. Upon request, the Browns arranged for exchanges between the two forms of domestic currency, but they transacted this business almost entirely through gold brokers and, therefore, took no responsibility for the rate. Because of this added step in the normal routine, there was some uncertainty in the customer's mind about the actual cost — or proceeds — of any given bill of exchange. This relationship between the two variables is illustrated in the following recapitulation of a transaction which the Baltimore agency prepared for one of its regular bill suppliers in 1868.[34]

Statement of Proceeds of Sterling Bills

4000 St.	3 d/s at 110 1/4		=	$19,577.77 G
$19,577.77 G at 142-7/8 %			=	27,971.74 Cy.
less 1/8 % Brokerage		24.47		
1/100% U.S. Tax		2.80		
Stamps on bills		12.00	=	39.27
Amount credited to your account				$27,932.47 Cy.

For the rate in the first conversion from sterling into gold dollars at 110 1/4, the Browns assumed responsibility; but for the second from gold into greenbacks at 142 7/8, they assumed none.[35]

Since the gold premium accounted for the vast amount of the price deviation away from the old antebellum gold par base of $4.86 to the pound, or a quoted rate of 109 1/2 percent, in transactions such as the one above, it is understandable why Milton Friedman and Anna Schwartz took the liberty of equating the gold premium with the sterling rate in their analysis of the foreign exchange mechanism during this period. Without challenging in any way the fundamental validity of their observation, it should nonetheless be noted that the Browns continued to quote an independent sterling rate, which fluctuated about the mint par rate of 109 1/2 percent in an interval similar to the one that prevailed before the war.[36] Unlike the earlier period, however, there was no discernible seasonality in the rates from 1862 to 1879.[37] Any tendency of the sterling rate to move in unison with the nation's seasonal import-export cycle was presumably thwarted by the activities of foreign exchange speculators, who were apparently an energetic group during the Greenback Era.

The Browns partially offset any sharp upward or downward movement in the gold premium by adjusting their sterling rate in the opposite direction. They did so, for instance, in September 1869, when Jay Gould and Jim Fisk unhatched their infamous plot to corner the gold market. From the time the gold premium started its steady climb early in the month, the Browns simultaneously lowered their sterling rates. The partners' quoted rate for 60 d/s bills fell from 108 1/4 on September 5, to 107 1/2 on the twentieth, to 106 on the twenty-third, and finally, at the height of the panic on the morning of the twenty-fourth to 104 1/2. From September 23 to 26 the Baltimore office received instructions to suspend entirely all purchasing activity. But there is no evidence that the flurry in the price of gold seriously affected any of the Browns' regular customers.

The gold episode was, in sum, primarily a political scandal, and its importance as a financial and economic crisis has at times been exaggerated.[38] The affair had no long-run significance, and the Browns' correspondence suggests that even its short run effect on the foreign trade sector was negligible. When the price of gold finally broke around mid-day of the twenty-fourth, the Browns immediately raised their quoted rates three and one half percentage points to 108. Several weeks later, the Baltimore agency sent news of the new climate to one of its regular bill suppliers in Petersburg, Virginia: "We are able to place the exchange at a better rate than has ruled for some time past . . . owing to the sudden break in the Gold Market which has stiffened exchange but depressed gold."[39] However, the agency failed to inform its customer that his net proceeds in greenback dollars would actually be less than in previous months due to a greater fall in gold than a rise in exchange.

During the late 1870s, the Baltimore office was transformed from a somewhat minor outpost in the Brown organization to an outlet of genuine importance. The explanation for this sudden rise in status is revealed in the port's foreign trade statistics. The nation's exports of agricultural products to Europe expanded rapidly during this period, and Baltimore was a port which benefited from the increased activity. The eastern railroads had assigned Baltimore a favorable freight rate differential vis-à-vis New York on the basis of the shorter route to Chicago and other inland markets, and the lower transportation costs aided the port in attracting midwestern commerce.[40] In the ten years from 1870 to 1880, Baltimore's pattern of foreign trade shifted from a net import deficit of $5.2 million to a net export surplus of $56.3 million. A fivefold increase in exports, which rose from $19.9 million to $76.2 million, was responsible for this dramatic reversal.[41]

Because of the huge excess of exports over imports, Baltimore's foreign exchange market was in a permanent state of disequilibrium by the late 1870s. The supply of foreign bills of exchange was almost four times greater than the local demand for them. As a result, the main activity of foreign exchange dealers was overwhelmingly the purchasing of bills. In this respect, the Baltimore market exhibited a striking resemblance to those in the southern cotton ports. The vast majority of the agency's purchases were offset through sales in the New York market, and close coordination via the telegraph became an essential feature of the operation of the joint exchange account.

Although the Browns and their agents enjoyed an upsurge in the volume of business during the late seventies, there was nonetheless one element in the general pattern of grain exports that was not compatible with the partners' traditional strategies. Because of the increasing European demand for American breadstuffs, a substantial number of ships headed directly for continental ports.[42] Therefore the bills of exchange created in the export sector were frequently drawn in currencies other than sterling. Although the Browns had always handled a small volume of "foreign bills" as a courtesy to important customers, the partners had generally confined themselves to the Anglo-American market for sterling bills. Unlike the Barings, Rothschilds, and other prominent London bankers, the Browns had no joint exchange account agreements with houses located in the important financial centers on the continent.

The expanded volume of bills drawn in francs on Paris and Antwerp became a progressively serious problem for the Baltimore agency in particular. An early signal of the difficulties that lay ahead arose in April of 1878. In a letter to the New York office, the agency reported that one of the port's largest grain shippers, James Knox & Co., had recently received a series of massive orders from Antwerp. The buyer had instructed Knox to draw 60 d/s bills in francs on the Bank of Antwerp. In responding to Knox's inquiry about purchasing the bills, Alex. Brown & Sons stated that it could do no more than follow the normal procedure prescribed by the main Brown organization. That is, AB&S was not permitted to purchase the bills outright at a firm rate, but it would accept them as a collection item, with the exact proceeds to be determined upon final payment or subsequent resale: "We told him we could only take the bills subject to final adjustment when advised of their outturn, not being willing to incur the risk of fluctuation in Continental Exchange."[43] As an alternative to an outright purchase, the agency asked the New York partners how much they might be willing to advance against a given bill subject to the eventual proceeds—or as they called it, the outturn. There was the prospect of a large business in francs, AB&S advised New York, and "we should prefer to control it, if possible, rather than have it go elsewhere—& perhaps divert some of the Sterling bills we do now get."[44]

The competitor AB&S feared most was Drexel, Morgan & Co., in London, and Drexel, Harjes & Co., in Paris. After the merger of the Drexel and Morgan firms in 1871, the allied houses began to challenge the Browns for the leadership position in the American foreign exchange market. In Baltimore an old associate of George Peabody, Robert Garrett & Sons, served as agent for the Drexel-Morgan alliance.[45] However, when local exporters drew an unusually large volume of exchange, Drexel & Co. in Philadelphia also entered the Baltimore market directly via the telegraph. With a branch in Paris and strong connections throughout Europe, the Drexel-Morgan organization was in a favorable position to supplant the Browns as the leading dealers in the Maryland port if the proportion of bills drawn in continental exchange rose dramatically.[46]

The agency's fears were soon confirmed. Although AB&S managed to obtain the first drawing of Knox & Co.'s franc bills upon offering a liberal advance, its success was short-lived. When Knox drew another group of bills two weeks later, Drexel & Co. promptly entered a firm bid for the exchange and took the business. Because AB&S anticipated that the Philadelphia house would now become a permanent interloper in the local market, the Baltimore managers were very apprehensive about the future. With the Drexels and Garretts indicating a willingness to purchase francs outright, William Graham and Stewart Brown were visibly disturbed: "We are not likely to get any more of them [francs], and we only hope that their loss may not imperil the Sterling drawings of these parties which we have heretofore retained."[47]

Other grain dealers in Baltimore were soon receiving a substantial number of orders for continental delivery. In reviewing the business prospects for the upcoming year in January 1879, AB&S saw little reason for optimism: "This season the bulk of shipments will be in francs, which will very much reduce our sterling bill purchases."[48] Several months later, William Graham and Stewart Brown strongly urged the main organization to form an alliance with one of the important banking houses in Paris.

The suggestion was not an unfamiliar one. The Browns actually had considered an expansion of franc transactions on several occasions in the past, but the impediments in the way of conducting active and profitable operations had appeared too formidable. In comparison with the sterling market, the U.S. market for francs was exceedingly thin. Even in New York the demand for franc bills was unsteady, and the partners anticipated that purchases of continental bills frequently would have to be offset with sales in sterling bills. On one occasion when AB&S purchased franc bills from a favored customer as an accommodation, the New York partners needed almost three days to negotiate a covering sale in the same currency.[49]

In addition, the English partners opposed the routine handling of continental exchange through the London office. They objected, in part, because the collection process normally took longer, but primarily because French law, in particular, required the holder of a collateralized franc bill to release the bill of lading for the merchandise to the payee on the date of formal acceptance. The Browns, of course, preferred to reserve for themselves the decision about re-

leasing the bills of lading on the acceptance date or on the final payment date, as they did in collecting all documentary sterling bills.
Thus when news arrived, late in January 1879, that the General
Assembly had modified the inhibiting laws on bills of lading, the
partners brought forward the proposal to engage in franc operations
for another review.

In the meantime, another important matter was demanding attention as well. Competitive pressures in Baltimore and elsewhere
had forced the partners to consider their response to the growing
futures market for bills of exchange drawn in both sterling and
francs. Futures markets for actively traded commodities such as cotton and grain were already an established part of the American
financial environment by the 1870s.[50] Thus the financial principles
underlying futures contracts were generally understood in the commercial community. In brief, a contract provided for the establishment of a fixed price that would be applied to bills of exchange
the seller delivered by a certain date in the reasonably near future.

In the situation at hand, it was grain exporters who hoped to sell
their future bill drawings to foreign exchange dealers like the
Browns. The prime motive of the grain shipper was to avoid the risk
of a substantial drop in exchange rates between the date he received
an order from across the Atlantic over the cable and the date his
cargo actually left port for its overseas destination. By selling an exchange future on the same day he received an order, the exporter
could calculate immediately his profit margin on the transaction.
The exchange "risk" normally inherent in filling foreign orders could
be entirely avoided, since the shipper was not forced to wait one or
two months before learning the exact proceeds of his bill. With this
uncertainty removed, the exporter could extend lower prices to his
foreign buyers and thereby increase his competitiveness in the transatlantic grain market. For the Browns, however, the main incentive
for engaging in such operations was the protection of their leadership
position in the foreign exchange market from the onslaughts of other
dealers.

The first hint of difficulties in the Baltimore market came in December 1878. In correspondence with the New York office, AB&S
casually mentioned that another of the port's important grain
dealers, Gill & Fisher, recently had sold Robert Garrett & Sons a
"block of £100,000" with the understanding that the bills would
"be delivered as the shipments are completed."[51] Two months later,
a trend toward an increased volume of transactions in futures had
definitely emerged, and there were signs that the movement was

gaining momentum. Exchange dealers in New York such as Hall-garten & Co. regularly quoted rates for futures through Baltimore exchange brokers.

When AB&S took up the subject with the Liverpool house in January 1879, the management was rather discouraged: "We have always declined to name rates for Exchange to be delivered in the future, as we believe is also the case with the New York House, and we do not see how it could be done under our system of closing the account each week."[52] In another letter the next month, the Baltimore managers discussed their situation further:

> As to your suggestion that we should confer with the New York House in regard to purchasing exchange for future delivery, we would say that we have understood that they never make such purchases, and they do not seem to have considered the subject with favor when we have suggested it to them. We would like to be able to meet this desire on the part of shippers but the difficulties that occur to us are that to make sure of a margin in the exchange it would be necessary to sell at once against such time purchases, which meanwhile would leave our account with you short remitted, and involve a charge of interest that we could hardly cover by the rate at which we purchased, as we hear that sales are made at about the rate for immediate delivery. Also we would thus be committed some time in advance to taking bills on parties whom we might afterward prefer to pass, but if you think that these difficulties can be overcome or in some way avoided, we will be glad to hear from you, as we feel that to control our share of the business here we must meet as far as possible what may appear to be the requirements of the trade.[53]

Apparently, the senior partners in New York and England felt the situation was serious too because in the coming months the implementation of the contemplated operations in futures became a major topic for discussion.

The questions the Baltimore agents asked during this period were the ones that any novice in the futures market might have logically raised. The fundamental issue was how the purchases of exchange futures could be covered with sales at a safe and predictable profit margin. Since there was little demand for futures arising from the import sector of the economy, AB&S felt that future purchases would have to be offset by current sales; otherwise the exchange risk would be forced upon the dealer. AB&S queried the New York partners about these matters in April 1879:

> In regard to the purchase of sterling for future delivery . . . is your idea that we should sell against such purchases at the time,

and, if so, from the short account [3 d/s] with BS&C . . . Is it your custom, when making such purchases, to give current rates, or are you guided simply by the prospective advance or decline in the market as may appear probable at the time of purchase, and on this basis make the best rate practicable.[54]

The answers AB&S received in reply have not survived, but when the New York office began quoting futures rates that summer, the partners offered their normal 3 day rate for bills delivered within one month and a rate $0.01, or 0.21 percent, lower for bills handed over within two months.[55]

In the course of establishing ground rules for the new operations, the interest rate Brown, Shipley & Co. was to charge on the anticipated deficit balances in the Baltimore firm's account became an issue of contention. Since the agency agreement had taken effect in 1867, the rate had been stipulated as 5 percent. Because AB&S had carefully matched sales and purchases, very little interest had been assessed against the account. But the basic plan for handling futures transactions called for the agency to sell an offsetting bill immediately after it had agreed to buy a bill drawn in the future. While this procedure assured a satisfactory profit margin on any given transaction, it still left AB&S open to some risk in the interest area. If the Baltimore office was unable to earn 5 percent or better on the proceeds from its bill sale during the interval from contract signing to the actual purchase date, then it would not offset completely the interest charges in London.

The Baltimore managers, William Graham and Stewart Brown, were unsure about earning any more than a 4 percent return on short term investments in the local money market. Either the London house should lower its rate, they argued, or the New York office should guarantee them a minimal 5 percent return on funds invested in the United States. Otherwise, the interest charges in England might offset a portion of the normal profit margin on the pure exchange transaction. Moreover, they felt that "these time transactions should be kept entirely separate from the current business."[56] A special account should be set up, they suggested, and "when transactions are finally closed by payment for the bills here, the balance, including such interest as we might be able to earn, [should] be then transferred to London." When the New York partners balked at any change in the 5 percent rate, which traditionally had been applied to all debit balances in England for over half a century, AB&S voiced its objections even more strongly. The maintenance of a 5 percent interest rate on all accounts involving futures while competitors "are working on the basis of current rates, of course, precludes the possibility of business," the Baltimore managers concluded. Eventually, the main organization and its agent settled their differences, although the exact terms are unknown, and they began preparations for handling futures transactions.

A brief analysis of the procedures outlined for conducting this new business in futures reveals striking similarities with the Browns' general strategies in the antebellum foreign exchange market. In both instances, prior bill sales were covered by later purchases. The offsetting of interest costs in England with interest revenue in the United States was likewise the same. Yet, there were important differences. Whereas the interval between sales and purchases in the earlier era was sometimes six months, the interval on futures operations was seldom longer than two months. But the main difference was in the area of profit margins. In the antebellum decades, the Browns relied on seasonal price movements to provide them with an adequate margin. In other words, they willingly assumed the exchange risk. In futures operations, on the other hand, the profit margin was assured, since bills were sold on the same day futures contracts with grain shippers were signed. In the latter period, only the "interest risk" remained, and despite the protestations of the Baltimore agency the issue was not critical because interest rates in the London money market were normally lower than those in other markets, including those in the United States.[57]

While the Browns formulated policies for their participation in the futures market, they also engaged actively in negotiations with bankers in Paris pursuant to their full scale entrance into the market for francs. No doubt the distressing reports emanating from Baltimore during the first half of 1879 spurred on the London partners in their efforts. In reviewing the overall situation in late April, AB&S told the London office that the outlook had not improved since last December: "Our principal drawers of Francs, Gill & Fisher, now sell regularly to Drexel & Co., and have not offered us a franc, or Sterling Bill on the continent . . . they and others . . . are now getting such very full rates that we could not at present hope to divert the business." Moreover, AB&S reported, "Hallgarten & Co. and other Jewish Bill buyers of New York are now offering by telegraph, through Brokers here, rates almost up to those quoted by the best drawers of Francs."[58]

Three months later, AB&S suddenly received instructions from the London branch to remit all franc bills either advanced against or purchased outright to Comptoir d' Escompte de Paris.[59] The announcement of the new alliance caught the Baltimore management by surprise: "It is the first intimation we have had of any arrangement having been made, and we are quite without instructions of a general character as to the conduct of the business."[60] In late August AB&S reviewed the precise details of the business arrangement with the Paris house. The main organization and Comptoir d' Escompte had agreed to divide equally the profits and risks. For its part AB&S was willing "to do the business here as proposed for one-fourth the profit . . . and . . . risk on operations at that point." The Baltimore managers felt they would confine their activities largely to bill purchasing, since there was little demand for francs from local importers. "We will be glad to receive your quotations for francs as promised," they told the New York office.[61]

The Baltimore agents then turned to another important topic. For the first time in the correspondence, AB&S discussed the possibility of purchasing francs for future delivery and the possibility that the New York office might, on occasion, be able to offset futures purchases, in both sterling and francs, with the sale of bills for future delivery. The handling of transactions on those occasions when the delivery dates on sales and purchases failed to coincide worried AB&S. The major concern of the Baltimore agency was that a local grain dealer might deliver his bills and demand payment a few days before the New York office had collected the funds from the offsetting futures sale. "Are your bills under time sales deliverable at your option within the time period stated," AB&S asked, "or would we come under advance for bills under such purchases which may be delivered to us prior to our reimbursement from you?" Although the response of the New York partners has not survived, it seems likely that naming the specific date of delivery within the allotted time span was an option reserved for customers under both sales and purchase contracts. Thus in those situations where offsetting contracts existed, dealers like the Browns had to assume the risk of losing a few days of interest.

In addition to the difficulties associated with entering the markets for francs and futures, the Baltimore agency — and presumably the entire Brown organization — found itself suffering from increasingly severe price competition. By the late seventies, sterling rates were no longer quoted in percentage deviations around 109 1/2, but in dollar and cents around the mint par figure of $4.8665. The quotation system had changed, but the Browns' pricing tactics remained roughly the same. At the beginning of 1879 the difference in the firm's quoted rates for sales and purchases was exactly 0.5 percent — the same differential that had been in force for approximately forty years. Under the new quotation system, the Browns named buying rates that were $0.025 below their current selling rates.

During the first half of the year, however, AB&S had difficulty making purchases at the old price differential. Much of the competition came from dealers in New York and Philadelphia, who quoted rates through local brokers. Some dealers offered to purchase bills at only $0.01 to $0.015 below their current selling rates, which meant that they were working on margins of 0.025 percent or less. At the same time, many dealers transacted business in francs at the same low margins previously reserved for sterling bills. Thus when the New York office finally began the regular quotation of rates for both francs and futures, AB&S still lost many opportunities because it could not meet the prices of other dealers. The agency concluded that it would either have to settle for smaller margins or lose the business entirely.

Neither alternative seemed very attractive. By early April the Baltimore managers were discouraged. "The competition is so great that we have to pay more than formerly, and the heavy concessions you make in sales for us leave but little margin to cover risks," AB&S told the New York office.[62] The story was much the same in July. "We have had to bid higher than the rates you name for sterling bills," they admitted; "We have had to meet the market or pass the bills, preference having been given *us* at the same rates." Preference at a competitive rate provided, at least, some incentive; in fact it became the basis for new pricing tactics. In bidding for the large drawings of the major grain shippers, AB&S extended rates that were competitive with those of out-of-town dealers. At the same time, it continued to do business with other exporters at the standard 0.5 percent margin.

The effects of a late entry into the market for francs and futures and the downward pressure on profit margins showed up in the yearly earnings statement. AB&S's one half share in joint exchange account profits for 1879 was $33,800 compared to $50,300 in 1878, a drop of about one third. For the main Brown organization, profits on foreign exchange operations dropped from $221,700 in 1878 to $176,100 in 1879, or 21 percent. The sharper decline in the agency's income is a further indication that much of the stimulus for readjustments in the Browns' strategies came from Baltimore.[63]

The year 1879 brought many changes in the firm's traditional pattern of operation. Once the partners recognized the seriousness of the threat to their leadership position in the foreign exchange field, they acted quickly to adjust their range of services to the demands of the market. What happened in Baltimore during the late seventies presumably occurred in other port cities as well. AB&S became concerned about the possible loss of business due to the inadequate facilities of the main organization in the spring of 1878. But it was not until the beginning of 1879 that the situation reached a critical point. By April the New York office had issued instructions of the handling of sterling purchased for future delivery. Three months later the formation of an alliance with Comptoir d'Escompte in Paris was announced. In August AB&S discussed the purchase of francs for future delivery and the possible sale of sterling and franc futures in the New York market. Meanwhile, the agency experienced increasingly sharp price competition from out-of-town dealers who were attracted to the Baltimore market by the growing volume of activity in the export sector. Eventually, the organization abandoned the policy of extending equal rates to all customers. In Baltimore the Browns offered the larger drawers higher, more competitive prices for their bills. The rates on large blocks of bills became negotiable, and the profit margin on many of these transactions fell from 0.5 percent to 0.25 percent in the space of six months. By the end of the year the House of Brown had become an active participant in the emerging market for foreign exchange futures.

Despite the richness of the data, the partners' correspondence fails to reveal the underlying reasons for the sudden appearance of a futures market for bills of exchange. The Browns were primarily interested in generating a response to the innovative tactics of competitors, not in analyzing the causes of their difficulties. Although the evidence is insufficient to develop a full explanation, it is nonetheless possible to describe the circumstances of the market's emergence and to suggest a few hypotheses about the forces responsible for the timing of its birth.

From an institutional standpoint, a brief survey of the historical development of futures contracts in the United States provides perspective. The futures contract was an outgrowth of the practice of selling merchandise while in transit from one destination to another, or "to arrive." The technique of selling on arrival was perfected in the Chicago grain market during the early 1850s, and later spread to the nation's other commodity markets. Out of the arrival sale evolved the futures contract; it called for the delivery of a specific, certified grade of a given commodity within the maximum time specified in the contract. The general adoption of this innovative financial device coincided with the formation of organized commodity exchanges in Chicago, New York, and other commercial centers. The commodity exchanges established uniform grading standards and stipulated the rules for the regular trading of futures contracts.[64]

A futures market for bills of exchange was the final step in the nineteenth century revolution in the overseas marketing and financing of agricultural commodities. It emerged only after refinements in the procedures for the handling of futures contracts had occurred on the commodity exchanges in the 1860s and 1870s. This broad relationship deserves special emphasis here because, generally speaking, independent studies of the evolution of futures contracts on the commodity exchanges and in the foreign exchange markets have failed to note the linkage.[65]

A review of the Browns' activities suggests that there were three exogenous developments which may have been responsible, either separately or jointly, for the emergence of a futures market for foreign exchange: increasing economies of scale, the transfer of financial technology from the European continent, and the resumption of specie payments in the United States after January 1, 1879.[66] From 1871 to 1879 the size of the foreign exchange market expanded rapidly; U.S. exports grew from $464.3 million to $728.5 million.[67] Increased European purchases of American agricultural products accounted for much of the rise in the export sector. Over the eight year period the shipment of crude foodstuffs to Europe rose 450 percent, with half of the increase coming in the last two years of the decade.[68] Since there was roughly a corresponding increase in the volume of foreign bills of exchange drawn in the U.S. market, economies of scale in matching buyers and sellers may have encouraged dealers to engage in futures transactions.

However, a closer examination of foreign trade statistics reveals an important shift in the pattern of U.S. exports which may be more relevant in this context. Although wheat shipments to Great Britain, traditionally the nation's best customer for agricultural products, fell by $13.5 million between 1878 and 1879, overall wheat exports rose 35 percent primarily because of a sevenfold increase in shipments to France, from $5.8 million to $46.7 million, and a twofold increase in trade with Belgium, from $4.8 million to $9.7 million.[69] American grain dealers therefore drew a corresponding volume of franc bills on Paris and Antwerp. It was, in short, primarily an expansion in the size of the market for continental exchange which coincided with the emergence of an active futures market.

There is some evidence that futures markets were functioning in the leading continental financial centers prior to this time. The leading historian of foreign exchange markets, Paul Einzig, believes that isolated transactions between bankers and their customers preceded the development of European markets. In the produce trade where profit margins were narrow, merchants frequently covered the exchange risk on business "between countries with stable currencies."[70] At the same time, another group of financial speculators, who had little connection with the foreign trade sector, also used futures contracts to profit from interest arbitrage. In Europe, Einzig concluded, it was impossible to determine whether commercial demand for futures facilities created a market, which was subsequently used by speculators, or "whether it was the speculators who created the market, which, once in existence, provided facilities also for genuine trade requirements." But an identifiable market had emerged in Vienna and Berlin by the 1880s and 1890s, and its functioning was encouraged by "progress in banking technique and the increase of confidence amidst relatively stable conditions in the second half of the 19th century."[71] If futures markets for foreign exchange already existed on the continent in the mid-1870s, then the development of a similar market in the United States might be viewed as essentially imitative.

There is additional support in the Browns' records for the hypothesis that the techniques of negotiating futures contracts in foreign exchange had continental origins. It was, after all, those exchange dealers with close ties to Paris, Antwerp, and other continental cities such as the Drexel-Morgan banking firm, who introduced these innovative practices to the American market. The Browns, on the other hand, lacked a strong network of continental correspondents. The partners' unfamiliarity with the procedures for handling futures can be explained perhaps by the paradoxical failure of London, the world's financial center in most respects, to develop an active futures market until the twentieth century.[72] Thus there is a fair amount of circumstantial evidence indicating that the financial technology associated with futures transactions came to the United States from the European continent, and that the stimulus for this transfer was the dramatic increase in the number of bills drawn in francs against shipments of wheat to France and Belgium in 1879.

There is a third possibility that the resumption of specie payments, after a seventeen year suspension, provided the stimulus for the emergence of a futures market. The immediate success of the government's resumption policy led foreign exchange dealers to anticipate an extended period of monetary stability, during which they expected exchange rates to fluctuate within a narrow band around mint par. Undoubtedly, this renewed stability contributed to the increasingly severe price competition which drove down profit margins on large transactions from 0.5 percent to 0.25 percent, and sometimes even less. At the same time, the reduced fears about the amplitude of exchange rate fluctuations may have encouraged some dealers to introduce new facilities for futures transactions. But this interpretation is not in accord with the generally accepted theory that the modern futures market arose in response to the destruction of confidence in foreign exchange rates after World War I. The assumption has been that greater uncertainty about exchange rate movements, rather than less uncertainty, was more conducive to the initiation of futures transactions.

The clue leading to a reconciliation of these opposing explanations is found in Einzig's research on the emergence of continental markets. There he associated the development of futures markets with the relatively stable monetary environment of the late nineteenth century, which inspired confidence.[73] Yet he could not identify which group—financial speculators seeking to profit from interest arbitrage or grain merchants seeking to avoid the exchange risk—was primarily responsible for creating the market. Meanwhile, the Browns' records indicate that, in the United States, grain dealers rather than speculators provided the stimulus during the late 1870s. Thus, it appears that futures markets for foreign exchange have arisen at different times in response to the demands of differing economic groups and that the initiation of futures transactions in the trade sector of the American economy coincided with the coming of more stable monetary conditions.

Summary and Conclusion

In his pioneering survey of the U.S. foreign exchange market in the nineteenth century, published in 1929, Arthur Cole emphasized the trends toward specialization and concentration.[74] By the 1880s he concluded, the business had fallen "wholly into professional hands" and the market "had attained a scope and a complement of devices which were indicative of maturity." Cole's broad analysis of the evolutionary process of development has held up without serious challenge for almost half a century, and the Browns' manuscripts tend to confirm the basic wisdom of his observations about the character of the market in the long run. At the same time, the Browns' description of the increasingly competitive nature of the market in the waning years of the antebellum era suggests that at least one, previously undetected detour may have been encountered along the way to a more concentrated market structure.

At the beginning of the nineteenth century, there were no foreign exchange dealers in the formal sense of the word. A few merchants like Alexander Brown performed the services of an exchange broker in addition to carrying out a wide variety of business functions. American foreign trade grew rapidly during this early period, and a number of merchants participated in the nascent foreign exchange market as a sideline. Entry into the market was relatively easy in the first quarter of the century. The situation changed, however, when Nicholas Biddle expanded the Second Bank's sterling operations shortly after he became its president. The Second Bank possessed superior capital resources, and through the alliance with the House of Baring, it drove profit margins down so much that many firms left the field entirely. A few merchants who had been more firmly entrenched in the market, but who were by no means specialists, stayed in the field to cover some of the gaps left by the Second Bank; among the remaining houses, the Browns were by far the most prominent. The dominant position of the Second Bank discouraged new entries into the exchange field. As a result the market became increasingly concentrated, with only one dealer that could be clearly identified as a genuine specialist in handling foreign exchange transactions exercising leadership.

Despite the expiration of the Second Bank's charter in 1836, the trend toward greater concentration was not immediately reversed. With the Second Bank's future seriously in doubt, the Browns, in 1834, decided to devote more of their energies to letter of credit activities and foreign exchange operations. Other firms generally awaited the outcome of the political battle over the Second Bank. Instead of new opportunities in the foreign exchange field, 1837 brought an unprecedented economic crisis that signaled the arrival of a depressed state of foreign trade in the early forties. Thus the financial panic and subsequent business contraction deterred the emergence of a more competitive foreign exchange market. The Browns, in the meantime, inherited the leadership position in the field and used the lull in economic activity to consolidate their hold on the market. By 1840 the house was committed to further specialization in the foreign exchange field.

After 1843 economic conditions improved and a host of new firms gradually entered the market. Following the example of the defunct Second Bank, many commercial banks in the south initiated sterling operations in conjunction with independent dealers in the northern ports. The advances in communications which followed the spread of the telegraph lines reduced risks substantially and led brokers and dealers alike to increase their activities. Although the Browns were formidable competitors, they did not have the market power to restrict entry into the field. By the late fifties price competition was sharp among exchange buyers in the south. In the aftermath of the panic of 1857, the Browns attempted to squeeze out some of their competitors by increasing their volume of business at lower margins. But the effort proved a failure. "We have neither beaten our Competitors out of the field, nor made a satisfactory result for ourselves," the Liverpool partners concluded in 1860.

The Civil War halted the movement toward a more open market

structure, however. The familiar patterns of business were disrupted, and once the country went off specie, exchange operations became unusually risky. The bulk of the business concentrated in the hands of those specialists with the most capital and experience. And this time, the shift toward a more oligopolistic market was irreversible. When the war ended, the nation was left with an irredeemable paper currency. Even after the northern economy had been restored to health, foreign exchange operations remained a dangerous venture for any dealer who could not generate sufficient volume to maintain a daily balance between bill sales and purchases. The complications associated with handling a growing volume of drafts with bills of lading attached was another factor discouraging new entries into the field. Thus, the private banking houses—led by the Browns and Drexel, Morgan & Co.—dominated the market in the two decades following the Civil War. With the expansion of futures transactions in the late seventies, the foreign exchange market had evolved from a simple, informal affair early in the century to, as Arthur Cole has written, "one of the most intricate and highly sensitive institutions of modern times."

Conclusion

Broadly speaking, the success of the House of Brown over the first eight decades of the nineteenth century can be explained in terms of a threefold combination of good fortune, intelligent management, and sound organization. Alexander Brown was fortunate to arrive in Baltimore at a time when the port's foreign trade was undergoing the most rapid expansion in its history. The year 1800 was thus an auspicious date for establishing an enterprise featuring the latest styles of imported Irish linens. While many merchants in Baltimore and other American ports found prosperity in the first decade of the century, only a few produced an heir qualified to carry the same entrepreneurial skills forward into the next generation. Alexander Brown and his wife Grace produced not only one competent heir, but four sons of superior business ability; in an era when family owned businesses dominated the economy, this was a remarkable achievement indeed.

It was another stroke of luck that the entire male side of the family was blessed with good health, and Alexander and his sons all lived long and productive lives. This longevity was an important factor in preserving continuity in the firm's management because of the vulnerability of the partnership form of business organization to dissolution upon the untimely death of one of its members. When Samuel Nicholson, the managing partner of the New Orleans branch, died in 1857, James Brown noted that it was only the third death of a partner in the over one half century since the founding of the firm, although three men, including Joseph Shipley and his brothers John and George, had been lost as a result of retirement. Finally, the Browns were fortunate to embark on business careers at a time when the leading merchant-banking houses were just beginning to develop a broad range of financial services for the international economy. Foreign exchange markets had only recently emerged in the major U.S. port cities. It was also coincidental that cotton, the one commodity with which the partners were most closely associated, had not begun its rise as the nation's most valuable export until the invention of the cotton gin eight years before the turn of the century. Fundamentally, therefore, the firm's first few decades of business operations were conducted during a transitional period between an age of barter in the foreign trade sector and the emerging new era of international finance, which was based more on bills of exchange and letters of credit.

Favorable circumstances and the partners' good health could, of course, only carry an enterprise so far. To benefit wholly from these opportunities, the Browns added a full measure of business sagacity. The depth of their managerial talents was evident in virtually every aspect of the administrative process: from grand strategy and the formulation of business policy to the most routine operational procedures. Two strategies associated with partnership merit special citation. From its founding, the firm concentrated its energies on the Anglo-American foreign trade sector; domestic commerce and domestic banking were strictly avoided. In time the partners eliminated most of their transatlantic merchandising activities and concentrated on financial functions, in particular foreign exchange operations and the financing of American importers through the issuance of letters of credit.

The second key strategy was the establishment of outlets in the major seaport cities, especially New York and Liverpool. By assigning most of their experienced partners to the latter two ports, the Browns stayed well informed about new developments in the Anglo-American trade. Beyond their dual Anglo-American head-quarters, the Browns' development of a chain of subsidiary branches, manned by the firm's employees, was an innovative strategy which was not duplicated by any of their competitors in the merchant-banking field.

Over the years, the Browns also formulated a distinctive set of operating policies. In their advancing and merchandising activities, the avoidance of speculation was a hallmark of the partnership. Some of the partners' business decisions coincided with the introduction of genuinely innovative policies. With the aid of the telegraph, the Browns were the first firm to establish a uniform schedule of foreign exchange rates in the main northern and southern seaports. In the letter of credit field, the partnership was a leader in insisting on prompt customer reimbursements and the issuance of predominantly secured credits. Indeed, it can be said that few firms contributed more to the development of the letter of credit as a tool of modern international finance than the House of Brown.

The final, and perhaps most important, factor contributing to the firm's success was its unique administrative structure. Except for the Second Bank of the United States and a few of the nation's first railroads, other business organizations failed to develop a comparable system of internal management during the first half of the nineteenth century. The original architect of a coordinated plan of management was the founder, Alexander Brown. He stressed the importance of maintaining a unified management structure over a geographically dispersed chain of branch offices. After Alexander established the basic principles for successful management, the task of developing them further fell mainly to his eldest son William and his youngest son James.

The partial breakup of the original family enterprise in the late 1830s, due to the withdrawal of George and John A. Brown from the partnership, was not a serious blow for the organization as a whole, since the two remaining brothers, William and James, were located in the crucial ports of Liverpool and New York. The management philosophy William and James developed over the years differed significantly from the one ascribed to by their retiring brothers. George and John were, of course, competent businessmen by any standard of measure, yet they retained many of the more conservative attitudes of the old-line merchant. After attaining a substantial degree of wealth, George and John began to crave security — not greater riches. Both men preferred to keep their business activities directly in front of them and under their personal control. After the death of their father in 1834 the responsibilities and risks associated with managing a large organization, at a time when communication was slow, became an unnerving experience for them; it left their affairs too susceptible to uncontrollable outside forces — like the panic of 1837. Moreover, both George and John realized that the branches in Baltimore and Philadelphia were moving outside the mainstream of important decision making within the firm.

William and James Brown were, in contrast, businessmen of a different stripe. By degrees, they came to view a large, interdependent merchant-banking organization as a source of strength rather than a point of vulnerability. In a fundamental departure from the business norms of the time, the two brothers realized that there were sound reasons for delegating authority to associates and subordinates located in distant ports, and they were prepared to see their plans through and make them work successfully. Since William and James were located in the ports where trading activity was the most intense, they were close to the pulse of the commercial world, and as a result they were not overcome with the same feeling of alienation and remoteness that affected George and John.

The general attitude William and James displayed toward administrative matters foreshadowed the modern approach to a management discipline. Even so, they were not the greatest spokesmen for the virtues of standardization and systemization within the firm. That honor belonged to Francis Hamilton and Mark Collet — two Englishmen who assumed responsibility for the Liverpool branch in the early 1850s. The branch structure and the broad commitment to coordinated management already existed when the two men began their tenure. Thus they were primarily concerned with refining administrative methods and devising new techniques of internal control. As a result of their critique of the firm's capital structure, the proliferation of outside investments ceased and the partners committed more funds to newly created reserve accounts. At one point Collet and Hamilton summed up their administrative philosophy succinctly: "Our idea is that concentration & a perfect system of management of our business are the objects to be aimed at." One step in this process was the development of a system for handling business transactions that subordinates and agents could apply uniformly in the firm's various outlets. Beyond that, the English partners took great pains to instill in their associates a correct attitude about the proper mode of conducting business. They left few stones unturned in their striving for a more rational administrative structure. Here was an early victory for the managerial mind in the realm of business affairs.

As overseers of the firm's development, William and James Brown were the perfect senior managers. For the most part, they gave a free rein to their younger associates who were deeply involved in organization building. Despite the occasional complaints of Hamilton and Collet that they were not granted a commensurate voice in the decision-making process, in truth they had a unique opportunity to experiment in the field of internal administration. A similar framework for the development of forward-looking management concepts could not be found in the other financial enterprises of the day.

In the first eighty years of its business operations, the enterprise built up an enviable record of successes. From 1815 to 1845 the partnership ranked among the two or three leading commission houses in Liverpool, one of the world's most active ports. In the United States the firm was the second largest foreign exchange dealer behind the Second Bank of the United States, and after the Bank's demise the partnership inherited the leadership position. In the letter of credit market, the Browns supplanted the House of Baring as the prime issuer during the 1840s.

This recapitulation of the firm's achievements calls attention to one dimension of its activities that failed to receive proper emphasis in the main body of the study—the interrelationships of the various functions the Browns performed. The gathering and assessment of credit information is a case in point. For example, the information accumulated on exporters seeking advances and importers applying for letters of credit also proved useful in the conduct of foreign exchange operations. The maintenance of up-to-date and reliable credit files reduced immeasurably the risks otherwise inherent in the performance of virtually all of the Browns' specialized services.

Of their three primary functions, foreign exchange operations were perhaps most crucial to the firm's long-run prosperity. The partners' involvement in the foreign exchange market permitted them to negotiate with ease the advances authorized against consignments to the Liverpool branch, and it enabled them to generate safe remittances for their letter of credit customers. Moreover, by following diligently the multitude of factors that affected foreign exchange rates, the Browns maintained close links with one of the most sensitive economic mechanisms of the gold standard and Greenback eras.

No survey of the firm's development would be complete without some acknowledgment of the extent to which the partners' strategies were related to the broader institutional changes in the Anglo-American trade sector. Economic growth and the accompanying increases in the size of the market encouraged many nineteenth century merchants to narrow the range of their activities. The Browns took advantage of these opportunities and concentrated their efforts on a limited number of specialized business services. Early in its history, the Liverpool branch handled a wide variety of American produce on consignment, but the house eventually earned much of its reputation from a close association with the expanding cotton trade.

The partnership followed shifts in the pattern of marketing American imports as well. When there were signs, during the late twenties, that the practice of selling foreign goods at auction was declining, the Browns reacted promptly by increasing their volume of American consignments. At the same time, they expanded the issuance of letters of credit to those importers who wanted to make overseas purchases on their own account. The letter of credit market grew so swiftly that the Browns decided in 1834 to cease most of their mercantile activities in the United States and to concentrate instead on financing the importations of other merchants. However, the partnership continued to negotiate advances against consignments of American cotton to Liverpool. In both their advancing and letter of credit activities, the Browns provided the broad credit facilities which were so essential to the functioning of a predominantly agrarian-commercial economic system. In the meantime, the firm's foreign exchange facilities permitted importers and exporters alike to exe-cute international financial transactions expeditiously and safely.

The Browns' strategies in the 1840s and 1850s were likewise con-sistent with general economic and institutional changes in the foreign trade sector. Whereas many merchant-banking firms such as the House of Baring shifted their emphasis from the solicitation of con-signments to outright purchases of raw cotton, the Browns decided to withdraw almost completely from this increasingly competitive mar-ket. The firm now placed more emphasis on the letter of credit mar-ket, which underwent a threefold expansion in the last fifteen years of the antebellum era. Because new firms found entry into this field a difficult or at best a lengthy process, the market structure remained decidedly oligopolistic.

By the outbreak of the American Civil War, the Browns had be-come primarily financial specialists. The bulk of their revenues came from letter of credit and foreign exchange operations, two speciali-zed fields in which the firm was a market leader. After the war, the foreign exchange field became increasingly oligopolistic as well. Be-cause of the continued existence of an irredeemable paper currency and the expanded use of documentary bills of exchange, the foreign exchange market fell almost completely into the hands of specialists during the last quarter of the century. Because the partners had cre-ated an organization of unusual strength, they possessed the flexibili-ty to seize the emerging opportunities in the international banking field; as a result, the House of Brown was able to dominate two fi-nancial markets in which the competition came almost exclusively from other members of the Anglo-American merchant-banking community.

A final measure of the Brown family's achievement was the rate of capital accumulation. The modest figure of $121,703 recorded in 1810 had grown to the immense sum of $5,626,420 by 1837. After George and John Brown withdrew their share of the assets from the firm in the late thirties, William and James managed to increase their joint capital from $3,014,860 in 1840 to $7,474,203 in 1856. After the latter date, William Brown began a systematic withdrawal of capital in anticipation of his death. As the following figures dem-onstrate, the most rapid period of growth occurred early in the firm's history:

Period	Percent
1811-1820	19.6
1821-1830	11.9
1831-1837	11.0
1841-1850	6.6
1851-1856	6.5

The rate of capital accumulation continued at a pace of 11 to 12 percent in the period from 1820 to 1836 and then leveled off to a steady, if less spectacular, 6 to 7 percent in the forties and fifties. The goal of earning a better-than-average return, without incurring undue risks, was largely realized.

In addition to the financial rewards, the partners derived a high degree of self-esteem from their association with the House of Brown. The firm was widely recognized as the leading merchant-banking firm in the Anglo-American trade. To the nonfamily members of the partnership, the firm was a vehicle for social and economic mobility. But the distinction the family and nonfamily partners savored most highly was the reputation the firm enjoyed among its peers in the commercial world. When James Brown's heirs, John Crosby Brown and Howard Potter, assumed a position of managerial leadership in the 1870s, the family not only had a monetary investment to protect but a long tradition of banking preeminence to preserve as well. By then, the business services which had been developed over the decades since Alexander Brown first opened the door of his linen shop in 1800 were thoroughly institutionalized. A primary objective of his heirs had become the preservation of the House of Brown as the strongest pillar supporting the merchant-banking heritage in the Anglo-American community. In the main their goal was achieved, and the firm remained the nation's foremost international banker well into the twentieth century.

Appendixes

Appendix A

Combined capital accounts of Alexander Brown, 1810-1833; George Brown, 1810-1839; John A. Brown, 1810-1837; James Brown, 1811-1856; and William Brown, 1815-1856.

Year	Capital as of 12/31/-	Gain or Loss	Adjustments	Rate of Increase (percent)
1810	$ 121,703			
1811	162,221	$ 40,518		33.0
1812	208,643	46,322		28.0
1813	251,211	42,568		20.0
1814	263,117	11,906		5.0
1815	395,782	132,665		50.0
	539,442	Add William's Capital = $143,640		-
1816	662,789	123,347		23.0
1817	840,184	177,395		27.0
1818	888,529	48,345		6.0
1819	836,454	(52,075)		(6.0)
1820	920,086	83,632		10.0
1821	1,015,574	95,488		10.0
1822	1,151,740	136,166		13.0

Year	Capital as of 12/31/--	Gain or Loss	Adjustments	Rate of Increase
1823	1,380,830	229,090		20.0
1824	1,530,899	150,069		11.0
1825	1,591,728	60,829		4.0
1826	1,788,702	196,974		12.0
1827	2,129,482	340,780		19.0
1828	2,475,568	346,086		16.0
1829	2,508,145	32,577		1.0
1830	2,838,896	330,751		13.0
1831	3,230,361	391,465		14.0
1832	3,623,902	393,541		12.0
1833	4,080,912	457,010		13.0
1834	4,610,321	529,409	150,000 [a]	17.0
1835	4,957,345	347,024		8.0
1836	5,912,034	955,689		19.0
1837	5,626,420	(285,614)		(5.0)
1838		Capital withdrawn by George		
1839		and John A. Brown = $ 2,150,000		
1840	3,014,860			
1841	3,176,160	161,300		5.5
1842	3,024,989	(151,191)	97,404 [b]	(1.5)
1843	3,240,238	215,249	104,821 [c]	10.5
1844	3,571,292	331,054		10.0
1845	3,718,283	146,991		4.0
1846	4,016,348	298,065	23,800 [d]	9.0
1847	4,046,408	30,060	50,000 [e]	2.0

Year	Capital as of 12/31/--	Gain or Loss	Adjustments	Rate of Increase
1848	4,612,876	566,468		14.0
1849	4,946,057	333,181	50,000 [f]	8.5
1850	5,149,217	203,160		4.0
1851	5,332,128	182,911		3.5
1852	5,749,195	417,067		8.0
1853	6,258,770	509,585		10.0
1854	6,812,859	554,089		9.0
1855	7,074,272	261,413		4.0
1856	7,474,203	399,931		5.5
1857	-	William Brown begins to withdraw		
1858	-	capital in anticipation of death		

Source: Historical Files, Brown Brothers Harriman & Co., New York.

[a] In 1834 a legacy of $150,000 was paid Mrs. Alexander Brown, the founder's widow.

[b] In 1842 William and James Brown gave the Junior partners $97,404.

[c] In 1843 the Juniors were given $54,821, and James Brown gave his daughter Grace $50,000.

[d] In 1846 James Brown gave his son James Alexander $23,800.

[e] In 1847 James Brown gave his son William Benedict $50,000.

[f] In 1849 James Brown gave his daughter Millie $50,000.

Explanatory notes

1. For the purpose of consolidating capital accounts, the Browns converted sterling to dollars at the rate of $4.50 to the pound from 1815 to 1833 and at the rate of $4.80 to the pound from 1834 to 1856.

2. After 1825 the figures understate the firm's total capitalization since they do not include the capital accounts of added members. In 1836, for example, the other partners had an investment of approximately $586,000 in the house, or about 9 percent of the firm's total capital.

3. Upon William Brown's death in 1864, it was revealed that he and James had apparently given their grandchildren a combined sum of $2,715,134, which had not been accounted for previously. If these gifts were made in the 1840's and 1850's, the brothers' rate of capital accumulation shown above may be understated by 4 or 5 percent per annum.

Appendix B

Appendix B

Allottment of partnership shares, 1846-1862 and 1863-1893

Partner	1846	1847	1848-50	1851	1852	1853	1854	1855	1856	1857	1858	1859	1860	1861-62
William Brown	218	222	202	188	184	163	139	150	145	168	163	153	153	126
James Brown	178	181	165	153	150	153	114	122	118	137	133	125	161	133
Joseph Shipley	40	40	40											
Stewart Brown	29	29	32	43	43	51	61	61	61	61	61	61	61	79
Samuel Nicholson	29	29	32	43	43	43	43	43	43					
William Bowen	16	16	19	25	25	30	36	36	36	36	36	36		
Francis Hamilton	8		17	28	28	33	40	40	40	40	40	40	40	51
J. M. Brown		9	11	12	20	24	29	29	29	29	29	30	30	39
Mark Collet				26	26	31	37	37	37	37	37	37	37	48
Wm. B. Brown						9	19							
Stewart H. Brown									9	9	9	10	10	13
George H. Brown											10	10	10	10
Charles Dickey												15	15	19

Partner	1863	1864	1865-68	1869-74	1875-77	1878-80	1881	1882-85	1886	1887-88	1889-90	1891-93
William Brown	118											
James Brown	97	86	100	100	100							
Stewart Brown	79	79	80	76	45	45						
Francis Hamilton	51	51	61	58	44	44	54	55	55	59	59	65
Mark Collet	48	48	58	55	43	43	53	54	54	58	58	64
J. M. Brown	39	39	53	50	42	42	52	53	53	57	57	
Stewart H. Brown	25	25	35	33	40	40	50	52	52	56		
Charles Dickey	25	25	39	37	41	41	57	52	52	56	56	62
Howard Potter	26	26	36	32	25	75	75	52	52	56	56	62
J. Crosby Brown	10	20	23	19	25	75	75	52	52	56	56	62
Herman Hoskier			20	30	37	37						
Fredrick Chalmers				15	25	25	36	40	46	50	50	56
John E. Johnson					25	25	36	40	46			
Alex. H. Brown					25	25	35	40	40	44	44	44
Clarence Brown			10									
Waldron P. Brown										25	25	31
C. D. Dickey, Jr.											15	26

Appendix C

Estimated profit margins on cotton shipments from New Orleans and New York to Liverpool, 1820-1860 (prices in cents/lb. of cotton)

Year	New Orleans prices	Freight costs	Net cost	Liverpool prices	Gain (or loss)	Percentage of cost	New York prices	Freight rates	Net cost	Liverpool prices	Gain (or loss)	Percentage of cost
1820	14.30	2.50	16.80	23.00	6.20	37	17.00	-	-	23.00	-	-
1821	15.20	2.00	17.20	16.46	(0.74)	(4)	14.32	-	-	16.46	-	-
1822	17.40	2.24	19.64	13.90	(5.74)	(29)	14.32	1.24	15.56	13.90	(1.66)	(11)
1823	11.50	2.00	13.50	14.42	0.92	7	11.40	1.50	12.90	14.42	1.52	12
1824	14.50	-	-	15.32	-	-	14.75	1.00	15.75	15.32	(0.42)	(3)
1825	17.90	2.00	19.90	20.20	0.30	1	18.59	1.36	19.95	20.20	0.25	1
1826	11.90	1.92	13.82	11.70	(2.12)	(15)	12.19	1.24	13.43	11.70	(1.73)	(13)
1827	9.30	1.60	10.90	11.58	0.68	6	9.26	1.24	10.50	11.58	1.08	10
1828	9.70	1.24	10.94	11.68	0.74	7	10.32	0.88	11.20	11.68	0.48	4
1829	9.80	1.12	10.92	10.64	(0.28)	(3)	9.88	0.76	10.64	10.64	0.00	0.00
1830	8.90	1.24	10.14	12.88	2.74	27	10.04	1.00	11.04	12.88	1.84	17
1831	8.40	1.50	9.90	10.76	0.86	9	9.71	1.12	10.83	10.76	0.92	9
1832	9.00	1.36	10.36	12.44	2.08	21	9.38	0.88	10.26	12.44	2.18	21
1833	10.00	1.24	11.24	15.74	4.50	40	12.32	0.88	13.20	15.74	2.54	19
1834	11.20	1.24	12.44	16.20	3.76	30	12.90	0.82	13.72	16.20	2.48	18
1835	15.50	1.00	16.50	18.26	1.76	11	17.45	0.76	18.21	18.26	0.05	1
1836	15.20	1.24	16.44	17.58	1.14	7	16.50	0.88	17.38	17.58	0.20	1
1837	13.30	1.50	14.80	12.18	(2.62)	(18)	13.25	1.12	14.37	12.18	(2.19)	(15)
1838	9.00	1.76	10.76	12.56	1.80	17	10.14	1.36	11.50	12.56	1.06	9
1839	12.40	1.40	13.80	14.38	0.58	4	13.36	1.24	14.60	14.38	(0.22)	(2)

Appendix C (Cont.

Year	New Orleans prices	Freight costs	Net cost	Liverpool prices	Gain (or loss)	Percentage of cost	New York prices	Freight rates	Net cost	Liverpool prices	Gain (or loss)	Percentage of cost
1840	7.90	1.76	9.66	10.84	1.18	12	8.92	1.36	10.28	10.84	0.56	5
1841	9.10	1.00	10.10	11.46	1.26	13	9.50	0.76	10.26	11.46	1.20	12
1842	7.80	1.00	8.80	9.72	0.92	10	7.85	0.62	8.47	9.72	1.25	15
1843	5.70	1.24	6.94	8.74	1.80	26	7.25	0.76	8.01	8.74	0.73	9
1844	7.50	1.00	8.50	9.42	0.92	11	7.73	0.76	8.49	9.42	0.93	11
1845	5.50	0.94	6.44	7.84	1.40	22	5.63	0.62	6.25	7.84	1.59	25
1846	6.80	1.00	7.80	9.60	1.80	23	7.87	0.62	8.49	9.60	1.11	13
1847	9.90	1.24	11.14	12.06	0.92	8	11.21	0.50	11.71	12.06	0.35	3
1848	7.00	0.92	7.92	7.86	0.06	1	8.03	0.38	8.41	7.86	(0.55)	(7)
1849	5.80	0.92	6.72	8.18	1.46	22	7.55	0.38	7.93	8.18	0.25	3
1850	10.80	0.74	11.54	14.20	2.66	23	12.34	0.38	12.72	14.20	1.48	12
1851	11.70	0.88	12.58	11.02	(1.56)	(12)	12.14	0.36	12.50	11.02	(1.48)	(12)
1852	7.40	0.92	8.32	10.10	1.78	21	9.50	0.44	9.94	10.10	0.16	2
1853	9.10	1.12	10.22	11.08	0.96	9	11.02	0.50	11.52	11.08	(0.44)	(4)
1854	8.80	1.38	10.18	10.66	0.48	5	10.97	0.56	11.53	10.66	(0.87)	(8)
1855	8.40	0.96	9.36	11.20	1.84	20	10.39	0.44	10.83	11.20	0.37	3
1856	9.10	1.00	10.10	12.44	2.34	23	10.30	0.38	10.68	12.44	1.76	16
1857	12.40	0.94	13.34	15.46	2.12	16	13.51	0.32	13.83	15.46	1.63	12
1858	11.20	0.96	12.16	13.82	1.66	14	12.23	0.38	12.61	13.82	1.21	10
1859	11.50	0.96	12.46	13.36	0.90	8	12.08	0.38	12.46	13.36	0.90	7
1860	10.80	1.12	11.92	11.94	0.02	1	11.00	0.50	11.50	11.94	0.44	4

Sources: Price data—Stuart Bruchey, *Cotton and the Growth of the American Economy, 1790-1860.* New York, Harcourt, Brace & World, 1967. Tables 3-A and 3-P. Freight rates—Douglass North, *The Economic Growth of the United States, 1790-1860.* New York, W. W. Norton & Co., 1961. Table B-X.

ᵃNo allowance was made for fluctuations in foreign exchange rates in the chart. Freight rates and Liverpool prices are converted to dollars at the uniform rate of $4.80 to the pound. No allowance was made for selling commissions, bankers' fees, and other incidental expenses.

Analysis of the data

1. Over the entire period from 1820 to 1860, owners shipping from New Orleans to Liverpool earned an average (mean) gross profit of 10.7 percent, while owners shipping from the New York market to Liverpool received a 5.3 percent return.

2. Shippers from New Orleans to Liverpool showed profits in 34 years, losses in 6 years, and no data existed for one year. Shippers from New York to Liverpool showed profits in 29 years, losses in 9 years, and there were insufficient data for two years.

3. The range of profit and loss for New Orleans shippers was a 40 percent gain in 1833 and a 29 percent loss in 1822. The New York range was a 25 percent gain in 1845 and a 15 percent loss in 1837. Owners shipping from New Orleans to Liverpool directly earned profits of 20 percent or better in 13 seasons, while shippers from New York earned similarly high profits in only two years.

4. The profit margins for shippers by decades were as follows (in percent):

	New Orleans-Liverpool	New York-Liverpool
1820s	3.4	1.7
1830s	13.3	6.5
1840s	15.9	9.6
1850s	10.4	3.0

5. The data reveal that there was no correlation between the absolute level of cotton prices and profit margins for shippers to the Liverpool market. Indeed, the best decade for shippers was the 1840s, a period when prices were generally low. This relationship supports the validity of the Browns' views about the most appropriate time for large cotton operations—when prices were substantially below their traditional norm.

Appendix D

Issuing and Processing Letters of Credit:

The Mechanism of International Finance

A thorough understanding of the role merchant-banking firms played in the Anglo-American economy requires some knowledge of the mechanics of international financial transactions. Moreover, the importance of these financial techniques and the legal documents supporting them in promoting economic growth has received a boost from several "new" economic historians who previously eschewed institutional analysis for quantification. Indeed, Robert Higgs has recently identified secure property rights, along with widening markets, as a key element responsible for sustained growth in the U.S. economy. "With English precedents as a starting point, judges set down new rules for the legal treatment of negotiable instruments like notes, bills of exchange and lading, and warehouse receipts," Higgs explains. "In an expanding and far-flung market, uniform standards for dealing with these commercial documents were essential."[1] The Brown partners were closely associated with these financial instruments, and an analysis of how they issued and processed letters of credit not only demonstrates the importance of the international banker in expediting trade but also reveals much about the development of international property rights in the nineteenth century.

Before proceeding, it may be helpful to concentrate on a few elementary definitions. An appreciation of the distinctions between secured and unsecured credits and between clean and documentary bills of exchange is likely to prevent confusion later in the discussion. A foreign bill of exchange with the bill of lading for the financed merchandise attached was generally called a documentary draft or a documentary bill of exchange. Since possession of the bill of lading conveyed ownership to the banker, or to any other holder, letters of credit which specified the drawing of documentary bills of exchange were, by definition, at least partially secured. Clean drafts, on the other hand, had no bills of lading or any other documents attached to them; they were completely free of encumbrances. Since unsecured letters of credit were not collateralized in any manner, it follows that all drafts and bills of exchange drawn under them were necessarily clean.

In the nineteenth century, however, there was a marked tendency to refer to a credit according to the type of bill normally drawn under it. Secured credits became documentary credits, while unsecured credits were casually referred to as clean credits. But these analogies were not totally accurate, and incorrect usage in that day and our own has frequently led to misconceptions and misunderstanding.

The difficulty was that a letter of credit calling for clean bills of exchange might, nonetheless, be a secured transaction. Besides the title to the merchandise, there were other alternative forms of collateral. Before granting a credit stipulating the drawing of clean drafts, a banker might require a customer to deposit cash, accounts or notes receivables, securities, or other acceptable assets. In short, the terms clean credit and unsecured credit were not synonymous. Moreover, a secured credit might call for either clean or documentary bills.

The Browns' correspondence indicates that many foreign merchants were prone to exaggerate the significance of a clean credit. In some overseas markets, many sellers automatically assumed that any buyer who held a letter of credit calling for clean bills surely had a good credit rating in his home port. Many American importers were thus anxious to obtain clean credits, the New York partners explained in 1857, in order to demonstrate, at least superficially, that they had "good standing with their bankers." Many customers purchasing merchandise in England discovered that an authorization to draw clean bills on an important Anglo-American banking house helped "give them credit with the factories," the partners continued. "Of course, they do not know what security we have," they added.[2]

The chief variables in the terms of the Browns' letters of credit were the percentage of the overall shipment costs that the partners were willing to finance (or more technically, to allow themselves to become contingently liable for as a guarantor) and the amount and type of security they required to back up their commitment. The starting point in formulating their policies was, of course, the customary practices followed by other bankers active in financing international trade. In the China trade, for instance, the firm generally conformed with the normal procedure of issuing unsecured credits for the full cost of a shipment. Overall, however, the Browns felt that customary practices were too liberal, and they added their own modifications.

From the Browns' standpoint, the safest credits were those that customers paid in full at the time of issuance. An applicant simply exchanged his dollars for sterling at the current exchange rate, and the American branch instructed the Liverpool office to credit the customer's account for the amount of the anticipated draft. These credits were clean, yet fully secured. The main advantage for an importer was that he did not need to carry along specie on an overseas trip. Many small dry goods merchants took out these credits before leaving to make their yearly purchases in Europe. Since cash payment was made in advance, practically any firm could obtain a credit of this type from the Browns. The partners also handled the majority of the traveling credits issued to tourists in this manner. A basic characteristic of prepaid credits was their relative small face value; in Baltimore for example the average credit in 1859 was for approximately $5,000.

The larger dry goods merchants could often obtain clean credits from the partnership after submitting suitable collateral. The deposited collateral was commonly referred to as the margin. Assets acceptable for the margin were defined as accounts or notes receivable, government bonds, and some corporate and bank securities if conservatively valued. Margin requirements on clean credits varied from the minimal 25 percent up to 100 percent, depending on the standing of the merchant and the amount of competition the Browns faced in a given port. As a rule, importers found it more convenient to make purchases overseas with bills of exchange which were not encumbered with bills of lading, evidences of insurance, and other documents. Thus many merchants preferred clean credits in spite of high margin requirements.

In addition to reducing risks generally, the Browns favored a strong margin requirement because it tended to hold customers to "their legitimate scope."[3] The partners were also extremely particular about the nature of the security they held. For example, "one-name paper," or an importer's own note, was not considered acceptable collateral. When the Baltimore branch manager told the New York office in 1859 that one of his customers wanted to give him one-name paper for the margin on a shipment of hides from South America, the partners were noticeably annoyed: "We cannot understand the object of parties offering their own paper for the margin, that is if they have any idea that it adds to our security—it is a ridiculous idea. If the parties cannot respond for the credit, the note would be worthless. When we take security, we want something that is security."[4]

Despite their predilection to confine activities to secured credits, the Browns were occasionally forced to deviate from their standard rules on margin requirements. For instance, transactions with the stronger importers in Boston's China trade were exempted because of the competition from the Barings. Since the Barings' chief American representatives, the Wards, were headquartered in Boston, the China trade was one bailiwick where they retained a large share of the letter of credit business. When the Browns opened a Boston office in 1844, the majority of their customers were younger merchants who imported goods under fully secured credits. However, as these new merchants prospered, the Barings began offering them the privilege of importing under unsecured credits. At first, the Browns resisted compromising the principle of margin requirements, but in the end they told the Boston branch manager to exercise his discretion on the matter. "Where customers can get clean unsecured credits from Barings, we shall have to meet them," the New York partners conceded in 1858.[5]

Besides depositing collateral in advance, there were other ways importers could satisfy the Brown's customary margin requirements. A customer might apply for a letter of credit that could be negotiated for only a portion of the total cost of an anticipated shipment. According to this arrangement, the difference between the percentage financed by the Browns and the total cost of the shipment served as the margin. Customers commonly received credits negotiable for two thirds or three fourths of shipment costs. Importers who were also involved in exporting American foodstuffs found these credits particularly useful, since the receipts from an outward cargo were often sufficient to provide their 25 percent contribution to the cost of a return voyage. In the coffee trade with South America, for example, the proceeds from an outward cargo of flour generally covered the shipper's margin on the return shipment.[6] Firms importing merchandise directly from Mediterranean ports frequently applied for three fourths cost credits as well.

At times, the Browns limited financing to a fraction of the invoice price of the merchandise. The importer then paid all the transportation costs on the homeward voyage in addition to a percentage of the cost of the goods. The partners periodically imposed this restriction because of the standing of a given customer or because of the risks associated with a certain commodity. When an economic expansion led to sharply rising prices or when trading in a specific commodity became unusually vigorous, the Browns often demanded higher margins from all their customers, no matter how good their credit rating. During the winter of 1859-60 coffee prices rose steadily, and the partners decided to limit financing to a fixed amount per bag, irrespective of other considerations.

The Browns were not inflexible in implementing their standard rules. The partners permitted some firms to submit collateral *after* they received the news that bills of exchange had been drawn under a credit. On other transactions such as guano shipments from Peru, the freight costs paid by the shipper often served as the only margin. Furthermore, it was not unusual for a customer who had reached his original credit limit to negotiate additional bills of exchange on the Liverpool branch, provided of course the foreign seller agreed to take them in payment. The customer then had to make hurried arrangements with the Browns' office in his home port in order to guarantee the acceptance of any additional bills in Liverpool. Naturally, importers took such liberties only on transactions involving small amounts.[7]

While margin requirements protected the Browns somewhat, the receipt of the bill of lading for the financed merchandise reduced their risk even further. And the vast majority of the Browns' letters of credit called for the drawing of documentary bills of exchange. From the time the financed goods were placed on board the vessel, legal title to them rested with the Browns. Cargoes were invariably insured, and the insurance policies specified the Browns as payees in case of loss.[8] When the vessel arrived in the designated American port, the ship captain delivered the bill of lading and other related documents to the Browns' local representative — not to the firm actually importing the merchandise.

Possession of the bill of lading gave the Browns absolute control over the goods at the time of their entry into the United States. With the bill of lading in hand, the partners could — if difficulties with the importer arose — sell the merchandise for their own account and transfer the proceeds overseas to cover the drafts accepted by the Liverpool branch. While they took this drastic action only in dire circumstances, such protective measures were at their disposal.[9] Since the merchandise was a vital part of the firm's security, the Browns generally restricted financing under documentary credits to those commodities that could be stored in warehouses for an extended period of time without deteriorating. Perishables like fruit were therefore normally ineligible for such financing.[10]

At times, the Browns requested bills of lading under credits which were nominally unsecured. On these occasions the duplicate bill of lading was attached to the bill of exchange merely to indicate that a shipment of goods had taken place; the original bill of exchange went directly to the importer and in no way served as security for the Browns. This procedure was an effective means of thwarting those merchants whom the partners believed to be primarily interested in drawing what were commonly called finance bills or financial bills.

A finance bill was a bill of exchange drawn for the purpose of raising cash for activities other than the conduct of international trade. Drawers used the proceeds for various speculative activities, usually involving securites or specie. Finance bills were difficult to identify because their outward appearance was similar to other bills of exchange; in fact, the only distinguishing characteristic was the motive of the drawer and all too often that determination could only be made with the benefit of hindsight. The finance bill was, in short, the hot money of the nineteenth century. Financiers shifted funds from one currency to another in order to take advantage of short-run profit opportunities, whether real or anticipated.

Although the Browns participated moderately in international financial speculation, they vehemently opposed the issuance of letters of credit to customers for that purpose. Any credit permitting the drawing of clean bills of exchange were vulnerable to abuse.[11] The receipt of the duplicate bill of lading was thus always welcomed by the Browns as confirmation that a shipment of merchandise had in fact taken place. The partners rarely issued a credit for any purpose other than the transfer of tangible merchandise, with the exception of a few credits that were integral parts of "legitimate" investment banking activities. For the most part the Browns were dedicated to financing bona fide trade exclusively.

Under the Browns' procedures for handling documentary bills, there were two ways an importer could obtain the original bill of lading and take possession of the merchandise. The most direct method was for the importer to provide the firm's local office with sufficient funds to meet the incoming draft on his Liverpool account. Releasing the bill of lading upon immediate cash reimbursement was a procedure a banker could safely follow with any importer. However, the Liverpool branch did not actually need the funds until the due date of the bill of exchange drawn under the importer's letter of credit, and most importers hoped to extend their financing up to the maximum time permissible.

Because the Browns had confidence in most of their customers, they frequently released bills of lading under various trust receipt arrangements. Once the importer had possession of the merchandise, he was in a position to make sales and thus generate funds for remittance to the Liverpool branch. The stated function of a banker's trust receipt was to preserve a lien on the financed merchandise after the customer had assumed physical control. The legal definition of this financial device underwent a process of refinement throughout the nineteenth century. The Browns' letterbooks indicate that there was much confusion among customers and the partners alike about the functions performed by these financial instruments. Indeed, even in the twentieth century, serious questions remain about the degree of protection the trust receipt mechanism actually provides for the apprehensive banker.[12]

When the Barings introduced the trust receipt to the Anglo-American trade in the 1830s, the concept was vaguely understood and its legal status widely questioned.[13] The Barings' receipt was incorporated in the standard letter of credit agreement; the importer pledged the property or its cash proceeds to the payment of any bills of exchange drawn under his credit. The fact that the Barings included the passage in nominally unsecured credits which called for clean bills is a good indication of the little regard they had for this clause. The bill of lading went directly to the customer, and the Barings merely reserved the option of claiming the merchandise or some other kind of security. Other banking houses adopted the same clause, and the U.S. court upheld its validity as a contractual agreement in an 1843 test case.[14] Thereafter, the receipt became a standard financial device for the secured lender.

When the Browns began the release of bills of lading to customers under trust receipts is unknown, but the earliest surviving form is dated October 1851:

Boston   October 2, 1851

Whereas, under several letters of credit upon Brown Shipley & Co. of Liverpool issued by Thomas B. Curtis Attorney, in Boston, for account of Benjamin Upton of Salem Mass. in pursuance of which Brown Shipley & Co. have come under acceptances to a large amount, of which Seven thousand pounds Sterling more or less is by the said Benjamin Upton not remitted for, and whereas we, Benjamin Upton, Benjamin Upton Jr. & Henry P. Upton, are interested in the proceeds of the goods purchased under said letters of credit — Be it known that we . . . do hereby jointly and severally agree with Brown Shipley & Co. to fulfil all the obligations . . . attaching to the said letters of credit, also, pledging & hypothecating for the specific purpose of reimbursing Brown Shipley & Co. for their acceptances . . . the entire cargoes of Barks "Russell," "Mermaid" & "Elizabeth Fulton," the proceeds thereof & the policies of insurance thereon together with the bills of lading to be held subject to the order of Brown Shipley & Co. on demand with authority to take possession & dispose of the same at discretion for their security.

	(Signed)		Benj Upton
Salem Oct 3 1851	,,		Benjamin Upton Jr.
	,,		H. P. Upton

Source: Historical Files, Brown Brothers Harriman & Co., New York

Despite the seeming preciseness of such contracts, many bankers found the agreements of little value during periods of widespread business failures. Although they often discussed proposals to make the trust receipt system more airtight, genuine progress proved difficult. Charles Dickey, a Brown partner who had previously headed the Mobile branch, reviewed the trust receipt problem with young J. P. Morgan while traveling to Liverpool in October 1861. Upon his arrival, Dickey related the details of these discussions to his associates back in New York: "On the passage coming over I had the opportunity of much conversation with Mr. J. P. Morgan who you are aware was brought up with Duncan Sherman & Co. . . . . He said that nearly all their heavy losses with credits had been in consequence of the bad faith of parties to whom they had entrusted the property." Morgan had assured him, Dickey revealed, that "Peabody & Co. and Duncan S. & Co. would be very glad to co-operate with the other Banking Houses in adopting any plan by which the security which was intended to be made perfect should actually be so."[15]

Later in October, within the context of a broad discussion centered primarily on personnel and administrative problems in the subsidiary branches, the partners examined again the matter of trust receipts. Collet and Hamilton charged that the Philadelphia office had been improperly managed for some time, and as proof they cited the mishandling of bills of lading on documentary credits. Just recently, the Liverpool partners claimed, they had been astonished to learn that the Philadelphia manager "had not been in the habit of taking receipts when handing out documents to good people . . . and it never seemed to have struck [him] that the endorsement of a Bill of Lading consigned to order & passing it over to the principal of the credit . . . invalidated our lien on the goods."[16]

Hamilton conceded, however, that there had been "a great deal of difficulty about these receipts which we are trying to remedy but they are a very uncertain security at best." And the difficulties were intensified when the partners dealt with importers whose goods were normally "broken up & distributed." In those situations the trust receipt proved of little value, Hamilton admitted, because experience had shown it was "almost impossible to follow or identify them."[17]

The successful completion of international letter of credit transactions relied in great part on the functioning of the firm's branch office in Liverpool and after 1863 in London. Because the pound sterling was the common medium of world trade, England served as a giant clearing house for the majority of international transactions involving not only Americans but also the merchants of all nationalities who used the oceans as an avenue of commerce. Thus bills of exchange drawn around the world under the credits granted by the American branches converged on Brown, Shipley & Co. for acceptance and payment.

While the vessel carrying a cargo financed through the Browns was in transit to the United States, the draft drawn by the foreign seller against the importer's account was simultaneously in route toward the Liverpool branch. Upon its arrival in England, the seller's local representative presented the draft to Brown, Shipley & Co. for formal acceptance. The Liverpool partners thoroughly inspected the draft and the documents attached to it, making certain that the bill of exchange had been properly drawn. They expected the shipping documents to conform to the stipulations set forth in the original letter of credit. If everything was in order, Brown, Shipley & Co. was by law required to accept the draft. The partners' acceptance meant the following: on the bill's maturity date the firm would have to pay the draft even if the American importer had failed, in the meantime, to remit sufficient funds to cover it.

If, on the other hand, the bill and its documents varied even slightly from the terms set forth in the letter of credit, the Liverpool partners could refuse to accept it. There was therefore a premium on clearness and preciseness in the initial working of a letter of credit. Naturally the Browns discouraged instructions which might be subject to varying interpretations. In December 1858, for instance, the Baltimore branch manager told the New York office that one customer regularly opened credits authorizing drafts for the "fair invoice price" of the merchandise purchased by his supercargo.[18] The manager questioned the wisdom of continuing the issuance of credits so vaguely worded because, he explained, "it throws upon Brown, Shipley & Co. the responsibility" of determining if the foreign seller was charging fair prices. Although the customer currently had a good credit rating, there was always the risk that he "might say the invoice was too high" and refuse to reimburse the Liverpool office. "Therefore," the manager added, "it would be better to insert [price] limits for each article." While such limits were practical in the sugar and coffee trade with South America, the Browns found them inappropriate elsewhere. In the Far Eastern trade especially, importers used credits to buy a variety of articles, and the New York partners characterized transactions in that part of the world as "difficult . . . to control."[19]

It is important to remember that Brown, Shipley & Co. only had the responsibility of ascertaining that the documents were in order. For the most part that meant merely that the duplicate bill of lading indicated merchandise had been properly shipped under the terms called for in the letter of credit. It did not mean that the Browns were responsible for verifying the actual quantity, quality, or condition of the goods. In other words, they did not inspect the merchandise itself; their duties were strictly financial. Even if, in an extreme case, a fraudulent seller shipped empty boxes to the American buyer, the Liverpool office was still obligated to accept a properly drawn draft so long as the bill of lading stated that boxes containing the actual merchandise had been put on board the designated vessel for the account of the American importer.

One of the difficult decisions the Browns and other issuers of letters of credit faced in the mid-nineteenth century was in defining those circumstances which might justify the disavowal of their outstanding guarantees. In financial jargon the terminology was to revoke a credit. Bankers generally agreed that the customer had the right to revoke the agreement, in whole or in part, if he did so prior to the formal, irreversible acceptance of a given bill of exchange. Customer revocations were usually selective, in the sense that they were aimed at specifically designated foreign merchants—a procedure comparable to stopping payment on a personal check today. The customer simply ordered the banker to accept no bills of exchange drawn against his account by a certain foreign seller. But if the customer's instructions reached the banker after acceptance, then they had arrived too late and had no effect.

The main controversy was over the prerogative of a banking house to repudiate unilaterally the guarantees in its outstanding credits. Early in the century, it was generally presumed that no such privilege existed; that is, a banker did not have the power to abrogate the contract under any circumstances. Searching for more flexibility, some houses began issuing credits which included a new clause permitting them to cancel the guarantee at their own discretion. The general understanding was that the clause would only become operational during a period of acute economic paralysis. It is difficult to pinpoint exactly when the first credits containing the cancellation clause were granted, but agents of George Peabody & Co., including the New York representative Duncan, Sherman & Co., were the most prominent issuers employing the device in the 1850s.

The Browns, in contrast, considered all their credits to be inherently irrevocable; to them a revocable letter of credit seemed a contradiction in terms—from both a legal and moral standpoint.[20] When the Boston branch manager suggested the inclusion of revocation clauses in 1856, the New York partners rejected the idea out of hand: "As regards obtaining the consent of parties to cancel credits . . . to have it with us to *cancel whenever we saw of it* would be tantamount to declining to open a credit since we could annul it at any moment."[21]

In England the act of acceptance by Brown, Shipley & Co. made any bill of exchange, no matter what the standing of the other parties associated with it, highly negotiable and therefore especially valuable. The holder of the acceptance could discount it in the very active English money market at any time prior to the maturity date. In addition, acceptance by a house with the stature of the Browns meant that the bill could be discounted at very favorable interest rates. The rates on prime foreign acceptances were usually just a fraction above or below the Bank of England's rediscount rate.

Upon presentation, the Liverpool office set the final maturity date for a sight draft and then relayed the pertinent information to the appropriate American branch. During the interval between acceptance and the bill's due date, the Liverpool partners expected the American importer to remit sufficient funds to cover the obligation through the firm's office in his home port. If an importer failed to transfer the funds by the bill's due date, the Browns' contingent liability immediately became a direct liability, and the firm had to pay the acceptance from its own capital resources. It was, of course, this guarantee of payment on the part of international bankers that made the bills of exchange drawn under their letters of credit so valuable to those merchants and factories selling goods to foreign buyers. During any normal year, defaults by American importers were rare; but when one occurred, the Browns were called upon to pay the acceptance and protect their own good name.

In the 1850s the partners expected importers to remit funds to Liverpool at least two weeks before a bill's maturity date. The Browns' ironclad rule on the promptness of remittances was one of the new policies introduced in response to the financial crisis in the mid-thirties. Prior to that time, international bankers had been customarily lax in requiring reimbursement. The Barings' policy in the early 1830s was, as described by Ralph Hidy, very flexible: "The managing partners willingly let trusted friends remit when they wished, allowed some postponements . . . and acquiesed in numerous delays . . . If the delay was not too long the Barings made no objections."[22] And generally speaking, the same could be said for the Browns. The Baltimore branch described its relationship with one of its prime customers, Peabody, Riggs & Co., in August 1836. George Peabody felt that he had made a good payment if he put the Liverpool house in funds within six months of the acceptance date. For strong firms like Peabody's, such accommodations were normally safe, George Brown believed, although he was "decidedly opposed to its being generally adopted as some houses are willing to do."[23]

However, by the end of 1836 the Browns had already tightened their terms. "In all credits now lodged we inform the parties that you must be put in possession of bills before you pay," George Brown wrote the Liverpool partners in November.[24] Peabody was told that he too would be expected to conform to the new rules on reimbursement. The same point was reiterated when Peabody's £15,000 credit line came up for annual review in January 1837. Because Peabody now planned to do business as a jobber as well as selling goods by the package, an as yet undetermined increase in his line was anticipated and readily acceded to by George Brown.[25] In reporting on Peabody's credit worthiness to the Liverpool branch, the Baltimore partner estimated his customer's capital at over $400,000 and then added the following remarks: "Unless he goes into some wild speculation (which we do not think likely) we consider his house safe . . . The only thing we do not like in Peabody is that we think he is too close with you & us about commissions & if he could save a little by doing his business with others we think he would be inclined to do so." But it was clearly understood that there were to be no more cash advances on acceptances. Peabody, Riggs & Co. was a good customer, George Brown continued, "yet they want unwarrantable accommodations & it may be better . . . to lose them than to put them on a different footing from others."[26]

In February 1837 George Brown summarized the firm's new operating policies in the letter of credit field.[27] Briefly stated, the rule on remittances went as follows: on the maturity date of an importer's acceptance, the partners expected the Liverpool branch to have in its possession a remitted bill of exchange due within 60 days or less. Thereafter, less of the firm's capital resources were normally tied up in letter of credit activities.[28] In his survey George Brown also emphasized the maintenance of a uniform set of rules in all three of the branches issuing credits—Baltimore, Philadelphia, and New York.

In remitting funds from the United States, importers had the option of buying pounds from the Brown firm itself or of handing in sterling bills acquired from an alternative source. In the first instance, the partners permitted customers to purchase sterling at a special rate, called the "settlement rate," which was no higher than the prices quoted by other first class foreign exchange dealers. Their regular sterling rate was often an eighth or a quarter percent above the settlement rate. The Browns used higher rates as the key device for decreasing demand whenever their overall position in the foreign exchange market dictated a temporary reduction in the volume of sales. But the partners considered it imprudent to ask letter of credit customers, who were providing the funds to meet the contingent liabilities of the Liverpool branch, to pay the higher sterling rate. Had they done so, it would have, at the very least, inconvenienced importers, who presumably would have purchased sterling elsewhere at the market rate, and it would have also given competitors a fine opportunity to solicit new accounts. Thus the partners deliberately extended competitive sterling rates to their letter of credit customers at all times.

The Browns permitted customers to hand in sterling obtained elsewhere for all or only a portion of their total obligation. Alternative suppliers of sterling bills were local exporters, domestic bill and exchange brokers, and other foreign exchange dealers. The partners' only stipulation was that the bill had to be drawn on a first class English payee, whatever its source.[29]

The Browns' policy was, in this respect, far more flexible than those adhered to by the Barings and George Peabody, who stood at opposite ends of the pole. Peabody was reluctant to receive any of his own sterling bills in remittances because he could not discount them readily in the short term money market. Indeed, his heavy reliance on the discount market was one practice that profoundly disturbed conservative English bankers.[30] The Barings, in contrast, financed their varied business activities without resort to the discount market, a general strategy that contributed greatly to their high esteem in the financial world. In their letter of credit operations the Barings much preferred, and sometimes insisted upon, remittances in the form of sterling bills drawn on themselves, presumably because they could thereby eliminate the risk of nonpayment.[31] By comparison, the Browns took no overt steps to pressure letter of credit customers to use one form of remittance in preference to another. They welcomed the opportunity to tie in foreign exchange sales with their letter of credit functions, but customers were free to shop around for better rates on first class bills. The Browns were, as a rule, moderate borrowers in the discount market, although the English partners aspired to a position of equality with the Barings.

Even though importers opened their credits in the American branches, the Browns maintained these accounts on the ledgers of the Liverpool office. A bill remitted in settlement of a customer's account usually reached Brown, Shipley & Co. a few days before his acceptance became due. Upon receipt the Liverpool partners presented the remitted bill to the payee for formal acceptance, and during the 60 days or so that they held this new asset awaiting final payment, the Browns charged interest against the customer's account. When the remittance was a bill drawn on the Liverpool house itself, the transfer of funds took place through internal bookkeeping procedures; but the net effect on the customer was the same because the partners charged interest on his account until the bill matured. Since the prices of 60 d/s bills in the United States were invariably lower than the "pure" dollar-sterling exchange rate due to the interest factor automatically built into them, the importer's interest expense in England was largely offset by the reduced price of sterling bills in his home port.

Even so, customers were generally sensitive about the level of interest rates on their overseas accounts. Consequently the Browns were content to restrict themselves to minimal earnings from interest charges on importer's accounts. Their practical goal was to charge rates sufficiently high to cover the interest expenses the Liverpool branch incurred in the discount market. Any interest income on letter of credit accounts over any given year was mostly incidental. Indeed, the firm's overall business strategy was to derive income primarily from commissions and foreign exchange margins; low, competitive interest rates were required to attract and then hold customers in the Anglo-American market.

During the first half of the century, the Browns' charge on customer accounts was a flat 5 percent interest, and they applied the same scale to credit as well as debit balances. Then in the 1850s the partners altered their policy. Although 5 percent still remained the standard rate, the Browns added a clause to the letter of credit agreement empowering them to charge interest at the Bank of England's rediscount rate whenever that rate rose above the 5 percent level. Despite the addition of this clause, there was much sentiment among the partners for retaining the standard, traditional rate irrespective of conditions in the English money market. The New York partners told the Boston branch manager in 1856 that the firm would probably be slow in reacting to any sharp, temporary rise in the rediscount rate.[32]

As the preceding analysis reveals, the issuing and processing of letters of credit was a complicated procedure which demanded a substantial amount of international coordination. For most merchant-banking houses in England, it required the cooperation of independent firms in the United States. For the Browns, on the other hand, the operations were strictly an intrafirm affair, and this fundamental difference explains, in large part, why the partnership was a dominant force in the market during much of the nineteenth century. Yet the basic mechanism was the same for all the firms actively financing American importers through the issuance of letters of credit. The development of this financial system and the evolution of the supporting documents laid the foundation for expanded world trade in the second half of the nineteenth century.

Notes
Bibliography
Index

ABBREVIATIONS USED IN THE NOTES

AB&S Alexander Brown and Sons

AB&SP Alexander Brown and Sons Papers

BB&C Brown Brothers and Company

BB&CP Brown Brothers and Company Papers

BS&C Brown, Shipley and Company

HF Historical Files, Brown Brothers Harriman and Company

W&JB&C William and James Brown and Company

Notes

INTRODUCTION

1. There are numerous secondary sources on the Browns' business enterprises and the family. The most recent book is John Kouwenhoven, *Partners in Banking: An Historical Portrait of a Great Private Bank, Brown Brothers Harriman & Co., 1818-1968* (Garden City, N.Y., 1968). For a complete list of related literature, see the special listing of sources on the Browns in the bibliography.

2. For a shorter work with a topical approach see Ralph Hidy, "The Organization and Functions of Anglo-American Merchant Bankers, 1815-1860," in *The Tasks of Economic History,* a supplement of the *Journal of Economic History,* 1 (1941).

3. A breakdown of the allocation of partnership shares is found in Appendix B. The allocation of shares determined a given partner's claim on the profits that remained *after* each partner's capital account had been credited with a minimal 5 percent in earnings. Prior to the mid-thirties, only Alexander Brown and his four sons were full members of the general partnership. Thereafter, new additions to the partnership were given a substantial number of shares, but the bulk of the capital invested in the firm continued to be held by the founders and their heirs.

4. Ralph Hidy, *The House of Baring in American Trade and Finance: English Merchant Bankers at Work, 1763-1861* (Cambridge, Mass., 1949).

I THE ROLE OF THE INTERNATIONAL BANKER

1. Douglass North, "International Capital Flows and the Development of the American West," *Journal of Economic History,* 16 (December 1956), 493-505.

2. George Green calls such a process the "monetization" of a barter economy in his *Finance and Economic Development in the Old South, 1804-1861* (Palo Alto, Calif., 1972) p. 47. Standard references on the subject are T. S. Ashton, "The Bill of Exchange and Private Banks in Lancashire, 1790-1830," *Economic History Review,* 15 (1945); G. H. Conder, "Bills of Exchange: The Part They Have Played in English Banking, Past and

Present,"*Journal of the Institute of Bankers* (October 1889), 415-441; Albert E. Feavearyear, *The Pound Sterling: A History of English Money* (Oxford, 1931); and A. P. Usher, "The Origin of the Bill of Exchange," *Journal of Political Economy* (June 1914), 566-576.

3. Rhondo Cameron, ed., *Banking in the Early Stages of Industrialization* (New York, 1967) pp. 1-25.

4. Shu-Iun Pan, *The Trade of the United States with China* (New York, 1924) p. 13.

5. Bernard Bailyn, *The New England Merchants in the Seventeenth Century* (Cambridge, Mass., 1955), chapters 4 and 7.

6. Joseph Klein, "The Development of Mercantile Instruments of Credit in the United States," *Journal of Accountancy*, 12 (1911), 321.

7. The new pattern of international payments had far-reaching economic repercussions. When the bill of exchange replaced specie as the normal medium of exchange in China during the late 1820s, it put an abrupt halt to the American silver outflow. Peter Temin has argued that the silver, which thereafter accumulated in the United States, dramatically increased bank reserves, and the result was the sharp inflation experienced by the economy in the early 1830s. Peter Temin, *The Jacksonian Economy* (New York, 1969), pp. 77-82.

8. W. T. C. King, *History of the London Discount Market* (London, 1936).

9. A market for acceptances did not arise in New York until 1913 after national banks were given the privilege of acceptance. Edgar S. Furniss, *Foreign Exchange* (Boston, 1922), pp. 366-404.

10. Margaret Myers, *The New York Money Market* (New York, 1931), p. 76, and Paul Einzig, *The History of the Foreign Exchange Market,* 2nd ed. (London, 1970), pp. 171-200.

11. Arthur H. Cole, "Evolution of the Foreign-Exchange Market of the United States," *Journal of Economic and Business History*, 1 (1928/29), 384-421.

12. Fritz Redlich, *The Molding of American Banking,* 2nd ed. (New York, 1968), pp. 124-133.

13. Robert L. Thompson, *Wiring a Continent: The History of the Telegraph Industry in the United States, 1832-1866* (Princeton, 1947), pp. 20-164.

14. Norman S. Buck, *The Development of the Organization of the Anglo-American Trade* (New Haven, Conn., 1925), p. 154.

15. The Barings' initial letters of credit were issued in 1777. R. Hidy, *House of Baring,* p. 16.

16. Norman Buck described the transaction this way: "This method of conducting business was profitable to all concerned; to a British manufacturer, because he received a bill of exchange which could be turned into cash immediately; to the American importer, because he got the benefit of lower prices for prompt payments; and to the British banking house, which

received a commission for accepting the bills of exchange, without having advanced any actual funds." Buck, *Organization of Anglo-American Trade,* p. 156.

17. The terms merchant banking and investment banking were not, of course, mutually exclusive. The Barings, for example, were active in both fields. The Browns were known mainly as merchant bankers.

18. Oelrichs & Lurman also sent grain consignments to one of the Barings' major competitors, George Peabody & Co. See Muriel Hidy, "George Peabody, Merchant and Financier, 1829-1854," (Ph.D. diss., Radcliffe College, 1939), p. 328.

19. Shelia Marriner, *Rathbones of Liverpool, 1845-73* (Liverpool, 1961), pp. 74-84.

20. Fletcher, Alexander & Co., for example, concentrated on the China and India trade. M. Hidy, "George Peabody," p. 139.

21. D. M. Williams, "Liverpool Merchants and the Cotton Trade, 1820-1850," in J. R. Harris, ed., *Liverpool and Merseyside* (London, 1969), pp. 182-211. In the years 1820, 1830, and 1839, the Browns' Liverpool branch was either the first or second largest importer of cotton — much of it on consignment. In 1839 they headed the list of importers and had their largest market share to date, 7.2 percent. Additional information on the Browns' important role in financing cotton shipments can be found in Stuart Bruchey, ed., *Cotton and the Growth of the American Economy: 1790-1860* (New York, 1967), pp. 221-245.

22. Harold A. Williams, *Robert Garrett & Sons: Origin and Development, 1840-1965* (Baltimore, 1965).

23. Another Baltimore house, Josiah Lee & Co., was given the power to grant credits in 1854, but the account was so inactive that it was soon closed. M. Hidy, "George Peabody," p. 315.

24. Bills on the Browns were accepted in Liverpool but paid in London. In 1821 a customer reported difficulty in passing bills on the firm in "foreign countries" that were not drawn directly on London. In order to accommodate foreign sellers the Browns made arrangements with their London correspondents, Denison Heywood Kennard & Co., to accept some of their bills. When the firm's name became better known in distant ports, the London option was no longer required. Until 1863, however, Denisons received a commission for paying the firm's monetary obligations. See Alexander Brown & Sons, Baltimore, to William & James Brown & Co., Liverpool, November 16, 1821, Alexander Brown & Sons Papers (Library of Congress).

25. Ralph Whitney, "The Unlucky Collins Line," *American Heritage,* 8 (February 1957), 48-53; and David Tyler, *Steam Conquers the Atlantic* (New York, 1939).

26. For the story of gaining Congressional approval and the firm's $153.75 of "entertainment" expenses see Kouwenhoven, *Partners in Banking,* p. 96.

27. See John G. Dow, "The Collins Line," unpub. masters' thesis,

Columbia University, 1937; and for a contemporary source Fessenden N. Otis, *Isthmus of Panama: History of the Panama Railroad: And of the Pacific Mail Steamship Co.* (New York, 1867).

II GROWTH AND EXPANSION

1. H. C. Lawlor, "Rise of the Linen Merchants in the Eighteenth Century," *Fibres & Fabrics Journal* (September 1941), 5. Alexander's father, William Brown, reportedly leased a bleachworks around 1760. His brother, Patrick, changed his name to John and lived in England as an insurance broker until his death in 1836.

2. Alexander's brother, Stewart, operated a firm in Baltimore for a few months in 1796. His partner was Moore Falls, origin unknown. They used the style, Falls & Brown, and Alexander inherited their old account books when he arrived in 1800. AB&SP.

3. Frank Kent, *The Story of Alexander Brown & Sons* (Baltimore, 1925), p. 44. The ad appeared in the *Federal Gazette and Baltimore Daily Advertiser* on December 20, 1800, and read as follows: "The Subscriber, lately arrived from Ireland, has brought with him a most complete assortment of 4-4 and 7-8 wide Irish linen which, upon examination will be found much lower than any inspected for three years past, and which will be sold by the box or piece for cash or good acceptance in the city on usual credit."

4. The figures are located in the firm's Historical Files. For further details see appendix A.

5. R. Hidy, *House of Baring*, p. 129.

6. Stuart Bruchey has already written a fine description of the various activities of another Baltimore merchant, Robert Oliver, during the first two decades of the nineteenth century. A detailed investigation of the early history of the Brown firm would almost certainly reveal many similarities between the two rising merchants. Stuart W. Bruchey, *Robert Oliver: Merchant of Baltimore, 1783-1819* (Baltimore, 1956).

7. David Gilchrist, ed., *The Growth of the Seaport Cities, 1790-1825* (Charlottesville, Va., 1967).

8. In 1810 Alexander considered sending John to Pernambuco, Brazil, to establish a house with one John McKee. During the War of 1812, he traveled to Lisbon and made arrangements with a Portuguese house to charter Russian ships to bring cotton from New Orleans to Lisbon and then on to William's Liverpool branch. John was later slated to join his brother in England, but for some reason James was sent instead.

9. James spent only a few years in Liverpool, however. By 1820 he was back in Baltimore and he spent much of the next five years substituting for John in Philadelphia. John went to New Orleans for several winters during the early twenties.

10. Robert G. Albion, *The Rise of New York Port, 1815-1860* (New York, 1939).

11. Thomas Whedbee, *The Port of Baltimore in the Making, 1828 to 1878* (Baltimore, privately printed, 1953).

12. Alexander Brown to William Cumming, Petersburg, April 8, 1803, AB&SP.

13. AB&S, Baltimore, to William Brown & Co., Liverpool, January 1, 1811, AB&SP.

14. AB&S, Baltimore, to William Cumming, Petersburg, December 27, 1813, AB&SP.

15. AB&S, Baltimore, to Durkin Henderson & Co., February 18, 1811, AB&SP. This firm was a Virginia tobacco dealer. The letter read as follows: "When shipments are made to William Brown & Co., the Bills of Lading sent us and Insurance ordered thro' us, we are at all times ready to negotiate a reasonable advance free of any commission."

16. AB&S, Baltimore, to William Brown & Co., Liverpool, May 1, 1811, AB&SP. The Liverpool house was informed of a cotton shipment coming to it from New Orleans—certainly among the first the branch received on consignment. Alexander Brown stated that insurance in the United States was much cheaper than in England, and the policy would be lodged with themselves. Later he decided holding insurance on consigned goods represented too great a conflict of interest.

17. Alexander Brown to George Brown, December 29, 1812, AB&SP. When William Brown brought his new wife to Baltimore for a visit, his brother George replaced him in Liverpool. For further information on wartime trade see Herbert Heaton, "The American Trade," in C. Northcote Parkinson, ed., *The Trade Winds: A Study of British Overseas Trade during the French War, 1793-1815* (London, 1948), pp. 194-226; and Freeman Galpin, *The Grain Supply of England during the Napoleonic Period* (New York, 1925).

18. Alexander Brown to William Brown, January 6, 1814, AB&SP.

19. AB&S, Baltimore, to D. C. Townes & Co., New Orleans, October 15, 1818, AB&SP.

20. AB&S, Baltimore, to Hugh Munro & Co., Lisbon, August 15, 1818, AB&SP.

21. AB&S, Baltimore, to William & James Brown & Co., Liverpool, October 27, 1819, AB&SP.

22. Alexander Brown to William Brown, August 7, 1820, AB&SP.

23. Ibid., August 21, 1821. The firm continued to underwrite the insurance on its vessels, however. In 1831 the Baltimore branch reported that the insurance account over the last eight years showed a $53,000 credit balance. AB&S, Baltimore, to W&JC&C, Liverpool, February 11, 1831, AB&SP.

24. AB&S, Baltimore, to W&JB&C, Liverpool, September 22, 1825, AB&SP.

25. Ibid., August 13, 1819. In 1820 the list of agents was as follows: Campbell & Cumming, Savannah; Adger & Black, Charleston; and McLanahan & Bogart, New Orleans. Johnston McLanahan's sister was married to George Brown, the second son. A number of the Browns' letters to their southern agents are included in the Stuart Bruchey, ed., *Cotton and the American Economy*, pp. 233-242.

26. Until the mid-thirties, outsiders were considered limited partners only in the branch office where they served, however.

27. AB&S, Baltimore, to W&JB&C, Liverpool, June 21, 1819, AB&SP.

28. Robert G. Albion, *The Rise of New York Port* (New York, 1939).

29. January 1, 1826, HF. For details of the circular see Kouwenhoven, *Partners in Banking,* pp. 41-42.

30. Brown Brothers & Co., N.Y., to S. & H. Stafford, Albany, January 27, 1826, HF.

31. AB&S, Baltimore, to W&JB&C, Liverpool, March 16, 1820, AB&SP.

32. Ibid., October 22, 1821.

33. Brown Brothers & Co., N.Y., to Benjamin Story, New Orleans, April 5, 1826, HF.

34. AB&S, Baltimore, to Adger & Black, Charleston, April 1, 1823, AB&SP.

35. AB&S, Baltimore, to William Cumming, Petersburg, April 24, 1819, AB&SP.

36. AB&S, Baltimore, to W&JB&C, Liverpool, March 15, 1820, AB&SP.

37. From the mid-twenties to the late 1870s, the Browns' buying rate was normally set 0.5 percent below the current selling price. In the antebellum era, seasonal operations generally increased overall margins. In the panic of 1837 the firm realized margins of 10 to 15 percent on some transactions.

38. AB&S, Baltimore, to W&JB&C, Liverpool, March 31, 1821, AB&SP.

39. Bray Hammond, *Banks and Politics in America: From the Revolution to the Civil War* (Princeton, 1957), p. 276. Brown and Stephen Girard were among the more important stockholders backing Langdon Cheves for the presidency, Hammond states. Alexander Brown had been a staunch supporter of the First Bank as well, and his letters in 1811 expressed much regret at its probable closing. The family's initial relationship with Nicholas Biddle was a cordial one. John A. Brown wrote him in 1824 recommending the directors and new head of the New Orleans branch. See John A. Brown to Nicholas Biddle, January 31, 1824, AB&SP.

40. In 1823 they allowed for a five months loss of interest on a specie shipment. The break even point between bills of exchange and specie was calculated at a sterling premium of 4.5 percent. See AB&S, Baltimore, to W&JB&C, Liverpool, May 14, 1823, AB&SP.

41. AB&S, Baltimore, to W&JB&C, Liverpool, June 13, 1835, AB&SP. Price differentials were sometimes caused by varying rates for domestic exchange.

42. For example, see Ralph Hidy, "The House of Baring and the Second Bank of the United States, 1826-1836," *The Pennsylvania Magazine of History and Biography,* 68 (1944), 269-285; Thomas Govan, *Nicholas Biddle, Nationalist and Public Banker, 1786-1844* (Chicago, 1959); Fritz Redlich, *The Molding of American Banking,* 2nd ed. (New York, 1968); Walter B. Smith, *Economic Aspects of the Second Bank* (Cambridge, Mass., 1953), and Hammond, *Banks and Politics.*

43. Arthur Cole, "Evolution of Exchange Market," pp. 384-421, and "Seasonal Variation in Sterling Exchange," *Journal of Economic and Business History,* 2 (1929/30), 203-218. Also see Lance E. Davis and J. R. T.

Hughes, "A Dollar-Sterling Exchange, 1803-1895," *Economic History Review*, 12 (1960), 52-78.

44. AB&S, Baltimore, to W&JB&C, Liverpool, August 13, 1836, AB&SP.

45. AB&S, Baltimore, to Adger & Black, Charleston, September 12, 1828, AB&SP.

46. AB&S, Baltimore, to W&JB&C, Liverpool, November 14, 1831, AB&SP.

47. Ibid., September 21, 1831.

48. Ibid., August 6, 1831.

49. Temin, *Jacksonian Economy,* p. 45.

50. Kent, *Story of Alex. Brown,* p. 123.

51. AB&S, Baltimore, to W&JB&C, Liverpool, September 5, 1834, AB&SP. Although there is no evidence that the bank was successful in obtaining a foreign loan, it is nonetheless worth noting that at least one American commercial bank looked abroad for excess reserves. Others may have done so as well. For example, the Barings loaned the Bank of New York £200,000 in 1823. See R. Hidy, *House of Baring,* p. 72.

52. AB&S, Baltimore, to W&JB&C, Liverpool, April 8, 1831, AB&SP.

53. Ibid., August 20, 1831.

54. In a letter to a correspondent in Princeton the Baltimore house indicated that William & James Brown & Co. had "a better knowledge for procuring iron for railroad than any other house in England." Alexander Brown was certain that much iron would be forthcoming, since he was completely satisfied that "if Rail Roads are properly made, they will supercede canals entirely in this country for both light & heavy traffic." AB&S, Baltimore, to John Potter, Princeton, October 14, 1830, AB&SP & HF. The firm also had some interesting comments on the iron market. In 1825 the Baltimore branch informed Liverpool that American iron sold for about $70-75/ton while "Swedish sells at around $90." The likely effect of railroads was already a matter of speculation: "So long as American Iron continues so low Foreign Iron cannot advance much. Rail Roads are a good deal talked of on this side & if they are found to answer with you they will soon be at work on them here, it will however take some time before this can affect the price of Iron on this side." AB&S, Baltimore, to W&JB&C, Liverpool, March 1, 1825, AB&SP.

III NEW STRATEGIES

1. In December 1832 the Baltimore branch wrote the Charleston agent the following: "The mother board of the U.S. Bank or rather their president, we believe is very jealous of our interfering so much with their exchange operations." AB&S, Baltimore, to James Adger, December 28, 1832, AB&SP.

2. James Brown to William Brown, April, 10, 1834, AB&SP.

3. George Brown to William Brown, June 21, 1834, AB&SP. The brothers continued to own a few sailing vessels throughout the antebellum period, and the Baltimore branch retained the primary managerial responsibility.

4. Ibid., July 12, 1834.

5. The exact figure for past due accounts was put at $545,715 in June 1834. James Brown to William Brown, June 17, 1834, AB&SP. James was visiting Baltimore when he wrote this letter.

6. George Brown to William Brown, July 12, 1834, AB&SP.

7. Kouwenhoven, *Partners in Banking,* p. 51. The name of the firm was Amory Leeds & Co.

8. George Brown to William Brown, September 27, 1834, AB&SP. Apparently others thought so as well. In 1832 the Liverpool firm of Cropper Benson & Co. described the Brown operations to an Edinburgh correspondent as "perhaps the most extensive in this country, entirely a commission House, & chiefly in the American trade." Kouwenhoven, *Partners in Banking,* p. 55.

9. George Brown to William Brown, January 9, 1835, AB&SP.

10. For a partial list of the firm's outstanding risks as late as 1836 see Kouwenhoven, *Partners in Banking,* p. 66.

11. Sterling balances were converted into dollars at the rate of $4.80 to the pound for the purposes of consolidating capital accounts. HF.

12. George Brown to William Brown, August 24, 1834, AB&SP.

13. AB&S, Baltimore, to Benjamin Story, September 1, 1834, AB&SP.

14. For cotton prices in New York from 1814-1860 see Table A-X in Douglass North, *The Economic Growth of the United States 1790-1860* (New York, 1961).

15. A detailed account of the Browns' resort to the Bank of England for aid during the panic is not included in this study, since the subject has been amply covered in the previous literature. The works by John Crosby Brown, *Hundred Years of Merchant Banking,* and Aytoun Ellis, *Heir of Adventure,* are especially good on this topic. There is also good detail in R. Hidy, *House of Baring,* pp. 205-234, and in his "Cushioning A Crisis in the London Money Market," *Bulletin, Business Historical Society,* 20 (1946), 131-145.

16. George Brown to William Brown, November 11, 1836, AB&SP. In a letter to the same correspondent, dated March 3, 1838, George expressed similar sentiments: "As respects stocks, I have made up my mind to keep clear of them as soon as we can lessen what we have, stock jobbing is a business of itself and only suits them that make a trade of it." AB&SP.

17. George Brown to William Brown, January 20, 1837, AB&SP.

18. AB&S, Baltimore, to Benjamin Story, April 6, 1837, AB&SP.

19. Ibid., July 29, 1837.

20. George Brown to William Brown, November 16, 1837, AB&SP.

21. Ibid., January 18, 1838.

22. Ibid., In a letter to William dated March 3, 1818, George confirmed his earlier statement: "We have not the least difficulty in selling our bills here at top prices as always, in fact there is more demand than we care to meet." If sales in New York were slow, George felt he could easily increase his own.

23. See Ellis, *Heir of Adventure,* pp. 36-51. The chapter is entitled "Joseph Shipley and the Panic of 1837" and includes Shipley's long letter to the Bank of England appealing for aid.

24. George was apparently more enthusiastic about expansion than James in the late 1830s. In a letter to William in 1838 James opposed the establishment of new agencies or anything "that will increase our business; we have enough to do now and more than I want . . . the actual & thinking labor (of any new business) is thrown here & it will wear us out, . . . there is so little to do at Balto. It is easy for Geo to sit in his armchair & talk of new houses." James Brown to William Brown, April 14, 1838, HF.

25. George Brown to James Brown, March 30, 1838, AB&SP.

26. Ibid., July 9, 1840.

27. George and William Brown to William Bowen, Mobile, March 19, 1839, AB&SP.

28. James Brown to William Brown, April 9, 1840, AB&SP.

IV SPECIALIZING IN FINANCE

1. William Bowen to Joseph Shipley, November 29, 1845, HF.

2. Ibid., November 7, 1844.

3. Brown Brothers & Co., New York, to Thomas Curtis, Boston, May 20, 1856, BB&CP.

4. Ibid., January 23, 1858.

5. Both statements are located in the firm's Historical Files. The 1859 statement is included in my "Financing Antebellum Importers: The Role of Brown Bros. & Co. in Baltimore," *Business History Review,* 45 (Winter 1971), 421-451.

6. R. Hidy, *House of Baring,* pp. 373-388.

7. See Joseph Shipley to Stewart Brown, New York, October 4, 1847, HF. Shipley explained that the £100,000 loan to Overends fell due in two weeks. Overends wanted to repay the loan with bills receivable that came due in November and December. He stated: "In other words to discount £100/M for them—I declined it." Shipley later learned that Denisons was holding security for their loans to Overends, so he wrote asking for similar collateral. At first they refused, but later sent over some bills. "I do not really think there is any risk," he added, "but they are not overscrupulous as to their means of protecting themselves so that in event of the worst it is as well to have the security."

8. Joseph Shipley to Stewart Brown, N.Y., January 20, 1848, HF.

9. Stewart Brown to Joseph Shipley, February 17, 1848, HF.

10. James Brown was the principal owner of the Novelty Iron Works which was located at the east end of 12th Street in New York. Howard Potter, a son-in-law who eventually joined Brown Brothers & Co., was associated with the firm in the fifties. For more details see Kouwenhoven, *Partners in Banking,* p. 84.

11. The shares in the partnership—or the claims on future profits after the payment of interest on capital accounts—was more evenly divided. For a yearly breakdown of share allotments from 1846-1880 see Appendix B.

12. In the spring of 1853 the house held $1,000,000 of Erie bonds. By August 1854 the Liverpool managers described the firm's association with

the Erie as the subject of "public gossip." After discussing a recent £50,000 loan to the railroad, Collet and Hamilton added the following: "You will excuse our repeating here our conviction that as a Firm it is our Policy not to meddle with Stocks or Bonds at all." See Brown, Shipley & Co., Lvpl., to William Brown, London, April 14, 1853, and Brown, Shipley & Co., Lvpl., to Brown Brothers & Co., N.Y., August 24, 1854, HF. William Brown was named a trustee of Illinois Central bonds in 1852.

13. For capsule biographies of Hamilton and Collet see Kouwenhoven, *Partners in Banking*, pp. 108-109.

14. Collet and Hamilton to William Brown, April 2, 1853, HF. The Liverpool managers did not like to entertain visiting Americans. Customers preferring more solicitous English bankers were received more warmly by the Barings and George Peabody.

15. Ibid., June 2, 1852.

16. Ibid., June 4, 1852.

17. Ibid.

18. Ibid, June 2, 1852.

19. Ibid., March 3, 1853.

20. Collet and Hamilton to William Brown, March 3, 1853, HF.

21. Collet to Hamilton, May 2, 1856, HF. For details on their railroad involvements see Kouwenhoven, *Partners in Banking,* passim.

22. Collet to Hamilton, May 2, 1854, HF.

23. Collet to Brown Brothers & Co., N.Y., February 9, 1855, HF.

24. Stewart Brown, New York, to James Brown, in Europe, October 27, 1864, HF. James Brown spent much of his time overseas during the Civil War.

25. An excellent book on the effects of the depression in England is J. R. T. Hughes, *Fluctuations in Trade, Industry, and Finances: A Study of British Economic Development, 1850-1860* (Cambridge, Eng., 1960). For a study of the United States see George W. Van Vleck, *The Panic of 1837* (New York, 1943).

26. By 1863 the firm had recovered all but $169,000 of its losses. The vast majority of the slow accounts were in Boston.

27. BS&C, Liverpool, to BB&C, N.Y., February 22, 1858, HF.

28. For example, see Stuart Bruchey, "Success and Failure Factors: American Merchants in Foreign Trade in the Eighteenth and Nineteenth Centuries," *Business History Review,* 32 (1958), 272-292.

29. They were worrying about the association with the Collins Line as early as 1852. At that time they cautioned that the firm should avoid an involvement "where the slightest ground for a suspicion against its integrity can arise." Even with increased Congressional grants, Collet and Hamilton doubted the line's profit potential. BS&C, Liverpool, to BB&C, New York, May 27, 1852, HF.

30. James Brown to BB&C, New York, November 15, 1860, HF.

31. In 1881, for example, Howard Potter sent the following note to J. P. Morgan: "We shall be glad to accept your offer of an eighth interest in your contemplated Syndicate to take two hundred millions of the forthcoming U.S. Funded Loan." February 10, 1881, HF.

32. The firm was closely associated with the Bangor & Aroostook Railroad Co., a line in the northern part of Maine, during the 1890s. At the turn of the century, the Browns were involved in financing the street railway system in St. Louis. See Kouwenhoven, *Partners in Banking,* pp. 173-182.

V THE MATURE FIRM

1. Several of Hamilton's letters during the war are found in Ellis, *Heir of Adventure,* pp. 67-85.
2. The Browns, incidentally, believed that the bonds and interest would be repaid in legal tender rather than gold. BS&C, London, to BB&C, N.Y., February 13, 1864, HF. Milton Friedman and Anna J. Schwartz hypothesized from the price data during the period that investors were treating the obligations as predominantly paper bonds. The Browns' correspondence tends to confirm their thesis. Friedman & Schwartz, *A Monetary History of the United States 1867-1960* (Princeton, 1963), p. 73.
3. The firm even began purchasing cotton on its own account—something it had not done for years. In late 1861 the Liverpool branch reported a profit of approximately $125,000 on recent activities. BS&C, Liverpool, to BB&C, N.Y., November 16, 1861, HF.
4. Kouwenhoven, *Partners in Banking,* p. 129. In 1864 the firm reported that only one third of its total acceptances were being generated by letter of credit activities whereas before the war almost two thirds of the total was based on credits. BS&C, London, to BB&C, N.Y., May 6, 1864, HF.
5. A branch in Cincinnati had already been seriously considered in early 1860.
6. BS&C, Liverpool, to BB&C, N.Y., August 30, 1861, HF.
7. Ibid., October 22, 1861.
8. The arguments pro and con are outlined in BS&C, Liverpool, to BB&C, N.Y., September 28, 1855, HF.
9. Hamilton to Collet, May 21, 1858, HF.
10. An announcement of the new firm's formation can be found in Kouwenhoven, *Partners in Banking,* pp. 110-111.
11. Herman Hoskier to BB&C, N.Y., May 27, 1863, HF.
12. BS&C, Liverpool, to BB&C, N.Y., January 28, 1863, HF. The produce referred to here was mainly cotton and some breadstuffs. The statement about handling bills of lading refers to the collection of bills of exchange. In collecting bills the firm normally had the option of releasing its control over the goods drawn against at the time of formal acceptance or, by holding the bill of lading, of retaining ownership of the goods until the bill of exchange was finally paid. These complicated procedures are explained in greater detail in a later chapter on foreign exchange operations.
13. Ibid.
14. Hamilton to Collet, May 25, 1858, HF.
15. BS&C, London, to BB&C, N.Y., October 14, 1864, HF.
16. James Brown to BS&C, London, December 5, 1864, HF.
17. John Crosby Brown to James Brown, July 12 and 14, 1865, HF.
18. "Cy." was the abbreviation for greenback currency as opposed to the

gold dollars in which all of the firm's foreign exchange transactions took place. When the currency was adjusted to a gold basis, the par ratio between dollars and sterling was maintained at the antebellum rate of $4.86 to the pound.

19. On the other hand, the English partners held one third of the partnership shares, an allocation proportional to their numerical representation in the firm. The allocation of shares determined the claim each partner had on the firm's profits after the 5 or 6 percent allowance on each partner's capital account. There was no connection between a partner's aggregate investment in the firm and the number of shares he held.

20. Potter to Clarence Brown, March 3, 1868, HF.

21. James Brown to BS&C, London, February 18, 1868, HF.

22. John Crosby Brown to Potter, April 14, 1868, HF.

23. The reverses during the panic of 1837 were the most notable even though they were not estimated at greater than 5 percent of capital. In both 1837 and 1857 the senior partners (the original brothers) wrote off most of the bad debts against their own capital accounts and set up a reserve account. As past due amounts were collected over the years, the surplus in this account was credited directly to the capital accounts of the men who had assumed the potential losses. The practice seems to have been a popular one, since the junior men were sheltered from temporary setbacks and anxiety over a possibly bad year. In 1857 the senior partners felt Thomas Curtis was responsible for many of their Boston losses, and although not a partner, his salary and commission accounts were debited slightly for several years. Their policy of alleviating the burdens of junior partners, who as members of the firm would be expected to share in the reverses, while at the same time assessing the account of an employee seems contradictory to this writer, but it does not seem to have appeared so to the Browns.

24. Potter to John Crosby Brown, May 25, 1868, HF.

25. Ibid., July 3, 1868.

26. At the end of 1867 Collet's capital account totaled about $745,000 Cy., and Hamilton's equalled about $723,000 Cy. They were certainly well off, but a long way from the status of the really wealthy.

27. For quantitative evidence on tourist expenditures see Matthew Simon, "The United States Balance of Payments, 1861-1900," in *Trends in the American Economy in the Nineteenth Century* (Princeton, 1960), p. 673.

28. T. J. Wertenbaker, *Norfolk: Historic Southern Port,* 2nd ed. (Durham, N.C., 1962).

29. Except for the articles by Morton Rothstein, which discuss very broadly the marketing of American agricultural products during the last half of the century, and a book by Harold Woodman, which analyzes the marketing of cotton, there are few secondary sources on the decline of middlemen in the Anglo-American trade. Morton Rothstein, "The American West and Foreign Markets, 1850-1900," in David Ellis, ed., *The Frontier in American Development* (Ithaca, N.Y., 1969), p. 381; "The International Market for Agricultural Commodities, 1850-1873," in D. T. Gilchrist & W.

D. Lewis, eds., *Economic Change in the Civil War Era* (Greenville, Del., 1966); "Antebellum Wheat and Cotton Exports: A Contrast in Marketing Organization and Economic Development," *Agricultural History,* 40 (April 1966), 91-100; and "America in the International Rivalry for the British Wheat Market, 1860-1914," *Mississippi Valley Historical Review,* 47 (December 1960), 401-418. Harold Woodman, *King Cotton and His Retainers: Financing and Marketing the Cotton Crop of the South, 1800-1925* (Lexington, Ky., 1968).

30. Hamilton to Potter, September 5, 1885, HF.

31. Additional research on this subject is needed from both a marketing and a financial standpoint.

32. Potter to James M. Brown, September 20, 1885, HF.

33. James M. Brown to BS&C, London, November 19, 1885, HF.

34. John Crosby Brown to BB&C, N.Y., February 17, 1871, HF.

35. Potter to John Crosby Brown, August 26, 1873, HF.

36. John Crosby Brown to Potter, March 21, 1895, HF.

37. Ibid., January 22, 1897, HF.

38. In the 1830s the family was among the wealthiest in the United States. By the end of the century the Brown family was far down on the long list of millionaire groups. For information on their earlier standing see Edward Pessen, "The Egalitarian Myth and the American Social Reality: Wealth, Mobility, and Equality in the 'Era of the Common Man,' " *American Historical Review,* 76 (October 1971), 989-1034.

SECTION 1. ADVANCES AND MERCHANDISING

1. For a different view on the role of exports in American economic growth see Irving B. Kravis, "The Role of Exports in Nineteenth Century United States Growth," *Economic Development and Cultural Change,* 20 (April 1972), 387-405.

2. Norman Buck, *The Development of the Organization of the Anglo-American Trade* (New Haven, Conn., 1925).

3. This conclusion about the market structure has been documented by an English historian, D. M. Williams, in his "Liverpool Merchants and the Cotton Trade, 1820-1850," in J. R. Harris, ed., *Liverpool and Merseyside: Essays in the Economic and Social History of the Port and Its Hinterland* (London, 1969), pp. 182-211.

4. Ibid, pp. 201-209. About 20 percent of the cotton arrived consigned "to order" and could not be identified with any specific importer. Several years ago, Bennett Wall of Tulane University did some preliminary research on the market shares of the leading firms which indicated that the Browns' percentage might have been significantly higher. The data were not published at the time, however, and during the interim his original notes have been mislaid. (Private correspondence of the author.)

5. Ralph Hidy, *House of Baring,* p. 256. The Barings imported approximately 100,000 bales in the 1837 season. If the raw cotton arriving from Egypt, Brazil, and other parts of the world was excluded from the total

Liverpool receipts, both Barings' and the Browns' share of the Anglo-
American trade could be increased by several percentage points in any given
year.

6. Williams, "Liverpool Merchants," pp. 201-209. Perhaps the most
interesting figure in Williams' tabulations is the 4.5 percent market share
assigned the firm of Humphreys & Biddle in 1839. For those historians
familiar with the debate over Nicholas Biddle's role in the cotton market
during the late 1830s, the relatively low market share of his chief Liverpool
consignee suggests that Biddle's influence in this field, in terms of the macro-
economic impact of his activities, may have been significantly exaggerated
by contemporaries and later scholars as well.

7. Harold Woodman, *King Cotton and His Retainers: Financing
and Marketing the Cotton Crop of the South, 1800-1925* (Lexington, Ky.,
1868), p. 293.

VI ANGLO-AMERICAN CONSIGNMENTS

1. David Gilchrist, ed., *The Growth of the Seaport Cities, 1790-1825*
(Charlottesville, Va., 1967).

2. Rhoda M. Dorsey, "The Pattern of Baltimore Commerce during the
Confederation Period," *Maryland Historical Magazine,* 62 (June 1967),
119-134.

3. Alexander Brown to William Brown, January 6, 1814, AB&SP.

4. AB&S, Baltimore, to D. C. Townes & Co., New Orleans, October 15,
1818, AB&SP.

5. For a brief survey of the effects of the panic see George R. Taylor, *The
Transportation Revolution, 1815-1860* (New York, 1951), pp. 334-338.

6. AB&S, Baltimore, to Jas. Carruthers, Savannah, March 23, 1819,
AB&SP.

7. AB&S, Baltimore, to W&JB&C, Liverpool, March 11, 1821, AB&SP.

8. Ibid., December 20, 1821.

9. Alexander Brown to William Brown, January 13, 1823, AB&SP.

10. The frequent references to auctions in both Baltimore and Philadelphia in the Brown manuscripts suggest that scholars may have overestimated the extent to which the auction system was an exclusive feature of
the New York market. See Ira Cohen, "The Auction System in the Port of
New York, 1817-1837," *Business History Review* (Winter 1971), 488-510. In
his statistical table showing auction sales as a percentage of total U.S.
imports, Cohen includes data from New York only. His percentages for auction sales are almost certainly understated, but it would take additional research on ports like Baltimore, Philadelphia, and Boston to determine how
far the figures are off the mark.

11. Copies of the circular are in the Historical Files of Brown Brothers
Harriman & Co. in New York.

12. James Brown to William Gihon, Ballymena, October 21, 1826, HF.

13. James Brown to John Patrick, Ballymena, February 28, 1827, HF.

14. James Brown to John & Daniel Curell, Belfast, March 15, 1827, HF.

15. Robert G. Albion, *The Rise of New York, 1815-1860* (New York, 1939).

16. In 1831 the Baltimore partners told a correspondent that while they did not refuse consignments, they strongly discouraged them. They had no salesman, the partners explained, and most of the goods simply went to auction. "We have received goods from others that did poorly yet they continue to send us more," the Baltimore management added. AB&S, Baltimore, to E. Wood & Sons, Burslem, September 16, 1831, AB&SP.

17. See Appendix A for a breakdown of the family's capital account from 1808 to 1856.

18. James Brown to W&JB&C, Liverpool, April 27, 1834, AB&SP.

19. George Brown to William Brown, July 12, 1836, AB&SP.

20. Alexander Brown had a brother John who lived in London and handled some of this business.

21. Alexander Brown to Beers & Sims, Savannah, January 20, 1803, AB&SP.

22. Williams, "Liverpool Merchants," p. 202.

23. The Barings, for example, did not open a branch office in Liverpool until 1833. R. Hidy, *House of Baring,* p. 173.

24. For discussions of the cotton trade and its importance to the economy see Douglass North, *The Economic Growth of the United States, 1790-1860* (New York, 1961); Stuart Bruchey, ed., *Cotton and the Growth of the American Economy* (New York, 1967); and Woodman, *King Cotton and His Retainers.*

25. AB&S, Baltimore, to W&JB&C, May 1, 1811, AB&SP.

26. AB&S, Baltimore, to Jas. Carruthers, Savannah, January 8, 1819, AB&SP.

27. On the tobacco trade, two articles by Jacob Price are essential reading: "The Rise of Glasgow in the Chesapeake Tobacco Trade, 1707-1775," *William and Mary Quarterly,* 11 (1954), 179-199; and "The Economic Growth of the Chesapeake and the European Market, 1697-1775," *Journal of Economic History* (1964), 496-511. For a good summary of the trade see Stuart Bruchey, ed., *The Colonial Merchant: Sources and Readings* (New York, 1966), pp. 119-125. Also see Samuel Rosenblatt, "The Significance of Credit in the Tobacco Consignment Trade," *William and Mary Quarterly* (1962), 383-399.

28. For a review of the relationship between planter and factor see Ralph Haskins, "Planter and Cotton Factor in the Old South: Some Areas of Friction," *Agricultural History,* 29 (January 1955), 1-14.

29. For production data refer to Bruchey, ed., *Cotton and Economic Growth.* The statistical tables at the beginning of the book are very comprehensive.

30. AB&S, Baltimore, to W&JB&C, Liverpool, March 11, 1821, AB&SP.

31. Ibid., July 25, 1821.

32. Ibid., March 25, 1823.

33. Albion, *Rise of New York Port,* pp. 95-121.

34. Bruchey, ed., *Cotton and Economic Growth,* Table 3-A.

35. AB&S, Baltimore, to W&JB&C, Liverpool, June 18, 1825, AB&SP.

36. Ibid., June 20, 1825.

37. BB&C, New York, to Reynolds, Byrne & CO., New Orleans, December 19, 1825, HF.

38. BB&C, New York, to T.R.D. Shepherd, Boston, January 10, 1827, HF.

39. See Appendix A for the figures on other years.

40. BB&C, New York, to Benjamin Story, New Orleans, November 14, 1825, HF.

41. AB&S, Baltimore to John Cumming & Son, Savannah, December 12, 1833, AB&SP.

42. Ibid.

43. AB&S, Baltimore, to Story, New Orleans, September 1, 1834, AB&SP.

44. Ibid., January 20, 1836. This letter along with several other selections is included in the Bruchey, ed., *Cotton and Economic Growth.*

45. AB&S, Baltimore, to Martin Pleasants & Co., Huntsville, January 19, 1836, AB&SP. The actual crop turned out to be 1,361,000 bales, so the estimate at this point was off by only a fraction.

46. AB&S, Baltimore, to Yeatman Woods & Co., New Orleans, January 19, 1836, AB&SP.

47. R. Hidy, *House of Baring,* p. 186. The Barings still received a substantial number of bales during these two seasons from customers who were in their debt for various reasons.

48. In order to understand why the panic was so severe, one must look closely at the timing of the break in the market. The price decline came in the interval from January to April, which was traditionally the height of the antebellum shipping season. Prices in New Orleans fell 18.5 percent in the first four months of 1837, and April prices were 30 percent below the previous year's level. Although there were other declines in average prices which were actually greater during the four decades prior to the Civil War than that recorded between 1836 and 1837, there was never a faster decline during the same crucial months in the marketing cycle. This unprecedented drop followed a period of five years in which the price of cotton had invariably risen during the interval from January to April. Thus, falling prices were totally unexpected by the vast majority of firms active in the Anglo-American cotton trade. According to the figures in Appendix C, shippers from New Orleans and New York to Liverpool lost an average of 18 and 15 percent respectively on cargoes in 1837. The only comparable year was 1851, when prices declined by 17 percent during the interval from January to April. Even so, cotton prices in 1851 were only slightly below the level that had prevailed in 1850, whereas prices in 1837 were much lower than those in 1835 and 1836. The price data are in Bruchey, ed., *Cotton and Economic Growth,* Table 3-P.

49. AB&S, Baltimore, to Story, New Orleans, April 5, 1837, AB&SP.

50. Ibid., April 8, 1837. In June, Story's instructions were modified again. Advances to the firm's debtors were to take precedence over purchases

of cotton. The goal was to get "something paid" by those planters and factors who were carrying over deficit accounts from the previous season.

51. Ibid., October 21, 1837.

52. Ibid., December 9, 1837.

53. AB&S, Baltimore, to James Adger, Charleston, March 14, 1838, AB&SP.

54. Williams, "Liverpool Merchants," pp. 206-207. Williams lists separate totals for William & James Brown & Co. and Brown, Shipley & Co. because of the change in the branch's name which took place on July 1, 1839. Even listed separately, the former ranked second on the list of the largest cotton importers while the latter received the number ten ranking. One fact revealed by the divided listing was that the branch received 48,238 bales during the first half of the year, and only 25,638 after July 1.

55. In contrast, commissions on the issuance of letters of credit were in the $300,000 range by the early fifties.

56. George A. Brown, Liverpool, to Stewart Brown, New York, July 5, 1848, HF. "But nothing can be better than Exc. operations," he added.

57. R. Hidy, *House of Baring,* p. 299.

58. In an article published in 1974, John Killick of the University of Leeds stressed excessive competition as the explanation for the Browns' exodus from the cotton market. See his "Risk, Specialization and Profit in the Mercantile Sector of the Nineteenth Century Cotton Trade: Alexander Brown and Sons 1820-80," *Business History,* 16 (January 1974), pp. 1-16.

59. BB&C, New York, to Thomas Curtis, Boston, January 23, 1858, BB&CP. Six pence was equal to roughly twelve cents in U.S. funds.

60. The firm's consignment activities were actually expanded for a brief period after the end of the Civil War, however. For more information of this subject, see chapter 7, "The Postwar Rejuvenation: An Indian Summer for Cotton Consignments," in "The House of Brown: America's Foremost International Bankers, 1800-1880" (Ph.D. diss., Johns Hopkins University, 1972).

Although the partners' primary association with American exports came through the cotton trade, the Browns were periodically involved in the marketing and financing of other commodities. Among them, the most important by far was tobacco — in terms of the absolute dollar value of the produce and the length of the partnership's involvement with the trade. The Browns occasionally financed the export of commodities like grain, flour, timber and copper ingots. In 1820, for instance, the Liverpool branch imported rice, turps, staves, and ashes from the United States as well as molasses from Demarara, British Guiana. Ten years later bark, apples, and hides had been added to the list of American goods entered at the customs office under the name of William & James Brown & Co.

Even in these minor markets, there was pressure on consignees to raise the level of their advances relative to anticipated market values. In the late 1850s, the Baltimore office was threatened with the loss of the business of the port's two large copper refiners after August Belmont offered higher advances against consignments of ingots on behalf of the Rothschilds. Besides financing commodities, the Browns also made advances to ship captains against the proceeds of outward freights. Advances on freights were sometimes offered as an indirect means of attracting consignments or bolstering the forwarding business of the Liverpool branch. However, in all these ancillary activities, the scale of operations was always small in comparison with the partners' cotton business and the magnitude of their other purely financial functions.

VII MANAGING COTTON OPERATIONS

1. The main source of information is the correspondence of the Baltimore office, which was the American headquarters until the late thirties, with agents, factors, and planters in the south and with the firm's own Liverpool branch. Because the Baltimore branch functioned, in part, as an intermediary between the Liverpool office and the other outlets in the chain, these letters reveal the broad guidelines the partners followed in managing their cotton business.

2. AB&S, Baltimore, to James Manning, Huntsville, April 27, 1827, AB&SP.

3. BS&C, Liverpool, to BB&C, New York, August 31, 1844, HF.

4. In fact, scholars like Peter Temin have only recently begun to analyze all the factors influencing cotton prices in the early nineteenth century. See Temin's article, "The Causes of Cotton-Price Fluctuations in the 1830's," *Review of Economics and Statistics,* 49 (November 1967), 463-470. Many of the conclusions are summarized in his later book, *The Jacksonian Economy.*

5. William Bowen, Philadelphia, to Joseph Shipley, Liverpool, September 14, 1843, HF.

6. AB&S, Baltimore, to McNeil & Kirkland, Fayettesville, N.C., December 17, 1824, AB&SP.

7. BB&C, New York, to Joseph Fowler, New Orleans, November 22, 1825, hf.

8. *William & James Brown & Co. v. Thomas McGran,* 14 Peters (U.S.), 479 (1840). The details of the case are discussed in Woodman, *King Cotton and His Retainers,* p. 62, and Kouwenhoven, *Partners in Banking,* p. 44. For a contemporary view of the case see *Hunt's Merchants' Magazine* (April 1840), 336-337.

9. BS&C, Liverpool, to BB&C, New York, August 16, 1859, HF.

10. AB&S, Baltimore, to W&JB&C, Liverpool, March 11, 1821, AB&SP.

11. Bruchey, ed., *Cotton and Economic Growth,* Table 3-M.

12. AB&S, Baltimore, to W&JB&C, Liverpool, March 25, 1823, AB&SP.

13. AB&S, Baltimore, to Martin Pleasants & Co., New Orleans, August 17, 1832, AB&SP. This firm had another office in Huntsville, Alabama, and perhaps elsewhere as well.

14. AB&S, Baltimore, to W&JB&C, Liverpool, September 7, 1820, AB&SP.

15. Ibid., April 17, 1821.

16. Ibid., March 14, 1835. The same facilities provided for foreign buyers

were occasionally extended to American residents as well. In some cases, the Browns arranged for the purchase of cotton and for the negotiation of an advance simultaneously. Such a transaction was outlined in correspondence with David Dunlop, a Petersburg, Virginia, merchant, in March 1838: "You are aware that our usual custom is to advance 2/3rds or 3/4ths the cost of cotton, . . . We would arrange the business as follows. You may give him [Story] an order for one thousand Bales or more on such terms as you may think proper and we will confirm the same by authorizing him to draw on our New York house or here if to be done on as good terms as 60 days sight . . . If we find the Cotton is likely to . . . leave a profit we will reimburse ourselves by drawing on Liverpool for the whole amount but if it's likely it will not leave cost . . . we would not like to draw on the Liverpool house for more than 80 or 90%, you paying the other 10 or 20% here. Mr. Story's commission would be 2½% for purchasing and ½% for drawing . . . we will reimburse ourselves . . . without any charge except ¼% brokerage which we have to pay. It is impossible now to negotiate drafts in New Orleans and Mobile on any place except New York . . . In giving the order be particular in making it clear as to price and the freight it is to be shipped at . . . We think money cannot well be lost by Cotton at the price it has got to." AB&S, Baltimore, to Dunlop, Petersburg, March 31, 1838, AB&SP. Based on an average price of 8¢/ lb. and a bale weight of 400 lbs., this order would have been in the range of $32,000.

17. AB&S, Baltimore, to Story, New Orleans, March 31, 1838, AB&SP.

SECTION 2. LETTERS OF CREDIT

1. The import data is from North, *Economic Growth of the U.S.,* Table C-VIII.

2. R. Hidy, *House of Baring,* p. 469. The only available data are on the aggregate of outstanding credits at the end of each quarter. From late in 1847 to a similar time in 1860, the outstandings averaged approximately £3,300,000. The Barings' credits were generally good for the full cost of a shipment. My assumption is based on full use of the credit lines and a once a year turnover, which seems fair for the China trade. The Barings then would have financed approximately $16,500,000 of American imports in 1858 and 1859—or about 5 percent of the 1859 total.

3. BS&C, Liverpool, to BB&C, New York, October 30, 1857, HF.

4. Other houses mentioned in the Browns' correspondence included Fruhling & Goschen; Drake, Kleinwort & Cohen, Rathbone Bros. & Co., Stuart & Co., Pickersgill & Co., and Wiggin & Co.

VIII THE RISE TO PREEMINENCE

1. AB&S, Baltimore, to William Brown & Co., Liverpool, July 24, 1811, AB&SP.

2. R. Hidy, *House of Baring,* pp. 114, 142.

3. AB&S, Baltimore, to W&JB&C, Liverpool, August 4, 1836, AB&SP. The agent referred to was a Mr. Pickersgill, who had married into the Riggs

family. Both families were among the elite in the Anglo-American commercial world. Elisha Riggs, the patriarch of the family, was instrumental in furthering the careers of several men who later became prominent financiers, among them George Peabody and W. W. Corcoran. George Brown also disapproved of the Wildes extending the normal reimbursement period from four to six months: "This we are decidedly opposed to & we think it is more our interest to decline all such arrangements as we have no fears of getting enough business for our means without running such risks." Ibid.

4. AB&S, Baltimore, to W&JB&C, Liverpool, November 11, 1836, AB&SP. George's failure to mention Thomas Wilson & Co. suggests that one member of the famous "3-W's" trio may not have been active in Baltimore.

5. In a letter to the Bank of England, written by Joseph Shipley, the firm's total liabilities were reported as approximately equal to the partners' capital of $6,750,000. Shipley stressed the fact that over two thirds of the firm's acceptances arose from financing American purchases of English manufactured goods. The letter is published in its entirety in Ellis, *Heir of Adventure,* pp. 45-47.

6. George Brown to William Brown, February 7, 1837, AB&SP.

7. BB&C, New York to Thomas Curtis, Boston, February 13, 1858, BB&CP.

8. R. Hidy, *House of Baring,* p. 351.

9. Curtis, Boston, to BB&C, N.Y., September 29, 1852, HF.

10. M. Hidy, "George Peabody," pp. 300-340. Peabody's policy was described by Mrs. Hidy in the following manner: "While many houses in London had agents in the United States to open credits on their principals, who assumed the responsibility of the risk, Peabody demanded that the firms in the United States with the power to open credits on him should guarantee the accounts." In short, she said, Peabody was a wholesaler of credits who forced the risk off on his retail outlets. Whether importers were fully aware of his limited responsibility is unknown. The Browns believed his credits to be inferior because the issuers generally reserved the privilege of revocation — a concept discussed in Appendix D.

11. The Browns discussed Peabody's policies in this regard in 1852. BS&C, Liverpool, to BB&C, N.Y., November 25, 1852, HF.

12. BB&C, New York, to Curtis, Boston, December 11, 1856, BB&CP.

13. BB&C, New York, to Graham, Baltimore, June 17, 1857, BB&CP.

IX MANAGING CREDIT OPERATIONS

1. Shipley to Stewart Brown, January 20, 1848, HF.

2. AB&S, Baltimore, to W&JB&C, Liverpool, September 7, 1836, AB&SP.

3. BB&C, New York, to T. Curtis, Boston, July 9, 1857, BB&CP.

4. Ibid., January 18, 1859.

5. BB&C, New York, to T. Curtis, Boston, January 23, 1858, BB&CP.

6. BS&C, Liverpool, to BB&C, New York, July 22, 1859, HF.

7. Ibid., August 2, 1859.

8. Ibid., September 25, 1851.

9. Ibid., October 31, 1855. All the words of restraint were not confined to the letters of the Liverpool partners. For instance, the New York partners were not especially disheartened in 1855 after the volume of credits declined by $2,500,000 from the previous year. In response to queries from the Boston manager, they indicated little uneasiness about the decline. "We do not think this branch of the business needs any new measures to increase it. We think our engagements are high enough and we even may decide to curtail." BB&C, New York, to T. Curtis, Boston, January 21, 1856, BB&CP.

10. James Brown to Joseph Shipley, November 17, 1857, HF.

11. Collet and Hamilton to William Brown, London, March 3, 1854, HF.

12. BS&C, London to BB&C, New York, May 5, 1866, HF.

13. Collet and Hamilton to William Brown, March 27, 1854, HF.

14. Shipley to BB&C, New York, March 10, 1848, HF. The rival Barings had been successful in reducing their outstanding credits in the mid-thirties after correctly anticipating an American recession. Their withdrawal from the market was timed with great precision, and the Barings avoided serious losses on letter of credit activities. The partners were not so fortunate in 1857, however. R. Hidy, *House of Baring,* pp. 456-457. For the Barings, shifts in and out of the market were relatively easy; one virtue of a loose organization was its flexibility. Moreover, the partners performed a broad range of financial services in many other countries, and any revenues lost in the American market could often be made up elsewhere. The Browns, in contrast, maintained a permanent organization which offered services exclusively in the Anglo-American market. Had the Browns periodically curtailed credit operations in the expectation of a possible recession, they would not only have sacrificed much of the firm's revenue but possibly its reputation as the leading house in the foreign trade sector. As a result, the partners did not seriously consider wholesale pullouts of the American market on the basis of vague apprehensions about future difficulties.

15. BB&C, New York, to Graham, Baltimore, October 31, 1857, BB&CP.

16. Hamilton to Shipley, November 23, 1857, HF.

17. BS&C, Liverpool, to BB&C, New York, January 18, 1863, HF.

18. See Stuart Bruchey, "Success and Failure Factors: American Merchants in Foreign Trade in the Eighteenth and Nineteenth Centuries," *Business History Review,* 32 (1958), 272-292.

19. Because of the inherent interrelationship of reports on the credit standing of merchants to the performance of the firm's financial functions, it would be a misrepresentation to assign the discussion of credit reporting techniques exclusively to any one section of the study. The information gathered on letter of credit customers was frequently valuable in the management of consignments and foreign exchange operations. Nonetheless, it can be said that the American branches had the primary responsibility for accumulating and evaluating information on those customers to whom the firm issued letters of credit, on customers to whom advances were made on

cotton and other produce, and on the various parties whose short term commercial paper was considered as an outlet for the investment of idle cash. The English branches, on the other hand, accumulated most of the information vital to foreign exchange operations.

20. AB&S, Baltimore, to W&JB&C, Liverpool, May 16, 1821, AB&SP. The rating system was described as follows: 1 — "We consider quite out of the power of chance"; 2 — "are in good Credit and safe for any engagement they may come under"; 3 — "are rather doubtful or rather we do not know enough of them." Both Baltimore and Philadelphia were covered in the report which rated 105 firms. Twenty merchants received a 1 rating; fifty-nine were rated 2; and twenty-seven were listed 3.

21. AB&S, Baltimore, to W&JB&C, Liverpool, November 13, 1837, AB&SP.

22. Ibid. Some of these houses were apparently still permitted to do business under completely unsecured credits in 1836. Most of the Browns' rule changes did not take effect until 1838.

23. Graham, Baltimore, to Browns & Bowen, Philadelphia, April 14, 1858, AB&SP.

24. BB&C, New York, to T. Curtis, Boston, May 14, 1858, BB&CP.

25. Ibid., January 28, 1858.

26. Ibid., January 15, 1859.

27. Ibid., January 28, 1858.

28. Many of the bills of exchange drawn in francs during the antebellum era were payable in London. Legal questions concerning the right of bankers to bills of lading seem to have discouraged the issuance of credits drawn on Paris. See AB&S, Baltimore, to W&JB&C, Liverpool, March 3, 1826, AB&SP.

29. Graham, Baltimore, to BB&C, New York, May 23, 1855, AB&SP. The customer in question was Maxwell Wright & Co., a large Brazilian coffee house, whose main American representative resided in Baltimore. The Wrights had already made some shipments to San Francisco, Graham stated, but they had been forced to delay drafts for 60 days in order to allow sufficient time for the vessel to arrive and sell the cargo. The Wrights were disappointed at the negative response, Graham remarked, because they felt the business "would pay well and would be a growing business."

30. BB&C, New York, to Graham, Baltimore, October 29, 1856, BB&CP. This time the customer was Birkhead & Co., an equally prominent house in the South American trade.

31. Collet to Kennard, December 11, 1851, HF.

32. Transactions with English importers never completely ceased, however. See, for instance, BS&C, Liverpool, to BB&C, New York, September 10, 1860, and AB&S, Baltimore, to BS&C, London, June 30, 1879, AB&SP.

33. BS&C, London, to BB&C, New York, November 3, 1866, HF.

34. The fee for accepting with "funds in hand" was only 0.5 percent in the 1820s. In the 1850s the rate for accepting against the security of an unmatured bill in hand was also reduced to 0.5 percent. The Browns opposed the

concession, but the Barings and Peabody decided to consider such transactions as "covered engagements" in 1856. The New York house wrote Boston about the shift this way: "We shall now conform to the practice of our neighbors but we reserve the right to reject any bills not first class." BB&C, New York, to T. Curtis, Boston, November 11, 1856, BB&CP.

35. The fee for internal credits, with drafts drawn on either the issuing branch or the New York house, was also 1 percent.

36. In late 1864 the Browns estimated J. S. Morgan's capital to be approximately £300-350,000 — or about the same as Timothy Wiggin & Co.

37. See BS&C, London, to BB&C, New York, December 14, 1864 and July 8, 1868, HF.

38. J. S. Morgan was later accused of having "undoubtedly a speculative turn." BS&C, London, to BB&C, New York, November 29, 1866, HF.

39. In 1878 Alexander Brown & Sons received an offer to issue credits from the English Bank of Rio de Janeiro, Ltd. Over the last half of the century, many commercial banks in England and the United States were entering the market on a limited scale. See David Joslin, *A Century of Banking in Latin America* (London, 1963).

40. In 1834 Peabody, Riggs & Co. was rebuffed when they hinted at a rate reduction. The Baltimore office reported the gist of a conversation with Peabody to the Liverpool branch: "We told him it was in his interest doing business with a house he knew was out of the power of chance . . . , there is no use in working for nothing for any house however respectable." AB&S to W&JB&C, August 20, 1834, AB&SP. But at least three parties can be identified as receiving preferential rates from the Baltimore house during the antebellum period — Wm. Wilson & Sons, Robert P. Brown (a cousin), and Maxwell Wright & Co., a Rio de Janeiro coffee firm.

41. BS&C, London, to BB&C, New York, April 24, 1866, HF.

42. Richard H. Leftwich, *The Price System and Resource Allocation,* 3rd. ed. (New York, 1966).

43. One Philadelphia house was granted a matching reduction in September 1852, however. The New York branch wrote William Bowen that a lower rate for Levy & Co. would be permissible because "during 1837 he acted so handsomely" paying up his debt to Liverpool at exchange rates as high as 22 percent over par. It was then felt, New York stated, that Levy & Co. was entitled to some concession on commissions. BB&C, New York, to Browns & Bowen, Philadelphia, September 30, 1852, HF.

44. The Barings came down in December 1852, but the Browns held out until June 1853. R. Hidy, *House of Baring,* p. 613.

45. Peabody had not decided to enter the letter of credit market until 1849. It was then that he actually began lending his name to third parties as a guarantor, and thereby became what was generally considered to be a merchant banker. M. Hidy, "George Peabody," p. 139.

46. BS&C, Liverpool, to BB&C, New York, November 16, 1861, HF.

47. The Browns did not lower their rates to competitive levels until 1870.

48. BB&C, New York, to Reynolds Byrne & Co., New Orleans, July 6, 1826, HF.

49. George Brown to William Brown, March 13, 1837, AB&SP.

50. AB&S, Baltimore, to BS&C, Liverpool, January 10, 1840, AB&SP.

51. AB&S, Baltimore, to BS&C, London, September 6, 1869, AB&SP.

52. For example, the Baltimore branch had difficulties with Wm. P. Lemmon in the late 1850s and finally declined the opening of new credits. In April 1858 William Graham, the branch manager, reported to his superiors in New York that Lemmon had subsequently taken out credits from McKim & Co. and Robert Garrett & Sons on Peabody. On a recent cargo, Lemmon's losses were so heavy that he was "ruined" and his bankers had been left with debts exceeding the margins they held as security. Graham to BB&C, New York, April 8, 1858, HF. Graham had a similar experience with a Baltimore exporter of oak timber, James Thornton. The Liverpool house refused to authorize any advances to him, but Thornton was able to persuade Robert Garrett & Sons to handle the transaction. The correspondence in the Garrett collection describes the difficulties that eventually ensued. George Peabody & Co. wrote Garrett in October 1859 that his bill on Thornton's brother, Benjamin, had gone to protest. Two months later Peabody deemed the chances of a full recovery to be "slender." See George Peabody & Co., London, to Robert Garrett & Sons, Baltimore, October 7, 1859, and December 6, 1859, Garrett Family Papers (Library of Congress).

53. In 1860 the Baltimore branch began adding the rate of commission to be applied by the English branch. Prior to that time, Brown, Shipley & Co. merely charged the customary rate and instructions from the American branches were not generally required. Graham, Baltimore, to BB&C, New York, June 30, 1860, AB&SP.

54. BB&C, New York, to T. Curtis, Boston, July 14, 1855, BB&CP.

55. For example, in January 1858 the Barings' Boston agent and chief American representative, Samuel Ward, traveled to Baltimore and offered all the Browns' first class customers the privilege of unsecured credits. For several weeks, the Baltimore branch manager feared the loss of the majority of his best accounts unless his superiors authorized an immediate liberalization in credit rules. But the next month, before the senior partners had been given enough time to consider an appropriate response, two of the recently solicited Baltimore importers told the manager they would continue to use the Brown credits. Applying to Ward in Boston, they explained, would be simply too long and cumbersome a procedure. The most interesting fact revealed by this episode was that the Barings' officially designated Baltimore agent, Oelrichs & Lurman, with whom a foreign exchange account was jointly operated, had no facilities for handling letter of credit transactions. Although Ward apparently found the recruitment of new customers in other ports a relatively easy task, the servicing of those accounts was another matter entirely. It was in the service field, of course, that the Browns' branch system excelled. Customer service was the one competitive advantage that no other banking house could even come close to matching.

56. BS&C, Liverpool, to BB&C, New York, November 16, 1861, HF.

57. Daniel Curtis, Boston, to BB&C, New York, August 1, 1867, HF.

58. Ibid., March 18, 1871.

59. BS&C, London, to BB&C, New York, November 2, 1868, HF.

60. A letter dated May 1868 expressed much satisfaction with the increased business in Baltimore after the old firm, Alexander Brown & Sons, had reassumed the agency duties. The London managers said it showed "what can be accomplished by increased vigor at the branches." BS&C, London, to BB&C, New York, May 23, 1868, HF.

61. BS&C, London, to BB&C, New York, May 23, 1868, HF.

62. BB&C, New York, to T. Curtis, Boston, February 3, 1858, BB&CP. The New York partners often asked Curtis to check with Ward about the Barings' policies and procedures. In December 1858 they heard that Thomas C. Baring and Henry Chapman were to become partners in the New York firm of Wood Campbell & Co., and Curtis was instructed to ask Ward if the house was now likely to begin opening letters of credit. Ibid., December 31, 1858.

SECTION 3. FOREIGN EXCHANGE

1. Despite the overall importance of the subject, little work has been done on the organization of foreign exchange markets since Arthur Cole's groundbreaking articles first appeared over forty years ago. Arthur H. Cole, "Evolution of the Foreign-Exchange Market of the United States," *Journal of Economic and Business History*, 1 (1928/29), 384-421, and in the same journal, "Seasonal Variation in Sterling Exchange," 2 (1930/31), 203-218.

X THE ASSUMPTION OF LEADERSHIP

1. AB&S, Baltimore, to W&JB&C, Liverpool, May 29, 1824, AB&SP.

2. Ibid., April 11, 1825.

3. Ibid., June 28, 1825.

4. Ibid., September 14, 1825. "Hypothecation" is the modern term used to describe this financial procedure—in which a borrower permits a lender to use his collateral in negotiating a subsequent loan from a third party.

5. Ibid., December 21, 1827. The war scare was related to problems in Greece and Turkey. The Liverpool partners apparently feared British involvement in the dispute.

6. The best source on this topic is Fritz Redlich's *Molding of American Banking*, 2nd ed. (New York, 1968), I, 127-145. Other books on Biddle and the Second Bank contain very little additional information on foreign exchange operations.

7. R. Hidy, *House of Baring*, p. 98.

8. See Redlich, *Molding of American Banking*, I, 131.

9. A very good source here is Bray Hammond, *Banks and Politics in America: From the Revolution to the Civil War* (Princeton, 1957). See chapter 16, "The Foundering of the United States Bank of Pennsylvania."

10. Lance Davis and J. R. T. Hughes, "A Dollar-Sterling Exchange, 1803-1895," *Economic History Review*, 12 (1960), 52-78.

11. George Brown to William Brown, January 13, 1832, and November 11, 1836, AB&SP. The firm's position vis-à-vis the Second Bank is also discussed at some length in chapter 3.

12. Ibid., January 20, 1837.

13. Thompson, *Wiring a Continent,* pp. 37-93.

14. In 1859 the firm earned $358,080 (£74,600) from letters of credit and $64,073 (£11,442) on foreign exchange operations. HF.

15. BS&C, Liverpool, to BB&C, New York, February 11, 1860. HF.

16. R. Hidy, *House of Baring,* p. 367.

17. Mr. Knight (first name unknown) had been previously employed by Glyn & Co. and the Bank of Montreal. At one time, the Browns had considered hiring him for their New Orleans branch.

18. BS&C, Liverpool, to BB&C, New York, February 23, 1860, HF.

19. Ibid., March 24, 1860.

20. Ibid., December 8, 1860.

21. R. Hidy, *House of Baring,* pp. 364-367, 469.

22. BB&C, New York, to William Graham, Baltimore, October 13, 1859, BB&CP.

23. Samuel Nicholson & Co., New Orleans, to BB&C, New York, December 1, 1857, HF. Nicholson was the senior partner in the New Orleans office, and until his death in 1857 the branch was known under his name. In 1858 it adopted the name Brown Brothers & Co. to coincide with the New York house.

24. BS&C, Liverpool, to BB&C, New York, August 21, 1860, HF.

XI MANAGEMENT AND ADMINISTRATION

1. BS&C, Liverpool, to BB&C, New York, February 18, 1852, HF.

2. Ibid.

3. Mark Collet to BB&C, New York, February 9, 1855, HF. For the Barings' attitude toward discounting see R. Hidy, *House of Baring,* p. 149.

4. Francis Hamilton to William Brown, June 4, 1852, and March 27, 1854, HF.

5. BS&C, Liverpool, to BB&C, New York, December 28, 1852, HF.

6. Ibid., January 1, 1858.

7. Ibid., January 1, 1859.

8. Ibid., August 3, 1858.

9. James Brown, Liverpool, to BB&C, New York, November 15, 1860, HF.

10. All the letters are located in the firm's Historical Files in New York.

11. BS&C, Liverpool, to The National Bank of Scotland, Glasgow, April 18, 1859, HF.

12. John Hart, Agent, The National Bank of Scotland to BS&C, Liverpool, April 21, 1859, HF.

13. BS&C, Liverpool, to BB&C, New York, April 23, 1859, HF.

14. Stewart Brown, New York, to Joseph Shipley, Liverpool, February 17, 1848, HF.

15. BS&C, Liverpool, to BB&C, New York, May 2, 1859, HF.

16. Ibid., November 25, 1852.

17. Ibid., January 25, 1859.

18. Arbitrage may be defined as purchasing in one market for immediate or instantaneous sale in another, more distant market.

19. AB&S, Baltimore, to BS&C, Liverpool, February 8, 1878, AB&SP.

20. Ibid., February 8, 1878.

21. For an examination of how the Browns' policies were implemented on the branch level see chapter 14, "Operations in Microcosm: Baltimore in the 1850's," Perkins, "The House of Brown." (unpublished).

22. In August 1855 the New York house told the Boston branch manager that since they had "plenty of money," they would remain "very firm" in their rates. BB&C, New York, to T. Curtis, Boston, August 15, 1855, BB&CP. In a letter to the Baltimore branch manager in January 1860, the partners stated that one reason sterling rates were low was the active demand for call loans at a 7 percent interest rate. BB&C, New York, to W. Graham, Baltimore, January 7, 1860, BB&CP.

23. For example, only 4 percent of the bills sold in Baltimore were drawn at less than sixty days in 1859, and 30 percent of those were for less than twenty pounds. Statements, AB&SP.

24. Demand bills sold at 1/8 a percent over 3 d/s bills. Cable transfers were priced at 1/4 percent over the three day rate plus the cost of the wire. Those fees were the equivalent of paying an additional interest rate of 15 and 24 percent respectively on an annual basis.

25. BB&C, New York, to W. Graham, Baltimore, October 13, 1859, BB&CP.

26. Ibid., January 6, 1860.

27. Graham, Baltimore, to BB&C, New York, December 14, 1859, AB&SP. Graham was upset because he had lost the commission on the sale of these bills. Normally, he earned 1/4 of a percent on the sale of bills drawn on Brown, Shipley & Co. in Baltimore.

28. BB&C, New York, to Graham, Baltimore, December 15, 1859, BB&CP.

29. Cole, "Evolution of Foreign Exchange Market, pp. 408-419.

30. BB&C, New York, to Graham, Baltimore, January 6, 1860, BB&CP.

31. Ibid., December 30, 1859.

32. Ibid., January 14, 1860.

33. Ibid., April 21, 1857.

34. In their selling activities, the Browns invariably charged discriminatory rates for all bills other than the standard 60 d/s bill. After the Civil War, however, the Browns were indifferent about whether their customers purchased a 3 d/s bill or a 60 d/s bill, and the variation in price was determined wholly by conditions in the English money market, since it was there that their own borrowing occurred.

35. Graham, Baltimore, to BS&C, Liverpool, April 2, 1860, AB&SP.

36. There were complaints about the laws on the continent in the early twenties. It was not until the late seventies that the law on bills of lading in France was adjusted to the satisfaction of the Browns. The change in the French law coincided with a sharp increase in American grain exports to France and the continent generally.

37. BB&C, New York, to Graham, Baltimore, September 21, 1859, BB&CP.

38. Why the Boston balance was not normally included in the summary is unknown.

39. In particular, Osker Morganstern, *International Financial Transactions and Business Cycles* (Princeton, 1959), pp. 176-191. Also see Davis and Hughes, "Dollar-Sterling Exchange," passim.

40. AB&S, Baltimore, to W&JB&C, Liverpool, May 14, 1823, AB&SP.

41. Generally speaking, the Browns' quoted rates compare very favorably with the early bill prices listed in the Davis and Hughes' article, Table A-4. The authors based their estimates on the actual purchases of sterling bills by the Philadelphia merchant, Nathan Trotter, from 1803 to 1895. The two series especially agree on the high and low points in bill prices.

42. AB&S, Baltimore, to W&JB&C, Liverpool, August 30, 1830, AB&SP. The figure of $20,905.45 was arrived at by converting the £4437.9.7 to dollars at a rate of 106 percent or $4.7064 to the pound. In subtracting, the Browns seem to have made a ten cent error.

43. By the 1850s, total transfer costs were down to 0.5 percent or less.

44. Paul Studenski and Herman Krooss, *The Financial History of the United States,* 2nd ed. (New York, 1963), pp. 108-109. The gold weight of the dollar was lowered to 23.2 grains while the silver dollar was maintained at 371.25 grains, thereby raising the coinage ratio to approximately 1 to 16. "Since the market ratio in Europe was about 1 to 15.75, the new mint ratio prompted the possessors of gold to bring it to the American mint."

45. AB&S, Baltimore, to W&JB&C, Liverpool, July 14, 1834, AB&SP.

46. AB&S, Baltimore, to James Adger—agent, Charleston, October 21, 1831, AB&SP.

47. Ibid., November 22, 1831. This statement suggests that the Second Bank used its market power to keep exchange rates within the effective gold points on at least some occasions.

48. BS&C, Liverpool, to BB&C, New York, April 29, 1859, HF.

49. Ibid., May 3, 1859.

50. James Brown to George H. Brown, May 18, 1859, HF.

51. BS&C, Liverpool, to BB&C, New York, July 29, 1859, HF.

52. The New York partners' remarks were quoted in BS&C, Liverpool, to BB&C, New York, August 26, 1859, HF.

53. Ibid.

54. BB&C, New York, to Graham, Baltimore, October 22, 1859, BB&CP.

55. Ibid., October 25, 1859.

56. The total amount of sterling remitted was £9,929,833 or approximately $44,640,000. All the figures are found in BS&C, Liverpool, to BB&C, New York, February 22 and March 24, 1860, HF.

57. On this point see Peter Temin, *The Jacksonian Economy* (New York, 1969), p. 145.

58. AB&S, Baltimore, to Benjamin Story, New Orleans, April 6, 1837, AB&SP.

59. Ibid., April 15, 1837.
60. Ibid., December 9, 1837.
61. BS&C, Liverpool, to BB&C, New York, November 5, 1857, HF.
62. Ibid., December 29, 1857.

XII FORMULATING NEW POLICIES

1. Until his death in 1857, the New Orleans branch was known as Samuel Nicholson & Co.
2. BS&C, Liverpool, to BB&C, New York, May 10, 1861, HF.
3. Ibid., December 4, 1861. The seriousness of the episode was compounded by the fact that Dickey had actually become a full partner in the firm about a year before this incident occurred. Therefore his actions were more embarrassing to the house than they would have been if he had only been a mere employee of the firm.
4. J. G. Randall and David Donald, *The Civil War and Reconstruction,* 2nd ed. (Lexington, Mass., 1969), p. 503.
5. BS&C, Liverpool, to BB&C, New York, December 4, 1861, HF.
6. Ibid., August 30, 1861.
7. For a good review of the politics of the period see Robert P. Sharkey, *Money, Class, and Party: An Economic Study of Civil War and Reconstruction* (Baltimore, 1959), and especially his initial chapter, "Origin of the Greenbacks." There is also some interesting information in Redlich, *Molding of Banking,* "Bankers and Civil War Finance," II, 85-95.
8. Gresham's law, that cheap money drives out dear money, was not applicable here; it only becomes effective when there is a fixed rate of exchange between two forms of money, such as coinage ratios.
9. Milton Friedman and Anna Jacobson Schwartz, *A Monetary History of the United States 1867-1960* (Princeton, 1963). The authors emphasize the fundamental correlation between the sterling rate and the premium on gold. In the antebellum period, the price of sterling in terms of the dollar varied in a fairly narrow interval around mint par. The costs of exporting and importing specie determined the width of this band. "Once the U.S. went off gold in 1862, the exchange rate was free to move outside these limits and, of course, did so. The dollar depreciated, which means that the greenback price of the pound rose and hence so did the greenback price of gold, since the pound price of gold was fixed with gold points by the Bank of England's buying and selling rates. Thereafter, until resumption in 1879, the exchange rate — and hence the premium on gold — was determined by the demand for and supply of foreign exchange" p. 60.
10. BS&C, Liverpool, to BB&C, New York, February 15, 1862, HF.
11. Ibid.
12. Ibid. In a letter dated July 22, 1862, the Liverpool partners reported that many people were selling their American securities, but they did not feel the sales would "exert a primary influence on Exchange; it will no doubt affect it according to the ordinary laws of supply and demand for Bills but the range of fluctuation from this cause is within moderate & almost ascertained

limits. Not so the effect of the depreciation of your currency, the limit of which it is impossible to predicate." Every fresh issue aggravated the rates, they stated, and caused doubts about the ultimate ability of the government to pay interest or redeem the notes in specie after the war.

13. In a technical sense the Browns were not really brokers because they did not resell the same bills they had previously purchased. But by drawing fresh bills at a pace that corresponded exactly with their rate of purchases, the net effect was the same.

14. For the many factors which made this level of foreign trade possible see Friedman and Schwartz, *Monetary History,* pp. 58-76.

15. These figures are located in BB&CP. Cy. was the abbreviation for greenback dollars — as distinguished from gold dollars (G).

16. BS&C, London, to BB&C, New York, May 6, 1864, HF.

17. The suggestion was made by Stewart Brown in his letter to J. M. Brown dated April 26, 1864, HF.

18. At this point their outstanding obligations were approximately twice the partnership capital. As of December 31, 1867, the total capital was $10,500,000 Cy.

19. A list of their various agencies from 1865-1870 reads as follows: *New Orleans*—Witherspoon & Halsey, Dec. '65 to Oct. '69; Halsey & Co., Nov. '69 to Dec. '70; *Mobile*—A. J. Ingersoll & Co., Dec. '65 to Aug. '67; Halsey, Goldthwaite & Co., Nov. '67 to Oct. '69; Goldthwaite & Co. Nov. '69 to Dec. '70; *Savannah*—Gourdin, Matthiessen & Co., Feb. '66 to Nov. '67; H. & R. N. Gourdin, Nov. '67 to Sept. '69; Gourdins, Young & Frost, Oct. '69 to Dec. '70; and *Charleston*—Adger & Co., 1865 to 1870. HF.

20. BS&C, London, to BB&C, New York, August 28, 1866, HF.

21. The New York partners calculated profits in greenbacks until 1868 when they shifted to gold dollars.

22. BS&C, London, to BB&C, New York, May 9, 1868, HF.

23. Because the dollar had depreciated, this percentage overstates the amount of sterling sold by about one half.

24. The potential outflow was estimated using the same methodology employed in the calculations on minimum market shares at the very beginning of the section. The original data is from Matthew Simon, "The United States Balance of Payments, 1861-1900," in *Trends in the American Economy in the Nineteenth Century* (Princeton, 1960), pp. 629-715.

25. Cole, "Evolution of Foreign Exchange Market," pp. 408-421.

26. The reasons for the increased use of documentary bills in the postwar period are discussed in chapter nine.

27. Barry E. Supple, "A Business Elite: German-Jewish Financiers in Nineteenth Century New York," *Business History Review,* 31 (1957), 143.

28. Redlich, *Molding of American Banking,* II, 75.

29. BS&C, London, to BB&C, New York, July 13, 1868, HF.

30. Ibid. The Seligmans reduced their risk to ten or fifteen days by discounting their remittances without recourse. If this was true, it seems likely that they would have had to pay a higher interest rate on these loans, and this would have offset some of the gains from a more rapid turnover.

31. Most of the names are found in *Merchants and Bankers Almanac* (New York, 1868).

32. For more information on these two banking families see Redlich, *Molding of Banking,* passim. From 1865 to 1868, the Drexels actually maintained their main English account with Brown, Shipley & Co. in London. Their business then appears to have been chiefly connected with securities.

33. There was generally separate coverage for 3 d/s bills and 60 d/s bills. On one day the Baltimore office might ask the New York house to sell £10,000 of 3 d/s bills and buy £15,000 of 60 d/s bills. The very next day, or possibly later the same day, it might request just the opposite. During some months of the year, the New York house allowed a 3/8 percent margin to their agents in Baltimore.

34. AB&S, Baltimore, to John Daingerfield, Alexandria, Virginia, July 23, 1868, AB&SP. The Daingerfield family had been a customer of the Browns since the early 1840s.

35. AB&S summed it up when depicting conditions in the gold market for one customer: "It is impossible to foretell the fluctuations." AB&S, Baltimore, to B. Lambert, Alexandria, Virginia, July 24, 1869, AB&SP.

36. The reason for the continued existence of an independent sterling rate was that gold dollars were in demand for other purposes besides their primary role in foreign exchange transactions. Indeed the tendency of the Browns' rates to fluctuate within a narrow interval around the mint par figure of 109 1/2 would suggest that the old gold point mechanism, or some substitute for it, was operational during the greenback era. In fact there are several references in the Baltimore letterbooks to gold shipments made by the New York house "during certain months of the year." A possible explanation for this behavior *might* proceed as follows. At any given level in the gold premium, there was always some room for slight fluctuations in sterling rates. If the rate moved too far away from the nominal par figure, then dealers would be given an incentive to ship gold instead of bills. All this is similar to the chain of events in the antebellum period. If, however, in the next stage, the rate moved even farther away from the par figure, then it would finally cause an adjustment in the gold premium itself. The price of gold would then change enough so that the sterling rate would, in turn, be forced back closer to par. In the antebellum era, of course, unusually deviant rates had led to the suspension of specie payment. Here in the greenback period, where suspension had already occurred, the response was merely an adjustment in the level of the premium. I hasten to add that this process is strictly conjecture at this point, but it seems plausible in light of the known facts and the evidence in the Browns' records.

37. Cole, "Seasonal Variation in Exchange Rates," p. 206.

38. For a somewhat jaded, yet lively, review of this episode see Matthew Josephson, *The Robber Barons* (New York, 1934), pp. 141-148.

39. AB&S, Baltimore, to Tennant & Co., Petersburg, Virginia, November 29, 1869, AB&SP. Alexander Brown was transacting business with tobacco exporters in Petersburg as early as 1803.

40. John B. Daish, *The Atlantic Port Differentials* (Washington, 1918)

and Thomas Whedbee, *The Port of Baltimore in the Making, 1828 to 1878* (Baltimore, 1953).

41. *Annual Report on the Commerce and Navigation of the United States,* U.S. Treasury Department, Bureau of Statistics (Washington, 1870 and 1880).

42. Morton Rothstein has written two important articles on American agricultural exports in the second half of the century—"America in the International Rivalry for the British Wheat Market, 1860-1914," *Mississippi Valley Historical Review* (December 1960), 401-418; and "The International Market for Agricultural Commodities, 1850-1873," in the D. T. Gilchrist and W. D. Lewis, eds., *Economic Change in the Civil War Era* (Greenville, Del., 1966) and reprinted in A. D. Chandler, S. Bruchey, and L. Galambos, eds., *The Changing Economic Order* (New York, 1968), pp. 312-320.

43. AB&S, Baltimore, to BB&C, New York, April 11, 1878, AB&SP.

44. Ibid.

45. Harold A. Williams, *Robert Garrett & Sons: Origin and Development, 1840-1965* (Baltimore, 1965).

46. The Barings were evidently not very active in the foreign exchange market during the late 1870s. At least the Browns did not refer to them as major competitors. In December 1878 AB&S wrote the following to one of its customers: "In regard to the rate for the bill on Baring Bro. & Co., we would say, as you perhaps are aware, that the Messers. Ward of New York, representing the Barings are not *dealers in Exchange,* and the rate given is not a criterion of the market. We rather apprehend it as a valuation at which they have been willing to assume a draft upon their principals." AB&S, Baltimore, to George Bain, Cashier, Exchange National Bank, Norfolk, Virginia, December 6, 1878, AB&SP.

47. AB&S, Baltimore, to BS&C, London, April 23, 1878, AB&SP.

48. AB&S, Baltimore, to BB&C, New York, January 25, 1879, AB&SP.

49. On another occasion in 1879, the New York partners had to go to the Baltimore market to cover one of its own transactions in francs. This never happened on sterling transactions.

50. Harold Woodman, *King Cotton and His Retainers,* pp. 289-294; "American Produce Exchange Markets," *Annals of the American Academy of Political and Social Science,* 38, (September 1911), 319-664; and Thomas Odle, "Entrepreneurial Cooperation on the Great Lakes: The Origin of the Methods of American Grain Marketing," *Business History Review* (Winter 1964), 439-455.

51. AB&S, Baltimore, to BB&C, New York, December 10, 1878, AB&SP.

52. AB&S, Baltimore, to BS&C, Liverpool, January 12, 1879, AB&SP. It is not clear why this letter and the one that follows were written to the Liverpool branch rather than to the more important outlet in London.

53. Ibid, February 7, 1879.

54. AB&S, Baltimore, to BB&C, New York, April 15, 1879, AB&SP.

55. The first regular quotations reached Baltimore on August 14, 1879. The rates were $4.79 for September delivery and $4.78 for October delivery.

56. AB&S, Baltimore, to BB&C, New York, June 24, 1879, AB&SP.

57. Sidney Homer, *A History of Interest Rates* (New Brunswick, New Jersey, 1963).

58. AB&S, Baltimore, to BS&C, London, April 29, 1879, AB&SP.

59. For information on this French firm see Rhondo Cameron, ed., *Banking in the Early Stages of Industrialization* (New York, 1967), p. 107.

60. AB&S, Baltimore, to BB&C, New York, July 31, 1879, AB&SP.

61. Ibid., August 27, 1879.

62. Ibid., April 5, 1879.

63. The Baltimore profits were greater than those of all the other outlets combined, including Boston, Philadelphia, and the various southern agencies. This was a dramatic change from the office's relative position in the antebellum period, or even as late as 1870. The main organization's earnings are found in BB&CP.

64. Pertinent monographs on futures trading in the commodity markets are the following: Henry Emery, *Speculation on the Stock and Produce Exchanges of the United States* (New York, 1896); Harold Irwin, *Evolution of Futures Trading* (Madison, Wis., 1954); Stanley Dumbell, "The Origin of Cotton Futures," *Economic History* (May 1927), I, 259-267; Odle, "Origins of Methods of Grain Marketing," and "American Produce Exchange Markets," *Annals of Political Science.* Futures markets for agricultural commodities developed in other business cultures too; for example, trading in rice futures was organized in Osaka in 1716. See Toyoda Takeshi, *A History of Pre-Meiji Commerce in Japan* (Tokyo, 1969), pp. 68-70 and E. S. Crawcour, "Changes in Japanese Commerce in the Tokugawa Period," in Hall and Jansen, eds., *Studies in the Institutional History of Early Modern Japan* (Princeton, 1968), p. 194. I am indebted to Les Mitchnick for calling these sources on Japan to my attention.

65. Paul Einzig, *The History of Foreign Exchange,* 2nd ed. (London, 1970) and *A Dynamic Theory of Forward Exchange* (London, 1961). Although Einzig found evidence of forward transactions as far back as the Middle Ages, the formation of organized futures markets came only in the nineteenth century. In his search for the antecedents of the modern foreign exchange futures contracts, he paid scant attention to the development of such contracts on the commodity exchanges.

66. Another possible influence—a sharp reduction in overseas communications costs—can be discounted as an important influence, since the undersea telegraph cable to Europe had become operational thirteen years earlier, in 1866. In theory, American grain exporters might have avoided the use of futures contracts by employing the alternative practice of hedging their position through a combination of the currency credit markets and the spot markets. However, the credit facilities for hedging in foreign currencies, which would have permitted exporters to follow the credit-spot route, apparently had not emerged as yet. The Browns' records contain no references to such facilities in the late 1870s. The failure of a speculative forward market to develop at this time can probably be laid to the high cost of information and prohibitive transaction costs. For discussions of the theory of forward markets see Einzig, *Dynamic Theory;* Egon Sohmen, *The Theory of*

Forward Exchange, Studies in International Finance (Princeton, 1966); and Fred R. Glahe, *An Empirical Study of the Foreign-Exchange Market: Test of a Theory,* Studies in International Finance (Princeton, 1967).

67. Robert Lipsey, *Price and Quantity Trends in the Foreign Trade of the United States* (Princeton, 1963), p. 154.

68. Matthew Simon and David Novack, "Some Dimensions of the American Commercial Invasion of Europe, 1871-1914," *Journal of Economic History,* 24 (1964), 594.

69. *Annual Statements on the Commerce and Navigation of the United States* (Washington, 1877-1879).

70. Einzig, *Dynamic Theory,* p. 9.

71. Ibid., p. 6. Einzig found indications that a large number of futures transactions took place in the Vienna money market during the political upheavals of the late 1840s.

72. The London foreign exchange market developed slowly, according to Einzig, because British merchants insisted on doing business solely in sterling; thus the necessary exchange transactions, whether spot or forward, occurred overseas. The situation was paradoxical, he observes: "Even though sterling was by far the most important international currency and London was by far the most important international financial centre, the turnover of the London Foreign Exchange market was distinctly smaller than that of a number of less important . . . centres." *History of Exchange,* p. 183. Moreover, it was not until after World War I that London finally became the major European market for foreign exchange futures.

73. Einzig, *Dynamic Theory,* p. 9.

74. Cole, "Evolution of Market," passim.

APPENDIX D

1. Robert Higgs, *The Transformation of the American Economy, 1865-1914* (New York, 1971), p. 54.

2. BB&C, New York, to T. Curtis, Boston, January 12, 1857, BB&CP.

3. Ibid, December 28, 1857.

4. BB&C, New York, to Graham, Baltimore, December 23, 1859, BB&CP. In March 1857 the partners told Graham they wanted no real estate for margins.

5. BB&C, New York, to T. Curtis, Boston, July 6, 1858, BB&CP.

6. Frank Rutter, *South American Trade of Baltimore* (Baltimore, 1897). Maryland flour was highly prized in Brazil, and Baltimore merchants retained a fair share of the coffee trade throughout the nineteenth century.

7. The Browns occasionally waived their margin requirements for those importers who could offer a strong endorser or guarantor. More often than not, the endorser was a relative. As a rule, however, the Browns discouraged the substitution of endorsers for tangible assets.

8. The firm acted as agents for various insurance underwriters and received a commission for its efforts. Customers were still free to make their own arrangements so long as the insurance company was reputable.

9. The Browns could also hold the merchandise for a more favorable

market. The firm assumed ownership of a large volume of goods in Boston during the 1857 financial panic, and the New York partners were not overly anxious to dispose of their collateral at the rock-bottom prices prevailing at the time: "While it is desirable to convert into money property held against credits, it is not advisable to force sales." BB&C, New York, to T. Curtis, Boston, December 26, 1857, BB&CP.

10. The Baltimore office financed a shipment of lemons from the Mediterranean area to New York in 1869, however. See AB&S, Baltimore, to BS&C, Liverpool, June 10, 1869, AB&SP.

11. In 1838 they explained to George Peabody their reasons for preferring documentary bills under their credits: "We attain the further very important object of knowing that our Credits can only be applied for the purpose for which they are given, and . . . there is no possibility of a House carrying on a System of finance by obtaining two or more Credits and drawing on one to pay off another." Quoted in M. Hidy, "George Peabody," p. 99.

12. Even in the twentieth century the same financial techniques have left ample room for fraud and chicanery. One of the greatest financial scandals in U.S. history, the Tony DeAngelis salad oil episode of the early 1960s, which resulted in tremendous losses for American Express and many large New York commercial banks and brokerage houses, grew out of the inadequate control devices seemingly inherent in the trust receipt system.

13. R. Hidy, *House of Baring,* p. 142.

14. Ibid. The firm named in the test case was Fletcher, Alexander & Co.

15. Dickey to BB&C, New York, October 25, 1861, HF. The Boston branch manager blamed many of his difficulties during the 1857 panic on the abuse of the receipt privilege. His letter to the Liverpool office in the fall of 1857 read as follows: "Since the failure of G. T. & W. P. Lyman it has turned out that we are left to come in as general creditors having been deprived of our lien upon goods imported, they having wholly ignored both the original obligation and the storage receipt given on endorsing over B/L . . . This blow follows hard upon the opinion expressed lately as to the reliance to be placed upon our customers. I am now concerting measures to increase the safety in giving over shipping documents, but where there is no want of principle there can be no safety. I have given credits for you thirteen years and this is only the second abuse of confidence, but times just now are such as to demand unusual care." T. Curtis, Boston, to BS&C, Liverpool, October 25, 1857, HF.

16. BS&C, Liverpool, to BB&C, New York, October 22, 1861, HF.

17. Ibid.

18. Graham, Baltimore, to BB&C, New York, December 2, 1858, AB&SP.

19. BB&C, New York, to T. Curtis, Boston, December 6, 1855, BB&CP.

20. The Baltimore branch manager was astonished to learn that Duncan, Sherman & Co. had repudiated its credits on George Peabody & Co. in the fall of 1857. "How can they do so if they are for a specified time as yours are and I should think no one would take a credit that could be revoked at pleasure," he wrote his superiors in November. Graham, Baltimore, to BB&C, New York, November 18, 1857, HF. (Graham's private notes to New

York were not recorded in the regular letterbooks, and a researcher must go
to the New York firm's Historical Files for the originals.)

21. BB&C, New York, to T. Curtis, Boston, July 1, 1856, BB&CP.
During the spring of 1861 the New York partners were on the receiving end
of a lecture about the sanctity of a letter of credit agreement. Due to the
wartime emergency, the American partners failed to negotiate bills under a
credit issued to an English buyer through the Liverpool branch. The New
York partners cited three factors which together seemed so potentially dangerous that they warranted revocation of the credit: possible destruction of
the cotton by civil action, capture at sea, and detention by the blockade. But
the Liverpool partners remained unconvinced. The first two instances were
covered by insurance, they argued, and the last was covered through the
continued possession of the bill of lading. Collet and Hamilton conceded
that such extreme and exceptional circumstances might arise which would
justify the failure to act under one of their credit agreements, but the current
situation was not, in their opinion, one of them. "These are our views on
what appears to us a most important matter in principle & practice," they
wrote. BS&C, Liverpool, to BB&C, New York, April 3, 1861, HF.

22. R. Hidy, *House of Baring*, pp. 144-145.

23. AB&S, Baltimore, to W&JB&C, Liverpool, August 20, 1836, AB&SP.

24. Ibid., November 11, 1836.

25. M. Hidy, "George Peabody," pp. 89-102.

26. AB&S, Baltimore, to W&JB&C, Liverpool, January 28, 1837,
AB&SP.

27. George Brown to William Brown, February 7, 1837, AB&SP.

28. Funds were invested in this area, but it was strictly a matter of choice;
the investments were mainly a function of their foreign exchange activities,
that is, the sale of sterling to customers who were importing goods under the
firm's letters of credit.

29. Although foreign exchange markets were fairly well developed in the
seaport cities during the antebellum era, sterling transactions had not as yet
concentrated in the hands of specialists. Exporters who occasionally drew
sterling bills on English buyers often sold their drawings to their importing
counterparts. This was especially true when exporters could sell at prices
above those tendered by foreign exchange dealers like the Browns, who
maintained a market and always stood ready to buy. Importers and
exporters with matching requirements found it advantageous to negotiate a
price somewhere within the dealer's normal profit spread. Domestic bill
brokers periodically offered foreign exchange for sale at reduced prices.
Their supplies usually came from nearby port cities temporarily experiencing a sterling surplus.

30. M. Hidy, "George Peabody," p. 325.

31. R. Hidy, *House of Baring,* p. 149.

32. BB&C, New York, to T. Curtis, Boston, November 2, 1856, BB&CP.
On customers' credit balances, the partners decided in 1855 to allow varying
rates which would fluctuate with the "value of money" in the short term
money market. By this date, market rates were often less than the 5 percent
interest traditionally allowed.

Bibliography

A Note on the Primary Sources

Primary sources on the House of Brown are located for the most part in Washington and New York. The Alexander Brown & Sons Papers in the Library of Congress are largely confined to the operations of the firm's Baltimore outlets. In terms of the scope of the business records included and the continuity of the material deposited, the Library of Congress collection is by far the most complete. With the exception of a few gaps early in the century, the letterbooks provide a continuous, daily record of the branch's outgoing correspondence with the other offices in the Brown organization and the branch's out-of-town customers from 1800-1879. The Alexander Brown & Sons collection is particularly useful during the period from 1800 to 1840, when the Baltimore branch served as the American headquarters for the firm's chain of offices.

Although less comprehensive in scope, the source material in the Historical Files of the surviving firm, Brown Brothers Harriman & Co., in New York City, is equally valuable in terms of its overall content. Here the emphasis is primarily on the second half of the nineteenth century, when the firm had become thoroughly involved in the performance of financial services for the American foreign trade sector. Especially revealing are the "private and confidential" letters written by the senior partners in the Liverpool and London branches to their counterparts in New York from 1851 to 1868. These letters, which were rarely written more often than once a week except during periods of economic crisis, were devoted almost exclusively to discussions of managerial and administrative policy. The whole collection was masterly organized and meticulously catalogued by Professor John Kouwenhoven of Barnard College, who directed the publication of a pictorial history of the enterprise in 1968. The firm plans to transfer the entire collection to the New York Historical Society in the very near future.

The Brown Brothers & Co. Papers at the New York library contain mostly account books and ledgers. The three or four letterbooks in the collection record the New York branch's outgoing letters to the Philadelphia, Baltimore, and Boston offices in 1859 and 1860. Photocopies of the correspondence in the Brown, Shipley & Co. Papers at the Liverpool Public

Library can be found in the Historical Files of Brown Brothers Harriman & Co. in New York City.

I. *Primary Sources*

Alexander Brown & Sons Papers, Library of Congress.
Brown Brothers & Company Papers, New York Public Library.
Brown Brothers Harriman & Company Historical Files, New York.
Garrett Family Papers, Library of Congress.
Joseph Shipley Papers, Eleutherian Mills Historical Library
Riggs Family Papers, Library of Congress.
Winans Family Papers, Maryland Historical Society.

II. *Government Publications*

United States Comptroller of the Currency, *Annual Reports*
United States Congress, *Commerce and Navigation Reports, 1830-1880*

III. *Newspapers*

Baltimore American and Commercial Advertiser
New York Tribune
The Porcupine (Liverpool)
Weekly Journal of Commerce and Price Current (Baltimore)

IV. *Periodicals*

De Bow's Review
Hunt's Merchants' Magazine and Commercial Review

V. *Secondary Materials*

A. LITERATURE ON THE BROWN FAMILY AND BUSINESSES

Brown, Cynthia. "The Business Activities of Alexander Brown and Sons, 1800-1860," manuscript, Columbia University, 1966.

Brown, John Crosby. *A Hundred Years of Merchant Banking.* New York, privately printed, 1909.

Brown, Mary Elizabeth (Mrs. John Crosby). *Alexander Brown and His Descendants,* privately printed, 1917.

Brown Brothers & Company. *Experiences of a Century 1818-1918.* Philadelphia, privately printed, 1919.

Browne, Gary L., "Business Innovation and Social Change: The Career of Alexander Brown after the War of 1812," *Maryland Historical Magazine,* 69 (Fall 1974), 243-255.

Davis, Henry A. "The Brown Partners in the Commerce and Politics of the Civil War," manuscript, Princeton University, 1965.

Ellis, Aytoun. *Heir of Adventure: The Story of Brown, Shipley & Co. Merchant Bankers.* London, privately printed, 1960.

Kent, Frank R. *The Story of Alexander Brown & Sons.* Baltimore, privately printed, 1925.

Killick, John. "Risk, Specialization and Profit in the Mercantile Sector of the Nineteenth Century Cotton Trade: Alexander Brown & Sons 1820-80" *Business History,* 16 (January 1974), 1-16.

Kouwenhoven, John A. *Partners in Banking: An Historical Portrait of a Great Private Bank, Brown Brothers Harriman & Co., 1818-1968.* Garden City, N.Y., Doubleday, 1968.

Perkins, Edwin J. "Financing Antebellum Importers: The Role of Brown Bros. & Co. in Baltimore," *Business History Review,* 45 (Winter 1971), 421-451.

_____ "The House of Brown: America's Foremost International Bankers, 1800-1880," Ph.D. diss., Johns Hopkins University, 1972.

_____ "Managing a Dollar-Sterling Exchange Account: Brown, Shipley & Co. in the 1850's," *Business History,* 16 (January 1974), 48-64.

B. BOOKS—GENERAL

Adger, John B. *My Life and Times, 1810-1899.* Richmond, Va., Presbyterian Committee of Publication, 1899.

Albion, Robert G. *The Rise of New York Port.* New York, C. Scribner's Sons, 1939.

Andreano, Ralph, ed. *The Economic Impact of the American Civil War.* Cambridge, Mass., Schenkman Publishing Co., 1962.

Bailyn, Bernard. *The New England Merchants in the Seventeenth Century.* Cambridge, Mass., Harvard University Press, 1955.

Barrett, Don Carlos. *The Greenbacks and Resumption of Specie Payments, 1862-1879.* Cambridge, Mass., Harvard University Press, 1931.

Barrett, Walter [pseud. of Joseph Scoville]. *The Old Merchants of New York City.* New York, Carleton, 1863.

Benns, Frank L. *The American Struggle for the West India Carrying Trade, 1815-1830.* Bloomington, Ind., Indiana University Studies, 1923.

Bisschop, W. R. *Rise of the London Money Market, 1640-1826.* London, P. S. King & Son, 1910.

Bourne, H. R. F. *English Merchants: Memoirs in Illustration of the Progress of British Commerce.* London, Chatto and Windus, 1886.

Bouvier, Jean. *Le Crédit Lyonnais de 1863 à 1882.* Paris, S.E.V.P.E.N., 1961.

Bruchey, Stuart. *Robert Oliver, Merchant of Baltimore, 1783-1819.* Baltimore, Johns Hopkins Press, 1956.

_____ *The Roots of American Economic Growth 1607-1861.* New York, Harper & Row, 1965.

_____, ed. *The Colonial Merchant: Sources and Readings.* New York, Harcourt, Brace & World, 1966.

_____, ed. *Cotton and the Growth of the American Economy.* New York, Harcourt, Brace & World, 1967.

Buck, Norman S. *The Development of the Organization of the Anglo-American Trade.* New Haven, Conn., Yale University Press, 1925.

Cameron, Rhondo, ed. *Banking in the Early Stages of Industrialization.* New York, Oxford University Press, 1967.

Catterall, Ralph. *The Second Bank of the United States.* Chicago, University of Chicago Press, 1902.

Chandler, Alfred D., Jr. *Henry Varnum Poor: Business Editor, Analyst and Reformer.* Cambridge, Mass., Harvard University Press, 1956.

Clapham, John. *The Bank of England: A History.* 2 vols. Cambridge, Eng., The University Press, 1944.

Clews, Henry. *Twenty-eight Years in Wall Street.* New York, J. S. Ogilvie Publishing Co., 1887.

Cohen, Henry. *Business and Politics in America from the Age of Jackson to the Civil War: The Career Biography of W. W. Corcoran.* Westport, Conn., Greenwood Publishing Corp., 1971.

Court, W. H. B. *A Concise Economic History of Britain: From 1750 to Recent Times.* Cambridge, Eng., Cambridge University Press, 1954.

Cramp, A.B. *Opinion on Bank Rate, 1822-60.* London, London School of Economics, 1962.

Cutler, Carl C. *Queens of the Western Ocean: The Story of America's Mail and Passenger Sailing Lines.* Annapolis, Md., U.S. Naval Institute, 1961.

Daish, John B. *The Atlantic Port Differentials.* Washington, W. H. Lowdermilk & Co., 1918.

Davis, Andrew M. *The Origin of the National Banking System.* Washington, G. P. O., 1910.

Easton, Harry T. *The History of a Banking House: Smith, Payne and Smiths.* London, Blades, East & Blades, 1903.

Einzig, Paul. *A Dynamic Theory of Forward Exchange.* London, Macmillan, 1961.

———— *The History of Foreign Exchange,* 2nd ed. rev. London, Macmillan, 1970.

Emery, Henry C. *Speculation on the Stock and Produce Exchanges of the United States.* New York, Columbia University, 1896.

Escher, Franklin. *Foreign Exchange Explained.* New York, The Macmillan Co., 1917.

Field, Henry M. *The Story of the Atlantic Telegraph.* New York, C. Scribner's Sons, 1893.

Foulke, Roy. *The Sinews of American Commerce.* New York, Dun & Bradstreet, Inc., 1941.

Friedman, Milton, and Anna Jacobsen Schwartz. *A Monetary History of the United States 1867-1960.* Princeton, Princeton University Press, 1963.

Galpin, W. Freeman. *The Grain Supply of England during the Napoleonic Period.* New York, The Macmillan Co., 1925.

Gates, Paul W. *The Farmer's Age: Agriculture 1815-1860.* New York, Holt, Rinehart and Winston, 1960.

Gibbons, J. S. *Banks of New York and the Clearing House.* New York, Appleton, 1859.

Gilchrist, David, ed. *The Growth of the Seaport Cities, 1790-1825.* Charlottesville, Va., University of Virginia Press for the Eleutherian Mills-Hagley Foundation, 1967.

———— and W. D. Lewis, eds. *Economic Change in the Civil War Era.* Greenville, Del., Eleutherian Mills-Hagley Foundation, 1965.

Goschen, George T. *The Theory of Foreign Exchanges.* London, E. Wilson, 1863.

Govan, Thomas P. *Nicholas Biddle, Nationalist and Public Banker 1786-1844.* Chicago, University of Chicago Press, 1959.

Greef, Albert O. *The Commercial Paper House in the United States.* Cambridge, Mass., Harvard University Press, 1938.

Green, George D. *Finance and Economic Development in the Old South, 1804-1861.* Palo Alto, Calif., Stanford University Press, 1972.

Greenberg, Michael. *British Trade and the Opening of China, 1800-1842.* Cambridge, Eng., University Press, 1951

Hall, C. C., ed. *Baltimore, Its History and Its People.* 3 vols. New York, Lewis Historical Publishing Co., 1912.

Hammond, Bray. *Banks and Politics in America: From the Revolution to the Civil War.* Princeton, Princeton University Press, 1957.

Harris, J. R., ed. *Liverpool and Merseyside: Essays in the Economic and Social History of the Port and Its Hinterland.* New York, A. M. Kelley, 1969.

Hedges, James B. *The Browns of Providence Plantation: The Colonial Years.* Cambridge, Mass., Harvard University Press, 1952.

Hidy, Muriel E. "George Peabody, Merchant and Financier, 1829-1854," Ph.D. diss., Radcliffe College, 1939.

Hidy, Ralph W. *The House of Baring in American Trade and Finance: English Merchant Bankers at Work, 1763-1861.* Cambridge, Mass., Harvard University Press, 1949.

Homer, Sidney. *A History of Interest Rates.* New Brunswick, N.J., Rutgers University Press, 1963.

Hughes, J. R. T. *Fluctuations in Trade, Industry and Finance: A Study of British Economic Development 1850-1860.* Oxford, Clarendon Press, 1960.

Hungerford, Edward. *The Story of the Baltimore and Ohio Railroad.* New York, G. P. Putman's Sons, 1928.

Hunt, Freeman, ed. *Lives of American Merchants.* New York, Hunt's Merchants' Magazine, 1858.

Irwin, Harold. *Evolution of Futures Trading.* Madison, Wis., Mimir Publishers, 1954.

Joslin, David. *A Century of Banking in Latin America.* London, Oxford University Press, 1963.

Josephson, Matthew. *The Robber Barons: The Great American Capitalists, 1861-1901.* New York, Harcourt, Brace & Co., 1934.

King, W. T. C. *History of the London Discount Market.* London, G. Routledge & Sons, 1936.

Larson, Henrietta M. *Jay Cooke, Private Banker.* Cambridge, Mass., Harvard University Press, 1936.

Leftwich, Richard. *The Price System and Resource Allocation.* 3rd ed. New York, Holt, Rinehart and Winston, 1962.

Waynesburg College Library

Waynesburg, Pa. 15370

Livingood, James W. *The Philadelphia-Baltimore Trade Rivalry.* Harrisburg, Pa., Pennsylvania Historical and Museum Commission, 1947.

Macaulay, F. R. *The Movements of Interest Rates, Bond Yields, and Stock Prices in the United States Since 1856.* New York, National Bureau of Economic Research, 1938.

McGrane, Reginald C. *The Panic of 1837: Some Financial Problems of the Jacksonian Era.* Chicago, University of Chicago Press, 1924.

Marriner, Shelia. *Rathbones of Liverpool, 1845-73.* Liverpool, University of Liverpool Press, 1961.

Mitchell, Wesley C. *Gold, Prices and Wages Under the Greenback Standard.* Berkeley, Calif., The University Press, 1908.

Morganstern, Oskar. *International Financial Transactions and Business Cycles.* Princeton, Princeton University Press, 1959.

Morison, Samuel Eliot. *The Maritime History of Massachusetts.* Boston, Houghton Mifflin, 1961.

Myers, Margaret. *The New York Money Market.* New York, Columbia University Press, 1931.

Nettels, Curtis P. *The Emergence of a National Economy 1775-1815.* New York, Holt, Rinehart and Winston, 1962.

Nishimura, Shizuya. *The Decline of Inland Bills of Exchange in the London Money Market.* Cambridge, Eng., Cambridge University Press, 1971.

North, Douglass. *The Economic Growth of the United States 1790-1860.* New York, W. W. Norton & Co., 1961.

Orchard, B. Guinness. *Liverpool's Legion of Honor.* Birkenhead, Eng., privately printed, 1893.

Otis, Fessenden N. *Isthmus of Panama: History of the Panama Railroad; and of the Pacific Mail Steamship Co.* New York, Harper & Brothers, 1867.

Pan, Shii-Lun. *The Trade of the United States with China.* New York, China Trade Bureau, 1924.

Pares, Richard. *Merchants and Planters,* supplement 4 of *The Economic History Review.* Cambridge, Eng., 1960.

Parkinson, C. Northcote, ed. *The Trade Winds: A Study of British Overseas Trade during the French War 1793-1815.* London, G. Allen and Unwin, 1948.

Payne, Peter, and Lance Davis. *The Savings Bank of Baltimore.* Baltimore, Johns Hopkins Press, 1956.

Phelps, Clyde W. *The Foreign Expansion of American Banks.* New York, Ronald Press, 1927.

Porter, Kenneth W. *John Jacob Astor: Business Man.* 2 vols. Cambridge, Mass., Harvard University Press, 1931.

———— *The Jacksons and the Lees.* 2 vols. Cambridge, Mass., Harvard University Press, 1937.

Price, F. G. H. *A Handbook of London Bankers.* London, Simpkin, Marshall, & Co., 1876.

Randall, J. G., and David Donald. *The Civil War and Reconstruction,* 2nd ed. Lexington, Mass., D. C. Heath and Co., 1969.

Redlich, Fritz. *The Molding of American Banking,* 2nd ed. New York, Johnson Reprint Corp., 1968.

Riggs, John Beverly. *The Riggs Family of Maryland.* Baltimore, Lord Baltimore Press, 1939.

Robert, Joseph. *The Tobacco Kingdom: Plantation, Market, and Factory in Virginia and North Carolina, 1800-1860.* Durham, N.C., Duke University Press, 1938.

Russel, Robert R. *Economic Aspects of Southern Sectionalism, 1840-1861.* Urbana, Ill., University of Illinois, 1924.

Rutter, Frank R. *South American Trade of Baltimore.* Baltimore, Johns Hopkins Press, 1897.

Seyd, Ernest. *Bullion and Foreign Exchanges.* London, E. Wilson, 1868.

Seaburg, Carl, and Stanley Paterson. *Merchant Prince of Boston: Colonel T. H. Perkins, 1764-1854.* Cambridge, Mass., Harvard University Press, 1971.

Shannon, Fred A. *The Farmer's Last Frontier: Agriculture, 1860-1897.* New York, Holt, Rinehart and Winston, 1945.

Shaterian, William S. *Export-Import Banking.* New York, Ronald Press, 1947.

Smith, Walter B. *Economic Aspects of the Second Bank.* Cambridge, Mass., Harvard University Press, 1953.

———— and Arthur H. Cole. *Fluctuations in American Business 1790-1860.* Cambridge, Mass., Harvard University Press, 1935.

Story, Joseph. *Commentaries on the Law: Bills of Exchange.* Boston, C. C. Little & J. Brown, 1843.

Studenski, Paul, and Herman Krooss. *Financial History of the United States,* 2nd ed. New York, McGraw-Hill, 1963.

Takeshi, Toyoda. *A History of Pre-Meiji Commerce in Japan.* Tokyo, 1969.

Taussig, Frank W. *The Tariff History of the United States,* 8th ed. New York, Johnson Reprint Corp., 1966.

Taylor, George Rogers. *The Transportation Revolution, 1815-1860.* New York, Holt, Rinehart and Winston, 1951.

Temin, Peter. *The Jacksonian Economy.* New York, W. W. Norton & Co., 1969.

Thistlethwaite, Frank. *The Anglo-American Connection in the Early Nineteenth Century.* Philadelphia, University of Pennsylvania Press, 1959.

Thompson, Robert L. *Wiring a Continent: The History of the Telegraph Industry in the United States, 1832-1866.* Princeton, Princeton University Press, 1947.

Todd, John A. *The Mechanism of Exchange: A Handbook of Currency, Banking and Trade in Peace and in War.* London, Oxford University Press, 1917.

Tooker, Elva. *Nathan Trotter: Philadelphia Merchant, 1787-1853.* Cambridge, Mass., Harvard University Press, 1955.

Tyler, David. *Steam Conquers the Atlantic.* New York, D. Appleton-Century Co., 1939.

Unger, Irwin. *The Greenback Era: A Social and Political History of Ameri-*

can Finance, 1865-1879. Princeton, Princeton University Press, 1964.

Walton, L. E. *Foreign Trade and Foreign Exchange: Their Theory and Practice.* London, Macdonald & Evans, 1956.

Watkins, James L. *King Cotton.* New York, J. L. Watkins & Sons, 1908.

Wertenbaker, T. J. *Norfolk: Historic Southern Port.* 2nd ed. Durham, N.C., Duke University Press, 1962.

Whedbee, Thomas. *The Port of Baltimore in the Making, 1828 to 1878.* Baltimore, privately printed, 1953.

Wilburn, Jean A. *Biddle's Bank: The Crucial Years.* New York, Columbia University Press, 1967.

Wilkins, Mira. *The Emergence of Multinational Enterprise: American Business Abroad from the Colonial Era to 1914.* Cambridge, Mass., Harvard University Press, 1970.

Williams, Harold A. *Robert Garrett & Sons: Origin and Development 1840-1965.* Baltimore, privately printed, 1965.

Woodman, Harold D. *King Cotton and His Retainers: Financing and Marketing the Cotton Crop of the South, 1800-1925.* Lexington, Ky., University of Kentucky Press, 1968.

C. ARTICLES

"American Produce Exchange Markets," *Annals of the American Academy of Political and Social Science,* 38. 2 (September 1911), 319-664.

Ashton, T.S. "The Bill of Exchange and Private Banks in Lancashire 1790-1830," *Economic History Review,* 15 (1945).

Bruchey, Stuart. "Success and Failure Factors: American Merchants in Foreign Trade in the Eighteenth and Nineteenth Centuries," *Business History Review,* 32 (1958), 272-292.

Catton, William E. "The Baltimore Business Community and the Secession Crisis, 1860-1861," manuscript, University of Maryland, 1952.

Clark, John G. "The Ante-Bellum Grain Trade of New Orleans," *Agricultural History,* 38 (July 1964), 131-142.

Cohen, Ira. "The Auction System in the Port of New York, 1817-1837," *Business History Review,* 45 (Winter 1971), 488-510.

Cole, Arthur H. "Evolution of the Foreign-Exchange Market of the United States," *Journal of Economic and Business History,* 1 (1928/29), 384-421.

—— "Seasonal Variation in Sterling Exchange," *Journal of Economic and Business History,* 2 (1929/30), 203-218.

Conder, G. H. "Bills of Exchange: The Part They Have Played in English Banking, Past and Present," *Journal of the Institute of Bankers* (October 1889), 415-441.

Crawcour, E. S. "Changes in Japanese Commerce in the Tokugawa Period," in John Hall and Marius Jansen, eds. *Studies in the Institutional History of Early Modern Japan.* Princeton, Princeton University Press, 1968.

Dorfman, Joseph, "A Note on the Interpretation of Anglo-American Finance, 1837-1841," *Journal of Economic History,* 6 (1951), 140-147.

Davis, Lance, and J. R. T. Hughes. "A Dollar-Sterling Exchange, 1803-1895," *Economic History Review,* 12 (1960), 52-78.

Dorsey, Rhoda M. "The Pattern of Baltimore Commerce during the Confederation Period," *Maryland Historical Magazine,* 62 (June 1967), 119-134.

Dow, John G. "The Collins Line," manuscript, Columbia University 1937.

Dumbell, Stanley. "The Origin of Cotton Futures," *Economic History,* 1 (May 1927), 259-267.

Fels, Rendigs. "American Business Cycles, 1865-1879," *American Economic Review,* 41 (June 1951), 325-349.

Graham, Frank D. "International Trade Under Depreciated Paper: The United States, 1862-79," *Quarterly Journal of Economics,* 36 (February 1922), 221-273.

Heaton, Herbert. "The American Trade," in C. N. Parkinson, ed. *The Trade Winds: A Study of British Overseas Trade during the French War 1793-1815.* London, G. Allen and Unwin, 1948.

Hidy, Ralph W. "Cushioning a Crisis in the London Money Market," *Bulletin, Business Historical Society,* 20 (1946).

_____ "The House of Baring and the Second Bank of the United States, 1826-1836," *Pennsylvania Magazine of History and Biography,* 48 (1946), 270-285.

_____ "The Organization and Functions of Anglo-American Merchant Bankers, 1815-1860," in *The Tasks of Economic History,* a supplement to the *Journal of Economic History,* 1 (1941).

Johnson, Helen. "Nathan Dunn's Letter Book: Canton, 1829-1830," manuscript, Connecticut College (New London, Conn.), 1966.

Klein, Joseph J. "The Development of Mercantile Instruments of Credit in the United States," *Journal of Accountancy,* 12 (1911).

Kravis, Irving B. "The Role of Exports in Nineteenth Century United States Growth," *Economic Development and Cultural Change,* 20 (April 1972), 387-405.

Lawlor, H.C. "Rise of the Linen Merchants in the Eighteenth Century," *Fibres and Fabrics Journal* (September 1941).

North, Douglass. "International Capital Flows and the Development of the American West," *Journal of Economic History,* 16 (December 1956), 493-505.

_____ "Ocean Freight Rates and Economic Development, 1750-1913," *Journal of Economic History,* 18 (1958), 537-555.

_____ "The United States Balance of Payments, 1790-1860," in *Trends in the American Economy in the Nineteenth Century* (Princeton, Princeton University Press, 1960), 573-627.

Odle, Thomas. "Entrepreneural Cooperation on the Great Lakes: The Origin of the Methods of American Grain Marketing," *Business History Review,* 38 (Winter 1964), 439-455.

Perkins, Edwin J. "The Emergence of a Futures Market for Foreign Exchange in the United States," *Explorations in Economic History,* 11 (Spring 1974), 193-212.

Pessen, Edward. "The Egalitarian Myth and the American Social Reality:

Wealth, Mobility, and Equality in the 'Era of the Common Man,' "
American Historical Review, 76 (October 1971), 989-1034.

Pettengil, Robert B. "United States Foreign Trade in Copper," *American Economic Review,* 25 (September 1935), 426-441.

Pratt, E. J. "Anglo-American Commercial and Political Rivalry on the Plata, 1820-1830," *Hispanic-American Historical Review,* 2 (August 1931), 302-335.

Price, Jacob M. "The Economic Growth of the Chesapeake and the European Market, 1697-1775," *Journal of Economic History,* 24 (1964), 496-511.

———— "The Rise of Glasgow in the Chesapeake Tobacco Trade, 1707-1775," *William and Mary Quarterly,* 11 (1954), 179-199.

Roeder, Robert E. "Merchants of Ante-Bellum New Orleans," *Explorations in Entrepreneurial History,* 10 (April 1958), 113-122.

Rosenblatt, Samuel M. "The Significance of Credit in the Tobacco Consignment Trade: A Study of John Norton & Sons, 1768-1775," *William and Mary Quarterly,* 19 (1962), 383-399.

Rothstein, Morton. "America in the International Rivalry for the British Wheat Market, 1860-1914," *Mississippi Valley Historical Review,* 47 (December 1960), 401-418.

———— "Antebellum Wheat and Cotton Exports: A Contrast in Marketing Organization and Economic Development," *Agricultural History,* 40 (April 1966), 91-100.

———— "The International Market for Agricultural Commodities, 1850-1873," in D. T. Gilchrist and W. D. Lewis, eds. *Economic Change in the Civil War Era.* Greenville, Del., Eleutherian Mills-Hagley Foundation, 1966.

———— "The American West and Foreign Markets, 1850-1900," in David Ellis, ed. *The Frontier in American Development.* Ithaca, N.Y., Cornell University Press, 1969.

Simon, Matthew, "The United States Balance of Payments, 1861-1900," in *Trends in the American Economy in the Nineteenth Century,* (Princeton, Princeton University Press, 1960), 629-715.

———— and David Novack. "Some Dimensions of the American Commercial Invasion of Europe, 1871-1914," *Journal of Economic History,* 24 (1964), 591-605.

Supple, Barry E. "A Business Elite: German-Jewish Financiers in Nineteenth Century New York," *Business History Review,* 31 (Summer 1957), 143-178.

Temin, Peter. "The Causes of Cotton-Price Fluctuations in the 1830's," *Review of Economics and Statistics,* 49 (November 1967), 463-470.

Tooker, Elva. "A Merchant Turns to Money-Lending in Philadelphia," *Bulletin, Business Historical Society,* 20 (1946), 71-85.

Usher, A. P. "The Origin of the Bill of Exchange," *Journal of Political Economy,* 22 (June 1914), 566-576.

Whitney, Ralph. "The Unlucky Collins Line," *American Heritage,* 8 (February 1957), 48-53.

Willett, Thomas D. "International Specie Flows and American Monetary Stability, 1834-1860," *Journal of Economic History,* 28 (March 1968), 28-49.

Williamson, Jeffrey G. "The Long Swing Comparison Between British and American Balance of Payments, 1820-1913," *Journal of Economic History,* 22 (March 1962), 26-46.

D. MISCELLANEOUS WORKS

Biographical Cyclopedia of Representative Men of Maryland and the District of Columbia. Baltimore, 1879.

Boyd's Directory of Washington and Georgetown with a Business Directory of Alexandria. Washington, 1867.

Financial Review. Published yearly by the *Commerical and Financial Chronicle.* William B. Dana & Co.

Homans, Isaac Smith. *A Cyclopedia of Commerce and Commercial Navigation.* New York, 1858.

Kirkland, Frazer. *Cyclopedia of Commercial and Business Anecdotes Compromising Reminiscences and Facts . . .* New York, 1865.

Matchett, Richard. *Matchett's Baltimore Directory.* Baltimore, 1796-1854.

Stephen, Leslie. *Dictionary of National Biography.* London, 1886.

Index

Harvard Studies in Business History

*Out of print